MODERN SCOTTIS
1707 TO THE PRESENT

MODERN SCOTTISH HISTORY
1707 *to the* PRESENT

VOLUME 5 : MAJOR DOCUMENTS

Edited by
Anthony Cooke, Ian Donnachie,
Ann MacSween and Christopher A Whatley

TUCKWELL PRESS

In association with
THE OPEN UNIVERSITY IN SCOTLAND

and
THE UNIVERSITY OF DUNDEE

First published in 1998 by
Tuckwell Press Ltd
The Mill House
Phantassie
East Linton
East Lothian EH40 3DG
Scotland

British Library Cataloguing-in-Publication Data
A catalogue record for this book is available on request
from the British Library

Designed by James Hutcheson

Typeset by Antony Gray

Printed and bound by
Cromwell Press, Trowbridge, Wiltshire

Preface

This volume and the series of which it is part have as their central purpose the study of the history of Scotland from 1707 until the present. The series seeks to combine the products of more recent research and general findings by some of the most prominent scholars working in the subject with the enthusiasm of those who wish to study it either in a systematic way or simply by reading one or more of these volumes at leisure.

Now is a particularly appropriate moment to bring this scholarship and the wider audience together. There is enormous latent enthusiasm for Scottish history, particularly, but not exclusively, of the modern period. This springs from a variety of sources: the new political agenda in Scotland following the 1997 Referendum; the higher profile of Scottish history in school, college and university curricula; the enhanced interest in local and family history; the success of museums and heritage ventures devoted to the more recent past; and the continuous flow of books on so many aspects of Scottish history. However, explicitly academic publications, with a few honourable exceptions, have been little read by any but specialists, so new findings have frequently had little impact on general perceptions of Scotland's more recent past.

There are two main aims encapsulated in these volumes, which are overlapping and complementary. The first is to present an overview of recent scholarly work, drawing on the approaches and findings of political, economic, social, environmental and cultural historians. This should be illuminating not only for those seeking an up-to-date review of such work, but also for anyone interested in the functioning of Scotland today - the essential historical background of present-day issues and concerns. The second, equally important, aim is to help readers develop their own historical skills, using the volumes as a tool-kit containing a wide range of primary sources and more detailed readings on specific topics. This and the other volumes in the series differ from most conventional academic publications, in that the focus is on **doing** history, rather than just absorbing the facts. The volumes are full of ideas on sources and methods that can be followed up by the interested reader.

Given the vast scope of the subject, we have had to put some limits on the coverage. The timescale is the early eighteenth century to the late twentieth century, a period for which sources not only abound but can also be readily understood and critically assessed. There is no attempt to give a detailed historical narrative of the period from the Union of 1707, which can readily be found elsewhere. Rather we present a blend of topics and themes, selected with a view to providing readers with a reasonably comprehensive introduction to recent work and a context and stimulus for further reading or investigation. Although there is an organisational divide at 1850, many of the themes are explored continuously over the whole period. Hence the first volume begins with the Union of 1707 and Jacobitism, and covers topics including industrialisation, demography, politics, religion, education, class, the environment, and culture, as well as looking at the differences between Highland and Lowland society and economy. The second volume from 1850 to the present also covers a wide range of topics. Some of these, such as industrialisation, demography, urbanisation, religion, class, education, culture and Highland and Lowland society are continued while new topics include the state, Scottish identity, leisure and recreation. The third and fourth volumes contain carefully selected readings to accompany the topic / theme volumes and are likely to prove an invaluable resource for any reader wishing to pursue a particular subject in greater depth or perhaps investigate it in a local or regional project. The fifth volume in the series is a collection of primary sources for the history of modern Scotland designed to accompany the other volumes. It makes accessible between the covers of one book many of the documents of national and local importance from the eighteenth century and beyond and provides a unique and detailed insight into the period.

This book forms one part of the University of Dundee-Open University collaborative course, Modern Scottish History: 1707 to the Present. This is an honours level undergraduate course for part-time adult learners studying at a distance, and it is designed to develop the skills, methods and understanding of history and historical analysis with modern Scotland as its focus. However, these volumes are designed to be used, either singly or as a series, by anyone interested in Scottish history. The introduction to recent research findings, together with practical exercises, advice on the critical exploitation of primary sources, and suggestions for further reading, should be of wide interest and application. We hope it will encourage users to carry their enthusiasm further by investigating, for example, some aspect of their own community history based on one or more themes covered in the series.

A series of this kind depends on the efforts of many people, and accordingly there are many debts to record. Our enthusiasm was shared by the Scottish Higher Education Funding Council which provided a generous grant to fund the development of the course. Within the University of Dundee, Professor

David Swinfen, Vice Principal, has played a valuable supporting role. The authors produced their contributions to agreed formats and deadlines. While they are responsible for what they have written, they have also been supported by other members of the writing team and our editorial and production specialists. The material was developed collaboratively, reflected too in the cooperation and support we have had from our publisher, Tuckwell Press. Particular thanks to Tracey Walker, the Project Secretary, for her administrative support. Thanks also to Karen Brough and Jen Petrie who transcribed some of the texts for the articles and documents volumes.

USING THIS BOOK

Activities

Volumes 1 and 2 are designed not just as a text to be read through but also as active workbooks. They are therefore punctuated by a series of activities, signalled by a different format. These include short questions, exercises, and prompts for the reader articles in Volumes 3 and 4 or documents in Volume 5. Conversely the readings and documents refer back to topics/themes discussed in detail in Volumes 1 and 2.

References

While this book is free-standing, there are cross-references to other volumes in the series. This is to aid readers using all the books. The list of books and articles that follows each chapter generally follows the scholarly convention of giving details of all works cited. They are not intended as obligatory further reading.

Series Editors

Acknowledgements

The editors would like to thank the following for permission to reproduce items in this collection:

Angus Council Cultural Services, Angus Archives: *doc 4*; British Museum: *doc 44*; Caledonian Books: *doc 114*; Canongate Books, Edinburgh: *doc 145*; Church of Scotland: *docs 20, 116*; Clydebank District Libraries: *doc 105*; Eyre and Spottiswoode, London: *doc 142*; Faber and Faber: *doc 137*; Harmondsworth: Penguin: *doc 144*; Keeper of the Records of Scotland: *docs 3, 14, 20, 33, 55, 78, 89, 101*; Macdonald Publishers, London: *doc 102*; Mitchell Library, Glasgow: *docs 124, 125*; National Library of Scotland: *docs 8, 10, 19, 26, 43, 91, 96*; National Museums of Scotland, Scottish Life Archive: *docs 120, 123*; Perth and Kinross Council Archives: *docs 3, 9, 78*; Polygon Books/BBC Scotland: *doc 133*; Public Record Office, London: *doc 126*; Routledge and Kegan Paul: *doc 143*; Scottish Gaelic Texts Society: *doc 42*; Skeffington, London: *doc 115*; Mrs Margaret Skilling: *doc 118*; *Scots Magazine*: *doc 135*; Smith Museum, Stirling: *doc 117*.

Introduction

There have been and are still available other splendid printed collections of Scottish historical documents. This documents volume, however, which comprises over 140 separate sources, is different in several respects. Most of the documents have been made available in this accessible format for the first time, as in the case of a pamphlet urging Scots in 1715 to support the Stuarts, even though the Pretender was a Catholic (**Document 10**). Only two copies of this document, both handwritten, are known to exist. Several documents have been drawn from archival holdings which have only recently been made available to the public; others are examples of categories of sources the potential of which historians have only recently recognised or which have been underutilised. An example of a relatively new type of source for historians is oral testimony, here taken from women and which provides revealing insight into women's attitudes to work, marriage and household in the first half of the twentieth century (**Document 117**). The *Statistical Account of Scotland*, produced by parish ministers in the 1790s, continue to be a unique and multi-seamed source for Scottish historians, much used hitherto, but still capable of producing fresh evidence, especially when evidence is drawn from them systematically, for comparative purposes. A similar case can be made for the *New Statistical Account* volumes of the 1830s and 1840s.

Another merit of this collection is that all the documents are drawn from the post-Union of 1707 period. This enables the reader to obtain a much deeper understanding of the last three momentous centuries in Scotland's history than would be the case with a collection of documents covering a longer time-span.

The volume provides an immensely rich resource for lecturers, teachers and their students to engage with much of the essence of Scottish social, economic, political and cultural life over the past three centuries. Any academically respectable course in Scottish social history of the eighteenth and early nineteenth centuries must pay some attention to issues such as demography, agrarian change (Highland and Lowland), industrialisation, urbanisation, labour, class and radicalism. Many of these are revisited, but in the the context of the later Victorian era and the twentieth century, as Scotland's economy lost its nineteenth-century dynamism (as well as its raw material base) and as, for example, the state played an increasingly active role in the Highlands, or in determining the nature of educational provision in the schools.

Few students of Scottish history will not spend some time examining the causes and consequences of the Union of 1707 or the series of Jacobite risings of 1708, 1715 and 1745. These topics are represented here, although in the last case the emphasis is on the 'Fifteen. Newer areas of historical investigation in Scotland such as environmental history and leisure, and the social history of religion (in the nineteenth and twentieth centuries as well as the better-known eighteenth century), are represented too, along with more standard topics such as the rise and decline of the heavy industries and their physically demanding employment for the 'hard men' of the older Scottish workplace, such as shipyard riveters.

The insights into Scottish society which can be provided by literature and art as well as the self-perceptions of Scotland and its identity (and identities) revealed by writers and poets can be found in a series of documents (67-75) which includes selections from Ramsay, Fergusson and Burns, as well as Hume, Smollett and Galt. From the present century, John Buchan, Hugh MacDiarmid, Edwin Muir and Alasdair Gray are also included, to telling effect (136- 145).

In their original format many of the documents were handwritten and have been seen previously only by those privileged by time and geographical proximity to visit the great national repositories such as the National Library of Scotland and the Scottish Record Office, both located in Edinburgh. The strong case for the return of primary records to the town or district whence they originated notwithstanding, the fact is that access can be made even more difficult for the non-professional historian who lives at the other end of the country. Here documents from local archives in Perth, Montrose and elsewhere are included. Others are from little-known printed sources or those which are now hard to find. In every case, however, whether the extract be long or short, the document has been chosen because of the way in which it can sharply illuminate an aspect of Scotland's past which might otherwise be difficult to communicate. Thus amongst several personal testimonies in this volume, one of the most searing in its impact is that of Christian Watt, a humble and acutely observant fisherwoman from near Fraserburgh, a devout servant of Christ but a passionate hater of the kirk session, which she labelled a 'bunch of hypocrites' (**Document 114**).

Revelation may not always be unambiguous, however; the sources also reflect the complexities of the past and the real difficulties historians face in interpreting the fragmentary and arbitrary evidence which forms the material base of their understanding of a period, topic or controversial issue. Thus, for example, **Documents 5 and 6** show pretty convincingly that 'political management', including bribery, was an important part of the Court Party's armoury in the process of making the Union of 1707, but they do not prove that promises of place or pensions changed their recipients' voting intentions. The apparent logic of the economic case for Union looks strong on paper and economic considerations feature in 19 of the 25 Articles of Union (**Document 1**), but how important were these when measured against, say, allegiance to party?

All document collections reflect to some extent the interests of their compilers and, quite properly, are designed to illuminate those historical topics and issues which are part of the canon of current historical debate. Both of these factors have governed the choice of documents for this collection, as has the fact that it has been compiled in the first instance to serve the needs of students studying the University of Dundee–Open University Distance Learning course in Modern Scottish History. Such readers will be given clear guidance about how to use this volume. Yet the documents published here also provide the general reader with a unique, fascinating and vivid exposure to the raw material related to several of the most important events and issues in Scottish history since the Union of 1707. Many of the documents required by university students as well as school pupils studying Scottish history to turn secondary reading into first-hand and secure understanding are to be found within these pages. Much pleasure however can be derived simply by browsing through the collection. It is to be hoped that this approach will lead to a more rigorous programme of reading or study in Scottish history. An alternative approach is to study a particular group of documents in conjunction with an appropriate secondary text. Some readers may be attracted by the prospect of enrolling for the Distance Learning course, or apply to another university where Scottish history is taught. The collection is arranged broadly chronologically, in accordance with the topics studied by students of the course, but this need not govern how the volume should be used. Individual teachers, students, pupils and other readers should utilise it to suit their own purposes.

Christopher A Whatley
University of Dundee

Contents

Part One 1707-1850

THE UNION OF 1707

JACOBITISM

ENVIRONMENT

CULTURE

EDUCATION

Part Two
1850 -1998

THE STATE

NATIONAL IDENTITY

CULTURE

Contributors

Robert Anderson, Professor of Modern History, Department of History, University of Edinburgh. Has published *Education and Opportunity in Victorian Scotland* (1983), *Education and the Scottish People, 1750-1918* (1995), and other works on Scottish educational history and modern French history.

Callum G Brown, Senior Lecturer, Department of History, University of Strathclyde. Has published extensively on religious, social and cultural history, including *Religion and Society in Scotland since 1707* (1997).

Ewen A Cameron, Lecturer in Scottish History, University of Edinburgh. Interests are Scottish and Irish rural history. Author of *Land for the People? The British Government and the Scottish Highlands, c. 1880-1925* (1996).

Gerard Carruthers, Lecturer, English Department, University of Strathclyde. Writes on eighteenth, nineteenth- and twentieth-century Scottish literature and culture, and is currently co-editing Walter Scott's *Reliquiae Trottcosienses* for publication in 1998.

Anthony Cooke, Senior Lecturer, Institute for Education and Lifelong Learning, University of Dundee. Has published widely on the history of adult education and on textile history including recent publications on the cotton mills at Spinningdale, Sutherland and on Stanley Mills, Perthshire for Historic Scotland.

Ian Donnachie, Senior Lecturer in History and Director of the Centre for Scottish Studies, The Open University in Scotland. Among his publications are *Historic New Lanark* (1993) and *The Companion to Scottish History* on CDRom (1996), both jointly with George Hewitt.

Richard J Finlay, Senior Lecturer in History, University of Strathclyde. Has published widely on Scottish identity and Scottish politics since 1700, including *A Partnership for Good?* (1997).

John Foster, Professor of Applied Social Studies, University of Paisley. Has published widely on working class and labour history in the nineteenth and twentieth centuries, including *A Class Struggle and the Industrial Revolution* (1974) and *Paying for the Piper: Capital and Labour in the Offshore Oil Industry* (1996), jointly with C Woolfson and M Beck.

W Hamish Fraser, Professor of History, University of Strathclyde. Has written extensively on aspects of social and urban history. Recent works include *Alexander Campbell and the Search for Socialism* (1996) and *Glasgow, Volume II: 1830 to 1912*, edited with I Maver (1996).

Michael Fry, Fellow, Centre for Research in Scottish History, University of Strathclyde. Author of *Patronage and Principle, A Political History of Modern Scotland* (1987) and *The Dundas Despotism* (1992).

Bob Harris, Senior Lecturer, Department of Modern History, University of Dundee. Specialist in eighteenth-century Britain and author of *A Patriot Press* (1993) and *Politics and the Rise of the Press: Britain and France, 1620-1800* (1996).

Christopher Harvie, Professor of British and Irish Studies at the University of Tübingen, Germany. Author among other works of *No Gods and Precious Few Heroes: Scotland since 1914*, which he is updating for its fourth edition.

William Kenefick, Lecturer in Scottish History, Department of Modern History, University of Dundee. Interests include labour history, particularly waterside labour and the role of the Irish; is currently preparing *Rebellious and Contrary: Glasgow Dockers, 1853-1932*.

Robert A Lambert, Institute for Environmental History, University of St Andrews. Writes on the environmental history of Britain, nature conservation, leisure, countryside recreation and tourism. Editor of *Species History in Scotland* (1997).

Ian Levitt, Professor of History, Department of Historical and Critical Studies, University of Central Lancashire. Has published widely on Government administration and the development of social provision, including *The Scottish Office, 1919-59* (1995).

Allan I Macinnes, Burnett-Fletcher Professor of History, University of Aberdeen. Has written extensively on covenants, clans and clearances, including *Charles I and the Emergence of the Covenanting Movement, 1625-41* (1991) and *Clanship, Commerce and the House of Stuart, 1603-1788* (1996).

Arthur McIvor, Senior Lecturer in History, University of Strathclyde. Research interests in labour and industrial relations history, women's history and the history of occupational health. Recently published *Organised Capital* (1996), and co-edited *Roots of Red Clydeside, 1910-1914* (1996) with W Kenefick.

Ann MacSween, Project Manager, Distance Learning: Modern Scottish History Project, University of Dundee. Author of a number of books and articles on the archaeology of Scotland, including *Prehistoric Scotland* (1990).

Irene Maver, Lecturer in Scottish History, Department of History, University of Glasgow. Research interests are Scottish social and political history, with particular focus on the urban and municipal dimension. Has recently co-edited, with W Hamish Fraser, *Glasgow, Volume II: 1830 to 1912* (1996), and is currently writing on Aberdeen and Glasgow.

RJ Morris, Professor of Economic and Social History, Department of Economic and Social History, University of Edinburgh. Author of several publications on urban history and the British middle classes including *Class, Sect and Party, 1800-1850* (1990). Founding editor of *History and Computing*.

Peter L Payne, Professor Emeritus of Economic History, University of Aberdeen and sometime Colquhoun Lecturer in Business History at the University of Glasgow, has written widely on many aspects of the modern Scottish economy, including *Growth and Contraction: Scottish Industry, c.1860-1990* (1992).

TC Smout, Director, Institute for Environmental History, University of St Andrews, and Historiographer Royal in Scotland. Author of various books on Scottish history, including *A History of the Scottish People, 1560-1830* (1969) and *A Century of the Scottish People, 1830-1950* (1986).

Gavin Sprott, Keeper of the Department of Social and Technological History in the National Museum of Scotland. He has published a range of papers on his two main areas of interest, farming history from the eighteenth century to the present, and the farming background of Robert Burns.

Neil Tranter, Senior Lecturer, Department of History, University of Stirling. His numerous publications on the history of population and social structure include *British Population in the Twentieth Century* (1996).

Christopher A Whatley, Professor of Scottish History, Department of Modern History, University of Dundee. Author of numerous publications on eighteenth-century Scottish economic and social history including *The Industrial Revolution in Scotland* (1997).

Ian Whyte, Professor of Historical Geography, Lancaster University. Author of many books and articles on the economic and social development of early-modern Scotland, including *Scotland before the Industrial Revolution* (1995).

Donald J Withrington, formerly Reader in History, University of Aberdeen. Has written widely on the ecclesiastical and educational history of Scotland since the Reformation.

Part One
1707–1850

THE UNION OF 1707

DOCUMENT 1

The Articles of the Treaty of Union of 1707, with the amendments* inserted by the Scottish Estates during the 'Explanations'

The Articles of Union are rarely published and read in full, and therefore only partial impressions of their range are given. The 'explanations' were a series of amendments to the Articles of Union which were added by the Scottish Parliament during the late autumn of 1706. Historians disagree about their significance, and also, of course, about the role of economic considerations in general in the 'making' of the Act of Union.

I   That the two Kingdoms of Scotland and England, shall, upon the first Day of May next ensuing the Date hereof, and for ever after, be united into one Kingdom by the Name of Great-Britain, and that the Ensigns Armorial of the said united Kingdom, be such as her Majesty shall appoint; and the Crosses of St. *Andrew* and St. *George* be conjoined in such a manner as her Majesty shall think fit, and used in all Flags, Banners, Standards, and Ensigns, both at Sea and Land.

II   That the Succession to the Monarchy of the united Kingdom of Great-Britain, and of the Dominions thereunto belonging, after her most sacred Majesty, and in default of Issue of her Majesty, be, remain, and continue to the most Excellent Princess Sophia, Electress and Duchess Dowager of Hanover, and the Heirs of her Body, being Protestants, upon whom the Crown of England is settled, by an Act of Parliament made in England, in the twelfth Year of the Reign of his late Majesty King William the Third, entitled, *An Act for further Limitation of the Crown, and better securing the Rights and Liberties of the Subject.* And that all Papists, and Persons marrying Papists, shall be excluded from, and for ever incapable to inherit, possess, or enjoy the imperial Crown of Great-Britain, and the Dominions thereunto belonging, or any Part thereof. And in every such Case, the Crown and Government shall from Time to Time descend to, and be enjoyed by such Person, being a Protestant, as should have inherited and enjoyed the same, in case such Papist, or Person marrying a Papist, was naturally dead, according to the Provision for the Descent of the Crown of England, made by another Act of Parliament in England, in the first Year of the Reign of their late Majesties King William and Queen Mary, entitled, *An Act declaring the Rights and Liberties of the Subject, and settling the Succession of the Crown.*

III   That the united Kingdom of Great-Britain be represented by one and the same Parliament, to be stiled the Parliament of Great-Britain.

---

* The amendments are italicised

IV   That all the Subjects of the united Kingdom of Great-Britain shall, from and after the Union, have full Freedom and Intercourse of Trade and Navigation, to and from any Port or Place within the said united Kingdom, and the Dominions and Plantations thereunto belonging; and that there be a Communication of all other Rights, Privileges, and Advantages, which do or may belong to the Subjects of either Kingdom, except where it is otherwise expressly agreed in these Articles.

V   That all Ships or Vessels, belonging to her Majesty's Subjects of Scotland, at the Time of *ratifying the Treaty of Union of the two Kingdoms, in the Parliament of Scotland,* though foreign built, be deemed, and pass as Ships of the Build of Great-Britain; the Owner, or where there are more Owners, one or more of the Owners, within twelve Months after the first of May next, making Oath, that, at the Time of *ratifying the Treaty of Union in the Parliament of Scotland,* the same did, *in whole, or in part,* belong to him or them, or to some other Subject or Subjects of Scotland, to be particularly named, with the Place of their respective Abodes; and that the same doth then, *at the time of the said Deposition,* wholly belong to him, or them, and that no Foreigner, directly or indirectly, hath any Share, Part, or Interest therein, Which Oath shall be made before the chief Officer or Officers of the Customs, in the Port next to the Abode of the said Owner or Owners: And the said Officer or Officers, shall be empowered to administrate the said Oath: And the Oath being so administrated, shall be attested by the Officer or Officers, who administrated the same. And, being registered by the said Officer or Officers, shall be delivered to the Master of the Ship for Security of her Navigation; and a Duplicate thereof shall be transmitted by the said Officer or Officers, to the chief Officer or Officers of the Customs in the Port of Edinburgh, to be there entered in a Register, and from thence to be sent to the Port of London, to be there entered in the general Register of all trading Ships belonging to Great-Britain.

VI   That all Parts of the united Kingdom, for ever, from and after the Union, shall have the same Allowances, Encouragements, and Draw-backs, and be under the same Prohibitions, Restrictions, and Regulations of Trade, and liable to the same Customs and Duties, and Import and Export. And that the Allowances, Encouragements, *and draw-backs,* Prohibitions, Restrictions, and Regulations, of Trade, and the Customs and Duties on Import and Export settled in England, when the Union commences, shall, from and after the Union, take place throughout the whole united Kingdom: *Excepting and reserving the Duties upon Export and Import, of such particular Commodities, from which any Persons, the Subjects of either Kingdom, are specially liberated and exempted by their private Rights, which, after the Union, are to remain safe and entire to them in all respects, as before the same. And that from, and after the Union, no Scots Cattle carried into England, shall be liable to any other Duties, either on the public or private Accounts, than these Duties, to which the Cattle of England are, or shall be liable within the said Kingdom. And seeing, by the Laws of England, there are Rewards granted upon the Exportation of certain kinds of Grain, wherein Oats grinded or ungrinded are not expressed, that from, and after the Union, when Oats shall be sold at fifteen Shillings Sterling per Quarter, or under, there shall be paid two*

Shillings and Six-pence Sterling for every Quarter of the Oatmeal exported, in the Terms of the Law, whereby, and so long as Rewards are granted for Exportation of other Grains; and that the Beer of Scotland, have the same Reward as Barley: And in respect the Exportation of Victual into Scotland from any Place beyond Sea, would prove a Discouragement to Tillage, therefore that the Prohibition, as now in Force by the Law of Scotland, against Importation of Victual from Ireland, or any other Place beyond Sea into Scotland, do, after the Union, remain in the same Force as now it is, until more proper and effectual Ways be provided by the Parliament of Great-Britain, for discouraging the Importation of the said Victual from beyond Sea.

VII   That all Parts of the united Kingdom be for ever, from, and after the Union, liable to the same Excises upon all excisable Liquors, *Excepting only that the thirty four Gallons English Barrel of Beer or Ale, amounting to twelve Gallons Scots present Measure, sold in Scotland by the Brewer at nine Shillings Six pence Sterling, excluding all Duties, and retailed, including Duties, and the Retailers Profit at two Pence the Scots Pint, or eighth Part of the Scots Gallon, be not after the Union liable on account of the present Excise upon excisable Liquors in England; to any higher Imposition than two Shillings Sterling upon the foresaid thirty-four Gallons English Barrel, being twelve Gallons the present Scots Meas-ure.* 'And that the Excise settled in England on *all other Liquors,* when the Union commences, take place throughout the whole united Kingdom.

VIII   That, from and after the Union, all foreign Salt which shall be imported into Scotland, shall be charged at the Importation there, with the same Duties as the like Salt is now charged with being imported into England, and to be levied and secured in the same manner. *But in regard the Duties of great Quantities of foreign Salt imported, may be very heavy upon the Merchants Importers, that therefore all foreign Salt imported into Scotland, shall be cellered and locked up under the Custody of the Merchant Importer, and the Officers employed for levying the Duties upon Salt; and that the Merchant may have what Quantities thereof his Occasions may require, not under a Weigh or forty Bushels at a Time, giving Security for the Duty, of what Quantities he receives, payable in six Months.* But Scotland shall, for the space of seven Years, from the said Union, be exempted from paying in Scotland for Salt made there, the Duty or Excise now payable for Salt made in England: but, from the Expiration of the said seven Years, shall be subject and liable to the same Duties as Salt made in England, to be levied and secured in the same manner, and with proportionable Draw-backs and Allowances as in England, with this Exception, *That Scotland shall, after the said seven Years, remain exempted from the Duty of two Shillings and four Pence the Bushel on home-Salt, imposed by an Act made in England in the ninth and tenth Years of King William the Third of England; and if the Parliament of Great-Britain shall, at, or before the expiring of the said seven Years, substitute any other Fund, in place of the said two Shillings and four Pence of Excise upon the Bushel of home Salt, Scotland shall, after the said seven Years, bear a Proportion of the said Fund, and have an Equivalent in the Terms of this Treaty.* And that, during the said seven

Years, there shall be paid in England for all Salt made in Scotland, and imported from thence into England, the same Duties upon the Importation, as shall be payable for Salt made in England, to be levied and secured in the same manner as the Duties on foreign Salt are to be levied and secured in England. And that, after the said seven Years, *how long the said Duty of two Shillings four Pence a Bushel upon Salt is continued in England, the said two Shillings four Pence a Bushel, shall be payable for all Salt made in Scotland, and imported into England, to be levied and secured in the same manner; and that during the Continuance of the Duty of two Shillings four Pence a Bushel upon Salt made in England,* no Salt whatsoever be brought from Scotland to England by Land in any manner, under the Penalty of forfeiting the Salt, and the Cattle and Carriages made use of in bringing the same, and paying twenty Shillings for every Bushel of such Salt, and proportionably for a greater or lesser Quantity, for which the Carrier as well as the Owner shall be liable, jointly and severally, and the Persons bringing or carrying the same, to be imprisoned by any one Justice of the Peace, by the space of six Months without Bail, and until the Penalty be paid. And, for establishing an Equality in Trade, that all Flesh exported from Scotland to England, and put on Board in Scotland, to be exported to Ports beyond the Sea, *and Provisions for Ships in Scotland, and for foreign Voyages, may be salted with Scots Salt, paying the same Duty for what Salt is so employed, as the like Quantity of such Salt pays in England and under the same Penalties, Forfeitures and Provisions, for preventing of such Frauds as are mentioned in the Laws of England:* And that, from and after the Union, the Laws and Acts of Parliament in Scotland for pineing, curing and packing of Herrings, white Fish and Salmon, for Exportation with foreign Salt only, *without any Mixture of British or Irish Salt*; and for preventing of Frauds, in curing and packing of Fish, be continued in Force in Scotland, subject to such Alterations as shall be made by the Parliament of Great-Britain; and that all Fish exported from Scotland to Parts beyond the Seas, which shall be cured with foreign Salt only, *and without Mixture of British or Irish Salt, shall have the same Eases, Premiums and Draw-backs, as are or shall be allowed to such Persons as export the like Fish from England:* And that for Encouragement of the Herring-fishing, *there shall be allowed and payed to the Subjects, Inhabitants of Great-Britain, during the present Allowances for other Fishes, ten Shillings five Pence Sterling for every Barrel of white Herring, which shall be exported from Scotland; and that they shall be allowed five Shillings Sterling for every Barrel of Beef or Pork salted with foreign Salt, without Mixture of British or Irish Salt, and exported for Sale from Scotland to Parts beyond Sea, alterable by the Parliament of Great-Britain.* And if any Matters of Frauds, relating to the said Duties on Salt, shall hereafter appear, which are not sufficiently provided against by this Article, the same shall be subject to such further Provisions, as shall be thought fit by the Parliament of Great-Britain.

IX That whenever the Sum of one Million nine hundred ninety-seven Thousand, seven Hundred and sixty-three Pounds, eight Shillings, four Pence Half-penny, shall be enacted by the Parliament of Great-Britain, to be raised in that Part of the united Kingdom, now called England, on Land and other Things usually charged in

Acts of Parliament there, for granting an Aid to the Crown by a Land-Tax; that Part of the united Kingdom, now called Scotland, shall be charged by the same Act, with a further Sum of forty-eight thousand Pounds, free of all Charges, as the Quota of Scotland to such Tax, and so proportionably for any greater or lesser Sum raised in England, by any Tax on Land, and other Things usually charged, together with the Land; and that such Quota for Scotland, in the Cases aforesaid, be raised and collected in the same manner as the Cess now is in Scotland, but subject to such Regulations in the manner of collecting, as shall be made by the Parliament of Great-Britain.

X   That, during the continuance of the respective Duties on stamped Paper, Vellum and Parchment, by the several Acts now in Force in England, Scotland shall not be charged with the same respective Duties.

XI   That, during the continuance of the Duties payable in England on Windows and Lights, which determines on the first Day of August, one thousand seven hundred and ten, Scotland shall not be charged with the same Duties.

XII   That, during the continuance of the Duties payable in England on Coals, Culm and Cinders, which determines the thirtieth Day of September, one thousand seven hundred and ten, Scotland shall not be charged therewith for Coals, Culm and Cinders consumed there, but shall be charged with the same Duties as in England, for all Coals, Culm and Cinders not consumed in Scotland.

XIII   That, during the continuance of the Duty payable in England on Malt, which determines the twenty-fourth Day of June, one thousand seven hundred and seven, Scotland shall not be charged with that Duty.

XIV   That the Kingdom of Scotland be not charged with any other Duties, laid on by the Parliament of England before the Union, except those consented to in this Treaty; in regard it is agreed, that all necessary Provision shall be made by the Parliament of Scotland, for the public Charge and Service of that Kingdom, for the Year one thousand seven hundred and seven; providing nevertheless, that, if the Parliament of England shall think fit to lay any further Impositions, by way of Custom, or such Excises, with which, by Virtue of this Treaty, Scotland is to be charged equally with England; in such Case, Scotland shall be liable to the same Customs and Excises, and have an Equivalent to be settled, by the Parliament of Great-Britain, with this further Provision, *That any Malt to be made and consumed in that Part of the united Kingdom now called Scotland, shall not be charged with any Imposition on Malt during this War.* And seeing it cannot be supposed, that the Parliament of Great-Britain will ever lay any sort of Burthens upon the united Kingdom, but what they shall find of necessity, at that Time, for the Preservation and Good of the whole; and with due Regard to the Circumstances and Abilities of every Part of the united Kingdom; therefore, it is agreed, that there be no further Exemption insisted on for any Part of the united Kingdom, but that the Consideration of any Exemptions beyond what is already agreed on in this Treaty, shall be left to the Determination of the Parliament of Great Britain.

XV   That whereas by the Terms of this Treaty, the Subjects of Scotland, for preserving an Equality of Trade throughout the united Kingdom, will be liable to several Customs and Excises now payable in England, which will be applicable towards payment of the Debts of England, contracted before the Union; it is agreed, That Scotland shall have an Equivalent for what the Subjects thereof shall be so charged, towards Payment of the said Debts of England, in all Particulars whatsoever, in manner following, *viz.* That, before the Union of the said Kingdoms, the Sum of three hundred ninety-eight Thousand, and eighty-five Pounds ten Shillings, be granted to her Majesty by the Parliament of England, for the Uses after mentioned, being the Equivalent, to be answered to Scotland, for such Parts of the said Customs, and Excises upon all excisable Liquors, with which that Kingdom is to be charged upon the Union, as will be applicable to the Payment of the said Debts of England, according to the Proportions which the present Customs in Scotland, being thirty thousand Pounds *per Annum*, do bear to the Customs in England, computed at one Million, three hundred forty-one Thousand, five hundred and fifty-nine Pounds *per Annum*: And which the present Excises on excisable Liquors in Scotland, being thirty-three thousand and five hundred Pounds *per Annum*, do bear to the Excises on excisable Liquors in England, computed at nine hundred forty-seven Thousand, six hundred and two Pounds *per Annum;* which Sum of three hundred ninety-eight Thousand, eighty-five Pounds ten Shillings, shall be due and payable from the Time of the Union: And in regard, that, after the Union, Scotland becoming liable to the same Customs and Duties payable on Import and Export, and to the same Excises on all excisable Liquors, as in England, as well upon that Account, as upon the Account of the Increase of Trade and People, (which will be the happy Consequence of the Union) the said Revenues will much improve beyond the before-mentioned annual Values thereof, of which no present Estimate can be made; yet, nevertheless, for the Reasons aforesaid, there ought to be a reasonable Equivalent answered to Scotland; it is agreed, That, after the Union, there shall be an Account kept of the said Duties arising in Scotland, to the end it may appear, what ought to be answered to Scotland, as an Equivalent for such Proportion of the said Increase, as shall be applicable to the Payment of the Debts of England. And for the further, and more effectual answering the several Ends hereafter mentioned, it is agreed, That, from and after the Union, the whole Increase of the Revenues of Customs, and Duties on Import and Export, and Excises upon excisable Liquors in Scotland, over and above the annual Produce of the said respective Duties, as above stated, shall go, and be applied, for the Term of seven Years, to the Uses hereafter mentioned, and that, upon the said Account, there shall be answered to Scotland, annually, from the end of seven Years after the Union, an Equivalent in Proportion to such Part of the said Increase, as shall be applicable to the Debts of England: *And generally, that an Equivalent shall be answered to Scotland, for such Parts of the English Debts as Scotland may hereafter become liable to pay, by reason of the Union, other than such for which Appropriations have been made by Parliament in England, of the Customs or other Duties on Export and Import, Excises on all exciseable Liquors, in respect of which Debts, Equivalents are herein before provided.* And as for the Uses to which the said Sum of three hundred ninety-eight Thousand, eighty-five Pounds ten Shillings, to be granted as aforesaid, and all other Monies which are to be answered or allowed to Scotland, as said is, are to be applied, it is agreed, *That, in the first place, out of the foresaid Sum,* what Consideration shall be found necessary to be had for any Losses which private Persons may sustain, by reducing the Coin of Scotland, to the Standard and Value of the Coin of England, may be made good. In the next place, that the capital Stock, or Fund of the African and Indian Company of Scotland, advanced together with the Interest for the said capital Stock, after the Rate of *5 per Cent. per Annum,* from the respective Times of the Payment thereof, shall be paid; upon Payment of which capital Stock and Interest, it is agreed, The said Company be dissolved and cease; and also, that, from the Time of passing the Act of Parliament in England, for raising the said Sum of three hundred ninety-eight Thousand, eighty-five Pounds ten Shillings, the said Company shall neither trade, nor grant Licence to trade, providing, *That if the said Stock and Interest shall not be paid in twelve Months after the Commencement of the Union, that then the said Company may from thence forward trade, or give Licence to trade, until the said whole capital Stock and Interest shall be paid.* And as to the Overplus of the said Sum of three hundred ninety-eight Thousand, eighty-five Pounds ten Shillings, after Payment of what Consideration shall be had for Losses, in repairing the Coin, and paying the said capital Stock and Interest; and also the whole Increase of the said Revenues of Customs, Duties, and Excises, above the present Value, which shall arise in Scotland, during the said Term of seven Years, together with the Equivalent which shall become due, upon the Improvement thereof in Scotland after the said Term *of seven Years*: and also, as to all other Sums, which, according to the Agreements aforesaid, may become payable to Scotland, by way of Equivalent, for what that Kingdom shall hereafter become liable, towards Payment of the Debts of England: it is agreed, That the same may be applied in the manner following, *viz. That all the public Debts of the Kingdom of Scotland, as shall be adjusted by the present Parliament, shall be paid: And that two thousand Pounds* per annum *for the space of seven Years, shall be applied towards encouraging and promoting the Manufacture of coarse Wool, within those Shires which produce the Wool; and that the first two thousands Sterling be paid at Martinmas next, and so yearly at Martinmas during the Space aforesaid.* And afterwards the same shall be wholly applied towards the encouraging and promoting the Fisheries, and such other Manufactories and Improvements in Scotland, as may most conduce to the general good of the united Kingdom. And it is agreed, That her Majesty be empowered to appoint Commissioners, who shall be accountable to the Parliament of Great-Britain, for disposing the said Sum of three hundred ninety-eight thousand and eighty-five Pounds, ten Shillings; and all other Monies which shall arise to Scotland, upon the Agreements aforesaid, to the Purposes before mentioned: Which Commissioners shall be empowered to call for, receive, and dispose of the said Monies in Manner aforesaid; and to inspect the Books of the several Collectors of the said Revenues, and of all other Duties, from whence an Equivalent may arise, and that the Collectors and Managers of the said

Revenues and Duties, be obliged to give to the said Commissioners, subscribed, authentic Abbreviates of the Produce of such Revenues and Duties arising in their respective Districts: And that the said Commissioners shall have their Office within the Limits of Scotland, and shall in such Office keep Books, containing Accounts of the Amount of the Equivalents, and how the same shall have been disposed of from time to time; which may be inspected by any of the Subjects who shall desire the same.

XVI   That, from and after the Union, the Coin shall be of the same Standard and Value throughout the united Kingdom, as now in England, and a Mint shall be continued in Scotland, under the same Rules as the Mint in England, *and the present Officers of the Mint continued*, subject to such Regulations and Alterations as her Majesty, her Heirs or Successors, or the Parliament of Great-Britain, shall think fit.

XVII   That, from and after the Union, the same Weights and Measures shall be used throughout the united Kingdom, as are now established in England: and Standards of Weights and Measures shall be kept by those Burghs in Scotland, to whom the keeping the Standards of Weights and Measures, now in use there, does of special Right belong. All which Standards shall be sent down to such respective Burghs, from the Standards kept in the Exchequer at Westminster, subject nevertheless to such Regulations as the Parliament of Great-Britain shall think fit.

XVIII   That the Laws concerning Regulation of Trade, Customs, and such Excises, to which Scotland is, by virtue of this Treaty, to be liable, be the same in Scotland, from and after the Union, as in England; and that all other laws in use, within the Kingdom of *Scotland*, do, after the Union, and notwithstanding thereof, remain in the same Force as before, (except such as are contrary to, or inconsistent with this Treaty) but alterable by the Parliament of Great-Britain, with this Difference betwixt the Laws concerning public Right, Polity, and Civil Government, and those which concern private Right: that the Laws which concern public Right, Polity and Civil Government, may be made the same throughout the whole united Kingdom; but that no Alteration be made in Laws which concern private Right, except for evident Utility of the Subjects within Scotland.

XIX   That the Court of Session, or College of Justice, do, after the Union, and notwithstanding thereof, remain, in all time coming, within Scotland, as it is now constituted by the Laws of that Kingdom, and with the same Authority and Privileges, as before the Union, subject nevertheless to such Regulations for the better Administration of Justice, as shall be made by the Parliament of Great Britain; *And that hereafter none shall be named by her Majesty and her Royal Successors, to be ordinary Lords of Session, but such who have served in the College of Justice as Advocates, or principal Clerks of Session for the Space of five Years; or as Writers to the Signet, for the Space of ten Years: with this Provision, that no Writer to the Signet be capable to be admitted a Lord of the Session, unless he undergo a private and public Trial on the Civil Law before the Faculty of Advocates, and be found by them qualified for the said Office, two Years before he be named to be a Lord of the Session: Yet so, as the Qualification made, or to be made, for capacitating Persons to be named ordinary Lords of Session, may be altered by the Parliament of Great-Britain.* And that the Court of Justiciary, do also, after the Union, and notwithstanding thereof, remain, in all time coming within Scotland, as it is now constituted by the laws of that Kingdom, and with the same Authority and Privileges as before the Union, subject nevertheless to such Regulations as shall be made by the Parliament of Great-Britain, and without Prejudice of other Rights of Justiciary: And that all Admiralty-Jurisdictions be under the Lord High Admiral, or Commissioners for the Admiralty of Great-Britain, for the Time being; and that the Court of Admiralty, now established in Scotland, be continued, and that all Reviews, Reductions, or Suspensions of the Sentences in Maritime Cases, competent to the Jurisdiction of that Court, remain in the same Manner after the Union, as now in Scotland, until the Parliament of Great-Britain shall make such Regulations and Alterations, as shall be judged expedient for the whole united Kingdom, so as there be always continued in Scotland, a Court of Admiralty, such as in England, for Determination of all Maritime Cases relating to private Rights in Scotland, competent to the Jurisdiction of the Admiralty Court, subject nevertheless to such Regulations and Alterations, as shall be thought proper to be made by the Parliament of Great-Britain; and that the heritable Rights of Admiralty and Vice-admiralties in Scotland, be reserved to the respective Proprietors, as Rights of Property; subject nevertheless, as to the Manner of exercising such heritable Rights, to such Regulations and Alterations, as shall be thought proper to be made by the Parliament of Great Britain; and that all other Courts now in being within the Kingdom of Scotland, do remain, but subject to Alterations by the Parliament of Great-Britain; and that all inferior Courts, within the said Limits, do remain subordinate, as they are now, to the supreme Courts of Justice within the same in all Time coming; and that no Causes in Scotland be cognizable by the Courts of Chancery, Queen's-Bench, Common-Pleas, or any other Court in Westminster-Hall; and that the said Courts, or any other of the like Nature, after the Union, shall have no Power to cognize, review, or alter the Acts or Sentences of the Judicatures within Scotland, to stop the Execution of the same. And that there be a Court of Exchequer in Scotland, after the Union, for deciding Questions, concerning the Revenues of Customs and Excises there, having the same Power and Authority in such Cases, as the Court of Exchequer has in England; and that the said Court of Exchequer in Scotland have Power of passing Signatures, Gifts, Tutories, and in other Things, as the Court of Exchequer at present in Scotland hath; and that the Court of Exchequer that now is in Scotland, do remain until a new Court of Exchequer be settled by the Parliament of Great-Britain, in Scotland, after the Union; and that, after the Union, the Queen's Majesty, and her Royal Successors, may continue a Privy-Council in Scotland, for preserving the public Peace and Order, until the Parliament of Great Britain shall think fit to alter it, or establish any other effectual Method for that End.

XX   That all heritable Offices, Superiorities, heritable Jurisdictions, Offices for Life, and Jurisdictions for Life, be reserved for the Owners thereof, as Rights of

Property, in the same Manner as they are now enjoyed by the Laws of Scotland, notwithstanding this Treaty.

XXI   That the Rights and Privileges of the Royal Boroughs in Scotland as they are, do remain entire after the Union, and notwithstanding thereof.

XXII   That by Virtue of this Treaty, of the Peers of Scotland, at the Time of the Union, sixteen shall be the Number to sit and vote in the House of Lords, and forty-five the Number of the Representatives of Scotland in the House of Commons of the Parliament of Great Britain; and that, when her Majesty, her Heirs, or Successors, shall declare her or their Pleasure, for holding the first or any subsequent Parliament of Great-Britain, until the Parliament of Great-Britain shall make further Provision therein, a Writ do issue under the Great Seal of the united Kingdom, directed to the Privy-Council of Scotland, commanding them to cause sixteen Peers, who are to sit in the House of Lords, to be summoned to Parliament, and forty-five Members to be elected to sit in the House of Commons in the Parliament of Great-Britain, according to the Agreement in this Treaty, in such Manner as by *an Act of this present Session of* the Parliament of Scotland, is, or shall be settled; *Which Act is hereby declared to be as valid as if it were a Part of, and engrossed in this Treaty*: And that the Names of the Persons so summoned and elected, shall be returned by the Privy-Council of Scotland, into the Court from whence the said Writ did issue. And that, if her Majesty, on or before the first Day of May next, on which Day the Union is to take place, shall declare under the Great Seal of England, that it is expedient, that the Lords of Parliament of England, and Commons of the present Parliament of England, should be the Members of the respective Houses of the first Parliament of Great-Britain, for, and on the Part of England, then the said Lords of Parliament of England, and Commons of the present Parliament of England, shall be the Members of the respective Houses of the first Parliament of Great-Britain, for, and on the Part of England. And her Majesty may, by her Royal Proclamation, under the Great Seal of Great-Britain, appoint the said first Parliament of Great-Britain, to meet at such Time and Place as her Majesty shall think fit, which Time shall not be less than fifty Days after the Date of such Proclamation, and the Time and Place of the Meeting of such Parliament being so appointed, a Writ shall be immediately issued under the Great Seal of Great-Britain, directed to the Privy-Council of Scotland for the summoning the sixteen Peers, and for electing forty-five Members, by whom Scotland is to be represented in the Parliament of Great-Britain: And the Lords of Parliament of England, and the sixteen Peers of Scotland, such sixteen Peers being summoned and returned in the Manner agreed in this Treaty; and the Members of the House of Commons of the said Parliament of England, and the forty-five Members for Scotland, such forty-five Members being elected, and returned in the Manner agreed in this Treaty, shall assemble and meet respectively, in their respective Houses of the Parliament of Great-Britain, at such Time and Place as shall be so appointed by her Majesty, and shall be the Houses of the first Parliament of Great-Britain, and that Parliament may continue for such Time only as the present Parliament of England might have continued, if the Union of the two Kingdoms had not been made, unless sooner dissolved by her Majesty: And that every one of the Lords of Parliament of Great Britain, and every Member of the House of Commons of the Parliament of Great-Britain, in the first, and all succeeding Parliaments of Great-Britain, until the Parliament of Great-Britain shall otherways direct, shall take the respective Oaths of Allegiance and Supremacy, by an Act of Parliament made in England, in the first Year of the Reign of the late King William and Queen Mary, entitled, *An Act for the abrogating of the Oaths of Supremacy and Allegiance, and appointing other Oaths,* and make, subscribe, and audibly repeat the Declaration mentioned in an Act of Parliament made in England, in the thirtieth Year of the Reign of King Charles the Second, entitled, *An Act for the more effectual preserving the King's Person and Government, by disabling Papists from sitting in either House of Parliament,* and shall take and subscribe the Oath mentioned in an Act of Parliament made in England, in the first Year of her Majesty's Reign, entitled, *An Act to declare the Alterations in the Oath appointed to be taken by the Act,* entitled, *An Act for the further Security of his Majesty's Person, and the Succession of the Crown in the Protestant Line, and for extinguishing the Hopes of the pretended Prince of* Wales, *and all other Pretenders, and their open and secret Abettors, and for the declaring the Association, to be determined at such Time, and in such Manner, as the Members of both Houses of Parliament of England, are by the said respective Acts, directed to take, make and subscribe the same, upon the Penalties and Disabilities in the said respective Acts contained.* And it is declared and agreed, that these Words, this Realm, the Crown of this Realm, and the Queen of this Realm, mentioned in the Oaths and Declaration contained in the aforesaid Acts, which were intended to signify the Crown and Realm of England, shall be understood of the Crown and Realm of Great-Britain; and that in that Sense, the said Oaths and Declaration be taken and subscribed by the Members of both Houses of the Parliament of Great-Britain.

XXIII   That in the aforesaid sixteen Peers of Scotland, mentioned in the last preceeding Article, to sit in the House of Lords of the Parliament of Great-Britain, shall have all Privileges of Parliament, which the Peers of England now have, and which they, or any Peers of Great-Britain, shall have after the Union; and particularly the Right of sitting upon the Tryals of Peers: And, in case of the Tryal of any Peer in time of Adjournment or Prorogation of Parliament, the said sixteen Peers shall be summoned in the same Manner, and have the same Powers and Privileges at such Tryals, as any other Peers of Great-Britain: And that, in case any Tryals of Peers shall hereafter happen, when there is no Parliament in being, the sixteen Peers of Scotland, who sat in the last preceding Parliament, shall be summoned in the same Manner, and have the same Powers and Privileges at such Tryals, as any other Peers of Great-Britain, and that all Peers of Scotland, and their Successors to their Honours and Dignities, shall, from, and after the Union, be Peers of Great-Britain, and have Rank and Precedency next, and immediately after the Peers of the like Orders and Degrees in England at the Time of the Union, and before all Peers of Great-Britain, of the like Orders and Degrees, who may be created after the Union, and shall be tried as Peers of Great Britain, and shall enjoy all Privileges of Peers as fully as the Peers of England do now, or as they or any other Peers of Great-Britain may hereafter enjoy the same, except the Right and Privilege of sitting in the House of Lords, and the Privileges depending thereon, and particularly the right of sitting upon the Tryals of Peers.

XXIV   That, from and after the Union, there be one Great Seal for the united Kingdom of Great Britain, which shall be different from the Great Seal now used in either Kingdom; and that the quartering the Arms, *and the Rank and Precedency of Lyon King of Arms of the Kingdom of Scotland*, as may best suit the Union, be left to her Majesty: And that, in the mean Time, the Great Seal of England be used as the Great Seal of the united Kingdom, sealing Writs to elect and summon the Parliament of Great-Britain, and for sealing all Treaties with foreign Princes and States, and all public Acts, Instruments, and Orders of State, which concern the whole united Kingdom, and in all other Matters relating to England, as the Great Seal of England is now used; and that a Seal in Scotland, after the Union, be always kept, and made use of in all Things relating to private Rights or Grants, which have usually passed the Great Seal of Scotland, and which only concern Offices, Grants, Commissions, and private Rights within that Kingdom: And that, until such Seal shall be appointed by her Majesty, the present Great-Seal of Scotland shall be used for such Purposes: And that the Privy Seal, Signet-Casset, Signet of the Justiciary Court, Quarter-Seal, and Seals of Courts now used in Scotland, be continued: But that the said Seals be altered and adapted to the State of the Union, as her Majesty shall think fit; and the said Seals, and all of them, and the Keepers of them, shall be subject to such Alterations as the Parliament of Great-Britain shall hereafter make: *And that the Crown, Scepter, and Sword of State, the Records of Parliament, and all other Records, Rolls and Registers whatsoever, both public and private, general and particular, and Warrants thereof, continue to be kept as they are, within that Part of the united Kingdom now called Scotland; and that they shall so remain in all Time coming, notwithstanding of the Union.*

XXV   That all Laws and Statutes in either Kingdom, so far as they are contrary to, or inconsistent with the Terms of these Articles, or any of them, shall, from and after the Union, cease, and become void, and shall be so declared to be, by the respective Parliaments of the said Kingdoms.

SOURCE: *History and Proceedings of the House of Commons*, IV 1742, London, 16–30.

Extract from William Seton of Pitmedden, younger, *A Speech in Parliament on the First Article of the Treaty of Union*, 1706

Seton was an eloquent advocate of Union, although it has been argued that his conviction was less than genuine, and dependent upon his obtaining a Court pension. Worth noting are the European and international dimensions of Seton's arguments.

My Lord Chancellor,

This Honourable House has heard the several *Articles of the Treaty of Union* twice read, has spent a considerable time in discoursing to each of them, and after much Debate is come to examine and determine upon the First: Notwithstanding all the Arguments offered against it, I cannot find the least Motive for altering the Opinion I had at Signing this Article, having had the Honour to be one of the Commissioners appointed by Her Majesty for that end; but that I may give all Satisfaction to every Member, I shall humbly offer in a plain manner my Thoughts in relation to it.

My Lord, This Article is the Foundation of the whole Treaty, and the Approving or Rejecting of it must determine Union or no Union betwixt both Kingdoms.

How far the Approving this Article conduces to our Happiness, appears evidently, by considering the three different Ways proposed for retrieving the Languishing Condition of this Nation; which are, That we continue under the same Sovereign with *England* with Limitations on his Prerogative as King of *Scotland*; That the two Kingdoms be Incorporated into one, or that they be entirely separated.

That the Union of Crowns with Limitations on the Successor is not sufficient to rectifie the bad State of this Nation, appears from these Positions founded on Reason and Experience.

Two Kingdoms subject to one Sovereign, having different Interests, the nearer these are one to another, the greater Jealousie and Emulation will be betwixt 'em.

Every Monarch, having two or more Kingdoms, will be obliged to prefer the Counsel and Interest of the Stronger to that of the Weaker: and the greater Disparity of Power and Riches there is, betwixt these Kingdoms, the greater Influence, the more powerful Nation will have on the Sovereign. Notwithstanding these Positions, I shall suppose the Parliament of *Scotland* is vested with the Power of making Peace and War, of rewarding and punishing Persons of all Ranks, of Levying Troops, and of the *Negative* it self.

I cou'd show the Inconveniences, that must attend such a State of Government in Disposal of Places and managing Publick Affairs; I cou'd likewise show the Improbability of attaining such Conditions, or keeping 'em if attained; but laying aside such Considerations, my humble Opinion is, That we cannot reap any Benefit from these Conditions of Government, without the Assistance of *England*: and the people thereof will never be convinced to promote the Interest of *Scotland*, 'till both Kingdoms are Incorporated into One: So that I conceive such a State of Limitations to be no better for *Scotland*, than if it were intirely separated from *England*, in which State there's little Appearance of procuring any Remedy to our present Circumstances, which appears from these uncontraverted Positions.

The People and Government of *Scotland* must be Richer or Poorer, as they have Plenty or Scarcity of Money, the common Measure of Trade.

No Money or Things of Value can be purchased in the Course of Commerce: but where there's a Force to protect it.

This Nation is behind all other Nations of *Europe* for many years, with respect to the Effects of an extended Trade.

This Nation being Poor and without Force to protect it's Commerce, cannot reap great Advantages by it, till it partake of the Trade and Protection of some powerful Neighbour Nation, that can communicate both these . . .

. . . Let us look to any other Part of the World, for Vent to our Product, and we'll find other Nations have prevented us.

If we attempt the *East-India* Trade, that is already Enhansed by the *Dutch, English, French, Spaniards* or *Portuguese,* from whom, we must expect Opposition, they themselves Opposing one another daily; and we of no Force to Debate the same, with the most inconsiderable of them . . .

My Lord, I'm sorry, that in place of Things we amuse our selves with Words; for my part I comprehend no durable Union betwixt *Scotland* and *England*, but that expressed in this Article by *One Kingdom,* that is to say, One People, One Civil Government and One Interest.

'Tis True, the Words, *Federal Union,* are become very Fashionable, and may be handsomely fitted to delude unthinking People; But if any Member of this House will give himself the Trouble, to examine what Conditions or Articles are understood by these Words, and reduce them into any kind of Federal Compacts, whereby distinct Nations have been United: I'll presume to say, These will be found Impracticable, or of very little Use to us.

But to put that Matter in a clear Light, these *Queries* ought to be duly examined, Whether a Federal Union be Practicable betwixt two Nations accustomed to a Monarchical Government? Whether there can be any sure Guaranty projected for the Observance of the Articles of a Federal Compact, stipulated betwixt two Nations; whereof the one is much Superior to the other in Riches, Numbers of People, and an extended Commerce? Whether the Advantages of a Federal Union do Ballance its Disadvantages? Whether the *English* will accept a Federal Union, supposing it to be for the true Interest of both Nations? Whether any Federal Compact betwixt *Scotland* and *England*, is sufficient to secure the Peace of this Island, or Fortify it against the Intrigues and Invasions of its Foreign Enemies? And whether *England* in Prudence, ought to Communicate its Trade and Protection to this Nation, till both Kingdoms are incorporated into one?

To clear this last *Querie,* I shall offer a Remark from History.

Of two Independent and distinct Kingdoms united by a Federal Compact under one Sovereign; the Weaker to preserve its Interest, has some times separated from the Stronger, unless prevented by open Force, or secret influence on its Government.

Spain and *Portugal* were subject to the same Sovereign, *Philip* II. And not withstanding the *Portuguese* got most Advantageous Conditions from *Spain,* they no sooner found a favourable Opportunity in the Reign of *Philip* IV. than they revolted from their Allegiance, and Elected the Duke of *Braganza* for their King.

Sweden and *Denmark* were united by a Federal Compact under one Monarch, but the *Swedes* judging a Separation more for their Interest, broke off, and choosed *Gustavus* the I. for their King . . .

. . . *My Lord*, I should now consider an Incorporating Union, as it is expressed in this Article by *One Kingdom;* but that I may not take up the time of the House, I shall only give one Historical Remark with Relation to it.

Two or more distinct Kingdoms or States, by Incorporating into one Kingdom, have continued under the same Sovereign, enjoying equally the Protection of his Government, and every part of the Body Politick, tho never so far remov'd from the Seat of Government, has Flourished in Wealth in proportion to the Value of it's Natural Product, or the Industry of its Inhabitants. To prove this Remark there are many Examples.

Spain was formerly divided into several Kingdoms, ten whereof are Incorporated into the one Kingdom of *Spain.*

France was formerly divided into 12 States, which are Incorporated into the one Kingdom of *France.*

England was formerly divided into seven Kingdoms, which are Incorporated into the one Kingdom of *England*; *Scotland* it self was formerly divided into two Kingdoms, which at present are Incorporated into the one Kingdom of *Scotland.*

I cou'd give some Account of the particular Advantages we'll obtain by an Incorporating Union with *England*, but there will be occasions to Discourse of these, as the other Articles fall under the Consideration of this Parliament. In general, I may assert, That by this Union, we'll have Access to all the Advantages in Commerce, the *English* enjoy; we'll be capable, by a good Government, to Improve our National Product, for the benefit of the whole Island; and we'll have our Liberty, Property and Religion, secured under the Protection of one Sovereign, and one Parliament of *Great Britain.*

Now, *My Lord*, If Limitations on the Successor can be of little or no Use to us; if an entire Separation from *England* brings no Advantage to this Nation: and if all Federal Compacts, as we are stated, have insuperable Difficulties, which in some measure I have cleared, there's but one of two left to our Choice, *to wit,* That both Kingdoms be united into one, or that we continue under the same Sovereign with *England* as we have done these 100 years past. This last I conceive to be a very ill State, for by it (if Experience be convincing) we cannot expect any of the Advantages of an Incorporating Union; but on the contrair, Our Sovereignty and Independency will be eclipsed, the number of our Nobility will Encrease, Our Commons will be Oppressed, Our Parliaments will be influenced by *England,* the

Execution of our Laws will be neglected; Our Peace will be interrupted by Factions for Places and Pensions; Luxury together with Poverty (tho' strange) will invade us; Numbers of Scots will withdraw themselves to Foreign Countries; and all the other Effects of Bad Government must necessarily attend us.

Let us therefore, *My Lord*, after all these Considerations approve this Article: and when the whole Treaty shall be duly examined and ratified, I'm hopeful, this Parliament will return their most Dutiful Acknowledgments to Her Majesty, for Her Royal Endeavours in promoting a Lasting Union betwixt both Nations.

SOURCE: William Seton of Pitmedden 1706 *A Speech in Parliament on the First Article of the Treaty of Union*. Edinburgh.

DOCUMENT 3

Petition, Stirling Town Council against the proposed incorporating union, 18 November 1706

This document, from a representative of the trading interest, reveals the dangers of assuming that the future of Scottish trade alone was an issue in burgh circles.

To His Grace Her Majesties high Commissioner and the Estates of Parliament. The Address of the provost Baillies Town Councill and other Inhabitants of the Burgh of Stirling.
Humbly Sheweth
That having had our most deliberat thoughts upon the great affair of the Union of the two Nationes, as Contained in the printed Articles, wee judge it our Indispensable duety to the Nation to this place, yea to posterity, with all Imaginable defference to your Grace and Honourable Estates of parliament humbly to represent, That though we are desirous that true peace and freindship be perpetually Cultivat with our neighbours in England, Up on Just and honourable termes consisting with the being, Soveraignitie & Independencie of our Natione and parliaments as defenders therof, Yet we judge your goeing into this Treaty as it now Lyes before you, will bring ane Insupportable burden of Taxationes upon this Land, which all the Grants of freedome of Trade will never Counterballance being so uncertain and precarious while still under the regulationes of the English in the parliament of Brittain, who may if they please discourage the most Considerable Branches of our Trade, if any way apprehended to interfer with their own. That it will prove, ruining to our manufactores, That it will ane expossing of our Religione, Church Government as by Law Established, our Claime of Right,

Lawes, Liberties & consequently all that's valuable, To be incroached upon, yea wholly Subverted by them, whose principles does, & Suposed Interests may Lead yr Unto, That it will be a depryving of us and the rest of the royall burghs in this Natione, in a great measure of our fundamentall right and propertie of being represented in the Legis Lative power, That therby one of the most ancient nationes so long and so gloriously defended by our worthie patriots will be supprest. Our parliaments the very hedge of all that is dear to us, Extinguished and we and our posterity brought under ane Lasting yoke which we will never be able to bear, The fatal consequences of which we tremble to think upon.

We therefore conforme to the privieledge allowed us in our Claim of right, most humbly Supplicat and firmly expect from your Grace and the Honourable Estates of parliament That ye will not conclude ane Incorporating Union Soe Destructive to many and Dangerous to the whole of these things which are dear to us, That ye will be pleased to Lay the evident Danger therof before Our Most Gracious Queen that some reliefs may be Granted untill some expedient be found out for the more universall Satisfactione of her majesties Good Subjects, That ye will so Setle the State of this Nation as the hopes and attempts of all popish pretenders Whatsomever may be forever defeat, That ye will maintain and support the true reformed protestant Religion the Government of this Nationall Church as now by Law established, The Soveraignity & Independency of this Natione in all its Liberties Sacred and Civill the undoubted properties of every Member of this Realme That ye will maintaine and defend the Rights and Being of our parliaments & our privilege of Still being represented therein without which we Cannot reckon our Selves secure in the possessione of those things soe valuable in themselves, and which we are resolved to defend with our Lives and fortunes According to our Laws and clame of right. Subscrybed be us at Stirling the eighteenth day of November 1706.

SOURCE: Perth and Kinross Council Archives, Perth Burgh Records, B 59/34/17/3.

DOCUMENT 4

Petition from the Burgh of Montrose in favour of the Union of 1707, 15 October 1706

A reflection of economic realism.

15 October 1706

Sederunt

Robert Turnbull Provost	Robert Arbuthnot Mr Hospitall
James Mudie	James Mill Late Provost
John Mill } Baillifs	Charles Ogilvie Late Provost
Alexr Rennald	Robert Petrie
David Skinner D of Gild	James Gentleman
James Ouchterlony Thesr	Alexr Arbuthnot
	George Caldercleugh

The which day the Council having thought fitt to write this day to James Scott younger of Logie Commissioner for this burgh to the Parliament to the effect after mentioned ordaine their Letter to him to be recorded whereof the tenor follows. Montrose the 15th Octr 1706 Sir We are not at all surprized to hear from you that there are sume who are not pleased with the Union, there never yet was any good Law made in Scotland (tho we have a great many very good) that was unanimously agreed to, some out of Caprice and humour, othrs from some disobligation from the Proposers and some out of interest still makeing some opposition and while these Gentlemen who are against the union will not do the nation the justice to print their reasons we will look on their opposition to proceed from some of the above reasons But not to mention the advantage of the Union which we think we are able [sic] to any to be many and great if the English Prohibitory Lawes which were repeal'd last Session of Parliament in order to facilitate the treaty do again take place as undoubtedly they will, We shall be deprived of the only valuable branch of our trade, the only trade by which the ballance is on our side and then one needs not the gift of Prophecy to fortell what shall be the fate of this poor miserable blinded nation in a few years. We therefor earnestly and unanimously Recomend to you to be active and zealous in common cause For we take this contest to be *pro aris et focis* You will also please write to us frequently especially to Inform us of any important occurences in Parliament that in matter of Consequence you may still have advice from Sr your affectionate Freinds subscribitur Ro: Turnbull Provost Jo Mudie Bailif John Mill Bailif Alexr Rennald Bailif David Skinner D. of Gild Ja: Oucherlony Tressr Robert Arbuthnot Mr Hospitall James Mill Council Clark.

SOURCE: Angus Council Cultural Services, Angus Archives, Montrose Town Archives, Montrose Burgh Minute Book, 15 October 1706.

DOCUMENT 5

Letter (abridged), James Ogilvy, 1st Earl of Seafield to Godolphin, 14 October 1706

An instance of 'political management' which in this case (the Duke of Argyll) appears to have made a difference.

Edr., Oct. the 14th, 1706.

MY LORD, – Since my last nothing has occurred befor nou worth your Lop. trouble. I have taken al the methods I was capable to use to keep the Neu Pairtie from conjoining with our Torie Pairtie, and the Marques of Montrose has concurred most activlie in this, and I doubt not bot that they will al concurr with us, which, I think, will make the cariing the Union certan . . .

. . . the constitution of this kingdom is intierlie altered by the treatie . . .

The Duke of Argyl is nou with us,[1] and seems readie to concurr, bot both he and his brother are most pressing with the Commissioner, the Secretaries, and myselfe, to desire that her Majestie may conferr on my Lord Archbald the title of ane Earle, and what ever objections ther may be to this, and of which they are fullie accquanted, yet I am sure they will not be pleased unless it be granted, and it is certanlie necessarie to keep them right at present. I promised my Lord Duke to concurr in using my interest, which I could not refuse, for I am much oblidged to him. Your Lo. will easilie determin what is fit to be done. I am for al measurs [that can] strenthen us in the carying the Union, and, if I be favored with ane ansuer, I desire it may be such as I may shou to my Lord Duke. I forbear to give your Lop. further trouble, and I am, with al respect, my Lord, etc.,

SEAFIELD.

NOTES

1 It was only after receiving the commission of a Major-General that Argyll consented to appear in Parliament and support the Union.

SOURCE: P Hume Brown (ed) 1915 *Letters Relating to Scotland in the Reign of Queen Anne by James Ogilvy, First Earl of Seafield, and others*, Edinburgh (Scottish History Society), 94–6.

DOCUMENT 6

Appendix to George Lockhart of Carnwath's *Memoirs*, in which it is alleged that 'Money was remitted to Scotland from England and employed in bribing Members of Parliament'

Lockhart's was the first widely broadcast intimation that some £20,000 had been disbursed by the Court in order to 'ease' the passage of Union through the Scottish Parliament. It should be noted, however, that Lockhart, a Jacobite, was not a disinterested party.

In the preceding Memoirs I have given a particular Account of what appeared to me, the Origine of the Treaty of Union, and of the several Views and Designs of the *Scots* and *English* Whiggs and Courtiers in carrying on and concluding the same, and have taken Notice of the many cross Accidents and Disappointments which happen'd to those who oppos'd it, and of the various, illegal, and arbitrary Methods that were made Use of to make the *Scots* Members swallow it down.

But since the compiling these Memoirs a further discovery hath been made, which evidently verifying what was with too much Reason suspected, *viz.* That Money was remitted to *Scotland* from *England* and employed in bribing Members of Parliament. I shall give a very distinct and clear Account of the Matter, as it was discover'd and reported to the British Parliament by the Commissioners, appointed in the Year 1711, for taking, stating, and examining the publick Accounts of the Kingdom.

These Gentlemen having got the scent, so closely pursued the Game, which they discovered from Sir D_____d N____n late Secretary Depute of *Scotland*, that the Sum of 20000 *l.* Sterling was remitted by the Treasury of *England* to the Earl of G____w, in the Year 1706. The occasion of which was this:

After the Treaty of the Union was concluded at *London*, the Ministers of State in *Scotland* being sensible that they'd meet with great Opposition in the carrying on their Designs in Parliament, and chiefly in the Affair of the Union, did conclude it was absolutely necessary to make Payment of part of the Arrears of Salaries and Pensions, lest some of the Persons to whom these Arrears were due, might prove humorous and ungovernable, and the *Scots* Funds being all anticipated, they applied to the Queen, laid a state of her *Scots* Revenue and Debts before her, and prevailed upon her to lend her *Scots* Treasury the sum of 20000 *l.* to be employed for Payment of part of these Arrears and Salaries. That this was the origin and pretence of that Loan, and remittance of Money is evident from the Queen's Letter to the Lords of that Treasury, a Copy whereof the said Sir D_____d N____n did upon Oath exhibit to the Commissioners of Accounts, which was by them delivered into the Parliament, and is as follows.

> *Right Trusty, and Right well beloved Cousin and Councellor, Right Trusty and entirely beloved Cousin and Councellor, Right trusty and well beloved Cousins and Councellors.*
> *We greet you well,*

'Whereas there has many Representations been made to us by our Servants, and by those who have been employed in our Service, desiring Payment of what is justly owing to them by us: We did thereupon Order you to lay before us the State of these Funds, and it appearing that they are entirely exhausted and pre-engaged for some Time to come, so that there remains nothing at present for defraying the Charges of our Government, or paying the Debts of the Civil Lists, And being desirous to do all that lies in our Power for defraying the Charges of our Government, which is so indispensible necessary for our Service, and to enable you in some Measure to pay such part of the Debts of the Civil List as we shall by particular Warrants direct, we have therefore remitted unto you the Sum of 20000 *l*. Sterling, to be disposed of by you for the Ends and Uses abovementioned, in such Manner as you shall find most fit for our Service, and for which sum you are to hold Account to us, and you are to pass an Act of Treasury, acknowledging that you have received the said sum in borrowing, to be refunded to us out of the Funds of the Civil List, or for paying the Debts thereof, and that at such time as we shall Demand the same: For doing of which, this shall be your Warrant, and so we bid you heartily farewell.'

> Given at our Court of *Windsor Castle* the 12th Day of
> *August* 1706, and of our Reign the 5th Year.
>> By Her Majesty's Command,
>>> L_____N.

After the *Scots* Ministers of State had prevailed with the Queen to write this Letter, and advance this sum, they went to *Scotland*, and finding the Country extremely bent against, and averse to the Union, they conceived it improper to deliver and read the Queen's Letter to the Treasury, and own the receiving of this Money from *England*, least it had afforded a Handle to strengthen and increase the Opposition to the Union; for at that Time of the Day, every Body would have believed that this Money was remitted to bribe Members of Parliament; to prevent which, they purposed to change the Course, in which the Queen had placed this Loan, and for that purpose wrote the two following Letters to the Earl of G___ ____n, then Lord High Treasurer of *England*; Copies of which Sir D___ d N____n likewise delivered on Oath to the Commissioner of Accounts.

My Lord,
'We are convinced, that what her Majesty by her Royal Letter to her Treasury here has promised to advance for defraying the necessary Charge of the Government, and paying some part of the Debts of the Civil List, is so needful, that the Government could not subsist without it, all the Funds of the Civil List being so far pre-engaged, as did plainly appear to her Majesty before granting of that Letter; neither can we think there can be any reasonable Objection to the doing of it, but because opposers will do every Thing in their Power to obstruct the Union, and might probably make some Noise if the Letter were read in the Treasury before the Meeting of the Parliament, and before the Treaty is well received; we think it therefore necessary for her Majesty's Service for some Time to delay making Use of

the Letter, and have thought it fit to represent this to your Lordship, and to desire that in the mean Time 10000 *l.* may be paid to Sir *D___d N____n* upon his Receipt to your Lordship; whereof the said Sir *David* is to retain 4500 *l.* on my Lord Commissioners Account, which sum his Grace, my Lord Commissioner, is to allow for his Equipage and daily Allowance, and for the remaining 5500 *l.* the said Sir *D___d N____ n* is to give an Obligation to your Lordship, to remit the same to the Earl of *G_____w*, who has given us obligation to disburse the said Sum by her Majesty's Order, or Acts of Treasury in *Scotland*, so soon as the same comes to his Hands, and the said Sir *David's* Receipt and Obligation in the Terms above mentioned, shall oblige us to procure to your Lordship's from the Treasury of *Scotland,* a Receipt in the Terms of her Majesty's Letter for the said 10000 *l.* in a short Time, when it may be more seasonable and convenient for her Majesty's Service to present it. We earnestly intreat your Lordship to grant this our Desire, being so necessary for her Majesty's Service.'

> We are my Lord,
>   Your Lordship's
>   most Obedient, and most Humble Servants,
>   Q_____y, S_____d,
>   M ____, L____n, G____w.

My Lord

'Your Lordship having complied with what was in our former Letter has been of great Use for her Majesty's Service. We now again find our selves obliged to desire, that the rest of that sum agreed to be lent to the Treasury of *Scotland*, being 10000 *l.* be likewise remitted as soon as possible; we have been obliged to give Promises to several Persons for a considerable part of Arrears, and without this sum they will be disappointed, which may prove of bad Consequence. We all agree in this, That it is unfit as yet to make use of Her Majesty's Letter to her Treasury here, or to have it known that her Majesty lends any Money to her Treasury; but afterwards we shall, in the safest and best Method, advise in what Manner, that her Majesty proposes in her Letter may be most effectually done; and in the mean Time, no Money to be remitted shall be employed but for the Commissioners daily Allowance, the Payment of the Salaries of the other Servants, and for payment of a Part of the Debts upon the Civil List, since her Majesty's Accession to the Crown. We desire your Lordship may pay in the Money to Sir *D____d N____n*, and take his Receipt for the same, together with his Obligation to remit the Money to the Earl of *G___w*, Lord Treasurer Depute. And we hereby declare, that his Receipt and Obligation, together with this Letter, shall be effectual for the Ends proposed in her Majesty's Letter to the Treasury here. We are with great respect,'

> My Lord,
>   Your Lordship's
>   most Obedient, and most Humble Servants,
>   Q_____y, S____d,
>   M_____r, L_____n, G_____w.

The Earl of G____n having nothing so much at Heart as the preventing of every thing which might obstruct the Union, was pleased to grant the desire of these Noble Lords, and though the Queen had expresly required that the *Scots* Lords of the Treasury should give her Treasury in *England* a publick security for the Re payment of that Money, did accept of these Lords missive Letters as a sufficient security for the same, and ordered the Money to be paid to Sir D____ d N_____n, who carefully, about the time that the *Scots* Parliament met, remitted it to the Earl of G____w, to be employed by his Lordship for promoting his Countries Ruine and Misery.

This Money being remitted after this Manner, was attended with another Advantage besides the concealing it was from *England*; for had the Loan been as the Queen designed it, publickly owned and received, all the several Persons, who had Arrears due to them would certainly have expected, and could not well have been refused a share thereof; but now the Ministers of State were absolute Masters of it, and could secretly (which was a great Point) dispose of it, to whom, after what Manner, and to what purposes they pleased. And fatal experience teaches us, That they did it to the best advantage by distributing it after the Manner, and to the Persons contained in the following Account, exhibited on Oath by the Earl of G____w to the Commissioners of Accounts.

	l.	*s.*	*d.*
To the Earl of M_____t	1104	15	7
To the Earl of C____ y	300	00	0
To the Lord P____ n H____ ll	200	00	0
To the Lord O___n, Lord Justice Clerk	200	00	0
To the Duke of M____se	200	00	0
To the Duke of A_____e	1000	00	0
To the Earl of B____s	500	00	0
To the Earl of D____e	200	00	0
To the Lord A____r	300	00	0
To Mr. S_____t of Castle S_____t	300	00	0
To the Lord E_____n	200	00	0
To the Lord F_____r	100	00	0
To the Lord C_____k, now P____h	50	00	0
To Mr. *John* C____ll	200	00	0
To the Earl of F_____r	100	00	0
To Sir K_____h M_____e	100	00	0
To the Earl of G_____n	100	00	0
To the Earl of K_____e	200	00	0
To the Earl of F_____ r	100	00	0
To *John* M____r Provost *of Air*	100	00	0
To the Lord F____s	50	00	0
To the Earl of S_____d Lord Chancellour	490	00	0
To the Marquiss of T_____e	1000	00	0

To the Duke of R____h	500	00	0
To the Lord E____s	50	00	0
To the Lord B____f	11	02	0
To Major C____m of E____t	100	00	0
To the Messenger that brought down the Treaty of Union	60	00	0
To Sir W____m S____p	300	00	0
To Patrick Coultrain, Provost of Wigton	25	00	0
To Mr. Alexander W____n	75	00	0
To the Commissioner for Equipage and daily Allowance	12325	00	0
	20540	17	7

Which Ballance of *540 l. 17 s. 7 d.* was as the Earl of G____w did acknowledge, paid him by the Earl of G____n, when he accounted to his Lordship for the 20000 *l.* he had received as aforesaid, and expended as by the particulars mentioned in the abovesaid Account.

The Commissioners of Accounts in their report of this Affair to the Parliament, do observe, That they are at a loss to explain some Expressions in these Letters (meaning two Letters from the *Scots* Lords to the Earl of G____n) such as that opposers to the Union would make some Noise if her Majesty's Letter were read in the Treasury; That they had been obliged to give Promises to several, and without the Sum desired, they would be disappointed, which might prove of bad Consequence; That they would not have it known that her Majesty lends any Money to her Treasury; and then these Commissioners add, That they will not presume to guess at the Reasons of these Insinuations; but humbly conceive, that if the Money had been fairly applied to the pretended purpose, there could have been no such occasion for so much Caution and Jealousy.

Such as endeavoured to justify the Conduct of the Ministers of State in this Matter, seem to wonder how the paying of just Debts can be reckoned a Fault, and especially a bribing of Members of Parliament.

To which I Answer, that it may with far more Reason be alledged, That the bestowing of Employments would not admit of such a Construction, since there must under all Governments, and in all Countries, be Employments and Persons appointed to Officiate in them, and yet, who is it that does not know, that often, nay, for the most Part, all Pensions and Employments have been bestowed, or continued, in order to procure Friends to assist the Designs of such as have the disposal of them.

But supposing that this Matter, when taken in a general View, might be fair, and could be justified, yet the Tables turn if you'll consider the particular Case and Circumstances of it; for tho' the Ministers of State in *Scotland* were very lavish in obtaining Pensions to stop the Mouths of hungry Gapers, yet they seldom or never paid them, but as a particular Favour, and upon particular Views; and who ever will impartially reflect upon the grand Affair under Agitation; when this pretended Payment of Arrears was made; and Place from whence the Money; the Clandestine Manner of obtaining and disposing of it; and lastly, that all the Persons (excepting the Duke of A____e) on whom it was bestowed, did Vote for and promote the Union: Whoever, I say, will impartially reflect upon these Particulars, must conclude, that the Money was designed and bestowed for bribing of Members of Parliament.

I mentioned that the Duke of A_____e, notwithstanding he got part of this, did oppose the Union; and this some would urge as an Argument, to prove the same was not applied as hath been alleged.

But alas! *One Swallow does not make a Summer*; and tho' his Grace did nevertheless stand his Ground, yet who knows what the Managers did expect, and with what Intention they gave it?

But what follows puts this Matter beyond all manner of Controversy; for the Commissioners of Accounts having required from the Auditors of the Exchequer in *Scotland*, an Account of all Pensions and Salaries due at any Time, from the Queen's Accession to the Throne, to the Commencement of the Union, to the Persons contained in the aforesaid Account, exhibited by the Earl of G ____w; and a particular Account of all Payments, and the Time when made, to such Persons, on Account of such Pensions and Salaries: It did appear from the Return, that several of these Persons, such as the Dukes of M___se and R____h, Sir K___h M_____e, the Earl of B_____s, Pat. C_____n, *John Muires*, the Lords F_____r, B____f, and E____k, had no manner of Claim, all that they on such pretence could have demanded, being paid to, and discharged by them a considerable Time before the distribution of this Money; and others, such as the Dukes of Q_____y and A____e, Lords E_____n and A_____r, Mr. S_____t of *Castle-Stuart*, Lord P____ll, and Marquiss of T_____e, gave no acquittance for, nor is there any Notice taken in the Records of the Treasury, of the Money they thus received from the Earl of G____w; so that in a few Months thereafter, when they obtained Certificates from the Lords of the Treasury of what was due to them on account of Arrears of Pensions and Salaries, some of them had no regard at all, and others only in part, to what they had received from the Earl of G_____w, and being thus entituled to the full of their Arrears out of the equivalent, many were consequently twice paid in whole or in Part.

These Facts being undoubtedly true, it evidently appears, that what was given in either of these Cases, must have been with some other View, and on some other Pretence, than Arrears of Pensions and Salaries.

The Duke of Q_____y having after the Union received the Sum of 22986 *l.* 12 *s.* 2 *d. Sterling* out of the equivalent, being the full of his Equipage Money and daily Allowance, as high Commissioner to the Parliament, did afterwards repay what he had received from the Earl of G____w on the same Account, But was it paid back again to the Treasurer as the Queen first designed it? But, as the Commissioners of Accounts discovered (after a great many Oaths and

Examinations of the Earls of *G____n*, and *G____w,* and Sir *D____d N_____n*, altogether repugnant and contradictory to one another) to the Queen her self, in a private clandestine Manner; and since the said Commissioners do affirm in their Report, That it was not applied to the Use of the Publick, People generally believe, that Her Majesty was pleased to return it to the Duke of *Q_____y* and the said two Earls, as a Reward for their good Services in carrying on the Union.

Murder will out, and what is thus discovered, is sufficient to satisfie any Man of the true Motives that induced the Ministry of *England* to lend this Money, and directed the Ministry of *Scotland* in the distribution of it.

It is abundantly disgraceful to be any manner of Way a contributor to the Misery and Ruine of ones Native Country; but for Persons of Quality and Distinction, to sell, and even at so mean a Price, themselves and their Posterity, is so Scandalous and Infamous, that such Persons must be contemptible in the Sight of those who bought them, and their Memories Odious to all future Generations.

FINIS.

SOURCE: George Lockhart of Carnwath 1714 *Memoirs Concerning the Affairs of Scotland From Queen Anne's Accession to the Throne to the Commencement of the Union of the two Kingdoms of Scotland and England in May 1707*, London, 405–20.

DOCUMENT 7

Letter, James Ogilvy, 1st Earl of Seafield, to Godolphin, on the progress of the Articles of Union in the Scottish Parliament, 7 November 1706

Further evidence of the steps thought necessary to ensure that the Articles of Union would be approved by the Scots.

Edr., Novr, the 7th, 1706.

MY LORD, – Since my last to your Lop., wee have caried by a majoritie of 32 vots the first article of the Union in the terms of the resolve I formerlie mentioned, bot, ther being a memorial concerning this and several other particulars, which my Lord Commissioner and her Majesties servants finds to be necessarie to obtain the Union to be past hier, I hope that wee will be aloued to make thes alterations. I shal give your Lop. no further trouble with relation to what is contained in it. Ther have been several adresses against the Union presented to the Parlament, bot what troubls me most is that from the Commission of the Assemblie, which declairs the Union inconsistant with ther principels, it being contrarie to the Covenant that the bishops sitt in the Parlament, bot I have not seen it.[1] I hear it is to be presented to morou. A copie of it shal be transmitted. The majoritie of a convention of borous have also addressed against it. After al wee hope, if the alterations be aloued, wee will carie it in Parlament. The Jacobit Pairtie continou to oppose it with violence. The Neu Pairtie, the E. of Marchmont and L. of Cromertie gives us al the assistance wee can desire. The D. of Argyl influences the M. of Lothean and his oun friends, so your Lop. sees wee have a majoritie that I hope will not fail us, bot without thes alterations nothing can be done that will pleas the treading peopel. The M. of Annandale continous to oppose the Union. The minuts will inform your Lop. of his proposel of a federal union or the succession with limitations, bot he had verie feu that concurred with him. Wee have given a first reading to the act for the Church, and wee have also given a first reading to ane act for a supplie. This could be delayed no longer, for the fonds are out and a great arear diu to the armie. Wee shal make what haist wee can, bot, tho wee continou with the majoritie wee have, wee cannot end so soon as is desired. I have onlie time to add that I am, with al respect, my Lord, etc.,

SEAFIELD

NOTES

1 On November 7, Mar wrote: 'One thing I must say for the Kirk, that, if the Union fail, it is owing to them.'

SOURCE: P Hume Brown (ed) 1915 *Letters relating to Scotland in the reign of Queen Anne*, Edinburgh (Scottish History Society), 101–2.

JACOBITISM

DOCUMENT 8

Reasons for appointing and observing a day of solemn fasting and humiliation . . .

*Episcopalians provided the bulk of active support for the Jacobite cause.
James Garden's sermon, composed for delivery at Aberdeen during the
'Fifteen, encapsulates the militancy of the political attitudes current amongst
the Episcopalians.*

The reasons drawn up in great part by Dr. James Garden I read from the pulpit in
the New Church of Aberdeen.

Reasons for appointing and observing a day of solemn fasting and humiliation,
to be read from the pulpit after the end of divine service on the Lord's Day
immediately preceeding, by the several ministers to whose hands this comes.

N.B. There was another draught sent from the Angus clergy, but they having
no right to impose on us, I did not obey.

The great corruption of all ranks and degrees both in Church and State within
the Kingdom, during the long course of prosperity, peace, and plenty, under the
auspicious reign of Charles the Second of happy memory, and that of his Royal
brother James the 7th, did provoke God in his just judgement to punish us with an
unhappy (dysmal) Revolution, which has proved a fruitful mother of many
miseries, and calamities under which this nation has groaned this twenty-seven
years past.

By it our (then) king was, against all divine and human law, deposed by a
prevailing faction of his own seditious and unnatural subjects, with the help of a
forraign prince, and forc'd into exile with his Royal Consort of the Crown, and
the Heir (our present king) in his cradle: the fundamental laws and constitution of
the kingdom subverted: the Hereditary right of the succession to the Imperial
Crown of this Realm diverted from the right line: and thereby the prospect of a
war entailed on us, and our posterity for many generations to come, even as long
as any of the Royal Family or their posterity excluded by the late Act of
Settlement, are in being.

By it the ancient Apostolick form of Church Government was abolished and
the true and faithful pastors of the Church deposed and violently thrust from their
offices, houses and livings, and exposed with their families to misery and want: the
rights of the Church usurped by Schismatical teachers, who have set up separate
communion from the Catholick Church of Christ in all ages: Lorded it over the
nobility and gentry and commons of this kingdom upon whom they did thruyst in
their preachers by armed force and violence in many places against the inclination
of the people, and even contrary to the rules of their own discipline, and ruled with
a rod of iron: and poysoned the minds of their hearers with factious and seditious

principles, and dangerous doctrines, tending to sour and imbitter the spirits of men, enervate the sacred truths of the Gospel and render them of no force towards the subduing of man's corrupt lusts and passions and advancing the kingdom of Jesus Christ in their hearts and lives.

Finally, by it the nation has become involved in the dreadful guilt of perjury, occasioned by the rigorous imposition of various oaths and those often to be repeated, upon all persons in any place, power or trust, Ecclesiastical, civil or military, which, it is to be feared, many have taken against the light of their own consciences and many ignorantly and unadvisedly: and under its shadow, Atheism and Irreligion have increased and abounded to a great degree, to the great dishonour of God and the decay of Christianity.

For these heinous sins and abominations of Rebellion, in justice, oppresssion, schism and perjury, God in his just wrath hath visited and plagued us with a long, a bloody and expensive war, several years of famine and extraordinary death, accompany'd with epidemical diseases and a great mortality, whereby the wealth and strength of this nation has been exhausted and our land in a great measure dispeopled: with the loss of the liberty, privileges and independency of this our ancient kingdom: with bondage under a forraign prince and with unsupportable burdens and taxes formerly unknown to us and our forefathers, that threaten utter ruin to us and our posterity.

As the banishment of the late K.J. gave rise to all the miseries and calamities that have ensued, so the only natural and proper remedy for removing the same, in subordination to the good and gracious Providence of God, is the restauration of his present Majesty, James the 8th. our natural and rightfull King, and with him, the settlement of our ancient laws and liberties, and re-establishment of our Legal Constitution both in Church and State, without which, nothing is left us but the dismal prospect of our misery and disgrace being derived and perpetuated to the succeeding generations.

Since it has pleased God at this time, to inspire many of the Nobility, Gentry, Burgesses and Commons, with a pious zeal and a generous courage for vindicating and asserting the rights of their King and country with the hazard of their lives and fortunes . . .

If moreover, when it was in the power of Pbrian teachers, by their influence upon the Nobility, Gentry and others of their (?way) to have preserved the liberties, priviledges and independency of this our ancient Kingdom, they allowed and tamely permitted the nation basely and shamefully to be sold and enslaved contrary to express remonstrances of most part of the Kingdom, under the specious name and pretence of the Union with England and this to the end that they might get the heavy yoak of Pbry unalterably wreathed on our necks, and the necks of our posterities to all generations for ever.

SOURCE: National Library of Scotland, MS 1012.

DOCUMENT 9

Information against Mr Thomas Murray, 30 March 1719

To qualify for toleration under the Toleration Act (1712), Episcopalian ministers had to pray for the sovereign. Evasion of this was commonplace and a source of great irritation and anger to many Presbyterians.

Information against Mr Thomas Murray Episcopal Preacher in the meeting house of Balledgerno within the parish of Inchsture and Presbytrie of Dundee

Mr Thomas Murray Episcopal Preacher in the Meeting house at Balledgerno in Manifest contempt of the Decreet & Sentence pronounced against him by the Sheriff of perth upon the   day of   Cost pyning and Amerciating him in Twenty pound Sterling for performing Divine Service in the Said Meeting house upon the dayes therin Mentioned without praying for Our Soveraign King George, The Prince and Princesse of Walls and all the royal familie in express words, and in open defyance and violation of the Laws of this Realm, continues still to exercise all the parts of the Ministerial function is to perform Divine worship in the Said Meeting house without praying for His Majestie, the Prince and Princesse and royal familie as above, and particularly Upon the Lords days following, To wit March the Twenty Ninth The Said Mr Murray in the Said Meeting House celebrate the Sacrament of the Lords Supper, preached on the fryday before & Sabbath preceeding being the Twentie Second day of the Said Moneth, all this unto a Considerarable body of Disaffected people, known and avowed enemies to the government both of Church and State who resorted from all Corners. As also the Said Mr Murray preached there upon the first, eight, fifteenth, and twenty second days of this current March, performed other parts of Divine worship without praying Nominatim for His Majestie King George the Prince and Princesse and royal family, and that before these witnesses Mr Patrick Greenhill late School Master in Longforgan & < . . . > baillie there James Kinnear & James Stewart both Grenars there and Alexander Low-Smith also there: James Ratry tennent in Balledgerno, Andrew Inst, James Coup, Francis Jackson, Patrick Inst all Tennents in Inchsture Further the said Mr Murray upon the fourth or fifth or Sixth or Seventh or eight days of February last, he Married in the Haltoun of Newtyle Henry Crawfoord Younger of Monorgan claindestinely without proclaimation of Bann with the only daughter of Mr James Paton late Minister of Kelin the said Monorgan being under Scandal and contumacious to the discipline of the Church before these witnesses the Said Mr James Patoun, & Patrick Smith of Over yeards above Mentioned.

This Information given by some Ministers of the Presbyterie of Dundee is by their appointment Signed at Inchsture – this thirtieth day of March One Thousand Seven hundred and Nineteen years . . .

SOURCE: Perth and Kinross Archives, Bell Public Library, B59/30/48.

Extracts from pamphlet 'To All True-Hearted Scotsmen, Whether Soldiers or Others', printed by Robert Freebairn in Perth in 1715

Fears about the possible political consequences of the restoration of a Catholic monarch were extremely difficult for the Jacobites to allay.

1   By the Earl of Mar's Manifesto we find, that the present Quarrel turns upon these two points, The restoring our Lawful Natural King, And the dissolving the Union; Both which should be seriously weigh'd by all Scotsmen, being of the utmost importance, both on the score of Conscience, Honour and Interest.

2   You are to fight against your Lawful & Rightful King, born in our own Island, of the Antient Stock of the Royal Family of the Stuarts, against whom there is not so much as a ground of Quarrel alledged, but what that he was born a Prince, and has a Right to govern us: For whatever might have been objected to his Father since he himself has done no wrong, 'tis against all the receiv'd notions of Justice & honour to punish the Innocent for the sake of Guilty . . .

5   Our Whole Nation either is, or pretends to be sensible of the mischief of the Union; we feel the weight of it to our cost; and the inconveniences will daily increase, as is obvious to any that will look before him . . .

6   But I am sufficiently aware that you are taught to say that you disclaim the King for his principles both in Religion & Politics, and were he a protestant, and had been bred with any Tolerable notions of the British constitution would think his government supportable, and would not oppose his restoration.

Pray, Gentlemen tell me where did you learn that a difference in Religion absolved the subjects from their allegiance to their lawful King? Did our Saviour or his Apostles think themselves excused from obedience to the Roman Emperors because they were Heathens? Or does the confession of faith, in the 23 article, teach any such doctine: is ther any Law of our Country that makes good this plea: I say any Law made by a lawful King & Parliament? Think better of it before you run such desperate courses upon so sandy a foundation.

Besides, pray what assurance have you of the King's being a Papist? Is it because he was educated in a popish country. He was so, more shame for those who were the occasion of it; and whatever mischief may be apprehended from that education, it is owing to the banishers of the Royal Family in the great Rebellions of 41 & 88. But did you never hear of a man of sense get over the prejudice of Education? Indeed, I cannot but say if all protestants follow your example, in going contrary to all received maxims of Religion and honesty by keeping your King from what is due by a more undoubted right than any man in Scotland holds his estates, it were bad encouragement for his Majesty to embrace a religion so plainly contrary to the principles of the Gospel. But as his Majesty well knows that the Injustice done him under the pretence of the protestant religion is not authorized by it, and has ground enough to be assured that it is disclaimed by the very best protestants in Britain, so I must still think that the force of truth which is certainly on our side, will convince him of the mistakes he may have formerly been subject to and his happy Restoration give him an opportunity to declare with safety that he truely is of the one Catholick Church, without the addition of Roman.

7   But let the King's religion be what it will, He has under his hand given us all the security we can ask, that he will maintain the protestant religion in these kingdoms & fence it from any danger by such laws, as shall by the advice of his Parliament, be thought necessary. And we have this demonstration of his being in earnest in his promise that no men of judgement & wisdom would venture the loss of his Dominions a second time for attempting what he plainly sees to be impracticall in Britain. And if I had no other reason to think the protestant religion secure by the King's Restoration, I can't but judge this consideration of great weight, viz – That the Pope & Popish Princes combined to destroy his Royal Father & himself, and his Protestant subjects are the chief asserters of his right, and promoters of his restoration. Let no body then amuse you with imaginary fears of Popery, for by your glorious revolution the Protestant, nay the Christian Religion suffered more in Britain by Atheism, Deism & contempt of God's true worship, than I tryst in God it shall ever do by the administration of our lawful sovereign.

SOURCE: National Library of Scotland, MS 1011.
Handwritten copy of a pamphlet printed by Robert Freebairn in Perth in 1715.

DOCUMENT 11

Letter from George Lockhart of Carnwath to the Old Pretender, 18 December 1725

George Lockhart, a leading Jacobite agent, offers his King, James VIII, advice on a number of important matters relating to staging a restoration attempt.

Sir,

. . . Taking it then for granted that in any attempt you're to make you'll be supported by a forreign force, such as may promise probable hopes of success, tis thought your grand effort will be in England, and the nearer to London the better. In which case all needful or expected from Scotland will be a diversion to the army in Scotland, so as to prevent that army's being called to England, or to embarass them in their march, so as to hinder a conjunction with the other forces. If with that view the army you sent to Scotland were able to make a stand against the Government forces then sure the best landing place is on the south side of the Firth of Forth, because they may be joined by your friends in the south of Scotland, and a communication will be secured with England, whereas if they land on the north side of the Firth of Forth these will be prevented, whilst your friends in the north of Scotland need no help. But if the army you send are not so numerous, then they should land in the Highlands, so as they may be quickly joyned by the Highlanders.

Whichever way you take, arms, ammunition, saddles, money, are all wanting here, and must be supplyed elsewhere, and it is very necessary to send a good number of officers, that is, a few of some rank, and as many subalterns and staff officers as possible. I have mentioned these particulars, because your friends are far from being in the same condition they were *anno* 1715. As the aversion to the Union dayly encreases, that is the handle by which Scotsmen will be roused to make a general and zealous appearance. This your enemies are so sensible of that on former occasions all pains were taken to buzz in the peoples' ears that they'd be disappointed in what they expected from the King, for that to please your subjects of England, you was to uphold the Union. Now as I am fully perswaded the better part of the English are far from thinking the Union beneficial to either Countrey, I cannot see but it is expedient for the King to gratify his friends in Scotland, and thereby advance your own intrest, and in order thereto that so soon as your army lands a manifesto should be published (as designed formerly) with respect to religion and containing an ample assurance of your design to maintain the two kingdoms in their ancient independent state by dissolving the Union pernicious to both. And it would be of great service if in this manifesto the King recommended to the electors in shyres and burrows to have their thoughts on proper persons to be by them chose to represent them in Parliament, which it is your intention should meet so soon as the state of affairs will allow, to consider and make such laws as may be judged necessary for securing [the] religion, laws and libertys of your ancient kingdom. Were some copies thereof printed and sent over beforehand, so as to be ready to be dispersed immediatly on a landing, it would answer the design to better purpose, but this must be done with great caution to prevent a discovery and seizure.

These are some of the cheif matters that occurrd to us in general, and to be more particular is not practicable, unless we know the nature and time of your design more particularly. The choise of a general is a matter of great importance, could one have his wish, he'd be native of a good rank and character, and well versed in both civil and military affairs, but one with these enduements is not, I am affrayd, to be got, and therefor it would appear that this defect must be supplyd by branching out these several powers into several hands. That is, that the management of your military be committed to a bred souldier (to which none affected towards the King now in this Countrey can pretend) who should correspond and live in perfect good terms with him or them where the supreme power in other matters is lodged, or perhaps in some degree of subordination thereto, who should be nevertheless particularly intrusted and required to move entirely by the advice and direction of the general in all military affairs.

Could harmony be effectually maintaind, this or some such in the present juncture would be the most probable scheme . . .

ENDORSED: 'George Lockhart to the King. Decyphered. December 18th 1725. Received by Mr Cameron Aprile 14th 1726.'

SOURCE: D Szechi (ed) 1989 *Letters of George Lockhart of Carnwath, 1698–1732*, Edinburgh (Scottish History Society), 251–53.

DOCUMENT 12

Letter from George Lockhart of Carnwath to Hay, 12 March 1726

While the Highlands remained the most likely source of armed support for a Jacobite rising in Britain after the 'Fifteen, this support could not be expected to be unqualified.

Sir,

... I come now to some other parts of your letter, to which you demand a particular answer, tho what has been represented in some former letters might suffice. If, as you lay down, a sufficient force be sent to England, 'tis a matter of less consequence where the landing place be in Scotland. However, to be somewhat more particular, if the armement for that Countrey consist of one thousand men, then I conceive some such place for landing must be chosen as will allow of an easy and speedy conjunction with the Highlanders, without whom such a body will not be able to make a stand against the regular forces now here. And in the case of two thousand, it would be so contrived that they might have it in their power to joyn the Highlanders, in case it was found necessary, and with this view I reckon the Firth of Clyde a proper situation, where are the ports of Irvine, Grenock and new port Glasgow, either of which may be chosen, as seems most proper at the time. The countrey thereabout (if right measures with respect to the Union and Scots Parliament as mentiond lately to the King be followd) will I beleive be found favourably inclined, and from Glasgow that number can force their way to the Highlands or wait till the Highland clanns force their way to them, if so be such a speedy conjunction was necessary.

How far a landing in the west of Scotland will correspond with the place of embarkation, we here can't pretend to judge, as we know nothing of that particular, but if there come three thousand, the Firths of Clyde or Forth are equally almost convenient as its an easy march to take possession of the capital and seat of Government, for I reckon such a body of men with those that will quickly joyn, especially if the Highlanders get out at the heels of the troupes quartred in the north of Scotland, if they move to the south of Scotland, will be a force sufficient against any opposition can be dreaded in this Countrey, unless England be entirely abandond, and the English army be sent to Scotland, which I could wish did happen, as it would make the game sure there.

On this subject I must caution you to neglect no means of timously preparing the Highlanders for such an affair, for much depends on them and their early appearance. Mr Cameron will I beleive very justly give a fair representation of their attatchment to the King, but as it is natural for all mankind to mention their own Countreymen with some favor, 'tis to be supposed he'll set the affairs of that Countrey in the best light he can, and which perhaps will hold good, but at the same time I think myself bound to tell you that I can on very good grounds assure you those people, tho perfectly well disposed, will act with more caution than formerly. They're a subtile cunning race, and will not move till they be assured that they'll be supported effectually, and it will require a good deal of prudence and address to satisfy them in this necessary article, so as they may resolve and prepare for it, and not run the hazard of discovery too soon. This I thought proper to mention as being a matter that deserves to be maturely considerd and prudently determined and executed. The questions that have of late been put to us about the choise of a General, landing place, etc, gives us great hopes that something for our relief is on the anvil, which is never more wanted, and would never be more joyfully received . . .

ENDORSED: 'George Lockhart. March 12th 1726. Decypherd.'

SOURCE: D Szechi (ed) 1989 *Letters of George Lockhart of Carnwath, 1698–1732*, Edinburgh (Scottish History Society), 270–2.

Letter from George Lockhart of Carnwath to the Old Pretender, 4 August 1727

Like many others, Lockhart was, by 1727, the year in which George I died, pessimistic about the prospects and likely consequences of a further restoration attempt, especially without the support of a major foreign power. His advice to James is all the more powerful for being so gently expressed.

Sir, Nothing could have surprised me more than my accidentall meeting with the bearer[1], but the account I got from him of you and your late resolutions being what indeed I did not in the least imagine or expect. Not being provided with some materialls twas with some difficultie I read yours. However, I made shift to understand the purport, and the same reason will prevent my writing so clearlie as otherwise I woud.

The subject of yours is a matter of the greatest consequence, and tho it was very naturall for you to desire to be in a condition to make benefite from any happy circumstances that might occur, yet I am much affraid nothing of that kind is like to happen at this juncture.[2] I have no intelligence from tother side of the water, but by the publick letters tis plain that the people of England are intoxicated at present, having forgot their late ailments by the (ill-ground) hopes of a better management, and till they find themselves dissapointed, I can form no hopes from them, especially seing you have no prospect of what you and all your advisers judgd essentially necessary, even under the fairest of veiws, for your support and others' encouragement. And as for Scotland, they can't possibly do any thing without being provided in many materiall things they want and ere that can be done much time and many difficulties must be surmounted, during which opposite preparations will be made on all hands.

I readily grant twere an double advantage to give the stroke in the beginning, least affairs at home and abroad grow worse and be rivetted, but then even under this consideration this is not to be attempted without necessary precautions and provisions, for without these, such, or any, attempt woud be too desperate and without miracles from heaven prove the utter ruin of all future hopes. I belive Scotland is much as I left it, that is, very well disposed, but withall so overrun and oppressd that it is impracticable for them to do anything but jointly and in concurrance with their neighbours of England, and I am pritty well assured this notion is so establishd and fixed in their breasts that they will scarce on any event divert from it, so that all depends on the people of England, and for a certain person to venture over without ane assurance of some support may prove pernicious to him and fatall to all that wish him well. I have with the bearer enterd into the particulars on which I found these my sentiments, which he'l narrate and explain more fully that I can write. No man living woud more gladlie see the dawning of a fair day, but when every airth of the compass is black and cloudie, I cannot but dread bad weather, such as can give no encouragement to a traveler, nay cannot well fail to prove his own and his dependents' ruin and destruction. What I have represented is from the very bottom of my heart and soul, which at the same time I submit with the greatest respect to your judgement.

[no farewell or signatures]

Endorsed (not in Edgar's hand): 'G Lockhart, August 4, 1727'.

NOTES

1 Allan Cameron.

2 The Old Pretender had made a dash from Rome to Lorraine with a view to getting to Britain quickly in the event of a revolt against the new king.

SOURCE: D Szechi (ed) 1989 *Letters of George Lockhart of Carnwath, 1698–1732*, Edinburgh (Scottish History Society), 312–3.

POLITICS

DOCUMENT 14

An exchange in the House of Commons, 1711

In the first few parliaments of the United Kingdom, Scots anti-unionists continued to be elected. This letter shows them congratulating themselves on scoring a point off the Government at Westminster. At this stage both sides were still using sharp language, but in time they grew more respectful of each other's sensibilities.

Jan[ua]r[y] 30 [1711]

Sir, My lord gives his Most humble service to You, and bids me tell you that Mr Fletcher[1] wa[s] going to giv[e] Carnwath[2] a Kiss for saying yesterday (he calls it) in the house of commons, one of the best things, to Mr Harley,[3] that ever was said. The Scots pleading that no further imposition should be laid on Scots linnen exported, that being our chiefe commodity, as wool was of England, Mr Harley said we had no reason to complain, for they had bought it, with the Equivalent.[4] Up rises Carnwath and said he was very glad to hear that, from so good a hand, for since he knew that we were bought it confirmed what he ay thought, that we were sold. This was much taken notice of by a house that loves free speaking. My lord adds, his father[5] never made a better Speech, tho it was shorte. Ther is no other news but it's said Kilsyth[6] and Blantire[7] are each of them to hav a new regiment. I am Sir your Most humble Servant, Ann Balmerino.[8]

NOTES

1 Andrew Fletcher of Saltoun (1653–1716), commonly called The Patriot, on account of his fierce opposition to the Union.

2 George Lockhart (1681–1732) of Carnwath, Jacobite MP Edinburghshire, 1708–15.

3 Robert Harley (1661–1724), MP New Radnor Boroughs, 1690–1711, Chancellor of the Exchequer, 1710–11, Lord Treasurer, 1711–14, created 1st Earl of Oxford and Earl Mortimer 23 May 1711.

4 This was the sum of £398,085 paid by England to Scotland at the Union as compensation for the failure of the Company of Scotland (the Darien project), and for the Scots paying, apart from a few exceptions, the same customs and excise duties as the English. See PWJ Riley 1964 *The English Ministers and Scotland, 1707–1727*, London, 203–29.

5 Sir George Lockhart (d 1689) of Carnwath, a highly successful lawyer well-known for his eloquence. He was President of the Court of Session. See D Szechi (ed) 1989 *Letters of George Lockhart of Carnwath, 1698–1732*, Edinburgh (Scottish History Society), xiv–xv.

6 William Livingston (1650–1733), 3rd Viscount Kilsyth, representative peer, 1710–15, took part in the Jacobite rising of 1715, was attainted and forfeited his title 1716.

7 Walter Stewart (1683–1713), 6th Lord Blantyre, representative peer, 1710–13. A follower of Argyll.

8   The author was wife of John, 4th Lord Balmerino (1652–1736), an opponent of the Union.

SOURCE: Letter from Lady Balermino, *Scottish History Society Miscellany* XII 1994, Edinburgh, 124–5, reproducing Scottish Record Office, GD45/14/352/3.

DOCUMENT 15

Scott's description of the 2nd Duke of Argyll

Injustice is a central problem of Sir Walter Scott's great novel The Heart of Midlothian *(1818). At both the personal and political level, right social relations are seen as the key to dealing with it. They place a special burden on those born at the top of the scale, and in Scott's view the 2nd Duke of Argyll amply fulfilled the obligations which that entailed. Injustice could, of course, also come out in the way a bigger England treated a smaller Scotland. In this passage, Scott indicates how Argyll's personal conduct and character averted injustice (though note that right at the end, the Duke suffers injustice himself).*

> My name is Argyle, you may well think it strange,
> To live at the court and never to change.
>
> *Ballad*

Few names deserve more honourable mention in the history of Scotland, during this period, than that of John, Duke of Argyle and Greenwich. His talents as a statesman and a soldier were generally admitted; he was not without ambition, but 'without the illness that attends it' – without that irregularity of thought and aim, which often excites great men, in his peculiar situation, (for it was a very peculiar one,) to grasp the means of raising themselves to power, at the risk of throwing a kingdom into confusion. Pope has distinguished him as

> Argyle, the state's whole thunder born to wield,
> And shake alike the senate and the field.

He was alike free from the ordinary vices of statesmen, falsehood, namely, and dissimulation; and from those of warriors, inordinate and violent thirst after self-aggrandizement.

Scotland, his native country, stood at this time in very precarious and doubtful situation. She was indeed united to England, but the cement had not had time to acquire consistence. The irritation of ancient wrongs still subsisted, and betwixt the fretful jealousy of the Scottish, and the supercilious disdain of the English, quarrels repeatedly occurred, in the course of which the national league, so important to the safety of both, was in the utmost danger of being dissolved. Scotland had, besides, the disadvantage of being divided into intestine factions, which hated each other bitterly, and waited but a signal to break forth into action.

In such circumstances, another man, with the talents and rank of Argyle, but without a mind so happily regulated, would have sought to rise from the earth in the whirlwind, and direct its fury. He chose a course more safe and more honourable.

Soaring above the petty distinctions of faction, his voice was raised, whether in office or opposition, for those measures which were at once just and lenient. His high military talents enabled him, during the memorable year 1715, to render such services to the house of Hanover, as, perhaps, were too great to be either acknowledged or repaid. He had employed, too, his utmost influence in softening the consequences of that insurrection to the unfortunate gentlemen, whom a mistaken sense of loyalty had engaged in the affair, and was rewarded by the esteem and affection of his country in an uncommon degree. This popularity with a discontented and warlike people, was supposed to be a subject of jealousy at court, where the power to become dangerous is sometimes of itself obnoxious, though the inclination is not united with it. Besides, the Duke of Argyle's independent and somewhat haughty mode of expressing himself in Parliament, and acting in public, were ill calculated to attract royal favour. He was, therefore, always respected, and often employed; but he was not a favourite of George the Second, his consort, or his ministers. At several different periods in his life, the Duke might be considered as in absolute disgrace at court, although he could hardly be said to be a declared member of opposition. This rendered him the dearer to Scotland, because it was usually in her cause that he incurred the displeasure of his sovereign; and upon this very occasion of the Porteous mob, the animated and eloquent opposition which he had offered to the severe measures which were about to be adopted towards the city of Edinburgh, was the more gratefully received in that metropolis, as it was understood that the Duke's interposition had given personal offence to Queen Caroline.

His conduct upon this occasion, as, indeed, that of all the Scottish members of the legislature, with one or two unworthy exceptions, had been in the highest degree spirited. The popular tradition, concerning his reply to Queen Caroline, has been given already, and some fragments of his speech against the Porteous bill are still remembered. He retorted upon the Chancellor, Lord Hardwicke, the insinuation that he had stated himself in this case rather as a party than as a judge: – 'I appeal,' said Argyle, 'to the House – to the nation, if I can be justly branded with the infamy of being a jobber or a partisan. Have I been a briber of votes? – a buyer of boroughs? – the agent of corruption for any purpose, or on behalf of any party? – Consider my life; examine my actions in the field and in the cabinet, and see where there lies a blot that can attach to my honour. I have shown myself the friend of my country – the loyal subject of my king. I am ready to do so again, without an instant's regard to the frowns or smiles of a court. I have experienced both, and am prepared with indifference for either. I have given my reasons for opposing this bill, and have made it appear that it is repugnant to the international treaty of union, to the liberty of Scotland, and, reflectively, to that of England, to common justice, to common sense, and to the public interest. Shall the metropolis of Scotland, the capital of an independent nation, the residence of a long line of monarchs, by whom that noble city was graced and dignified – shall such a city, for the fault of an obscure and unknown body of rioters, be deprived of its honours and its privileges – its gates and its guards? – and shall a native Scotsman tamely behold the havoc? I glory, my Lords, in opposing such unjust rigour, and reckon it my dearest pride and honour to stand up in defence of my native country, while thus laid open to undeserved shame, and unjust spoliation.'

Other statesmen and orators, both Scottish and English, used the same arguments, the bill was gradually stripped of its most oppressive and obnoxious clauses, and at length ended in a fine upon the city of Edinburgh in favour of Porteous's widow. So that, as somebody observed at the time, the whole of these fierce debates ended in making the fortune of an old cookmaid, such having been the good woman's original capacity.

The court, however, did not forget the baffle they had received in this affair, and the Duke of Argyle, who had contributed so much to it, was thereafter considered as a person in disgrace.

SOURCE: Walter Scott 1818 *The Heart of Midlothian*, Edinburgh (Constable), Chapter 35.

DOCUMENT 16

The electoral campaign for a Scots burgh district, 1789

*This letter concerns the campaign in a typical district of burghs – Aberdeen,
Arbroath, Brechin, Inverbervie and Montrose – in the months before the
General Election of 1790. The franchise lay in the town councils which each
cast one vote, so the victorious candidate had to get three councils on his
side. The sitting member, Sir David Carnegie, was attached to the opposition
at Westminster. Here we see his efforts to hang on against a push by the
Government, with a candidate in David Callander, to dislodge him. There
are no holds barred: carrots and sticks are wielded with equal abandon. But
the decisive argument was probably that 'it is the duty of every member for
Scotch boroughs to support the Minister of the day'. Carnegie lost.*

Sir David Carnegie *to* William Adam, 14 *November* 1789

Endorsed by Adam's clerk: David. Carnegie/14th Novr. 89
Endorsed by Portland: 21 Novr/Adam

Dear Sir
. . . I am sorry to say that the state of the matter is such, as not to warrant me to be
sanguine, though I do not look upon it as desperate. The history of it is briefly
this – after many private assurances & an apparently favorable michaelmas
election[1], I took the field; & in a couple of days after my circular Letter, Montrose,
Aberbrothock[2], & Brechin gave me answers, signed by almost every individual in
each council, that they would support me. I went to . . . Aberdeen to endeavour to
make the matter sure by securing them, but I found they had already associated
against me at the instigation of Mr Barclay of Ury.[3] In the mean time Mr Scott,[4] the
India Director, & our county member elect, started Mr Callander[5] against me at
Montrose; & the arguments used by these nabobs[6] there have had such an effect
that, of seventeen who signed my letter, nine have avowed a determination to break
their engagement, & they are joined by two others who had not signed; making the
division at present eleven against me; & eight, partly for me & partly
undetermined . . . It is possible that I may reclaim some of the eleven; but besides
that many of them may be secured by *presents*, the share that they all expect in the
distribution of custom house & other places fascinates them – & they cannot be
disappointed, as my opponents openly avow that it is the duty of every member for
scotch boroughs to support the Minister of the day; & that if a change were to
happen, they would wheel about of course. This system may not appear a bad one
alltogether to *you* – in the contemplation of future events; but I cannot combat
such strong arguments myself; & they treat me very disagreably in Montrose,
where contrary *to precedent* all custom house places have been given to strangers
ever since I was their representative. I would however state one idea for your
consideration, & I shall not press it, if thought improper. There is a belief at
Montrose that the collector of the customs has not long to live, & the hopes of

succeeding him has certainly drawn off one principal man, if not more from me: Views of inferior posts have probably debauched others. Now though it is common to consider those offices when once obtained as being for Life, I think myself, that in a case where they are obtained by such uncommon perfidy as the breach of a written engagement, common rules should not be observed; & that I should have authority from our friends to say, if I see it proper, that should *they* ever have the power, they will at my request dismiss such rascals from whatever employments they may chance to have got possession of. This threat might be of use, & I would not employ it if I did not find a proper occasion. As I must have tired you with this long Letter I shall only add to it that if any change happen for the better I shall let you know – & I hope if you have any good news to communicate, you will not let me be the last to be informed of it. I am with great regard

      Dear Sir
        Yours faithfully
        DAVID CARNEGIE
Kinnaird 14th Novr 1789

NOTES

1 Town Councils were elected at Michaelmas (end of September).

2 Arbroath.

3 Robert Barclay Allardice (1732–1799), of Urie (Kincardine). He had inherited and acquired through his second marriage large estates in Kincardineshire and the Aberdeen Burghs. He was attached to Government, it was thought because he was seeking to revive the Scottish Earldoms of Strathearn, Monteath, and Airth in his wife's line. In 1788 he had been returned for his county with the assistance of Henry Dundas. See Sir Charles Elphinstone Adam (ed) 1887, *View of the Political State of Scotland in the Last Century,* Edinburgh, 12, 183–184, and Sir Lewis Namier and John Brooke (eds) 1964 *History of Parliament: The House of Commons, 1754–1790,* 3 vols, London.

4 David Scott (*c.* 1746–1805), of Dunninald, MP Forfarshire 1790–1796, Perth Burghs 1796–1805. He was the Ministerial candidate for the county (Adam *Pol. State,* 158).

5 Alexander Callander (1741–1792), of Crichton.

6 'Nabob' was the popular nickname for people who had made a fortune in India.

SOURCE: Letter from Sir David Carnegie, *in* DE Ginter 1967 *Whig Organization in the General Election of 1790,* Berkeley (University of California Press), 126.

DOCUMENT 17

Henry Dundas's speech on the Union, 1799

Rebellion in Ireland in 1798 led the British Government to adopt a drastic solution to that country's chronic problems, a Union with Great Britain on lines similar to those of the Anglo-Scottish Union of 1707. Dundas, one of the most senior ministers, advocated it in the House of Commons on the grounds that Ireland could expect the same advantages as Scotland had won during the past century. Here is an extract from his main speech setting out that view, which he develops by considering the criticisms of the Union made by its enemies. Dundas's intervention in the debate was reckoned one of the most decisive. The Union of Great Britain and Ireland came into force on January 1, 1801.

Many melancholy pictures, in the shape of prophecies, were presented to the public view on that memorable occasion. Among other false prophecies, permit me to make a few remarks on that celebrated speech of lord Belhaven[1]: 'I think I see', exclaimed his lordship, 'a national church voluntarily descending upon an equal level with the Jews, Papists,' &c. Now to prove his lordship a false prophet in this, I not only think I see, but I actually do see, that very national church, founded upon a firm foundation, at the distance of ninety years from the passing of the act of Union; and that very national church so firmly secured in all her privileges, that it is very likely she will continue to possess them, unimpaired, for ever! In truth, her simplicity and her poverty will remain to her an impregnable security against the plunder and rapine of all ruffian hands! 'I think I see,' continues his lordship, 'the noble and honourable peerage of Scotland, now divested of their followers and vassalages, and put even on an equal footing with their own very vassals.' If the union has had a tendency to break asunder the bands of feudal vassalage[2], which prevailed to too great an excess in that country, wise and virtuous men will not be disposed to consider this as one of the evil consequences to be lamented in the formation of a legislative union of the two kingdoms. As to the peerage of Scotland, considered as a body in the state, it may be true they suffered some transitory mortifications in consequence of the union[3]; but I believe there is no candid or good man in that whole respectable body who would wish to change their present situation for all the pomp and poverty they enjoyed previous to the union. 'I think I see,' adds his lordship, 'the royal state of boroughs walking their desolate streets,' &c. On the contrary, I see that the boroughs, instead of being desolate, are most of them ten times improved in population, in industry, and in wealth! To prove this, it is only necessary to mention the names of Edinburgh, Glasgow, Aberdeen, Perth, Montrose, Dundee; and, in short, every other town of any name or consequence in that part of the united kingdom. 'I think I see our learned judges,' continues lord Belhaven, 'laying aside their practices and decisions, studying the common law of England,' &c. Now I see no such violation or alteration of the municipal law of Scotland, which is as purely administered now as it was before the union took place. But although the Scotch judges do not study the common law of England, by way of introducing it into their courts, I certainly must do my lord Belhaven the justice to acknowledge, that at all times the northern part of the island has produced some of the brightest luminaries of the law of England, who never would have emblazoned Westminter-hall with their transcendant talents, had not the union taken place between England and Scotland. 'I think I see', adds his lordship, 'the valiant and gallant soldiery of Scotland, all their old corps broke up, the common soldiers left to beg, and the youngest English corps kept standing.' Now I do see, that the natives of Scotland, both in the army and the navy, from the common soldier, and the man before the mast, to the general in the field, and the admiral on the ocean, instead of being worse treated than the English, are put upon the most equitable footing with the soldiers and the sailors of this part of the united kingdom, according to their respective merits! I do see nothing but the most liberal rewards and provisions made for the Scottish as well as the English hero; both of whom have consolidated their strength, by a politic and glorious union, for the general benefit of every part of the British empire! 'I think I see,' continues this noble false prophet, 'the honest industrious tradesman drinking water in the place of ale; eating his saltless pottage, and petitioning in vain for encouragement to his manufactories!' – The increase of excise, in Scotland, since the time of the union, is certainly no proof that this part of the prophecy has been fulfilled; or that water has become the beverage of the people of Scotland. But I need not enlarge on this topic. The reverse of the prophecy is notoriously the truth, in every respect. 'I think I see the laborous ploughman,' adds this visionary, 'with his corn spoiling upon his hands, for want of sale, cursing the day of his birth,' &c. – Now I do see on the contrary, the mere ploughman enjoying treble wages, and treble comforts; while his master, the farmer, instead of his corn spoiling upon his hands, for want of sale, reaps such profits from its immediate sale, as enables him to live almost upon an equal footing, in point of every social enjoyment, with even the hereditary landed gentleman, the possessor of the soil itself! 'I think I see', continues his lordship, 'the pretty daughters of our landed gentlemen petitioning for want of husbands, and their sons for want of employment.' – Now I do see, and I believe every one in this House sees, that the pretty daughters of the Scotch nobility and gentry, so far from petitioning for husbands, bear, at the present moment, a very high premium in the hymeneal market of the English aristocracy!

I need not enlarge on a topic which is proved to every man's observation, by the examples daily passing before them. In truth, nothing has tended more to accelerate the happy connexion which now subsists between the two parts of the island, than the intercourse of friendship, habits, and affection, arising from the union of the beauty, wealth, and talents, produced by the intermarriage of the inhabitants of the opposite sides of the Tweed. And as to their sons petitioning for want of employment, let me do justice to this liberal nation by declaring, that we need only look into every profession in life, from the Scotch gardener, baker, and hair dresser; up to the Scotch merchant, the Scotch physician, the Scotch general, the Scotch admiral, and the Scotch lawyer, to prove, that, since the union, merit has been equally rewarded throughout the whole island, whether its possessor was rocked in his cradle on the south, or on the north side of the Tweed! The noble lord concludes this prophetic reverie, with an allusion to the death of Julius Cæsar, which he compares to the murder of 'Mother Caledonia', by her own sons in the Scotish parliament. The comparison is so wild and inapt in all its parts, that it would be a waste of time to pursue it. If the Scotch parliament had been such a tyrant as the comparison would suppose, there was real patriotism in her instant annihilation. But in justice to the memory of my ancestors, I disclaim any such charge, as imputable to the ancient Scotish legislature. Whoever will take the trouble of perusing the acts and regulations of the Scotch parliament, will find a fund of much wisdom and good policy to admire. But the union of the two kingdoms is ill understood, and ill defended, by those who conceive that it proceeded either from want of wisdom, or want of virtue in the Scotch parliament; it proceeded from a principle of rendering the exertions of its members more extensively useful, by enlarging its functions; and making them, as they now are, sharers in the deliberations of that legislature, which is the only truly exalted assembly, for the rational and practical freedom, for the security and the felicity of man, on the whole surface of the habitable globe!

NOTES

1 Lord Belhaven, an opponent of the Union, made his speech to the Scots Parliament on 2 November, 1706.

2 A reference to the abolition of heritable jurisdictions.

3 Mainly because only 16 representatives, rather than the whole peerage, sat in the House of Lords at Westminster.

SOURCE: *Parliamentary History* 1799 XXXIV, c 345–65.

DOCUMENT 18

Letter from Henry Cockburn to Thomas Kennedy, 26 April 1827

With the resignation of Lord Liverpool as Prime Minister in the Spring of 1827, the broad-bottom Tory administration which had ruled for more than twenty years began to break up. George Canning, Liverpool's successor, was hated by the high Tories and had to win support from the Whigs. This letter shows some of the repercussions in Scotland. Thomas Kennedy and Henry Cockburn are Whigs wondering how they could work in government with Tories they have always opposed. But they are happy at the prospect of getting rid of a special Minister for Scotland. The Whigs' plan was that Scottish affairs should be overseen directly by the English Home Secretary as a cure for alleged corruption in Scotland.

Edinburgh, 26th April, 1827

My dear Kennedy[1],

I have been for several days in a state of excessive errancy, and have got your letter only this moment on coming home from Inverness.

I shall write to you fully in a day or two, but I cannot lose a moment in telling you some things which may be safely acted upon in so far as Scotland is concerned.

In the first place the Liberals here are all in raptures with the defeat of the Tories and the rise of the Whigs, and instead of excluding themselves by stickling for everything right, the decided opinion of the wise here is that it is the duty of the Whigs to take office, and to do what good they can, though with the minimum of power.

Secondly, neither Rae[2] nor Hope[3] have the smallest intention of resigning – not the slightest. Rae will be very glad to go into the retirement of the Exchequer Bench[4], and Baron Rattray[5] will be very glad to make room for him if his son be made a Sheriff; all of which would be quite right. But Rae cannot afford to resign and wait.

Thirdly, I do not believe that there is any sane Whig here who would hesitate to take office even in combination with John Hope. Hope will be perfectly liberal as soon as liberality is in vogue, and no man is entitled to risk the rising cause of Scotland by rejecting its advancement in his company.

Fourthly, and ABOVE ALL, save us from the continuance of the horrid system of being ruled by a native jobbing Scot[6]. Hope is in extacy at the prospect of getting quit of Rae, and getting in Binning[7], *i.e.* himself. Now if we are to be the slaves of the Hopes, we had much better have remained subject to the old hereditary rule[8] . . .

Ever yours,
H. Cockburn.

NOTES
1 Thomas Kennedy, Whig MP for the Ayr burghs 1818–34.

2 Sir William Rae, the Tory Lord Advocate (1818–34), out of Parliament at this point, having lost his seat at the General Election of 1826.

3 John Hope, the Tory Solicitor-General.

4 The Scottish Court of Exchequer dealing with financial cases had five judges, called Barons. It was later abolished.

5 James Rattray, Baron of Exchequer.

6 A reference to the Scottish system of political management.

7 Thomas Hamilton, Lord Binning, another contender to take over the Scottish system.

8 A reference to the previous managers, Henry and Robert Dundas, Viscounts Melville.

SOURCE: Henry Cockburn 1874 *Letters chiefly connected with the affairs of Scotland*, London (W Ridgeway), 153–4.

DOCUMENT 19

Memorandum for the private consideration of those principally concerned in maintaining the Conservative Interest in the County of Midlothian, March 1833

This provides an interesting insight into how Conservative 'machine-politics', personified by the lawyer David Horne, responded to defeat in Midlothian following the Reform Act. The first General Election under the reformed system was held in December 1832 and resulted in many Conservative losses including the seat of Sir George Clerk.

Although Sir George Clerk[1] was unsuccessful in the late contest for the County – the first since the formation of a new constituency – there is good reason for hoping that the same result would not follow another contest.

Considering the state of the times – the excitement in the public mind at the time the Election took place – and the intimidation exercised over the voters and the consequent breaking of pledges – it is perhaps surprising that the majority was not greater than it was.[2] It is not likely that all these causes will operate again – or at least to the same extent – at another Election; and as it is almost certain that a considerable number who voted for Sir John Dalrymple at the late Election against their private feelings – (some because he was first in the field, but most because they considered themselves bound to give their first vote to the party who got them the franchise) – will on the next occasion support Sir George Clerk. It is quite well known that many now regret the course they followed; and there were also several of Sir George's friends who were frightened to come forward at that time, who will probably give their votes in different circumstances.

For these reasons, and considering that there was nothing very formidable in the majority by which the Election was carried, there does not appear to be any cause for despondency in regard to the state of the County.

But it appears to be absolutely necessary, in order to ensure success, that means be taken in the meantime, not only for keeping up the interest of the party, but also for strengthening and extending it; the more so as it may be said that the two Parties are nearly equally balanced, and that almost the whole landed interest, which must in the end have its legitimate influence, and so turn the balance, is on the Conservative side.

With this view it is suggested that those principally concerned in keeping up the interest of the Party in this county should immediately come to some understanding in regard to the future, and give some authority and directions for their interests being attended to at the next and subsequent Registration of voters. Many claims of friends, which were rejected at last Registration, may be rectified; and many more may be brought forward – but none of this will be done if left to the parties themselves.

The acquisition of property, and the introduction of a friendly and respectable Class of Voters, is another very important object which should always be kept in view, and acted upon when occasion may offer.

This plan has already been acted upon to a certain extent, and some considerable purchases have been made and friends found, who have been willing and ready to take them, and who will be enrolled next August. But in these cases purchasers had been previously found who were willing to take Qualifications. There are various properties affording votes, which could be bought just now (almost all belonging to Voters of Sir John Dalrymple) but they cannot be purchased until some persons are found ready to be the purchasers. And, while matters continue on this footing, the Case cannot be otherwise, and thus frequent opportunities of purchasing properties (which are from [time] to time coming into the market) will be lost, and possibly the property may be bought by the opposite party.

It appears evident that there is no way in which the landed proprietors can so surely, or so legitimately and fairly maintain their influence in the county as by purchasing Ten Pound properties in the villages, *and so getting them out of the hands of a class of men who cannot be depended upon at any time.*

Whenever a desirable purchaser can be found, a sufficient qualification can be given to him; but if the property is not sold, or given in liferent, it is almost certain to let, and in general a very good return can be got for the purchase money.

It may be stated that in the Town of Dalkeith alone 16 votes have been made, since the Election, by purchases in favour of friends who will be enrolled next August, and many more can be so made though not now in time for the first Registration. The price of the Qualification to each gentleman is generally from £210 to £230 for the best purchases, and properties affording only one qualification may be had for £150. All these yield rents equal to from Six to Seven and a half per Cent of the purchase money.

It is manifest that very little can or will be done in this way by the opposite party, compared with what may be done by the Conservative Party, and there can be no doubt that if this course is steadily and quickly pursued that the Conservative Interest will ere long be so materially strengthened in this county as to ensure the return of a member in that Interest.

Another matter connected with the purchase of property, and the making of votes, which requires to be provided for, is the expence attending the same.

It will often happen that, although friends are found ready to purchase, it may not be prudent to put them to the expence of the purchase – and also that in some cases the seller must be relieved of any expence. Although this is a secondary consideration yet it should be kept in view as it will often afford considerable facility in arranging such transactions.

There are also many other modes of making votes, but it is not necessary to enter into particulars here. All that is now submitted is that some plan should be agreed upon and put in operation for having the interests of the Party properly looked after and kept up. For, unless this is done, all the trouble and expence of the late contest will have been thrown away, and it will be in vain to attempt another. Whereas if proper means are now taken there is every prospect of the interest of the Party being again firmly established, and pre-dominant, in this County, notwithstanding of the Reform Bill.

[Donald Horne Esq., WS]

NOTES
1 Clerk, the Tory candidate, won the seat in 1835 but lost it again in 1837.
2 Sir John Dalrymple had a majority of sixty-five.

SOURCE: JI Brash 1974 *Papers on Scottish Electoral Politics*, Edinburgh (Scottish History Society), 6–8, reproducing National Library of Scotland, Melville Papers, MS 2, fos 175–8.

RELIGION

The Case of Christian McGregor and Robert Monteath (and child), 1794–6

This document concerns a typical charge or 'libel' of fornication brought before a Church of Scotland kirk session. This case started in 1794 in Aberfoyle Parish in the Trossachs. Over several meetings of the session, you can see the details of the alleged offence unfold as those charged and the witnesses give evidence. Note how the second woman involved, Agnes McMurrick, is quite cagey about her own actions so as to protect herself against possible charges. Once all the evidence is heard, the Aberfoyle session is unable to decide, and the case is passed up to the superior court, the Presbytery of Dunblane, which is much less hesitant. In the interim, however, Christian's case is settled, but Robert's part is not completed for almost another two years.

Aberfoyle 13th July 1794
The Session being met & duly constituted, Sederunt the Revd Mr. Graham Moderator, Walter Graham, John Macfarlan, Andrew McInnes & John Swan Elders – Voluntarily compeared Christian McGregor in Dasher of this parish, Acknowledging herself to be with child; and after being solemnly exhorted by the Moderator to speak the truth, and nothing but the truth, she declared that Robert Monteath, in the Barony of Duchray and Parish of Drumen [Drymen], was the Father of her Child: she was summoned, apud acta, to attend the Session on Sabbath the 27th. Inst. – and it was resolved to take the proper steps to procure the Attendance of the said Robert Monteath. Closed with prayer.

Aberfoyle 27th July 1794
The Session being Met & constituted – Sederunt the Rev. Mr. Graham Moderator, Walter Graham, John Macfarlan, Andrew McInnes, Duncan Macfarlan & John Swan Elders. Compeared Robert Monteath in Duchray accused by Christian McGregor in Dasher as being the father of her child, & being solemnly exhorted by the Moderator to tell the truth, and nothing but the truth; and being interrogated as to his Guilt with Christian McGregor, solemnly declares in the negative. Closed with prayer.

Aberfoyle 17th August 1794
The session being met and constituted . . .
Robert Monteath in Duchray and Christian McGregor in Dasher being called compeared. Christian McGregor being interrogated, declared again, that she has no other father of her child to give up, except Robert Monteath: and the said

Robert being also interrogated, persisted in denying all guilt.

Christian McGregor being desired to condescend upon some circumstances tending to fix the Guilt, declares that two or three nights before the latter fair of Doun[e], (that is, before the 5th day of Nov. last) while she was in bed with Agnes McMurrick, her fellow servant in the house of her Master John Macfarlan in Blarvaigh, Drumen parish, the said Robert came into her bed: that Agnes McMurrick then left the bed; and that she and Robert were seen together in bed, by the said Agnes McMurrick, Alex. Stewart, & Hugh Mcphie, also servants in Blarvaigh. The Session resolved to take the proper steps to summon the said Agnes McMurrick, Alex. Stewart & Hugh Mcphie before the Session for Examination. Closed with prayer.

Aberfoyle 14th September 1794
The Session being met and constituted . . .
In Consequence of a summons executed by the kirk Offices of the parish of Drumen – compeared Alex. Stewart servant to John Macfarlan in Duchray Drumen Parish. – And being solemnly exhorted to declare the truth in the cause of Christian McGregor & Robert Monteath: he declares that a few nights before the latter fair of Doun, and as he thinks on a Thursday, Robert Monteath being a night at his Master's, John Macfarlan, about the time the family were going to bed, instead of going to bed with the declarant, went into bed with the two Girls Christian McGregor & Agnes McMurrick: that he saw him in bed with them, and that he is fully convinced that both he and the women had all their clothes off: that he continued in bed with them for a considerable time, & at length came to bed with the declarant: being interrogated whether Agnes McMurrick left the bed when Robert Monteath came in, he replies that he cannot say whether she did or not.

In the same cause and summoned by the same Authority – compeared also Hugh Mcphie servant to John Mcfarlan in Blarvaigh, and being solemnly exhorted to delare the truth, and nothing but the truth, he declares, that as far as he recollects, it was on the Thursday before Christian McGregor left her service /that is the Thursday before the 5th. day of Nov./ that Robert Monteath, being in his Master's house, and to sleep with him and Alex. Stewart, put off his clothes at the bed side, and then went into bed with Christian McGregor & Agnes McMurrick, who slept in the same room, and were in their bed naked: that the said Robert staid in bed with the women for a long time, – at least an hour, and then came to bed with the declarant: that he knows not whether Agnes McMurrick left the bed or not.

Compeared also in the same cause and summoned by the same Authority, Agnes McMurrick, servant to John Macfarlan in Blarvaigh, and being solemnly exhorted to declare the truth, and nothing but the truth, declares that as far as she recollects Christian McGregor left her service on Friday before the 5th. Day of Nov.: that on the night before, as She & Christian were lying in their naked bed, Robert Monteath, being there that night, after putting of his clothes at the other bedside, came in to them; that she, the declarant lay on the back side of the bed – and Christian on the foreside. – That Robert lay down on the foreside, so that

Christian was in the middle; that she the declarant desired Robert to leave the bed; which he not doing, she turned her back to them, and thought no evil would happen: that Robert continued in bed with them a considerable time, and then went to his own bed. Being interrogated whether she left the bed she declares, that she does not exactly remember whether she did or not; but that it is very possible she did; but cannot be certain.

Being interrogated whether she had an opinion of their being guilty that night, she replies that she had no suspicion of them.

The Session after deliberating on the matter, unanimously resolve to refer the whole cause simpliciter to the Rev. Presbytery of Dunblane to meet there on the second Tuesday of Nov. next – for direction and advice – and they summon the said Christian McGregor, apud acta, to attend said presbytery: and they appoint the Moderator to procure Robert Monteath to be summoned by the Session of Drumen to attend said meeting of presbytery. Closed with prayer.

Aberfoyle 19th October 1794
[Following another case of fornication:] . . . Christian McGregor in Dasher was also publickly rebuked before the Congregation for her sin of fornication: the Session appointed her to compear next Lord's day to be rebuked and pay her fine for the School of the Poor [ten shillings and sixpence] with the Clerk's and beadles fees [one shilling to the clerk, sixpence to the beadle, making a total of twelve shillings]. Closed with prayer.

Extract from the Records of the Presbytery of Dunblane.
Dunblane 11th November 1794
The Presbytery of Dunblane being met & constituted – A Reference from the Session of Aberfoyle in the cause of Christian McGregor & Robert Monteath was read, and parties being called & suitably exhorted, Robert Monteath judicially acknowlegded before the presbytery that on the night alleged he, having all his clothes off, was in bed with Christian McGregor & Agnes McMurrick. The Presbytery therefore, tho' he persists in denying the guilt, do unanimously find him censurable as guilty of Fornication with the said Christian McGregor, and allow her to purge the Scandal according to the Rules of the Church: and parties being called in, this Sentence was intimated to them.

Aberfoyle 21st June 1796
This day Robert Monteath underwent Church Discipline & satisfied the Session of Aberfoyle for his sin of Fornication with Christian McGregor of this parish having paid a fine of twenty Shillings Sterl. with the Clerk's & B's dues: he is now absolved from the Scandal.

SOURCE: Stirling Archive Services, Register of Church Discipline of the Session of Aberfoyle, CH2/704/4.

DOCUMENT 21

Parishioners as described by various ministers in *The Statistical Account of Scotland*

The Statistical Account of Scotland *(or Old Statistical Account as historians refer to it) was published in the 1790s. In it, every parish minister in Scotland was invited to provide an account of the topography, economy, religion, education and society of the parish; however, some ministers failed to do so and some entries were written by others. This document provides extracts from a collection of parishes in which Church of Scotland ministers talk of the parishioners.*

a) *Kirkmichael (Ayrshire)*

As to their religious character, there is certainly less apparent seriousness, and less respect to the external ordinances of religion, than there were to be seen in former times. It is to be regretted, that a proper respect to religion should ever be diminished; it gives ground to suspect that there is not a real regard to it. If this increases, and becomes general, the consequences will be dreadful. Morals, among the bulk of mankind, will stand upon a precarious foundation, as they will be without the restraints necessary to keep them from going astray.

b) *Kinnaird (Perthshire)*

Their religion may be often tinctured with superstition, but it is seldom heated with enthusiasm. If, where it is in truth, it is accompanied with little fervour, it however operates as a calm, rational, steady principle of wise and virtuous conduct.

c) *Kintail (Ross-shire)*

Reasons for the growth of Popery;

The [Church of Scotland] Presbytery of Lochcarron in 1778 entered into a resolution, and passed an act obliging every member [ie minister] thereof to keep regular registers of baptism. And that, instead of the usual due, one shilling should in future be exacted, to enable the schoolmasters to keep up and preserve the registers. Many of the most ignorant in Glenelchaig hearing of the new act, considered it as a heavy grievance; and to avoid its consequence, applied to Roman Catholic priests for baptism, and in the heat of passion dragged whole families after them.

Popery has increased by intermarriages. When a Protestant man marries a Roman Catholic woman he has very little domestic peace or happiness till he professes that religion, in which, he is often told by the wife, salvation can only be expected. This is a web which catches many a filly-fly.

It is to be regretted that the people are subject to low and melancholy fits, which (as is conjectured) arises from too much hazy and damp weather; on these occasions a priest with whom the art of exorcism is supposed to be found, attends for relief to the distressed. If it happens that a kind providence thereafter removes the malady, the glory of the cure redounds to human frailty, and the pretended miracle becomes the ground and ostensible reason of conversion.

Lastly, the people in the district of Glenelchaig, where Popery prevails most, are extremely ignorant, and easily become the dupes of trafficking priests . . .

d) Loth (Sutherland)

As to the moral and religious character of the common people, they are generally sober, serious, and industrious, attentive to their business and credit, humane in their deportment, respectful to their superiors . . . No doubt there are exceptions, especially amongst the lowest class: of whom there are many addicted to pilfering, when they expect to escape detection, or to come off with impunity. The better sort have an high veneration for the forms of religion, and are very strict in the exercises of devotion in their families, and in attendance on public worship, of which there is no form but that of the established church in the parish. This uniformity of opinion as to doctrine and worship is not confined to this parish, but extends over all the country [ie county]: which is an uncommon appearance in a free nation, and amongst protestants, not owing to any thing peculiar in the inhabitants of Sutherland, but entirely, to their local situation, and external circumstances. However though there be no open schism to divide them in public worship, they have their lay-leaders, some of the boldest and most conceited speakers at fellowship meetings, whom they implicitly believe, merely on account of their high pretensions and affected sanctity, by which they impose upon the people, and frequently mislead them. Of late, they have begun to keep fellowship meetings amongst themselves, without the prescence of a minister. To these meetings they convene at certain fixed periods from different parishes, propose questions in divinity, explain scriptures, and give a sanction to any doctrines or opinions that are considered as orthodox by the presiding saint. The evil consequences of these meetings on the heads and hearts of the people are begun to be too clearly seen by the clergy; but they have not been able as yet to devise a method of suppressing them; if they are allowed to proceed, it is not easy to say, in what they will terminate at last.

e) City of Edinburgh

[Letters sent to the Edinburgh contributor by William Creech, publisher, in December 1792]

In 1763 – It was fashionable to go to church, and people were interested about religion. Sunday was strictly observed by all ranks as a day of devotion; and it was disgraceful to be seen on the streets during the time of public worship. Families attended church, with their children and servants; and family worship was frequent. The collections at the church doors, for the poor, amounted yearly to L.1500, and upwards . . . The clergy visited, catechised, and instructed the families within their respective parishes, in the principles of morality, Christianity, and the relative duties of life.

In 1783 – Attendance on church was greatly neglected, and particularly by the men; Sunday was by many made a day of relaxation; and young people were allowed to stroll about at all hours. Families thought it ungenteel to take their domestics to church with them: The streets were far from being void of people in the time of public worship; and, in the evenings were frequently loose and riotous, particularly owing to bands of apprentice boys, and young lads. Family worship was almost disused. The collections at the church doors for the poor had fallen to L.1000. . . . Visiting and catechising were disused (except by a very few), and since continue to be so: Nor, perhaps, would the clergy now be received with welcome on such an occasion . . .

In 1791 – The collections at the church doors had risen to L.1200.

f) *Abbey Parish of Paisley*
Sunday schools, though upon a small scale, have been lately established, both in the town of Paisley and Abbey parish: Institutions that have become highly necessary since the introduction of the cotton spinning, which engages children before they have got almost any education of any kind, and which occupies them from morning to night throughout the week.

g) *Carluke*
Amongst those who attend the Established Church, there is scarce an instance, either of wild enthusiasm, or of a persecuting and cruel spirit . . . The discipline of the church has been always exercised with mildness. In ordinary cases, only one appearance is now required [before the congregation], and antenuptial fornication dismissed with a sessional rebuke, like a private marriage; so that none are hardened by frequent appearances; and marriage is encouraged in all.

h) *Glenorchay and Inishail (Argyll)*
 . . . with us of the church of Scotland, many of our country kirks, are such dark, damp, and dirty hovels, as chill and repress every sentiment of devotion. They, besides, endanger the health of every class of worshippers, and encourage the indifferent and indolent . . .

i) *Edzell (Forfarshire)*
The people are nearly of one class and condition. Their way of living arises, either wholly or in great part, from the culture of the ground. Their manners are suitable to their condition . . . It is beyond a doubt, that the people are much improved since last century, both in morals and in manners. In the old [kirk session] records there are instances of persons subjected to discipline for dragging nets on the Sabbath; and farmers, with their wives and servants, convened in parties for drinking, fighting and scolding, on the Lord's day during divine worship. Such irregularities would now cause horror.

j) *Harris (Island of)*
[In relation to] the rude state of the poor people, in regard to civil and religious improvement . . . too clearly indicates neglect on the part of those whose interest

and whose duty it was to have enlightened them. Their vices are such as must be supposed, among a people professing Christianity, to proceed from difficulty of access to gospel ordinances, and from a total want of police. We would therefore spread a veil over them.

k) *Barony of Glasgow*
(a parish extending from Shettleston in the east, then north-westwards to the north of the Cathedral, past Port Dundas and then south-westwards to Anderston.)

[Breakdown of total population as they adhered to each denomination:]

Connected with Church of Scotland	12,369
Relief [Church]	2,793
Burghers [A branch of the Secession Church]	1,564
Antiburghers [Another branch of the Secession Church]	1,054
Reformed Presbytery [the successors of the old covenanters]	220
Episcopalians	171
Independents, or Congregationalists	162
Methodists	64
Baptists	25
Roman Catholics	20
Quakers	4
Bereans [a presbyterian-orginating evangelical sect]	3
Glassites [another similar sect]	2
Total	18,451

l) *Shotts (Lanarkshire)*
The Seceders are much more numerous than the members of the Established Church . . . After a [patronage] struggle which lasted upwards of six years, the settlement of Mr. Laurence Wells, late incumbent [parish minister] in Shotts, was at length effected in the year 1768. Soon after this, a meeting-house was built, to which the great majority of the people called a Burgher clergyman.

m) *Peterculter (Aberdeen)*
[Some young people attend a Church of Scotland chapel-of-ease in Aberdeen rather their local parish church.] It is pretended that they go to hear favourite preachers, those eminent for popularity; but I have heard it alleged, that they are drawn thither by motives not purely of a religious nature.

n) *Kilmadock or Doune (Perthshire)*
Language – The language of the common people in this parish, like many of the parishes in the neighbourhood, is a mixture of Scotch and English. This jargon is very unpleasant to the ear, and a great impediment to fluent conversation . . . In the quarter towards Callander, the generality of the inhabitants speak Gaelic; and this is perhaps still more corrupt than even the Scotch, in the other quarters of the

parish. It is impossible to conceive any thing so truly offensive to the ear, as the conversation of these people . . .

Character of the People – In this district, a simplicity of manners, peculiar to rural felicity, has, for a long time, prevailed. A stranger to deceit, the honest farmer whistles along the lawn, is quite careless of modern refinement, trusting his success and prosperity to the kind hand of providence, and the faithful bosom of the earth. He is now, however, beginning to perceive, that man was not formed a simple passive being, but inquisitive, active, persevering, and industrious. The genial warmth of religion, and the piercing rays of philosophy, begin to expand his ideas . . .

SOURCE: DJ Withrington and IR Grant (eds) 1983 *The Statistical Account of Scotland 1791–1799 edited by Sir John Sinclair*. East Ardsley (EP Publishing).
Vol VI Ayrshire, 382 (parish of Kirkmichael)
Vol XI South and East Perthshire, Kinross-shire, 288 (parish of Kinnaird)
Vol XVII Inverness-shire, Ross and Cromarty, 528–9 (parish of Kintail)
Vol XVIII Sutherland and Caithness, 465–6 (parish of Loth)
Vol II The Lothians, 48 (City of Edinburgh)
Vol VII Lanarkshire and Renfrewshire, 859–60 (Abbey Parish of Paisley)
Vol VII Lanarkshire and Renfrewshire, 145 (parish of Carluke)
Vol VIII Argyll (mainland), 126 (parish of Glenorchy and Inishail)
Vol XIII Angus, 224–6 (parish of Edzell)
Vol XX The Western Isles, 94 (parish of Harris)
Vol VII Lanarkshire and Renfrewshire, 350 (parish of Barony of Glasgow)
Vol VII Lanarkshire and Renfrewshire, 573 (parish of Shotts)
Vol XIV Kincardineshire and South and West Aberdeenshire, 652 (parish of Peterculter)
Vol XII North and West Perthshire, 501–2 (parish of Kilmadock or Doune).

Rev Micah Balwhidder's arrival at Dalmailing

John Galt (1779 –1830) was born in Irvine in Ayrshire and set Annals of the
Parish *(1821) in that county. At times humorous, the story centres on Rev
Micah Balwhidder for whom the reader is invited from the very start to feel
sympathy. This is the beginning of the book.*

Year 1760

The Ann. Dom. one thousand seven hundred and sixty was remarkable for three
things in the parish of Dalmailing. First and foremost, there was my placing; then
the coming of Mrs. Malcolm with her five children to settle among us; and next, my
marriage upon my own cousin, Miss Betty Lanshaw, by which the account of this
year naturally divides itself into three heads or portions.

First, of the placing. It was a great affair; for I was put in by the patron, and the
people knew nothing whatsoever of me, and their hearts were stirred into strife on
the occasion, and they did all that lay within the compass of their power to keep me
out, insomuch, that there was obliged to be a guard of soldiers to protect the
presbytery; and it was a thing that made my heart grieve when I heard the drum
beating and the fife playing as we were going to the kirk. The people were really
mad and vicious, and flung dirt upon us as we passed, and reviled us all, and held
out the finger of scorn at me; but I endured it with a resigned spirit,
compassionating their wilfulness and blindness. Poor Mr. Kilfuddy of the Braehill
got such a clash of glar on the side of his face, that his eye was almost extinguished.

When we got to the kirk door, it was found to be nailed up, so as by no
possibility to be opened. The sergeant of the soldiers wanted to break it, but I was
afraid that the heritors would grudge and complain of the expense of a new door,
and I supplicated him to let it be as it was; we were, therefore, obligated to go in by
a window, and the crowd followed us, in the most unreverent manner, making the
Lord's house like an inn on a fair day, with their grievous yellyhooing. During the
time of the psalm and the sermon, they behaved themselves better, but when the
induction came on, their clamour was dreadful; and Thomas Throl, the weaver, a
pious zealot in that time, he got up and protested, and said, 'Verily, verily, I say
unto you, he that entereth not by the door into the sheepfold, but climbeth up some
other way, the same is a thief and a robber.' And I thought I would have a hard and
sore time of it with such an outstrapolous people. Mr. Given, that was then the
minister of Lugton, was a jocose man, and would have his joke even at a solemnity.
When the laying of hands upon me was a-doing, he could not get near enough to
put on his, but he stretched out his staff and touched my head, and said, to the great
diversion of the rest, 'This will do well enough, timber to timber,' but it was an
unfriendly saying of Mr. Given, considering the time and the place, and the temper
of my people.

After the ceremony, we then got out at the window, and it was a heavy day to
me, but we went to the manse, and there we had an excellent dinner, which Mrs.
Watts of the new inns of Irville prepared at my request, and sent her chaise-driver

to serve, for he was likewise her waiter, she having then but one chaise, and that not often called for.

But, although my people received me in this unruly manner, I was resolved to cultivate civility among them; and therefore, the very next morning I began a round of visitations; but oh, it was a steep brae that I had to climb, and it needed a stout heart. For I found the doors in some places barred against me; in others, the bairns, when they saw me coming, ran crying to their mothers, 'Here's the feckless Mess-John'; and then when I went into the houses, their parents would no ask me to sit down, but with a scornful way, said, 'Honest man, what's your pleasure here?' Nevertheless, I walked about from door to door, like a dejected beggar, till I got the almous deed of a civil reception, and who would have thought it, from no less a person than the same Thomas Thorl that was so bitter against me in the kirk on the foregoing day.

Thomas was standing at the door with his green duffle apron and his red Kilmarnock nightcap – I mind him as well as if it was but yesterday – and he had seen me going from house to house, and in what manner I was rejected, and his bowels were moved, and he said to me in a kind manner, 'Come in, sir, and ease yoursel'; this will never do, the clergy are God's gorbies, and for their Master's sake it behoves us to respect them. There was no ane in the whole parish mair against you than mysel', but this early visitation is a sympton of grace that I couldna have expectit from a bird out the nest of patronage.' I thanked Thomas, and went in with him, and we had some solid conversation together, and I told him that it was not so much the pastor's duty to feed the flock, as to herd them well; and that although there might be some abler with the head than me, there wasna a he within the bounds of Scotland more willing to watch the fold at night and by day. And Thomas said he had not heard a mair sound observe for some time, and that if I held to that doctrine in the poopit, it wouldna be lang till I would work a change. 'I was mindit,' quoth he, 'never to set foot within the kirk door while you were there; but to testify, and no to condemn without a trial, I'll be there next Lord's day, and egg my neighbours to be likewise, so ye'll no have to preach just to the bare walls and the laird's family.'

SOURCE: John Galt 1821 *Annals of the Parish*, Edinburgh (Blackwood), Chapter 1.

Thomas Chalmers and the Large City

Thomas Chalmers wrote extensively on the problems of the churches in large cities. Based on his experiences in successively Glasgow and Edinburgh, he generated ideas on how the working classes could be turned from what he and many of the middle classes perceived to be godless living in the slums of industrial and urban districts. Here, three of his writings are quoted, the most influential of these being The Christian and Civic Economy of Large Towns, *published in 1821, in which Chalmers outlined his solution to the insecurities and inadequacies of urban life.*

a) *A Sermon delivered in the Tron Church on the occasion of the death of Princess Charlotte* (1817)
This is the age of moral experiment, and much has been devised in our day for promoting the virtue, and the improvement, and the economical habits of the lower orders of society. But in all these attempts to raise a barrier against the growing profligacy of our towns, one important element seems to have passed unheeded, and to have been altogether omitted in the calculation. In all the comparative estimates of the character of a town and the character of a country population, it has been little attended to, that the former are distinguished from the latter by the dreary, hopeless, and almost impassable distance at which they stand from their parish minister. Now, though it be at the hazard of again magnifying my office, I must avow, in the hearing of you all, that there is a moral charm in his personal attentions and his affectionate civilities, and the ever-recurring influence of his visits and his prayers, which, if restored to the people, would impart a new moral aspect, and eradicate much of the licentiousness and the dishonesty that abound in our cities. On this day of national calamity, if ever the subject should be adverted to from the pulpit, we may be allowed to express our rivetted convictions on the close alliance that obtains between the political interests and the religious character of a country. And I am surely not out of place, when, on looking at the mighty mass of a city population, I state my apprehension, that if something be not done to bring this enormous physical strength under the controul of Christian and humanized principle, the day may yet come, when it may lift against the authorities of the land, its brawny vigour, and discharge upon them all the turbulence of its rude and volcanic energy.

b) *The Christian and Civic Economy of Large Towns* (1821)
We hold the possibility, and cannot doubt the advantage of assimilating a town to a country parish. We think that the same moral regimen, which, under the parochial and ecclesiastical system of Scotland, has been set up, and with so much effect, in her country parishes, may, by a few simple and attainable processes, be introduced into the most crowded of her cities, and with as signal and conspicuous an effect on the whole habit and character of their population – that the simple relationship which obtains between a minister and his people in their former

situation, may be kept up with all the purity and entireness of its influences in the latter situation; and be equally available to the formation of a well-conditioned peasantry; in a word, that there is no such dissimilarity between town and country, as to prevent the great national superiority of Scotland, in respect of her well-principled and well-educated people, being just as observable in Glasgow or Edinburgh, for example, as it is in the most retired of her districts, and these under the most diligent process of moral and religious cultivation. So that, while the profligacy which obtains in every crowded and concentrated mass of human beings, is looked upon by many a philanthropist as one of those helpless and irreclaimable distempers of the body politic, for which there is no remedy – do we maintain, that there are certain practicable arrangements which, under the blessing of God, will stay this growing calamity, and would, by the perseverance of a few years, land us in a purer and better generation.

One most essential step towards so desirable an assimilation in a large city parish, is a numerous and well-appointed agency. The assimilation does not lie here in the external framework; for, in a small country parish, the minister alone, or with a very few coadjutors [ie elders] of a small [kirk] session, may bring the personal influence of his kind and Christian attentions to bear upon all the families. Among the ten thousand of a city parish, this is impossible; and, therefore, what he cannot do but partially and superficially in his own person, must, if done substantially, be done in the person of others. And he, by dividing his parish into small manageable districts – and assigning one or more of his friends, in some capacity or other, to each of them – and vesting them with such a right either of superintendence or inquiry, as will always be found to be gratefully met by the population – and so, raising, as it were, a ready intermedium of communication between himself and the inhabitants of his parish, may at length attain an assimilation in point of result to a country parish, though not in the means by which he arrived at it. He can in his own person maintain at least a pretty close and habitual intercourse with the more remarkable cases; and as for the moral charm of the cordial and Christian acquaintanceship, he can spread it abroad by deputation over the part of the city which been assigned to him. In this way, an influence, long unfelt in towns, may be speedily restored to them; and they, we affirm, know nothing of this department of our nature, who are blind to the truth of the position – that out of the simple elements of attention, and advice, and civility, and good-will, conveyed through the tenements of the poor, by men a little more elevated in rank than themselves, a far more purifying and even more gracious operation can be made to descend upon them, than ever will be achieved by any other of the ministrations of charity . . .

There is no large city which would not soon experience the benefit of such an arrangement. But when the city is purely commercial, it is just the arrangement which, of all others, is most fitted to repair a peculiar disadvantage under which it labours. In a provincial capital, the great mass of the population are retained in kindly and immediate dependence on the wealthy residenters of the place. It is a resort of annuitants, and landed proprietors, and members of the law, and other learned professions, who give impulse to a great amount of domestic industry, by

their expenditure; and, on inquiring in to the sources of maintenance and employment for the labouring classes there, it will be found that they are chiefly engaged in
the immediate service of ministering to the wants and luxuries of the higher classes
in the city. This brings the two extreme orders of society in to that sort of
relationship, which is highly favourable to the general blandness and tranquillity of
the whole population. In a manufacturing town, on the other hand, the poor and the
wealthy stand more disjoined from each other. It is true, they often meet, but they
meet more on an arena of contest, than on a field where the patronage and custom of
the one party are met by the gratitude and good will of the other. When a rich
customer calls a workman into his presence, for the purpose of giving him some
employment connected with his own personal accommodation, the general feeling
of the latter must be altogether different from what it would be, were he called into
the presence of a trading capitalist, for the purpose of cheapening his work, and
being dismissed for another, should there not be an agreement in their terms. We do
not aim at the most distant reflection against the manufacturers of our land; but it
must be quite obvious, from the nature of the case, that their intercourse with the
labouring classes is greatly more an intercourse of collision, and greatly less an
intercourse of kindliness, than there is that of the higher orders in such towns as
Bath, or Oxford, or Edinburgh. In this way, there is mighty unfilled space interposed
between the high and the low of every large manufacturing city, in consequence of
which, they are mutually blind to the real cordialities and attractions which belong
to each of them; and a resentful feeling is apt to be fostered, either of disdain or
defiance, which it will require all the expedients of an enlightened charity to do
away. Nor can we guess at a likelier, or a more immediate arrangement for this
purpose, than to multiply the agents of Christianity amongst us, whose delight it
may be to go forth among the people, on no other errand than that of pure good-
will, and with no other ministrations than those of respect and tenderness.

On the Influence of Locality in Towns

We do not know how the matter is ordered in London; but, in the second-rate
towns of our empire, it will often be found that, when a philanthropic society is
formed in them for any assigned object, it spreads its operations over the whole
field of the congregated population. This holds generally true both of the societies
for relief [of the poor], and of the societies for instruction . . .

We do offer at present to discuss the specific merits of these societies; . . . but,
through them, to illustrate a principle of philanthropic management, for which we
can find no better designation, than the influence of locality in large towns.

In most of the Sabbath school societies with which we are acquainted, this
principle is disregarded. The teachers are indiscriminately stationed in all parts of the
city, and the pupils are as indiscriminately drawn from all parts of the city. Now, what
we affirm, is, that the effectiveness of each individual teacher is greatly augmented, if
a definite locality be given to him; and that a number of teachers spread over any
given neighbourhood on this principle, is armed, in consequences of it, with a much
higher moral power, over the habits and opinions of the rising generation.

Let a small portion of the town, with its geographical limits, be assigned to such a teacher. Let his place of instruction be within this locality, or as near as possible to its confines. Let him restrain his attentions to the children of its families, sending forth no invitations to those who are without, and encouraging as far as it is proper, the attendance of all who are within. Under such an arrangement, he will attain a comfort and an efficiency in his work, which, with the common arrangement, is utterly unattainable. And, we farther conceive, that, if this local assignation of teachers were to become general, it would lead to far more precious and lasting consequences of good to society . . .

There is nothing in the mere circumstance of being born in a town, or of being imported into it from the country, which can at all obliterate or reverse any of the laws of our sentient nature. That law, in virtue of which a feeling of cordiality is inspired, even by a single act of recognition, and in virtue of which it is augmented into a fixed personal regard by many such acts, operates with just as much vigour in the one situation as it does in the other. In towns, everything has been done to impede the reiteration of the same attentions upon the same families. The relationship between ministers and their parishes has, to every moral, and to every civilising purpose, been nearly as good as broken up. Every thing has been permitted to run at random; and, as a fruit of the utter disregard of the principle of locality, have the city clergyman and his people almost lost sight of each other . . .

c) *The Right Ecclesiastical Economy of a Large Town* (1835)

It is difficult to imagine, indeed, how, under such a system of local surveillance, headed by the minister, and powerfully seconded by the auxiliaries of an eldership, each looking after, and with no very oppressive and formidable labour, the state of his own manageable district, – it is difficult, we say, to imagine how, under such an economy like this, the families of our working classes, at all times alive to the observation and moral suasion of their superiors, could in any sensible numbers have fallen away from the habits and the decencies of their forefathers; and, far more, how the present and frightful degeneracy and disease should have ever taken place, breaking out into the frequent and ever-enlarging spots of a foul leprosy, till at length we have spaces in many a town, and most distinctly in our own [Edinburgh], comprehensive of whole streets, nay, of whole parishes, in a general state of paganism. An entire disruption has taken place between the people and their minister, – they never at his church, he seldom or never in their houses . . . we speak of the deep and dense irreligion, which, like the apathy of a mortification or paralysis, has stolen imperceptibly on the great bulk of our plebeian families . . .

SOURCES: Thomas Chalmers
1817 *A Sermon delivered in the Tron Church on the occasion of the death of Princess Charlotte*, Glasgow, 30–1.
1821 *The Christian and Civic Economy of Large Towns*, Glasgow, 25–9, 53–4, 126–7.
1835 *The Right Ecclesiastical Economy of a Large Town*, Edinburgh, 20–1.

DOCUMENT 24

Lord Kames' Statute Law abridged

This summary of the laws against Catholics in the eighteenth century shows how religious toleration was slow to come to Scotland.

All seminary priests found in the realm, all receptors of these if found a third time in fault, all sayers of mass, and all wilful hearers of mass and concealers of the same, are subjected to the pains of death, and confiscation of their moveables. A Protestant servant, if he become a Papist, is to be punished, and must be dismissed his service. If a Papist purchase land, the deed of sale is declared null, and the seller is entitled to retain both the land and the price. No professed Papist shall be capable of succeeding to an estate;[1] and if a Protestant become a Papist he forfeits his estate. Neither shall it be allowed to any professed, or even *suspected* Papist, to teach any art, science, or exercise of any sort, under the pain of 500 merks; and the above penalties may be sued for by any Protestant subject for his own behoof as his reward.

That no adjudication or real diligence shall be competent at the instance of a Papist; neither shall a Papist be capable of becoming tutor, curator, or factor; and if any person or persons presume to employ a Papist, *or such as are suspected* of Popery, in any of the above trusts, they must purge themselves of Popery, under the penalty of a year's valued rent, or a fine of 1000 merks. No Papist past the age of 15 shall be capable to succeed as heir, nor bruik, nor enjoy any estate by disposition or conveyance from any person to whom the said Papist is apparent heir, until he purge himself of Popery. The heir under 15 must purge himself of Popery before succeeding as heir, and if he refuse to do so his right shall go to the next Protestant heir. Presbyterians are appointed to summon before them all Papists, and those suspected of Papistry, in order to satisfy the Kirk; and if Papists do not produce sufficient certificates of their having given due satisfaction to the Kirk, they shall be declared rebels, put to the horn, and both their single and life-rent escheated. Further, that whoever receipts, supplies or entertains, such persons after denunciation aforesaid, shall incur the penalty of single and life-rent escheat.[2]

NOTES

1 *Scots Magazine* 1774, 279 – 'Died at Fetteresso, Peter Lesslie Grant, Esq, of Balquhain, which estate was decreed about a dozen years ago to belong to him, as *Protestant heir*, after a keen litigation against him by Antonius and Charles Catejan Lesslies, German Counts, against whom he pleaded their being *Papists* and *aliens*.'

2 *Scots Magazine* 1756, 100 – 'On the 1st of March, 1756, Hugh M'Donald, brother of M'Donald of Morra, was tried at Edinburgh before the High Court of Justiciary, at the instance of the Lord Advocate, for refusing to purge himself of Popery. Being asked "whether he was willing to take the formula prescribed by Act 1700–3" he declared ' "that he was not at freedom of conscience to do it." He was then found guilty in terms of the libel, and sentenced to be banished the kingdom, never to return under pain of death.'

SOURCE: Lord Kames' Statute Law Abridged, quoted in Senex (pseud) 1884 *Glasgow Past and Present* Vol II, Glasgow, 263–4.

DOCUMENT 25

The 'Encrease of Popery' in the Highlands

This is one of a number of reports written by groups of Highland ministers of the Church of Scotland concerning the growth of Roman Catholicism in the Highlands. In much of the area, Presbyterianism had never been fully established, but during the first half of the eighteenth century the attempt to presbyterianise the people was seen as the key to the 'hearts and minds' element of suppressing Jacobitism. These accounts show how Catholicism was relatively flourishing and how the work of the presbyterian clergy was difficult.

Dated 29 May, 1714

Particular condescendance of some grievances from the encresce of poperie, and the Insolence of popish priests & Jesuits.

[*In margin*: Strathbogie] In the bounds of the presbytery of Strathbogie popish priests are very insolent, some of them have their dwelling houses and farms and Live as openly and avowedly as any Minister within the Presbytery, particularly Mr Alexander Alexander at Burned, and the papists in that Country do repair to their Idolatrous Mass as publickly as protestants do to the Church. Priest Frazer and several papists in the nighbourhood of that Country avowed resetters and harbourers of priests, were banished by the Lords of Justiciary, and yet they live openly and avowedly in their former dwellings. Priest Frazer is intertained in The duke of Gordon's family. As also there is one Mr Peter Reid who preaches and says Mass in the said bounds, particularly at Kinore Abathie and Rabston, and Mr Charles Stewart says Mass and preaches at dumbennan Mr Alexander Sirnamed Mein has lived at Bornend in dumbennan these nine or ten years he says Mass & preaches ordinarly in the house of James Dalgarno in Raws of Huntly. Mr John Gordon Priest Lives at Cormelat in the paroch of Rathven & Botarie and is a busie traffiquer. By means of those there are above a hundered in the paroch of Rathven perverted to poperie within these tuo years or thereby. Mr Alexander Bruce Alias Bishop Bruce, and James donaldson priest have their dwelling at Presham, and they with Charles Stewart priest, have frequent meetings and Masses at Letterfurie, Gellochie and Cofurach. Mr John Irwing priest keeps Mass at Castlegordon, and Mr Patrick ffrazer priest at ffochabers in a fixed place in the house of Robert Edward there, There are above Six hundred papists in the paroch of Bellie, & in Kinnore & dumbennan the papists are equal in numbers to the protestants. In the Countreys of Glenlivet & Strathaven in the presbytery of Aberlour, priests are very Insolent & busie, and have seduced some to apostatize, and others who had renounced popery are now fallen back to their former delusions. William Gordon in Upper drummen an apostate, resetts Mr John Gordon a priest, and has built a Mass house to which the people do as openly resort to hear Mass as protestants do to their paroch Churches, The said priest Gordon travels up & doun that Country and says Mass and baptizes Children, They proclaim banns in that Mass house in order to marriage, and do marry avowedly. One of the teachers of the grammer schooll of ffochabers is popish, and Children of popish parents from diverse remote places are sent thither to be taught, and priest Stewart brother to Stewart of Boigs in the Enzie not long ago gathered about thirty boys of good expectation having the Irish tongue, and carried them abroad, to qualifie them at their return to make prosleyts to Rome, The papists in the said bounds have of Late set up privat Schools which are taught by popish women. The priests also Instruct women, and send them through the Country to propagat their delusions, and when they find any easily to be practized upon, they acquaint their priests and the priests perfite what they have begun. In that country some protestant ministers have no house to preach in, or any Shelter against the cold in winter or heat in Summer, and yet not only is the priest provided in a convenient house there, but in the nighbouring paroch of Kirkmichael his hearers had bought for him a Large and Convenient house to which he & they do ordinarily resort for worship. There are in the paroch of Inveraven two hundred and seventy papists, of whom fifteen have apostatized within these [*blank space in original*] years. [*In margin:* Lochabber] In the paroch of Lochaber the priests swarm Like Locusts, running from house to house, gaining multitudes to their anti Christian Idolatry, Baptizeing and marrying. In the presbytery of Abernethie the priests keep publick meetings, visite, preach, declare people marryed & say Mass without fear of the Laws. There are four large tracts of ground in the presbytery of Lorne upon the continent vizt: Muidart, Arasaig, Morhirr & Knoidart contiguous to one another, which are altogether popish Except one gentleman, They have one Mr Gordon a priest always residing among them saying Mass publickly each Sabbath, and who of late is become so bold that he encroaches upon the adjacent paroches which are planted with Ministers of the Established Church. He perverts the people and marries and Baptizes, particularly he Baptizes Children begotten in fornication and takes the parents obliged to be of the Communion of the Church of Rome, and such delinquents resort to him to evade discipline which weakens the hands of the Protestant Ministers, he frequents Glenavait, Kenloch and Muidart their houses, where he keeps Mass openly, [*In margin*, Isles] The Isles of Rum, Egg & Canna are all popish They keep their priest and pay him their tithes. The Isle of South Uist is all popish, They have a priest who resides besides with Clanronald & Benbecula, and says Mass publickly. These Countreys and Islands were never Reformed from Popery, And generally all the relations followers & tennants of Clanronald, through all his Lands both in the Continent & Isles are all papists. The Isle of Bara and other adjacent Lesser Isles have a priest, who resides in the house of Mc : Neil of Bara. In these countreys there are to the number of two thousand papists, there are six priests and a mendicant friar still resideing and officiating among them, They have their respective paroches where they ordinarily reside & officiat as if formally fixed and countenanced by authority, and it's said they are duly maintained from abroad They keep their meetings under the inspection of their popish Bishop, who comes to their bounds to administrat their pretended Sacrament of Confirmation. The proprietars of these Countreys are but fourteen, of whom Eight are popish, who all Countenance the priests in perverting the people.

SOURCE: NM Wilby 1966 'The "Encreasce of Popery" in the Highlands, 1714–1747', *Innes Review* 17, 92–4.

RURAL TRANSFORMATION AND LOWLAND SOCIETY

DOCUMENT 26

'Improving' lease, Lockhart of Lee Estate, Lanarkshire, 1799

This document provides a good example of the conditions which the tenant of an improved farm at the end of the eighteenth century would have had to agree to. A generation earlier leases on most estates were still fairly simple, straightforward documents with few regulations regarding farming practices. The lease below is very detailed and specific regarding how the tenant was to cultivate the land, giving him little scope for initiative and experiment. This illustrates the rather authoritarian and heavy-handed approach of many early improving landowners.

ARTICLES AND REGULATIONS,
SETTLED BY THE
TUTORS & CURATORS OF
CHA. LOCKHART-WISHEART, Esq; of Lee;
TO BE OBSERVED BY
The TENANTS of the Lands belonging to him, whose
Tacks shall be made to bear relation to the same.

Dated 21st
And recorded in the books of Session, 24th January, 1791

I   All assignees, whether legal or voluntary, and all sub-tenants, are excluded. – Heirs portioners are also excluded, the eldest being to succeed without division; but power is given to a tenant having children, to appoint any of his children he pleases to succeed him in his lease.

II   The tenants must reside with their families upon their farms, and always have a sufficient stock thereupon.

III   The lands shall be managed and cropped by the tenants during their tracks in the following manner, viz. – The old croft land, together with such a proportion of the field lands as the tenants shall be taken bound to labour and cultivate, must within the first five years of the tack, be put into ten divisions, as nearly equal as the nature of the fields will admit; five of these divisions at least must be in grass, the other five may be in tillage, and cropped in the following order.

1. Oats			1.	Oats
2. Pease			2.	Barley
3. Barley	or		3.	Oats
4. Oats			4.	Pease
5. Fallow			5.	Fallow

When land is new plowed out of old lee, the rotation of crops may be: –

1. Oats		1.	Oats
2. Oats		2.	Oats
3. Barley		3.	Pease
4. Oats		4.	Oats
5. Fallow		5.	Fallow

The division or field that falls yearly to be in fallow, must be equal to a tenth part of the lands to be cultivated; but it must get at least four plowings in the season, and be manured at the rate of sixty cart loads of good dung, or ten cart loads of lime shells to the acre. Turnips may be sown on the fallow field after it has been laboured and manured as aforesaid, and along with the following crop, it must be sown with grass seeds, at the rate of two bushels of rye grass, and twelve pounds of clover seed to the acre. Thereafter it must remain in grass five years, in one of which years it may be cut for hay. The farms being all thus fallowed and manured, the same round of fallowing and manuring as above specified is to be begun again. The tenants are bound strictly to observe, that the part of the fallow field to be first limed in the second round of fallow, is to be that which got no lime in the first round. Tenants who may have less than the half of the manured land in tillage after the whole has been once fallowed and manured, shall only be obliged to fallow and manure yearly one-fifth part of what they reap in tillage. Liberty is given to tenants to put their respective farms into eight divisions in place of ten; but, in this case, one eighth part of the lands to be cultivated shall be yearly fallowed and manured as above mentioned, till the whole is gone over, and thereafter one-fourth part of what is in tillage is to be in fallow. Those who follow this method may leave the pease crop out of the rotation. The field lands that may be by agreement left out of the above-mentioned divisions and method of management, shall at no time be plowed, unless it be to have them fallowed and manured with dung or lime, thereafter to be sown with grass seeds, along with the third crop, and not be plowed again unless when it is to undergo the same course of management. At any rate, it must remain in pasture grass six years after being sown off.

The small possessions in the crofts of Carnwath, and other places, must be put into four equal divisions; one of which divisions shall be yearly fallow, or turnips; one barley; one red clover, one oats. The half of the fallow division may be potatoes in place of turnips; but when it is, it must be dunged after the crop is taken out of the ground. No lint is to be sown, except upon the oat division, when the land is to be in fallow the following season. Declaring, That if the tenants shall at any time contravene any of the articles of management above mentioned, he shall be obliged to pay the sum of Three Pounds Sterling of additional rent, for every acre managed contrary to the regulations above specified, and that along with the first rent falling due after the contravention has taken place; and shall also pay Six Shilling Sterling for each cart load of lime-shells, and One Shilling Sterling for each cart load of lime-shells, and One Shilling Sterling for each cart load of dung that is not laid on the fallow field, or division, as before specified.

IV The tenants shall be bound to allow the proprietor, or in-coming tenant, to sow grass along with the last crop, and to hain and preserve the grass that shall be so sown by them the last year of their possession, and not to pasture, or allow any of their bestial to trespass thereupon, after the separation of the crop from the ground, under the penalty of paying One Pound Sterling for every horse, cow, or other cattle, that may be found pasturing on the same.

V   The tenants shall be bound to consume with their cattle, upon their respective farms, the whole straw and fodder (hay excepted) that shall grow thereupon, and to lay on the whole dung that shall be made upon the same; and upon no account to sell or five away any of their fodder or dung; and they shall be obliged to leave the whole dung made upon their farm the last year of their possession, carefully gathered together, for the use and behoof of the proprietor to whom the same shall belong. Declaring, That if they, notwithstanding hereof, take upon them to sell or give away any of the said fodder or dung, they shall be bound to pay the proprietor the sum of Four Shillings for every threave of straw or fodder, and Two Shillings for every cart-load of dung so sold or given away.

VI The proprietor, at any time within the first five years of the lease, is to have it in his option and power to inclose and subdivide the old croft land, and twenty acres of the field-land of each respective farm, with ditch and hedge, stone or seal dykes, or drains, whichever of these is best adapted to soil and situation; the rentee being obliged to pay 5 per cent. per ann. for the cost or money laid out on such inclosing. The which cost or outlay is to be ascertained by the workmen's receipts, or an accompt certified under the hand of the person employed to direct the work. Where the proprietor does not incline to make any inclosures, in terms of this article, the tenant himself may inclose as above; and, at the end of the tack, he shall be entitled to receive from the proprietor the original cost of making such inclosures; provided that the fences be then in good order and repair; and that the lines of division of the inclosures be first approved of by the factor or doer on the estate, at the time such inclusures are made.

VII The tenants shall be bound and obliged to maintain and uphold, in good and sufficient condition and repair, yearly, the whole houses, offices, dykes, ditches and hedges, and drains or gates, that are upon their respective farms at their entry, or which may be built thereupon during the currency of their tacks; and to leave them, at their removal, in the like good and sufficient repair, all upon their own charges and expences.

VIII   In cases where a tenant may find it necessary to alter the situation of any of the houses, or to repair or rebuild any of them upon a better plan, he is to have liberty to bring a proof of the value of the said houses (they always being considered as in good and sufficient repair and condition at the time if such proof is brought); and the value being ascertained, it is to be recorded in the court-books of the barony of Carnwath; and, at the expiry of the lease, the houses shall be again valued, and the proprietor shall allow to the tenants the increase of value of the houses, provided that the alteration and improvement of the same have been executed on a plan approved of by the proprietor, his factor, or doer, at the time such alterations shall take place.

IX   In case the proprietor (his factor or doer for the time) shall, at any time, find the houses, dykes, drains, hedges, ditches, and gates neglected, and in disrepair, power and liberty are expressly reserved to him to order the same to be put in proper and sufficient repair and condition; and the expence thereof being ascertained by the workmen's receipts, or by an accompt certified by the factor, the tenants shall be obliged to pay the same, with interest from the date of the receipts or said certified accompts.

X   In case it shall be judged proper to make any alteration in the farms, either by straighting marches, or by excambing lands with neighbouring heritors or tenants, the tenants shall be obliged to concur and acquiesce therein; and the variations thereby occasioned in their rent, whether increase or decrease, shall be determined by two neutral persons to be named by the proprietor and tenant.

XI   The proprietor reserves all mines, metals, and coal, quarries of stone and lime, marl, and other fossils whatsoever of the like kind, within the bounds of the lands let, with liberty to work, win, and carry away the same; for that purpose, to sink pits, build houses, make roads, and erect any necessary works thereupon, the tenants being allowed such surface damages, and such abatement of rent as shall be determined by two neutral persons, to be mutually appointed by the parties.

XII   The tenants are to be thirled to the mills to which their respective lands have been in use to be astricted, and shall pay mill-dues, and perform services to mill and kiln, confirm to use and wont.

XIII The tenants are to have the liberty and privilege of casting, winning, and leading home peats for feuel, for the use of their families residing in their respective lands, from such moss or mosses, or parts of the same as shall be allotted and set off to them yearly by the officer of the barony, or others having the proprietor's authority for that purpose.

XIV The tenants shall attend the courts of the barony within which their respective farms lie, when summoned thereto, and obey the acts, decrees, and regulations thereof according to law.

XV   Whatever the term of entry may be, the term of removal from that part of the farm that is in tillage the last year of the tenant's possession, shall be at the separation of the crop from the ground of each respective field, so that whenever one field is cleared, the incoming tenant may enter to it, for the purpose of plowing only, although the crop may not be separated from the other fields. And we, as tutors foresaid, consent to the registration hereof in the books of Council and Session, or of any other proper Court, therein to remain for preservation; and constitute

our Procurators. In witness whereof, these presents, consisting of this and the four preceding pages, are written upon stamped paper, by Robert Stewart, writer in Edinburgh, and subscribed by a majority and quorum of the said tutors at Edinburgh, the twenty-first day of January. One thousand seven hundred and ninety one years, before these witnesses, James Haldane, writer in Edinburgh, and Joseph Thorburn, servant to the said John Wauchope.

		Signed	{	William Miller.
Signed	{ James Haldane, witness.			John Pringle.
	{ Joseph Thorburn, witness.			Geo. Cumin.
				John Wauchope.

SOURCE: National Library of Scotland, Acc 4322, Lockhart of Lee Papers, Box 17.

DEMOGRAPHY

DOCUMENT 27

The potato, inoculation and mortality

Despite the losses caused by emigration, rates of population growth in Scotland rose in the second half of the eighteenth century, chiefly, it is currently believed, as a result of falling rates of mortality. In this document it is argued that this was principally a combined consequence of the spread of potato cultivation and the introduction of inoculation against smallpox.

Population, Manner of Living, &c.- Within these 40 years, the population is more than doubled.

The number, at present, is, of males,	640
– females,	694
	——
In all,	1334
In Dr. Webster's report, the number is only	613
	——
Increase,	721
The present number of families is	279

As there was a considerable emigration from this country to North America, in 1770, and a large drain of young men to recruit the army during the late war[1], it is difficult to assign adequate causes for this rapid increase of population. It cannot be accounted for, from any change in the division of farms, most of which have been bounded by the same marches for upwards of a century, and still possessed by what may be called the *Aborigines* of the country, often descending, from father to son, in the same family, to the fourth generation. The cultivation of potatoes, introduced here about 45 years ago, (which, with various kinds of fish, now constitute the greatest part of the food of the people,) seems to have principally contributed to it. Their mode of farming, requiring little of their attention, during the summer and beginning of harvest, they are much employed in fishing of sythe, (a small species of the cole fish), herrings, and sometimes ling, cod and skate. The sythe are eat fresh; the herrings are pickled, to be eat with the potatoes during the harvest, winter, and spring. Though 63 boats be employed in this manner, there are no fish exported from the parish. Communicating the small-pox by inoculation, now become universal over this coast, and practised with success, has also very much contributed to preserve the lives of the people[2]. The emancipation of the lower classes, too, from the remains of feudal oppression, and their circumstances greatly improving, under the fostering care of a liberal landlord, enables them to marry earlier in life, and to provide with more ease for a rising family.

NOTES

1 Since writing the above, the proprietor, who is now raising a regiment, raised here upwards of 40 volunteers in 2 days.

2 About 40 years ago, when inoculation was not practised here, this virulent distemper, visiting them in the natural way, gave cause to many unhappy parents, to bewail the loss of a whole family of children.

SOURCE: DJ Withrington and IR Grant (eds) 1981 *The Statistical Account of Scotland 1791–1799 edited by Sir John Sinclair,* Vol XVII Inverness-shire, Ross and Cromarty, 548–9 (parish of Lochalsh, Ross and Cromarty). East Ardsley (EP Publishing).

DOCUMENT 28

Employment and population growth

According to Alex MacLean, though inoculation against smallpox made some contribution to the increase in rates of population growth in late eighteenth-century Scotland, its significance was diminished by a widespread reluctance to accept it and outweighed by the effects of increasing employment opportunities made possible by agricultural and industrial development.

Population – In Dr Webster's list in 1755, the numbers were rated at 858. In the year 1764, the whole population amounted to 680 souls, of which the Ferry-town of Cree (now Creetown) then contained 104. As the country part of the parish has altered very little in point of population, since that period, it will be necessary to show the increase that has been in Creetown at all the different periods since that time.

	Families	Under 10 Yrs of age	Above 10 Yrs of age	Total	Births	Marriag.	Deaths.
In 1764, Creetown contained	34	20	84	104	4	0	1
In 1774, ditto	120	73	294	367	11	2	3
In 1784, ditto	145	88	354	442	15	3	6
From the 1st November 1793 to ditto 1794	183	142	409	551	19	6	23[1]
In 1794, the whole parish contains	289	249	839	1088	38	9	27

Causes of Population. – The increase of population, not only in this place, but also in many other places in Scotland, is principally owing to these three following causes:

1   To the beneficial effects of inoculation for the small-pox, by which the lives of numbers of children are preserved; and, general as the practice is become, yet, still there are many of these little innocents, that fall victims to the inattention, stupidity, and superstition of their parents, who are so wedded to their ancient prejudices, that rather than part with them, they will consign over half-a-dozen fine children to the ravages of this terrible disorder, or, perhaps, to the gloomy mansions of the tomb.

2   To the improvement of waste lands, by which numbers are employed and maintained.

3   To the recently established branches of manufactures. By the first, life is preserved, and by the two last, emigration is prevented.

NOTES

1   Of the 23 children that died in Creetown last year, 12 died of the small-pox.

SOURCE: DJ Withrington and IR Grant (eds) 1983 *The Statistical Account of Scotland 1791–1799 edited by Sir John Sinclair,* Vol V Stewartry of Kirkcudbright and Wigtownshire, 229–30 (parish of Kirkmabreck, Kirkcudbright). East Ardsley (EP Publishing).

DOCUMENT 29

Hostility to inoculation

Historians continue to disagree over the part played by inoculation against smallpox in the decline in mortality which occurred during the late eighteenth and early nineteenth centuries. In contrast to the views of some of his contemporaries, Rev Thomas Pollock argued that its contribution was far more restricted than it should have been.

Small Pox. – This disease . . . rages here, at times, with the utmost violence, and is often extremely fatal. In the summer and autumn of 1791, upwards of 90 children had the natural small pox, and more than one half of them died. The chin-cough and natural small pox not unfrequently prevail at the same time. When this happens, as was the case at the above period, the ravages committed by this last disease, are truly dreadful. The coincidence of these diseases might, in a great measure, be prevented by inoculation. But though in this, and in every other respect, inoculation is attended with the happiest consequences, it is only practised here in two or three families. From ignorance, and the most superstitious preju-dices, the parents, regardless, or insensible of consequences, instead of inoculating their children, crowd into those houses in which the disease is of the most malignant nature, and at a time when it is the most infectious. The very worst kind of this dangerous and loathsome disease is, in this manner, communicated and spread, and thousands of valuable lives are lost to the community. This impious presumption, these illiberal and groundless prejudices, are not peculiar to this parish; in every other country parish in Scotland, the great bulk of the people think and act pretty much in the same way. It is well known, at least to the clergy, that every argument in support of inoculation, however conclusive or self-evident, makes no impression upon their minds. To make a law, obliging all persons, without distinction, to inoculate their children, would be thought inconsistent with the liberty of British subjects, and even with the common principles of humanity. But as the prosperity, nay the very existence of every country, is inseparably connected with the number of its inhabitants, something certainly ought to be attempted, to render, if possible, inoculation in Scotland more general than it is at present.

SOURCE: DJ Withrington and IR Grant (eds) 1982 *The Statistical Account of Scotland 1791–1799 edited by Sir John Sinclair*, Vol VI Ayrshire, 341–3 (parish of Kilwinning). East Ardsley (EP Publishing).

DOCUMENT 30

The causes of population decline

In this document Rev John Dunbar reminds us that the phenomenon of population growth was not shared by all parishes in Scotland in the second half of the eighteenth century. By forcing people to emigrate in search of employment, a combination of declining numbers of farms and a failure to develop manufactures sometimes led to population decrease.

Causes of the Decline of Population – The population of this parish, as far as can be guessed by multiplying the average of births by 31⅓, would seem, from the above Tables, to have been, in 1677, as high as 2200. From that period there are three visible causes of its subsequent decline.

1   One unavoidable cause, was the overwhelming of the populous barony of Culbin[1], by a violent drifting of sand from the Maviston hills; and, excepting a small remnant farthest from the coast, the depopulation of that barony was completed before the close of the last century.
2   Another cause, affecting all the other estates in the parish, is the change that has taken place since the rebellion, 1745, in the size and number of farms. Formerly

they were very small and numerous, running from 4 to 16 bolls of rent; now they are larger, and not half so numerous as they were. A multitude of small farms is very favourable to population; yet the enlargement of farms, to a certain degree, was needful in this parish, where the grounds so much needed rest, and where milk, butter, and butcher-meat were so scarce; and, had there been manufactures sufficient to employ the hands superseded from tillage, the enlargement of farms might have been favourable to agriculture, without diminishing the population. But this not being the case,

3 The neglect of manufactures may be stated as a third cause, and the greatest of any, affecting the population of this parish. The present possessors, finding that there are not so many rooms as formerly for farmers, breed their children to handicrafts; and these, not finding employment at home, push their way to Edinburgh, Glasgow, Paisley, or London, from whence they seldom find their way back to settle here. This cause affects most of the northern districts, where manufactures do not meet with the attention and encouragement that they deserve. This is what occasions yearly emigrations, during the seasons of summer and harvest work, to places where there is more employment and higher wages; and these short excursions frequently end in a removal to manufacturing towns at the last.

NOTES

1 The sand had been making great encroachments before it overwhelmed the mains and garden of Culbin. But that event, which completed the business, must have happened considerably earlier than the date assigned in Shaw's History of the Province; because it is specially mentioned in the Act of Parliament, against pulling of bent, passed in 1695, intitled, for Preservation of Lands adjacent to Sand-hills, and is mentioned as one of the reasons for passing that act, K. Wil. III. I Par. 5 Sef. Act XXX.

SOURCE: DJ Withrington and IR Grant (eds) 1982 *The Statistical Account of Scotland 1791–1799 edited by Sir John Sinclair.* Vol XVI Banffshire, Moray and Nairnshire, 559–60 (parish of Dyke and Moy, Morayshire). East Ardsley (EP Publishing).

DOCUMENT 31

The causes of Highland emigration

By the early nineteenth century emigration was already a well-established feature of the demography of many Highland parishes. As Rev Alexander Beith observes, it was usually not the most destitute who left for overseas destinations. The lure of opportunities overseas was just as important a motive for emigration as the push of poor conditions at home.

III – POPULATION

Population in	1801	.	2834
	1811	.	2611
	1821	.	2807
	1831	.	2874

The ancient population must have been very considerable, probably double at least of what it is now. The decrease is to be accounted for solely by emigration; for to such an extent has this prevailed, that America too rejoices in a Glenelg, with a population, at least equal to that which the parent parish still possesses. This emigration was at first of necessity and not of choice. The letting of large tracts of land to single individuals caused the original banishment of the hardy and numerous race, who had for so many generations possessed the soil. This class of emigrants did not quit their native shores empty-handed. On the contrary, they carried with them the means of procuring a comfortable home beyond the Atlantic. The population which remained consisted of those who were too poor to follow, and of a few others, who, willing to forego some advantages for the privilege of residing in their much loved native land, tried to content themselves with sadly reduced possessions, until, finding that thus they were losing their all, and induced by the flattering tidings which reached them from the western continent, they too, though in different circumstances from their predecessors, bade farewell to a country, to which they had clung till they could do so no longer. Of this description of inhabitants few (that is, not more than a dozen families,) are left behind; and of those, as they are able to effect their object, occasional families take their flight to what they consider a happier shore. Besides the tacksmen of the large possessions into which the country has been divided, – four of whom possess Glenelg Proper, and about as many more the other districts, – besides them and the shepherds and servants whom they require, the population consists of those who dwell in villages near the sea; – divided into two classes, – such as possess from one acre to perhaps six of arable ground, and the grazing of from one to three cows, and others who have nothing but the cottage that shelters them, who depend on the kindness of neighbours for patches of ground for potatoes, and supply all their other wants by fishing, and such work as they may obtain at home or abroad. It is but fair to remark, that the banishment of the original population, and the throwing of the country into a few large possessions, took place long before the time of the present race of proprietors, so that, whether matter of regret or satisfaction, to them belongs neither the blame nor praise. Whatever the views of political economists on this interesting topic, as to the nation's loss or gain, it is impossible not to contemplate it in reference to those exiles themselves, and, in doing this, not to lament, especially, over the injury sustained by them in a moral point of view. Amidst the plenty for their bodily support which they enjoy in America, they dwell there in a barren wilderness as to provision for their souls. Deprived of the ordinances of religion, or but scantily and occasionally supplied, deprived also of the means of instruction for their children, the many careless and indifferent who go thither become confirmed in their spiritual deadness, whilst those of them who quit their native land under more serious impressions, also yield to the secularising influence of such an order of things; and though *they* retain their integrity, and hold fast their profession in their day, yet, leaving no successors, the harps which for a time had awakened echoes, that previously enjoyed an unbroken sleep, are at last hung upon the willows, and the Songs of Zion cease to be heard by the streams of the foreign land! How worthy this subject of the consideration of a patriotic and parental Legislature! Nay, how imperative that the thousands who yearly go to swell the population of our growing colony, should not be left to perish for the lack of knowledge!

SOURCE: *New Statistical Account of Scotland* 1845 Vol XIV Inverness, Ross and Cromarty, 135–7 (parish of Glenelg, Inverness-shire). Edinburgh and London (William Blackwood & Sons).

DOCUMENT 32

Influences on population growth

The balance of forces for and against population growth in the individual communities of eighteenth- and early nineteenth-century Scotland was invariably complex and subject to substantial periodic fluctuation. Nowhere is this better demonstrated than in the Argyll parish of Morvern.

III – POPULATION

The population of the Highlands has undergone many fluctuations. No doubt, in ancient times, the country was populous. While the power of the feudal chief was estimated or his possessions secured by his vassals and retainers, efforts were made to augment their numbers. At a later period also, during the prevalence of war, and the prosperity of kelp manufacture, similar efforts were resorted to; and, accordingly, almost every spot was occupied, not only along the sea coasts, but also in the inland glens. The introduction of sheep-farming, and the failure of kelp manufacture, have introduced a different system. The tenure of land, as held by the poorer classes, is simple in the extreme, and their hamlets removable with as great ease, and to others with as little detriment, as a temporary encampment, and, accordingly, humanity alone has obstructed, in causing the more general recourse to the depopulation system, – a system, let it be remembered, held at no distant period in such dread, when emigration to America seemed to offer to the people themselves so many inducements, – Morvern participated to no small extent in these fluctuations. It is evident that the population was great, previous to 1755. It appears to have come, at and from that period, to the amount at which it has, with no inconsiderable variations, continued down to the present day, or, at least, to the period of the last census.

Amount of population in	1755	.	1223
	1795	.	1764
	1801	.	2000
	1831	.	2036
	1841	.	1781

But while it appears that the population of 1831, which considerably exceeds that of the present period, is not much more than that of 1795, and is not greater than the extent and resources of the country are capable of supporting, it is necessary, in drawing conclusions from these and the following numerical statements, to advert to the very different mode in which the inhabitants of the country are now located.

The fact is, the two opposite systems of depopulating and over-peopling are here in full operation. To the former there are strong inducements. The country, undoubtedly, is, to a great extent, a pastoral district, and, of whatever improvements the soil may be susceptible, and whatever fertility it may, and, in some districts, really does possess, the variable character of the climate renders the raising of crop precarious; and, besides, the price of sheep and wool has of late years maintained an entire ascendency over that of black-cattle and agricultural produce. Accordingly, on the sale of the Argyle estates, and the breaking up of the old tack leases, the sheep system came into more general operation. The people, though in some cases partially continued, from motives of compassion, have but slender holdings. In other cases, they have wholly removed. This process has again facilitated the introduction of another, in one point of view, certainly the most commendable, but, on the whole, perhaps not the least pernicious in its effects; for, in place of repairing to the south, in search of steady employment, or taking the more decided and advisable step of emigrating, the dispossessed tenantry have here and elsewhere become the occupants of small allotments in wretched villages, where idleness exercises its unhappy influence over them, and lands them in penury and wretchedness.

These remarks are made, not as advocating either of the systems, or reproaching any of the respected individuals by whom they are severally practised. Each system has its advantages and disadvantages, as judiciously or injudiciously acted on. Both are to be condemned, when carried to an undue extremity. The evil effects of the allotment system are obvious; but, in addition to its more immediate, but perhaps temporary effects on the condition of the people, the other system referred to will, in all probability, yet be seen to produce evils of great magnitude. It will suspend the reclaiming of waste land, and, while the arable now or lately in cultivation will soon become overrun, as it has a strong tendency to do, with fog, heath, and brushwood, the existing dikes and farm-steadings will become dilapidated; and then, should the price of black-cattle, as it is not improbable, regain its former amount, will the acknowledgement be more readily given than at present, that a system, combining, as formerly, the agricultural and the pastoral, is of all the most conducive to the improvement of the country, the comfort of the people, and the interest of the proprietors.

SOURCE: *New Statistical Account of Scotland* 1845 Vol VII Renfrew and Argyle, 185-6 (parish of Morvern, Argyle). Edinburgh and London (William Blackwood & Sons).

INDUSTRIALISATION

Contract of Co-partnership for Stanley cotton mills, Perthshire, 1 January 1787

This is a legal contract registered in the Sheriff Court of Perthshire. It gives details of the partners in the Stanley Company, including the amount of capital invested, agreement for sharing profit and loss and banking arrangements. Other details include the involvement of the Duke of Atholl in leasing the land and water rights, the Duke's advance of a loan for building houses and arrangements for training the Stanley workforce at Cromford, Derbyshire.

At Perth the first day of January Seventeen hundred and Eighty Seven Registered In presence of David Smyth Esqr Advocate Sheriff Depute of Perthshire Patrick Duncan and James Chalmers Procurators.

It is Contracted and Agreed upon Betwixt Richard Arkwright Esquire at Cromford Derbyshire South Britain George Dempster Esquire of Dunichen Robert Graham Esquire of Fintry William Sandeman Merchant in Perth Patrick Stewart Merchant there and Andrew Keay Merch^t, Whereas the Said parties Having intended to enter into Co-Partnership for the purpose of carrying on the business of preparing and Spinning cotton-wool in this Country in the way and manner in which it is carried on by the Said Richard Arkwright at Cromford afore-Said and other branches of Trade connected therewith Did in prosecution of their Said intention enter into a Submission with his Grace John Duke of Atholl for a Lease of the Cornmiln at Stanly aquaduct thereat and exclusive priviledge of the water and for certain grounds adjacent to the Miln and parts of the Lands of Stanely to the Said Richard Arkwright Sole Arbiter conform to Submission of date the Sixteenth day of May last upon which the Said Richard Arkwright Pronounced his Decreet arbitral dated the Seventeenth day of the Said which with the Said Submission is Registered in the Sheriff Court Books of Perthshire that same day By which Decreet arbitrall, The Said Duke is Decerned to grant Leases of the Mill water and grounds therein mentioned for the periods therein Specified to the Said parties and they are Decerned to pay rents for the Same as mentioned in the Said Decreet as also to pay rents for the Same as mentioned in the Said Decreet as also to pay Seven and an half per Cent yearly to the Said Duke for Two thousand pounds Sterling to be advanced by him in erecting Houses or otherwise at Stanly for the aforesaid intended business, as the Said Submission and Decreet Arbitrall containing Sundry other Clauses more Bear and whereas the Said William Sandeman Patrick Stewart William Marshall and Andrew Keay did in Contemplation of the aforesaid Co-Partnership an business enter into Sundry Indentures with different persons to be sent to the Said Richard Arkwright at Cromford aforesaid to be taught the constructing and making of the Machinery used by him in preparing and Spining of the Said wool itself which Indentures having been entered into for the general interest and behoof of the Said intended Co-partnership, They therefore Do hereby now assign Convey and Make over the Same to the Said Richard Arkwright George Dempster and Robert Graham and to themselves the Said William Sandeman Patrick Stewart and William Marshall and Andrew Keay their Heirs and Assignies according to the Shares and proportions they are to hold in the Said intended Co-Partnership as after mentioned and the Said Parties mutually and jointly Bind & oblige themselves their heirs and executors to relieve the Said William Sandeman Patrick Stewart William Marshall and Andrew Keay of the above obligations they have have come under by the aforesaid Indentures in behalf of the Said Company and Whereas a Compleat and regular Contract of Co-partnership cannot at present be conveniently entered into, and that it is necessary for the carrying on the business of the Said intended Company in the meantime that a temporary Contract and agreeement Should be entered into betwixt the Said parties Therefore the Said Richard Arkwright George Dempster Robert Graham William Sandeman Patrick Stewart William Marshall and Andrew Keay Do hereby mutually agree to associate themselves into a Company or Co-Partnership for the purpose of carrying on the business of preparing and Spinning Cotton-wool as aforesaid And In order that the business & concerns of the Said Comp^y may be the more properly conducted and carried on untill a regular Contract of Co-partnership be entered into by them They in like manner for that purpose agree to the following rules and regulations First They hereby Ratify and approve of all and every Act and Deed done or execute by either of the Said parties relative to the forwarding and carrying on the aforesaid intended business and mutually oblige themselves to relieve each other of all obligations they or any of them have come under thereanent and particularly of an Agreement made by the Said William Sandeman Patrick Stewart William Marshall and Andrew Keay with James Stewart Fleeming Esquire of Moness relative to a Few of part of the Grounds of Pitcastle where a Cotton Miln was intended to be erected Second That the Said Company's concern Shall be divided into Seven Shares and that each of the Said Parties Shall Severally hold one of the Said Shares in his person Third That the Capital Stock of the Said Company Shall be Seven thousand pounds Sterling, of which Sum each of the Said parties Shall advance one thousand pounds Fourth that the Said parties shall have a right to draw the profites and must Sustain the losses in the aforesaid business according to their Several interests therein above mentioned But no profites are to be drawn exceeding the yearly interest of the Sum advanced by each partner to the Stock of the Company, untill a Majority of the Comp^y Shall agree thereto, and that after any debt that may be resting by the Company Shall be paid and Discharged Fifth That none of the Said parties Shall have liberty to Sell or Dispose of his Share in the Company except it be to one of the members thereof, or to the Company in general without the consent of a Majority of the Partners Provided alwise That the Said Richard Arkwright whenever the Spining of Cotton at the Said Mill Shall So far Succeed as to become a profitable concern Shall be at liberty to assign his Share in the Said Mill to the Said George Dempster and in case of the Said George Dempster's declining to accept of his Said Share at a valuation then the Said Richard Arkwright may Sell or assign his Share in any manner he Shall See fitt Sixth That the said Andrew Keay Shall be manager for the Company and have the charge of their whole affairs at Stanly, For which he shall have such reasonable allowance yearly as Shall be agreed on betwixt the Company and him, and that all bills, orders letters and other Deeds necessary to be Subscribed in the prosecution of the Ordinary business of the Company Shall be Signed by him the Said Andrew Keay But untill he return from Cromford where he now is Shall be Signed either by by the Said Patrick Stewart or William Marshall for and in behalf of the Company which shall be binding on all the partners Seventh that regular Books of accompts shall be keept by the Said Andrew Keay of the whole transactions relative to the business of the Company and ballanced upon the　　　　　　　　　　day of　　　　　　　　　　yearly, and that in the management of the affairs of the Company he Shall be directed by two or more of the partners to be chosen as a Committee for that purpose Eight That each of the aforesaid partners Shall be obliged to advance and pay in to the Said Andrew Keay or in his absence as aforesaid to the Said Patrick Stewart or William Marshall their aforesaid proportions of the above Capital Stock or at least Such parts thereof as Shall be necessary from time to time for carrying on the business and concerns of the Company and that within thirty days after the Same is demanded and Such of the Said Partners as Shall fail to do So Shall not only forfeit such Sum or Sums as Shall have been paid in by him But also Shall in all time thereafter have no further interest or concern in the Company Ninth That for the better conveniency of carrying on the business of the Company the parties agree to take out a Cash Acco^t from the Perth united Company or any other Banking Company to the amount of three thousand and to grant their joint Bond for the Same. Lastly the Said parties agree with all convenient Speed to enter into and Subscribe a Regular Contract of Co-Partnery containing such rules and regulations agreeable to the Tenor of this Contract as Shall be thought proper and necessary by them, or by a Majority of the Partners in point of interest in the Comp^y For the better conducting and carrying on the affairs and concerns of the Company and everything relative thereto and to the Heall premises the Said Parties Bind and Oblige them hinc inde to one another and the failzier to pay to the observers or willing thereto the Sum of five hundred pounds Sterling of Liquidate penalty in case of faillie by and Attour-performance Consenting to the Registration hereof in the Books of Councill and Session Sheriff Court Books of Perthshire or others Competent therein to remain for preservation and if need be to receive all Execution necessary on a Simple charge of Six days only And thereto They Constitute

Their Prois In Witness whereof these presents consisting of this and the two preceeding pages with one marginal note on the Second page are wrote upon Stampt paper by James Miller Writer in Perth and Subscribed by the parties as follows viz By the said George Dempster at London the twentieth day of July one thousand Seven hundred and eighty five years before these Witnesses Alex^r Anderson Esqr, Merchant in London and Roderick MacLeod Servant to the said George Dempster By the Said Richard Arkwright at Cromford the Second day of December and year last above mentioned before these Witnesses Mr David Dale Merchant in Glasgow and William Greatorex Servant to the Said Richard Arkwright By the Said William Sandeman Patrick Stewart William Marshall and Andrew Keay at Perth the twelfth day of the Said month of December and year foresaid before these Witnesses Alexander Bennet Writer in Perth and Walter Irvine Servant to the Said Patrick Stewart And by the Said Robert Graham at Perth the Thirty first day of January one thousand Seven hundred and eighty Six years before these Witnesses Thomas Marshal Vintner in Perth and Alexander Davenie his Servant The above Witnesses being also Witnesses to the parties Subscriptions to the marginal note on the Second page The respective places dates witnesses names and designations being insert and filled up by the Said Alexander Bennet/Signed/Richd Arkwright George Dempster Robt Graham Willm Sandeman Pat Stewart William Marshall Andrew Keay David Dale Witness Wm Greatorex Witness Roderick McLeod Witness Alex Bennet Witness Walter Irvine Witness Tho Marshall Witness Alex^r Davenie Witness.

SOURCE: Scottish Record Office, SC49/48/104.

DOCUMENT 34

Charles Hatchett visits industrialised Scotland, 1796

Charles Hatchett, FRS was a scientist in the Enlightenment era. Here he describes Carron and Clyde Ironworks before providing us with a valuable pen-portrait of New Lanark. Tours of this kind were not uncommon, but few visitors had his eye for technical detail.

WEDNESDAY JULY 13TH Set out with Mr. Jameson from Edin'h. at ½ past 10 o'clock, road good and country well cultivated arrived at Linlithgow a small Town not handsome. 16 M. changed chaise & horse; went to Falkirk 8 M – dined – went to Carron to see Iron Works. They say they employ 1000 Men but I do not believe it. They have 5 blast furnaces 36 feet by 18 each make from 2½ Tons to 3 Tons. Here they cast Cannon, Shells, Shot and all sorts of Iron Kettles etc. The Ore is Argillaceous (not rich) found in the neighbourhood. The coal also – the Limestone is brought from Fyfe. To each Blast Furnace they have 4 Cylinders. They cast twice in 24 hours. *Not* equal to Mr. Walkers Works. They do not allow the boring of the cannon to be seen. Make coke on the spot – only use the Ore of the country.

MONDAY JULY 25TH After Breakfast at ¼ before 10 oClock we set out from Glasgow – the road was near the Clyde in a level cultivated country. At about 3 Miles from Glasgow we stopped to see the Clyde Iron Works which belong to Messrs. Edingtons who have given a small share to Mr. Bigbie late of St. Petersburgh. These works are about ½ a Mile out of the road to the right or west and are near the river. They are extensive and have three Blast Furnaces each about 36 feet high by 15 in the widest part – when the works goes on well each of these Furnaces will produce about 25 Tons of Iron per week. They employ about 400 men. There are several Air Furnaces as at the other Iron Works and a small Blast Cone as at Carron for the Scrap Iron. The ore is brown Argillaceous Stone with calc: spar which with the coal is found in the neighbourhood. The coal is even raised within sight of the Works at less than ¼ of a Mile distance. The Lime Stone used as a Flux is hard and of a dark grey but not bituminous. At these works they cast and bore cannon of all sizes likewise all sorts of Vessels, Cylinders etc. Their Blowing Cylinders & Boring Machines are worked by the common Steam Engines.

We continued our route through a level county (at least for the chief part) and arrived at Hamilton a small Town which gives the title to the Duke of Hamilton who has a seat in the neighbourhood. Hamilton is 11 Miles from Glasgow.

Changed Horses and pursued our Journey through a country diversified with Hill & Dale, well wooded and cultivated. The road was chiefly near the Banks of the Clyde – passed a fine seat belonging to the Earl of Hyndford – at about 4 Miles before we reached Lanark we stopped to see Stone Byre one of the falls of the Clyde which is about 50 feet in Depth and is very beautiful and Picturesque. Reached Lanark a small Town by ¼ past 4 PM. After dinner went to see the Cotton Mills belonging to Mr. Dale. These are about 1 Mile from the Town and consist of 4 immense Buildings of 6 stories in which by Machines worked by a water wheel and attended principally by Children, cotton is carded and spun into yarn. In these Works above 400 Children are employed but it is said that in all Works belonging to Mr. Dale 1600 Persons are employed. Afterwards went to see Cora Lin waterfall of the Clyde about ½ a Mile from the Mills and also Bonnetin[1] falls ½ a Mile beyond Cora. These are in the lands of Sir Charles Lockhart Ross who has a fine seat near them. The country and cliffs on all sides are thickly covered with wood and these falls have a most beautiful and Romantic appearance – Cora is about 55 or 60 feet deep and Bonnetin about 40. Bonnetin is the first fall. Cora is the 2nd and Stone Byre the 3rd. Of these Cora appeared to me as the most beautiful.

Slept at Lanark. Lanark is 15 Miles from Hamilton.

NOTES
1 Bonnington.

SOURCE: A Raistrick (ed) 1967 *The Hatchett Diary: A Tour through the counties of England and Scotland in 1796 visiting their mines and manufactories*, Truro (D Bradford Barton Ltd), 89, 99–100.

Evidence of Robert Owen to the Select Committee on the State of Children Employed in Manufactories, 1816

The large number of children employed in mills and mines was beginning to cause concern among social reformers. Here Owen presents evidence of the situation he inherited at New Lanark, describing the changes he introduced, especially in schooling.

What is your situation in life? – I am principal proprietor and sole acting partner of the establishment at New Lanark, in Scotland.

How many persons, young and old, are immediately supported by the New Lanark manufactory and establishment? – About 2,300: Upon the first of January last the numbers were 2,297, I believe.

To how many out of that number do you give employment? – This number varies occasionally, but upon the average about sixteen or seventeen hundred.

The remainder of the 2,300 are the wives and children? – Children too young, and persons too old, of the same families; some of the wives are employed.

Do you mean that the 2,300 are the number composing the whole of the families, some parts of which are employed in the works? – Yes; the difference between those immediately employed in the works and the number first stated, are those who are too young for work, or too old, or wives who are obliged to attend families too young for work.

What is the population of the village? – About 2,300.

At what age do you take children into your mills? – At ten and upwards.

What are your regular hours of labour per day, exclusive of meal times? – Ten hours and three quarters.

What time do you allow for meals? – Three quarters of an hour for dinner, and half an hour for breakfast.

Then your full time of work per day is twelve hours, out of which time you allow the mills to cease work for an hour and a quarter? – Yes.

Why do you not employ children at an earlier age? – Because I consider it would be injurious to the children, and not beneficial to the proprietors.

What reason have you to suppose it is injurious to the children to be employed in regular manufactories at an earlier age? – The evidence of very strong facts.

What are those facts? – Seventeen years ago, a number of individuals, with myself, purchased the New Lanark establishment from the late Mr. Dale of Glasgow; At that period I found there were 500 children, who had been taken from poor-houses, chiefly in Edinburgh, and those children were generally from the age of five and six, to seven and eight; they were so taken because Mr. Dale could not, I learned afterwards, obtain them at a more advanced period of life; if he did not take them at those ages, he could not obtain them at all. The hours of work at that time were thirteen inclusive of meal times, and an hour and a half was allowed for meals. I very soon discovered that, although those children were extremely well fed, well clothed, well lodged, and very great care taken of them when out of the mills, their growth and their minds were materially injured by being employed at those ages within the cotton mills for eleven hours and a half per day. It is true that those children, in consequence of being so well fed and clothed and lodged, looked fresh, and, to a superficial observer, healthy in their countenances; yet their limbs were very generally deformed, their growth was stunted, and, although one of the best schoolmasters upon the old plan was engaged to instruct those children regularly every night, in general they made but a very slow progress, even in learning the common alphabet. Those appearances strongly impressed themselves upon my mind to proceed solely from the number of hours they were employed in those mills during the day, because in every other respect they were as well taken care of, and as well looked after, as any children could be. Those were some, and perhaps they may be considered by the Committee sufficient, facts to induce me to suppose that the children were injured by being taken into the mills at this early age, and employed for so many hours; therefore, as soon as I had it in my power, I adopted regulations to put an end to a system which appeared to me to be so injurious.

In consequence then of your conviction that children are injured by being employed the usual daily hours in manufactures, when under ten years of age, you have for some time refused to receive children into your works till they are ten years of age? – Yes.

Do you think the age of ten to be the best period for the admission of children into full and constant employment for ten or eleven hours per day, within woollen, cotton, or other mills or manufactories? – I do not.

What other period would you recommend for the admission to full work? – Twelve years.

How then would you employ them from ten to the age of twelve? – For the two years preceding, to be partially instructed; to be instructed one half the day, and the other half to be initiated into the manufactories by parties employing two sets of children in the day, on the same principle that two sets of children were employed when proprietors thought it their interest to work day and night.

If such be your opinion, how happen you not to have acted upon it? – Had the works been entirely my own, I should have acted upon that principle some time ago, but being connected with other gentlemen, I deem it necessary in practice not to deviate so much from the common regulations of the country as I otherwise would have done; and, besides, it required some time to prepare the population for so material a change from that to which they had been previously accustomed . . .

Do you give instruction to any part of your population? – Yes.

What part? – To the children from three years old, upwards; and to every other part of the population that chuse to receive it.

Will you state the particulars? – There is a preparatory school, into which all the children, from the age of three to six, are admitted at the option of the parents; there is a second school, in which all the children of the population, from six to ten, are admitted; and if any of the parents, from being more easy in their circumstances, and setting a higher value upon instruction, wish to continue their children at school for one, two, three, or four years longer, they are at liberty to do so; they are never asked to take the children from the school to the works.

Will you state who supports the schools? – The schools are supported immediately at the expense of the establishment; they are indeed literally and truly supported by the people themselves.

Will you explain how that is? – New Lanark was a new settlement formed by Mr. Dale; the part of the country in which these works were erected was very thinly inhabited, and the Scotch peasantry generally were disinclined to work in cotton mills; it was necessary that great efforts should therefore be made to collect a new population in such a situation, and such population was collected before the usual and customary means for conveniently supplying a population with food were formed, the work people therefore were obliged to buy their food and other articles at a very high price, and under many great disadvantages; to counterbalance this inconvenience, a store was opened at the establishment, into which provisions of the best quality, and clothes of the most useful kind, were introduced, to be sold at the option of the people, at a price sufficient to cover prime-cost and charges, and to cover the accidents of such a business, it being understood at the time that whatever profits arose from this establishment, those profits should be employed for the general benefit of the work people themselves; and these school establishments have been supported, as well as other things, by the surplus profits, because in consequence of the pretty general moral habits of the people, there have been very few losses by bad debts, and although they have been supplied considerably under the price of provisions in the neighbourhood, yet the surplus profits have in all cases been sufficient to bear the expense of these school establishments; therefore, they have literally been supported by the people themselves.

What effects have you experienced from these plans of instruction? – The best possible. It perhaps may be useful, as there are many gentlemen present who are interested in these questions, and who may not have had the experience I have had, to state, that when these schools were opened, it was not considered sufficient that attention should be paid merely to instructing the children in what are called the common rudiments of learning, that is, in reading, writing, arithmetic, and the girls also in sewing, but was deemed of much greater importance, that attention should be given by the masters to form the moral habits of the children, and their dispositions; and in consequence, the moral habits of the children have been improved in such a manner as that from the 1st of January last to the time I left the establishment, about a week ago, out of two hundred and about twenty children, who are in school in the day, and three hundred and eighty or ninety, who are in school at night, there has not been occasion to punish one single individual; and as the school is arranged upon such principles as are calculated to give the children a good deal of exercise and some amusement, the children are more willing and more desirous of attending the school and the occupations which they are engaged in there, than of going to their ordinary play; the most unpleasant time they have in the week is the Saturday afternoon, which is necessarily a holiday, in consequence of the schools, in which they are taught, being washed and cleaned on that day. I have found other and very important advantages, in a pecuniary view, from this arrangement and these plans. In consequence of the individuals observing that real attention is given to their comforts and to their improvements, they are willing to work at much lower wages at that establishment, than at others at no great distance, which are esteemed to be upon the best plans in the country, with all the newest improvements . . .

What length of time per day, at school, do you conceive would be necessary to give boys common instruction in reading and writing? – That depends very much upon the capacity of the children, and more materially upon the plans adopted by the teachers: Under the best system I have ever witnessed, at which indeed I was present this morning at the National School, the children are taught to read not only well, but better than any other children I have heard, not only in a small number but in the gross, in twelve months: There can be no doubt, children may be taught to read and write, and understand accounts, and the girls also to sew, by attending to those rudiments one hour a day for a given number of years; but if they attend two hours a day, it will be done in less than one half of that time.

The town of Lanark is entirely dependent upon your manufactory? – Entirely so.

Do you think that the regulations which are in force at New Lanark, would apply to a large populous manufacturing town, where the inhabitants are not entirely dependent upon a manufactory? – The same principles, I conceive, may be applied, under different modifications, to any situation, either where there are few or many.

What employment could be found for the children of the poor, in those situations, till ten years of age? – It does not appear to me that it is necessary for children to be employed, under ten years of age, in any regular work.

If you did not employ them in any regular work, what would you do with them? – Instruct them, and give them exercise.

Would not there be a danger of their acquiring, by that time, vicious habits, for want of regular occupation? – My own experience leads me to say that I have found quite the reverse, that their habits have been good in proportion to the extent of their instruction.

That proceeds upon the supposition that they are to be instructed? – Most assuredly: if the children are not to be instructed, they had better be employed in any occupation that should keep them out of mischief.

SOURCE: 'The Select Committee to Enquire into the State of Children employed in the Manufactories of the United Kingdom', 1816, *Parliamentary Papers*, iii, 20.

URBANISATION

DOCUMENT 36

Proposals for carrying on certain public works in the City of Edinburgh, 1752

The development of the New Town, although commenced in 1767, had been widely discussed during previous decades. In 1752 the Convention of Royal Burghs was one of several guiding influences behind the publication of a pamphlet expressing the urgent need for Edinburgh's regeneration. Practical considerations, especially the easing of population congestion, combined with a desire to enhance the city's prestige and commercial prosperity. The successful examples of New Town construction in other European cities were to the forefront of contemporary thinking, as was the more competitive concern to place Edinburgh on a par with London, and show that Scotland was a dynamic and equal partner in the United Kingdom.

So necessary and so considerable an improvement of the capital cannot fail to have the greatest influence on the general prosperity of the nation. It is a vulgar mistake, that the greatest part of our principal families chuse to reside at LONDON. This indeed is true with regard to a few of our members of parliament, and some particular families who were settled there before the union. The rest go only occasionally; and if their stay be long, and their expense by consequence greater than this country can well bear, it must be entirely imputed to the present form and situation of EDINBURGH. Were these in any tolerable degree remedied, our people of rank would hardly prefer an obscure life at LONDON, to the splendour and influence with which they might reside at home. An uninterrupted country-life, is what they will never be brought to submit to. Attention to the forming an interest, the pleasures of retirement, or a taste for agriculture, may induce them possibly to pass some part of their time at their country-seats; more cannot reasonably be expected. It might indeed be otherwise in ancient times, when the feudal customs prevailed, with their large dependancies and extensive jurisdictions. The institution of our government is now different: our manners must be different also. A nation cannot at this day be considerable, unless it be opulent. Wealth is only to be obtained by trade and commerce, and these are only carried on to advantage in populous cities. There also we find the chief objects of pleasure and ambition, and there consequently all those will flock whose circumstances can afford it. But can we expect, that persons of fortune in SCOTLAND will exchange the handsome seats they generally possess in the country, for the scanty lodging, and paltry accommodations they must put up with in EDINBURGH? It is not choice, but necessity, which obliges them to go so frequently to LONDON. Let us improve and enlarge this city, and possibly the superior pleasures of LONDON, which is at a distance, will be compensated, at least in some measure, by the moderate pleasures of EDINBURGH, which is at home.

It has been objected, That this project may occasion the centre of the town to be deserted. But of this there can be no hazard. People of fortune, and of a certain rank, will probably chuse to build upon the fine fields which lie to the north and south of the town: but men of professions and business of every kind, will still incline to live in the neighbourhood of the exchange, of the courts of justice, and other places of public resort; and the number of this last class of men will increase in a much greater proportion, than that of the former. *Turin, Berlin*, and many other cities, shew the truth of this observation. In these cities, what is called the *new town*, consists of spacious streets and large buildings, which are thinly inhabited, and that too by strangers chiefly, and persons of considerable rank; while the *old town*, though not near so commodious, is more crouded than before these late additions were made. The national advantages which a populous capital must necessarily produce, are obvious. A great concourse of people brought within a small compass, occasions a much greater consumption than the same number would do dispersed over a wide country. As the consumption is greater so it is quicker and more discernible. Hence follows a more rapid circulation of money and other commodities, the great spring which gives motion to general industry and improvement. The examples set by the capital, the nation will soon follow. The certain consequence is, general wealth and prosperity: the number of useful people will increase; the rents of land rise; the public revenue improve; and, in the room of sloth and poverty, will succeed industry and opulence . . .

Such being the nature and end of these proposals, we can have little doubt but they will meet with general encouragement. Whoever is warmed with a sincere concern for the prosperity of his country, will chearfully contribute to so national an undertaking. Extensive projects, which little minds are apt to condemn as impracticable, serve only to excite generous spirits to act with greater industry and vigour. Peace is now generally established; the rage of faction in this country is greatly abated: there is a concurrence of almost every circumstance, which can prompt us to undertake, or enable us to execute great designs. Such of our young men of rank and fortune as are not sunk in low pleasures, must find employment of some kind or other. If the great objects of war and faction no longer present themselves, may they not find a more humane, and not less interesting exercise of their active powers, in promoting and cultivating the general arts of peace? In the reign of Queen *Elizabeth*, ENGLAND was but a forming state, as SCOTLAND is now. It was then that the spirit of the ENGLISH began to exert itself. Ships were fitted out, nay fleets were equipped, by private gentlemen. In the same manner public buildings were erected, colonies were settled, and new discoveries made. In a lesser degree, the same disposition begins to discover itself in this country. Building bridges, repairing high-roads, establishing manufactures, forming commercial companies, and opening new veins of trade, are employments which have already thrown a lustre upon some of the first names of this country. The little detail of an established commerce, may ingross the attention of the merchant: but it is in prosecution of greater objects, that the leading men of a country ought to exert their power and influence. And what greater object can be presented to their view, than that of enlarging, beautifying, and improving the capital of their native country? What can redound more to their honour? What prove more beneficial to SCOTLAND, and by consequence to UNITED BRITAIN?

SOURCE: Quoted in AJ Youngson 1966 *The Making of Classical Edinburgh, 1750–1840*, Edinburgh (Edinburgh University Press), 9–12.

DOCUMENT 37

Dundee in the 1790s

Rev Robert Small was one of Dundee's Church of Scotland ministers, charged with the responsibility of describing the city for The Statistical Account of Scotland. *In his detailed narrative, Small showed that he was very much aware that Dundee was in a transitional stage of development towards the end of the eighteenth century. However, as this extract reveals, he was also conscious that there were both positive and negative dimensions to urban change.*

The principal advantages of Dundee are, – the noble river on which it is situated, opening to the inhabitants, a ready communication, not only with the London market, but with those of the principal and most opulent countries of Europe; and also giving them a considerable extent of inland navigation: – The fertile countries in its neighbourhood, the Carse of Gowrie especially, full of thriving, rich, and intelligent farmers; whose industry, if it was first set in motion by the opulence of towns, and their increasing demand for country produce, now amply returns the favour, by equal demands on the towns for their merchandise and manufactures: – The industry, sobriety, and frugality of its inhabitants, which virtues, having been confirmed by long habit, will probably continue to be reputable for a long period to come. In addition to these, it must draw the most signal benefits from the excellent turnpike roads lately constructed, and continuing to be extended through all the principal districts of Angus, and the neighbouring parts of Perthshire. For these the town is entirely indebted to the exertions of a few country gentlemen; and though its inhabitants have had no share, either in the trouble or the risk of the undertaking, they will be probably the principal sharers in the profits; for their markets instead of being often shut up, and becoming inaccessible, will now be open at all seasons of the year, for the heaviest goods; and the people in distant parts will no longer be under the necessity of repairing to the less abundant markets of inferior towns. But if Dundee enjoys these advantages, it is not without its disadvantages and defects. Among these the following seem to be the most remarkable: – The lanes, and even several streets are uncommonly narrow, and the dwellings of the inhabitants too close upon one another; – the greatest part of the families living by half dozens, as formerly in Edinburgh, under the same roof, with common stairs, without back yards or courts, and many possessing only single rooms: – The late additional suburbs have been built without any general plan, and without the least regard to health, elegance or cleanliness; though no situation perhaps in the world, presented better opportunities to provide for all the three: – There is an almost total want of public walks and open places, to which sedentary or delicate people may resort, and children be carried for air and exercise . . .

SOURCE: DJ Withrington and IR Grant (eds) 1981 *The Statistical Account of Scotland 1791–1799 edited by Sir John Sinclair* Vol XIII Angus, 190–1 (town and parish of Dundee). East Ardsley (EP Publishing).

DOCUMENT 38

Dundee in the 1830s

Some forty years after the publication of The Statistical Account of Scotland, *the* New Statistical Account of Scotland *updated the commentary on Scotland's parish communities, and included a lengthy analysis of the progress of industry and commerce in Dundee. The description of the city during the 1790s had been borne in mind by the assorted contributors to the second volume, who took pains to point out intervening changes to the urban fabric and population profile.*

Of late years the progress of improvement, especially in manufacturing towns, has been rapid beyond all former experience; and perhaps a better illustration of this can nowhere be found than in Dundee. In looking to the public works, the harbour, seminaries, spinning–mills, and opening of new streets, – the greater number of them have been undertaken within the last few years; and there seems scarcely a limit, except change of trade, to the advancement and prosperity of the town. Nor in the midst of public measures have more minute details been neglected. The rough pavement of our streets, which formerly seemed only of use for proving the springs of carriages, or affording exercise to the invalid within, is giving way to the system of Macadam; and our burying–ground, which lately presented an aspect gloomy to the eye, and uncomfortable to the foot, has been beautified with walks and shrubs . . .

In concluding this account of the parish of Dundee, it seems unnecessary to add any farther remarks of our own. To draw a comparison betwixt what it is now, and what it was forty years ago, when the last Report was published, would almost be to repeat what we have written. Its population has been more than doubled; its charities have risen from L.1900 to L.7000; its shipping has increased fourfold; and its linen trade been almost entirely called into existence. But the reverse side of the picture must not be concealed. The assessment for the poor has advanced tenfold. In 1791 it was L.400; it is now L.4000. This, perhaps, is an evil inseparable from prosperous communities. The poor generally flock to, or are rapidly increased in them; and where multitudes are gathered together at various employments, example does not always favour economy, industry and virtue. Nor is it easy, amidst the spirit of enterprise which is abroad, to suggest any improvement for the town, which is not in the course of being attempted. A new Jail and Bridewell, or perhaps House of Refuge, a supply of water, and a new burying-ground – the present one being fearfully over-crowded, – are generally believed to be indispensably necessary; and measures, as before intimated, are in progress to procure them. In population, manufactures, and trade; in the luxury and comfort which prevail, Dundee has perhaps advanced faster than any similar town in the kingdom. There are men alive in it who remember when its population was only *one-fifth* of what it is now; when its harbour was a crooked wall, often inclosing but a few fishing or smuggling craft; when its spinning-mills were things unknown and unthought of; and its trade hardly worthy of the name. And curious would it be could we anticipate the future; and tell what will be its state, when another generation shall have passed away, and other hands shall perhaps be called to prepare a record of its progress or decline.

SOURCE: *New Statistical Account of Scotland* 1845 Vol XI Forfar-Kincardine, 52–3 (parish of Dundee). Edinburgh and London (William Blackwood & Sons).

DOCUMENT 39

Comments on Glasgow's Fever Epidemic, 1818, by Robert Graham, MD

Robert Graham combined the responsibility of Regius Professor of Botany at Glasgow University with work as a physician in the city's Royal Infirmary. In 1818, during the height of a typhus epidemic in Scotland, Graham wrote a detailed assessment of the condition of patients he examined, in order to help explain the causes and treatment of this little-understood disease, then called 'continued fever'. As can be seen here, his conclusions were uncompromising in their criticisms of Glasgow's rapidly deteriorating fabric.

Origin and propagation

If any man wonders at the prevalence of continued fever, among the lower classes in Glasgow, or at its spreading from their habitations, let him take the walk which I did to-day with Mr. Angus, one of the district Surgeons. Let him pick his steps among every species of disgusting filth, through a long alley, from four to five feet wide, flanked by houses five floors high, with here and there an opening for a pool of water, from which there is no drain, and in which all the nuisances of the neighbourhood are deposited, in endless succession, to float, and putrify, and waste away in noxious gases. Let him look, as he goes along, into the cellars which open into this lane, and he will probably find lodged, in alternate habitations, which are no way distinguished in their exterior, and very little by the furniture which is within them, pigs, and cows, and human beings, which can scarcely be recognised till brought to the light, or, till the eyes of the visitant get accustomed to the smoke and gloom of the cellar in which they live. I have been to-day in several dens of this kind, where I did not see persons lying on the floor near me, till Mr. Angus, whom a previous visit had taught where to find them, inquired after their health. I was in one closet, measuring twelve feet by less than five, on the floor of which, he told me, six people had lain, affected with fever, within these few days, and where I saw the seventh inhabitant now confined. We found, in one lodging-house, fifteen feet long, by nine feet from the front of the beds to the opposite wall, that fifteen people were sometimes accommodated; and when we expressed horror at the situation in which they were placed, the woman of the house, somewhat offended, and, I believe, a little alarmed lest we should cause some enquiry to by made by the Police, said, in support of the character of her establishment, that *each family* was provided with *a bed*, and that she very seldom had any body lying on the floor. I shall only mention one other instance of misery. In a lodging house, consisting of two rooms, separated by boards, the first thirteen feet by eleven, the other fifteen by eight, twenty-three of the lowest class of Irish were lately lodged. To-day there are fourteen, of whom two are confined with fever, three are convalescent, and one only has hitherto escaped. There are only three beds in this house, (denominated, with that facetiousness which enables an Irishman to joke with his own misery, Flea Barracks,) one of them in a press half-way up the wall, the others wooden frames, on which are laid some shavings of wood, scantily covered with dirty rags. A man, two sons, and an adult daughter, were lying side by side on the floor of the first room, their bedding of the same materials with the others, and the boys being destitute of shirts. Could imagination feign a combination of circumstances more horribly conducive to disease and immorality? . . .

Prevention & removal

. . . if the statements which I have made in the last section regarding the origin of contagion, are well founded, then the principles which ought to regulate all our attempts at preventing it, are obvious. If it is true that the great source from whence contagion springs, is a crowd of human beings confined in an ill-ventilated room; then it is also true that if we can prevent this crowd, or if we can ventilate the apartment in which it meets, we shall at least make the occurrence of contagion much less frequent, and as it is a matter of dispute whether it has any other source, it is possible, that by this means we may prevent the origin of contagious fever altogether.

As it may be found extremely difficult, however, to keep the houses of the poor under strict regulation in these respects, we must look to the circumstances which favour the operation of contagious matter, that by checking them also as much as we can, we may render this more manageable, if unfortunately it should at any time be generated. The principal of these I have stated to be filth, damp, scanty or unwholesome food, and generally every circumstance which promotes inaction and debility. If we can prevent or lessen these concomitant circumstances, it is probable we shall be able to prevent contagious matter from acquiring that degree of concentration which will enable it to produce disease.

I am afraid it will be found nearly impossible to ventilate the houses of a great body of the poor in Glasgow, as they are at present accommodated. The construction of the houses is such that on this account it would be extremely difficult; but perhaps a more insuperable impediment still we should find in the excessive apathy of the people, and their dislike to ventilation. To a person unacquainted with the habits of the lower classes, this aversion would be nearly incredible; but every one who is in the habit of going among them, knows it well. It is a constant battle which their medical attendants have to fight, and I recollect one particularly aggravated case, where I only succeeded in preventing the shutting of the window whenever my back was turned, by sending for a carpenter, and making him carry it away with him.

An important step towards ventilation would be effected, if we could even open up the lanes in which the lower classes live. In Glasgow, the hovels which they inhabit are collected into dense masses of very great size between some of the larger streets. I believe it would greatly add to the healthiness of the place, if some improvements which I have heard talked of were effected, and straight and wide streets carried in different directions through these depositories of wretchedness. It would not, I think, be easy to devise a more judicious charity, than the building of houses for the poor on an approved plan and in a good situation. The avidity with which such houses are sought after, shows too, that it is a kind of benevolence which would cost very little money, if indeed it did not pay a speculation.

SOURCE: Robert Graham 1818 *Practical observations on continued fever, especially that form at present existing as an epidemic, with some remarks on the most efficient plans for its suppression*, Glasgow, 56–8, 62–4.

DOCUMENT 40

Report on the general and sanitary condition of the town of Greenock by WL Laurie, MD

The 1842 Reports on the Sanitary condition of the labouring population of Scotland *revealed that serious environmental problems existed in a broad cross-section of towns and cities. The author of the report for Greenock was WL Laurie, a local doctor, who provided graphic and disturbing examples of conditions in the town's less salubrious quarters. However, Laurie attempted to redress the balance by commenting on what he perceived as the more positive aspects of urban life.*

I have hitherto only alluded to the poorest class of the inhabitants; of course there is a numerous body of respectable operatives, who live in comfort, and who feed and clothe their families well, and also give their children an education suited to their circumstances, and who even manage to save a little each week from their earnings, which is proved by the great success of the savings' bank, which has now been in operation for 26 years. Amongst this class of the community, notwithstanding the unmerited opposition it has met with, teetotalism has effected a great moral reformation; it has brought comfort and independence to many a fire-side which formerly knew only misery and degradation.

Excluding those who are addicted to the immoderate use of ardent spirits, the conduct of the working-classes is praiseworthy; the greater bulk of them attend church regularly, and likewise contribute more in proportion than the higher classes do to the various Christian charities.

Trade has for many years past been in a flourishing condition in this town, consequently the workmen are well paid: while other places are suffering from fluctuations in trade, the depression is little felt here.

A great body of the operatives have established friendly societies, which are well supported, and which in time of illness afford their sick brethren a weekly aliment sufficient for their maintenance. Several of these societies pay a medical man for attending their members while sick. It would be well for the working population if these benefit societies were more general, as too many of them are very improvident, laying past nothing, but, on the contrary, spending their whole gains, and when laid on a sick bed, depending on credit for their support; they thus run largely into debt, and when able to resume their employment, feel little disposed to pay what they owe; they thus lose all self-respect, and are degraded in their own and in the eyes of their fellow men.

Like other towns in Scotland, Greenock has a large pauper population; the great bulk of these (I would say three-fourths) are natives of other places, having come here in search of employment, and from destitution, disease, and other causes, have been thrown a burden on the community. A great number come from Ireland and the Highlands with the express purpose of making a settlement, that is, supporting themselves in the best way they can for three years, when they can have a legal claim for relief from the parish. There are many who, though not claimants for public relief, suffer much, especially during winter, from want of food and fuel. We still here and there find some remains of that spirit of independence which would rather suffer than complain, still it must be a matter of regret to think that many, feeling unable to maintain that spirit of independence, are induced from their destitution to commit crime, perhaps their first offence, or fall a prey to disease in its most malignant form.

SOURCE: *Reports on the Sanitary condition of the labouring population of Scotland* 1842, London (HMSO), 252–3.

HIGHLAND SOCIETY

DOCUMENT 41

Thomas Telford's proposals for the Highlands, 1802

The rehabilitation of the Highlander through imperial service required more than cultural appreciation, argued Thomas Telford, following his survey of the inadequate commercial infrastructure in the Highlands. Although his report of 1802 led in the following year to parliamentary authorisation for a programme of canal, road and bridge building under his direction, his plea that civil engineering must be complemented by social engineering fell on deaf ears.

In one point of View it may be stated, that, taking the mountainous Parts of Scotland as a District of the British Empire, it is the Interest of the Empire that this District be made to produce as much human Food as it is capable of doing at the least possible Expence; that this may be done by stocking it chiefly with Sheep; that it is in the Interest of the Empire the Food so produced, should not be consumed by Persons residing among the Mountains totally unemployed, but rather in some other Parts of the Country, where their Labour can be made productive either in the Business of Agriculture, Fisheries, or Manufactures . . .

In another point of View it may be stated, that it is a great Hardship, if not a great Injustice, that the Inhabitants of an extensive District should all at once be driven from their native Country, to make way for Sheep Farming, which is likely to be carried to an imprudent Extent; that in a few Years, this Excess will be evident; that before it is discovered, the Country will be depopulated, and that Race of People which has of late Years maintained so honourable a Share in the Operations of our Armies and Navies will then be no more; that in a Case where such a numerous Body of People are deeply interested, it is the Duty of Government to consider it as an extraordinary Case . . .

SOURCE: Thomas Telford 1802 'Survey and Reports of the Coasts and Central Highlands of Scotland in Autumn of 1802', *in* 'Reports of the Select Committee on the Survey of the Central Highlands of Scotland', *Parliamentary Papers* IV, 16.

Duncan Ban Macintyre: Gaelic post-clearance poem

A less focused but more poignant critique of deserted settlements has come from the Gaelic poet, Duncan Ban Macintyre, a former forester who commemorated his removal from Glenorchy in 1766 by praising foxes for attacking sheep in 'Orain nam Balgairean'. Relocated in Edinburgh, he won favour from the Highland Society of London during the 1780s for poems on such culturally acceptable themes as the association of the Gael with bagpipes and the imperial service of Highland regiments.

An iad na caoraich cheannriabhach
Rinn aimhreit feadh an t-saoghail;
Am fearann a chur fàs oirnn
'S am màl a chur an daoiread?
Chan 'eil àit aig tuathanach,
Tha bhuannachd-san air claonadh;
Is éigin dhà bhith fàgail
An ait anns an robh dhaoine.

Na bailtean is na h-àirighean
Am faighte blàths is faoileachd,
Gun taighean ach na làraichean,
Gun àiteach air na raointean.
Tha h-uile seòl a b' àbhaist
Anns a' Ghàidhealtachd air caochladh,
Air cinntinn cho mì-nàdurra
'Sna h-àitean a bha aoigheil.

[Are these the sheep of bridled face that caused dispeace throughout the world; the land to be laid waste to us, and the rent to become dearer? There is no place for a farmer, his revenues have dwindled; he is compelled to leave the place where his forbears had resided.

The villages and sheilings where warmth and cheer were found, have no houses save the ruins, and no tillage in the fields. Every practice that prevailed in Gaeldom has been altered, and become so unnatural in the places that were hospitable.]

SOURCE: A MacLeod (ed) 1952 *Orain Dhonnchaidh Bhain: The Songs of Duncan Ban Macintyre*, Edinburgh (Scottish Gaelic Texts Society), 346–7.

DOCUMENT 43

William Thom's views on Highland chiefs, 1773

---

*The commercial motives promoting the demise of clanship were not
necessarily enlightened. A pungent critique of the clan élite's continuous
drive to push up rents came in an anonymous pamphlet attributed to
William Thom, minister of Govan. Having lambasted the unfettered recourse
to competitive bidding for leases as a principal cause of emigration, he
attested that the bad harvests and failures of the droving trade in the past
three years were divine warnings.*

God has taken to himself, in his Providence, what was to have been a prey to the
avarice of those who think all that their dependants are possessed of belongs to the
master. In short, there is such a concurrence of causes at present working out the
ruin of the people betwixt the hard seasons on the one hand, and the severity of
masters on the other, that it would look as if providence was beginning to bring
about some remarkable change in the Highlands of Scotland, and intended to
remove the ancient inhabitants of it. Thus, making the superiors of the country
defeat their own purposes, by their own general measures, which in the end will
turn out to be a punishment for their conduct. It is plain then, that our Chieftains
are manifestly acting against their own interest, as their conduct has already
contributed very much to ruin their people and to promote a spirit of emigration
among them to a degree that is much more alarming than has as yet been seriously
attended to.

SOURCE: National Library of Scotland, A Highlander 1773 *The Present Conduct of the
Chieftains and Proprietors of Lands in the Highlands of Scotland towards their clans and
people, considered impartially.*

DOCUMENT 44

John MacVicar's proposals for public works in the Highlands (c. 1750)

Despite the decline in militarism by 1700, the role of the clans in the front line of successive Jacobite risings raised cries not only for exemplary reprisals, but for exemplary measures to civilize the Highlands after the 'Forty-Five. A Highlander who had served against the Jacobites, John MacVicar, late Captain in Lord Murray's Regiment, tempered his strictures against clanship by an agenda for public works designed to increase the commercial activity already manifest in the southern Highlands.

As all sorts of Industry are carried on at a Vast Expence in England, a great many Boys & Girls might be brought from the Highlands and employed there in Manufactures.

A great many Young able fellows who are now outlawed and live by Rapine to the great Disadvantage of their Neighbours, might be invited to serve in our Army and hold the Plough. Great numbers of the poorer sort might be employed in making Roads through the Highlands, and in other publick Works, such as Fortifications, tho' the same might be attended with more Expences than it might have been done for by the Troops.

It is said that there are very promising Lead mines in Suinart in Argyle shire and in Glengarry in Inverness shire, which are places abounding with Cow Steallers and other troublesome Idlers, who might be very usefully employed in improving these.

The Seas to the West and Northwest of Scotland are said to abound with cod and other kinds of Fish, that might for the advantage of undertakers be sent to foreign Markets, which makes it wished that some such merchants would join in Company, and advance a Competent Fund for that purpose and for working these Mines.

It would certainly be of great benefit to the Publick if the raising of Hemp and Lint were duely encouraged . . . Spinning Houses ought to be built in different corners of the Highlands, especially on Crown lands, with houses to accommodate several dozens of Boys & Girls who ought to be furnished with lodging and provision while learning to spin, and dress the flax of hemp & lint.

When once the people apply themselves heartily to the raising of flax, lint mills might be built at convenient places and factory houses furnished with weavers and other artificers that will be capable to teach the youth.

SOURCE: British Museum, Hardwicke papers, vol DX: *Political Tracts Relating to Scotland, c. 1745–50*, Add.MSS 35,858, fos 17–60. *A Scheme for Civilizing the Clans in the North of Scotland*, (c. 1750).

DOCUMENT 45

Rev Dr John Walker's opinion of the Highlanders, 1771

As part of their flagship endeavours for exemplary improvements, the Commissioners of the Annexed Estates in 1764 despatched the Rev Dr John Walker, then minister of Moffat (subsequently Professor of Natural History at Edinburgh University), to the Hebrides. His report, which was eventually completed in 1771, identified the improvement of the Hebrides as 'a great National Object' that required the constructive employment of erstwhile clansmen in agriculture, fisheries and manufactures.

I call them laborious, contrary indeed to a received Opinion. But it is only from a superficial View, that they are represented as inconquerably averse to Industry and every kind of Innovation. The Culture of their Fields, carried on by the Spade, with the Strength of their Arms, instead of that of Cattle, and many other Operations, in their rude System of Husbandry, exhibits powerfull though indeed ill directed Efforts of Industry. Their extensive Cultivation of Potatoes, by Hand Labour: their Hardships and Assiduity in the Manufacture of Kelp: the Success of the Linen Manufacture, wherever it has been introduced and the amazing Progress of Inoculation; show, that the Highlanders are as capable to judge of, are as ready to embrace and can as vigorously pursue any Innovation that is advantageous or Salutary as any other People whatever.

SOURCE: MM McKay (ed) 1980 *The Rev Dr John Walker's Report on the Hebrides of 1764 and 1771*, Edinburgh (John Donald), 35.

DOCUMENT 46

Rev John MacLeod, Harris, on the kelp industry (1790s)

The particular fragility and vulnerability of crofting communities to market forces had clearly been identified prior to the advent of the Napoleonic Wars, which led to an embargo on barilla as an alternative to kelp. The minister for Harris, Rev John MacLeod, delivered his admonition prior to the price of kelp being driven up to £20 per ton while wages rarely rose above £3 per ton in the Western Isles.

Kelp is the staple, and, excepting the few cows sold to the drovers, the only valuable article of exportation which the country produces. This manufacture is thought to be brought to its utmost extent of late, in consequence of high prices some years ago, which encouraged the people to convert all the sea ware produced by these shores into kelp, regardless of the detriment to their corns and pastures, which have degenerated much through want of the manure formerly afforded by the shores . . . The people of Harris are very expert and industrious at it. The whole quantity now made amounts to 450 tons. The shores are held in tack along with the landed possession. The manufacturers are paid at the rate of so much per ton . . . for the easiest shores the least paid is L1 5s; for the more difficult from L1 10s to L1 15s per ton. For manufacturing such ware as is cut at low ebbs on such rocks, which must be ferried in boats to drying grounds at a distance, there is in some instances paid from L2 10s to L3 per ton.

The introduction of this manufacture . . . has been a great blessing to the poorer tenantry, who, in the summer quarter, have no other object on which their industry can be profitably exerted. Yet its benefit does not extend to them so far as might be wished; as every kelp dealer is desirous to have his kelp made as early as possible . . . the tacksman, for the sake of expediting the manufacture, portions out his shores in small lots to as many manufacturers as he can find; so that for the most part, the man who gets more than a ton for his lot may reckon himself lucky . . . We reckon 350 hands employed in this work which, in a dry season, they finish in the course of 5 or 6 weeks. The employer supplies them in meal, at as easy a rate as it can be purchased; and were it not that in a season of scarcity, they are obliged to buy of this article a quantity sufficient to serve their families till the harvest, they would be generally enabled by their earnings, at the kelp manufacturing, to pay their land rents. The kelp is either sold to a merchant in the country, or sent to market at the risk of the original owner. Some years ago, it fetched in the country from L5 to L6 per ton. The price has been much on the decline for three years back, owing, it is said, to the quantity of barilla allowed to be imported from a foreign kingdom, almost free of duty.

SOURCE: DJ Withrington and IR Grant (eds) 1981 *The Statistical Account of Scotland 1791–1799 edited by Sir John Sinclair* Vol XX The Western Isles, 66–8 (parish of Harris). East Ardsley (EP Publishing).

DOCUMENT 47

Alexander Hunter on emigration schemes, 1827

The economic recession which followed the conclusion of the Napoleonic Wars not only exposed the fragility of the crofting community, but led to a dramatic change of attitude on the part of government, landowners and their agents in favour of emigration. As evident from the testimony of Alexander Hunter, the Edinburgh lawyer who supervised the clearance of the island of Rhum in July 1826, medical efficacy was not to get in the way of cost effectiveness for assisted passages.

If Government think seriously of being at any expense in sending out emigrants, I think it can be done a great deal cheaper than it has hitherto been done . . . According to the present rate of freight to Cape Breton, or any of these places, New Brunswick or Nova Scotia, a ship could be freighted for 25s. per ton; at present two tons are allowed for every adult passenger, and the crew are included; but if government, for so short a voyage, would allow the crew not to be included, but let them go extra, it would be a very considerable saving of expense; and for so short a voyage, the captains of ships in that trade, who have gone with emigrants, and with whom I have conversed, say it would not be the least inconvenience. There is also the additional expense of a surgeon for so short a voyage, which is a very great additional expense. Then there are the provisions according to the Act of Parliament, a certain quantity of beef; now by substituting what the Rum people were allowed by government, oatmeal instead of beef, the expense would be greatly reduced, and they are not accustomed to beef, they live altogether on oatmeal: in fact, on potatoes principally. In this way I make the expenses per adult 4l. 14s. 6d. I am allowing the twelve weeks provision in this calculation, because when they land they must have some provisions to maintain them until they raise a crop.

SOURCE: Testimony of A Hunter, WS on 10 April 1827, 'Report of the Select Committee appointed to inquire into the Expediency of encouraging Emigration from the United Kingdom', *Parliamentary Papers* V 1826–7, 291–2.

DOCUMENT 48

CR Baird on Highland distress, 1841

The majority of migrants from the Highlands did not go overseas but to the
industrial towns and cities of Britain. Drawing on his successful endeavours
in raising £36,511 through the Glasgow committee for famine relief in the
Highlands after the successive failures of the potato crop in 1836–7, CR
Baird articulated urban concerns about the impact of unbalanced land use,
rural congestion and inequitable tenurial conditions within crofting
communities.

. . . I may state generally what I thought were the principal causes of the distress:
One is the absenteeism of the landlords. Another is the want of capital amongst the
people. The principal cause, I think, is ignorance, the excessive want of education
. . .

Another cause is the errors in the Government system of emigration, which
took away the able-bodied, those who were able to labour, and left the old and
infirm, the young and helpless, and the very poor; also the want of employment by
the cessation of the kelp trade, and the alteration in the fisheries, and so on . . . [The
immediate cause of distress of these two years were] bad harvests, the failure of the
herring fishery and the want of employment, which greatly aggravated the distress
which had been going on for seven or ten years previously.

In the greater part of the Outer Hebrides, as well as in part of the mainland, the
lands are let either at the will of the landlord or from year to year, or on short
leases, and in some cases, only on the promise of a lease from seven to twelve years
duration; this I consider very prejudicial ultimately to the landlord, and immediately so to the tenant. He will not go on improving the land which he holds from
year to year, or as a tenant at will, as he would do were a lease given to him. Then
these poor people who are tenants at will are often driven out in great numbers,
which has happened in the case of several estates, and they are sent in upon the
large cities, particularly upon Glasgow, where their condition is most miserable;
they are peculiarly subject to the worst of diseases on coming to a city, particularly
to fever and to small-pox.

SOURCE: Testimony of CR Baird on 3 March 1841, 'First Report from the Select Committee on Emigration from Scotland', *Parliamentary Papers* VI(i) 1841, 49–50.

DOCUMENT 49

George Douglas Campbell (8th Duke of Argyll) on the Great Famine

In recounting his response to the Great Famine that became endemic throughout the crofting community in 1846, George Douglas Campbell, the 8th Duke of Argyll, was particularly sanguine about the expenditure he incurred personally to promote not only relief but restructuring. But he glossed over the £10,000 he was able to borrow from government as compensation for the abolition of the Corn Laws; a sum which not only matched his personal outlay during the famine but was repayable over thirty years.

When the potato famine came in 1846, the destitution of the people was as severe as under such circumstances it could not fail to be. Not only was there great distress, but there was danger of actual starvation . . . A large sum was spent in providing meal for the people, and another large sum in assisting as many as were willing to emigrate to Canada. I have not beside me at this moment any note of the exact number who went to Canada, but during the course of four years it exceeded a thousand souls. The whole of this was purely voluntary emigration, for a great portion of which I paid the whole cost myself, whilst assisting the expenses of the remainder . . . I saw, however, that emigration was not the only remedy which the condition of the Island required. Active steps were taken to give employment to the people in draining, in the making of roads, and various other agricultural improvements. As the rents of the crofters could not be generally collected, these outlays had to be provided for out of other resources; in fact, I was myself compelled to borrow a large sum . . . Nor did this condition of affairs pass off immediately, or even soon. During the four years from 1846 to 1850 the sum spent on improvements in Tyree and the Ross of Mull was £7919, or, including incidental expenses, upwards of £8000, of which the greater part – about £6373 – was in drainage alone. This was in addition to the sums spent in emigration and in the distribution of meal . . . during [these] four years there had been expended on wages and gratuities to the inhabitants a sum exceeding the whole revenue derived from the property by £4680.

SOURCE: The Duke of Argyll 1883 *Crofts and Farms in the Hebrides being an Account of the Management of an Island Estate for 130 Years*, Edinburgh, 20–1.

DOCUMENT 50

Robert Somers on landowners and the Great Famine, 1846

A more sentient perspective was provided by the journalist Robert Somers who travelled extensively through the famine districts in 1846. He condemned the waste of land, the waste of human resources and, above all, the waste of capital exposed by the Great Famine. Ironically, the noble house of Sutherland, traditionally vilified for promoting the Clearances, were exempted from his injunctions against landlords and large-scale tenant-farmers for their failure to accumulate and reinvest capital in the Highlands.

The annual rental of the four counties of Sutherland, Ross, Inverness, and Argyle, is £597,496 18s.; but how much of this, after paying the interest of money-lenders and family incumbrances, really goes into the hands of the nominal proprietors? Perhaps a third, a fourth, or not more than a fifth. Then three-fourths of the proprietors receiving this fraction of the annual rental are absentees, and squander their incomes on personal enjoyment in foreign lands. The remnant of annual rental . . . requires, therefore, to be reduced to a still lower fraction, in order to represent the sum which goes into the hands of proprietors resident in the Highlands; and of this sum . . . a very insignificant portion can be saved from consumption, for the formation of capital, and for purposes of improvement. Thus a magnificent rental of upwards of half-a-million, from which it would not be too much to expect an annual saving of one or two hundred thousand pounds, is frittered away, wasted, and lost to the Highlands, by the extravagance either of present or former proprietors. As for the large farmers, they are also in a great measure an absentee class. The sheep-walks are principally held by gentlemen who have farms in the south, and who carry away with them the profits and savings accumulated in the Highlands. It was this fact which induced the Duke of Sutherland, one of the few Highland proprietors who lays out his income where it is produced, to resolve upon breaking down his grazing farms to a smaller size. That excellent nobleman saw that it was in vain that he let his farms at low rents, and expended a princely income year after year upon improvements, so long as he tolerated a class of non-resident graziers who carried away from the estate all that they produced from the soil, or could squeeze from a too liberal landlord. He therefore resolved to do what every wise man would do in the same circumstances, namely, to break down the sheep-walks to such a size as will secure the constant residence of the tenants. The absentee graziers do not waste the capital saved by them in the Highlands; they are men who generally know what to do with their money; but they carry it out of the Highlands, and thus complete the dispersion of that surplus produce which is the life-blood of industry, the germ and the food of improvement.

SOURCE: R Somers 1848 *Letters from the Highlands on the Famine of 1846*, Inverness (The Melvin Press, 1985), 168–9.

CLASS

Adam Smith on social inequalities

*Adam Smith (1723–1790) succeeded Francis Hutcheson to the chair of
Moral Philosophy at the University of Glasgow in 1752 where he joined
John Millar who was Professor of Law there. His immensely influential*
Wealth of Nations *was published in 1776. Smith was no crude advocate of
unregulated markets but was always conscious of the moral implications of
economic decisions and concerned about the inequalities which the
development of capitalism was producing.*

In a Society of a hundred thousand families, there will perhaps be one hundred who
don't labour at all, and who yet, either by violence, or by the more orderly
oppression of law, employ a greater part of the labour of the society than any other
ten thousand in it. The division of what remains too, after this enormous
defacation, is by no means made in proportion to the labour of each individual. On
the contrary those who labour most get least. The opulent merchant, who spends a
great part of his time in luxury and entertainments, enjoys a much greater
proportion of the profits of his traffic, than all the Clerks and Accountants who do
the business. These last, again, enjoy a greater deal of leisure, and suffering scarce
any other hardship besides the confinement of attendance, enjoy a much greater
share of the produce, than three times an equal number of artizans, who, under
their direction, labour much more severely and assiduously. The artizan again, tho'
he works generally under cover protected from the injuries of the weather, at his
ease and assisted by the convenience of innumerable machines, enjoys a much
greater share than the poor labourer who has the soil and the seasons to struggle
with, and, who while he affords the materials for supplying the luxury of all the
other members of the common wealth, and bears, as it were, upon his shoulders the
whole fabric of human society, seems himself to be pressed down below the ground
by the weight, and to be buried out of sight in the lowest foundations of the
building.

SOURCE: 'An Early Draft of the Wealth of Nations', *in* WR Scott 1937 *Adam Smith as
Student and Professor,* Glasgow, 327–8.

Demands for Parliamentary Reform

The reintroduction of Corn Laws in 1815 restricting the importation of foreign grain was one of the main issues which politicised the middle class. The Corn Laws were regarded as the self-serving action of a landed aristocracy who monopolised political power. The result was stagnation in foreign trade, and distress among the working population. The demands for Parliamentary Reform which had been subdued during the Napoleonic Wars burst forth once peace was restored. An expansion of the press gave increased opportunities for publicising reforming activities.

Distress of the People

Agreeable to intimation, a PUBLIC MEETING of the BURGESSES, and other INHABITANTS of the BOROUGH of POLLOKSHAWS, was held on Tuesday, 5th instant, to consider the propriety of Petitioning his Royal Highness the Prince Regent, on the unprecedented Distress of the Country;

Mr Henry Patrick, in the Chair.

The following Resolutions were unanimously agreed to:–

RESOLVED,

1st   That the present deplorable state of the nation, our unprecedented sufferings and misery, are owning to a corrupt House of Commons and want of an equal, fair, and free Representation of the People.

2d   That our blood and treasure have been wasted in an unjust and unnecessary war, which has entailed endless misery on ourselves, and blasted the fair prospect of freedom to Europe; that such unjust policy was contrary to the avowed purpose of the war, subversive of the right of nations, and disgraceful to our country.

3d   That our present sufferings and misery have arisen to a melancholy pitch, unprecedented in the annals of our country; that we have long groaned under the most incessant toil, submitted with the most patient fortitude to privation of every kind, that we are loaded by the most grievous and intolerable taxation, and the public money is notoriously squandered among an host of sinecure pensioners, who are rolling in splendour and profusion at the expense of every comfort of a laborious population.

4th   That our Ministers are making the most rapid and dangerous strides towards a Military Government, by tenaciously holding a powerful and expensive Army in a time of peace and universal distress; confident in their power they have already shown the utmost disregard of the united voice of the People, raised against the late impolitic, unjust, iniquitous, and calamitous Corn Bill, the baneful effects of which are too universally felt to require any illustration.

5th   That the Commercial Interests of the Country have been disregarded and shamefully neglected in the late numerous and expensive Treaties; that our Manufacturers are carefully excluded from the ports of Europe, by the very Princes restored by British bayonets; hence the long, gloomy, and swelling list of ruinous bankruptcies; hence the dire necessities that have impelled Britons to raise their hands for the scanty charity of a Frenchman and a Bourbon.

6th   That the Nation is divided into two classes, a neglected and wretched Populace, and a more favoured and overgrown Landed Interest; that our most able mechanics are compelled to wander in foreign climes in search of an asylum, where they may reap the reward of their industry and experience those comforts of life denied them in their own.

7th   That a Petition be presented to his Royal Highness the Prince Regent, intreating him to give ear to the united voice of a loyal, but wretched People, praying him to assemble Parliament, and demand an instant abolition of all sinecures, pensions, grants and emoluments not merited by public services, to introduce the most rigid economy in every department of public expenditure, and restore the People their just and valuable right of annually choosing their own Representatives.

8th   That it is the opinion of this Meeting that the inhabitants of every City, Town and Village in the Empire should come forward with their Petitions, and use every lawful and constitutional effort to forward a Reformation of the Commons House of Parliament.

9th   That the Thanks of this Meeting be given to Major Cartwright, Sir Francis Burdett and Lord Cochrane, to the Editor of the Statesman, Globe and Morning Chronicle Newspapers, to Messrs Cobbett and Hunt, and the Members of the Hampden Club, for their unwearied exertions in the Cause of Reform, and in the honourable cause of a suffering People.

10th   That these resolutions be published in the Glasgow Chronicle, and thanks of the Meeting be given to the Editor.

HENRY PATRICK.

SOURCE: *Glasgow Chronicle*, 12 November 1816.

DOCUMENT 53

James Hogg 'On the Changes, Amusements and Condition of the Scottish Peasantry'

The high demand for foodstuffs during the years of the Napoleonic Wars had brought great prosperity to farming and encouraged the development of capitalist methods in farming. Although the changes were most obvious in the rich farming areas of the Lothians, they soon spread to the Borders where the poet, James Hogg, 'the Ettrick Shepherd', lived. An increasing number of landless labourers became full-time wage earners and the social distance between farmer and farm-worker widened.

But ever since the ruinous war prices made every farmer for a time a fine gentleman, how the relative situations of master and servant are changed. Before that time every farmer was first up in the morning, conversed with all his servants familiarly, and consulted what was best to be done for the day. Now, the foreman, or chief shepherd, waits on his masters, and, receiving his instructions, goes forth and gives orders as his own, generally in a peremptory and offensive manner. The menial of course feels that he is no more a member of the community, but a slave; a servant of servants, a mere tool of labour in the hand of a man who he knows or deems inferior to himself, and the joy of his spirit is mildewed. He is a moping, sullen, melancholy man, flitting from one master to another in hopes to find heart's ease and contentment – but he finds it not; and now all the best and most independent of that vulnerable class in our community are leaving the country.

SOURCE: *Quarterly Journal of Agriculture* III, February 1831, 258–9.

DOCUMENT 54

Rev Thomas Chalmers to William Wilberforce, 18 April 1820

Both Chalmers, who was minister of St John's Church in Glasgow at the time of the 'radical war' of April 1820, and his fellow evangelical Christian, William Wilberforce, MP, the campaigner against black slavery, were deeply conservative figures who had little sympathy with those who were pressing for radical political change. Both emphasised that moral improvement had to take precedence over material improvement. Chalmers' hopes that the deference and control of rural society could be maintained in an industrial city were to be disappointed.

My Dear Sir, – As far as I know of our disaffections in this city, I would say that there are perhaps not half a dozen instances of people befriending Radicalism who are possessed of more than £200 a year. Its most active instigators appear to be well-paid workmen of cotton mills and other manufactories where there has been little or no decline of wages, though the depression that obtains in the weaving department gives them without doubt the advantage of such materials as encourage them greatly to prosecute the designs of agitators. I ought also to have mentioned that among the weavers themselves, who, speaking generally, are a highly intelligent order of men, there are not a few who act as delegates and leaders to the rest, and are well qualified for the whole business of counsel and committeeship. Of these there are certainly some who have acquired their taste and their talent for public management, I think, from the circumstance of being the members of a dissenting congregation, and thus offer the melancholy combination of a fierce restless and dangerous politics, with a regular and respectable habit of attending upon the ordinances. But still this is so far from being generally the case, that the aspect here of radicalism upon the whole is just what it is with you, an aspect of infidelity and irreligion, the great majority of the men of ascendancy among them being of this stamp and verily all, I believe, who have stated their determination to the extent of actual war and bloodshed, having just as little of the profession of Christianity as they have the substance of it.

SOURCE: Rev Wm Hanna 1850 *Memoirs of the Life and Writings of Thomas Chalmers* Vol II, Edinburgh, 262–4.

Placard which appeared in Glasgow and the West of Scotland on the night of 1–2 April 1820

It has never been entirely clear whether this placard which appeared on walls in Glasgow was genuinely the work of a radical group or a forgery by agent provocateurs who wanted to flush out the radicals. But the tone was authentic enough to convince groups of workers that it was the prelude to an insurrection and to trigger widespread strikes in the West of Scotland. The atmosphere had been very tense in the city for some days before the placard appeared.

ADDRESS

TO THE

Inhabitants of Great Britain and Ireland;

FRIENDS AND COUNTRYMEN,

ROUSED from that torpid state in which We have been sunk for so many years, We are at length compelled, from the extremity of our sufferings, and the contempt heaped upon our Petitions for redress, to assert our RIGHTS, at the hazard of our lives; and proclaim to the world the real motives, which (if not misrepresented by designing men, would have United all ranks), have reduced us to take up ARMS of the public redress of our *Common Grievances* .

The numerous public meetings held throughout the Country has demonstrated to you, that the interests of all Classes are the same. That the protection of the Life and Property of the *Rich Man*, is in the interest of the *Poor Man*, and in return, it is the interest of the Rich, to protect the poor from the iron grasp of DESPOTISM; for, when its victims are exhausted in the lower circles, there is no assurance but that its ravages will be continued in the upper: For once set in motion, it will continue to move till a succession of Victims fall.

Our principles are few, and founded on the basis of our CONSTITUTION, which were purchased with the DEAREST BLOOD of our ANCESTORS, and which we swear to transmit to posterity unsullied, or PERISH in the Attempt. – Equality of Rights (not of Property,) is the object for which we contend; and which we consider as the only security for our LIBERTIES and LIVES.

Let us show to the world that We are not that lawless, Sanguinary Rabble, which our Oppressors would persuade the higher circles we are – but a Brave and Generous PEOPLE, determined to be FREE, LIBERTY or DEATH is our *Motto*, and We have sworn to return home in *triumph* or return *no more!*

SOLDIERS,

Shall YOU, countrymen, bound by the sacred obligation of an Oath, to defend your County and your King from enemies, whether foreign or domestic, plunge your Bayonets into the bosoms of Fathers and Brothers, and at once sacrifice at the *Shrine of Military Despotism,* to the unrelenting Orders of a Cruel Faction, those feelings which you hold in common with the rest of mankind? SOLDIERS, Turn your eyes towards SPAIN, and there behold the happy effects resulting from the Union of Soldiers and Citizens. Look to that quarter and there behold the yoke of hated Despotism, broke by the unanimous wish of the People and the Soldiery, happily accomplished without Bloodshed. And, shall You, who taught those soldiers to fight the battles of LIBERTY, refuse to fight those of your own Country? Forbid it Heaven! Come, forward then at once, and Free your Country and your king, from the power of those that have held them *too* , *too* long in thraldom.

FRIENDS AND COUNTRYMEN,

The eventful period has now arrived where the Services of all will be required, for forwarding of an object so universally wished, and so absolutely necessary. Come forward then, and assist those who have begun in the completion of so arduous a task, and support the laudable efforts, which we are about to make, to replace to BRITONS, those rights consecrated to them, by MAGNA CARTA, and the BILL of RIGHTS, and Sweep from our shores that Corruption which has degraded us below the dignity of MAN.

Owing to the misrepresentations which have gone abroad with regard to our intentions, we think it indispensably necessary to DECLARE inviolable, all Public and Private Property. And, We hereby call upon all Justices of the peace, and all others to suppress PILLAGE and PLUNDER, of every description; and to endeavour to secure those Guilty of such offences, that they may receive that Punishment, which such violations of Justice demand.

In the present state of affairs, and during the continuation of so momentous a struggle, we earnestly request all to desist from their LABOUR, and from and after this day, the FIRST OF APRIL; and attend wholly to the recovery of their Rights, and consider it as a duty of every man not to recommence until he is in possession of those Rights which distinguishes the FREEMAN from the SLAVE; viz.: That of giving consent to the laws by which he is to be governed. We, therefore, recommend to the Proprietors of Public Works, and all others, to Stop the one, and Shut up the other until order is returned, or we will be accountable for no damages which may be sustained; and which after this Public Intimation, they can have no claim to.

And We hereby give notice to all those who shall be found carrying arms against those who intend to regenerate their Country, and restore to its INHABITANTS their NATIVE DIGNITY; We shall consider them as TRAITORS to their Country, and enemies to their King, and treat them as such.

By order of the Committee of Organization,

for forming a PROVISIONAL GOVERNMENT.

Glasgow, 1sr April 1820.

Britons – God – Justice. – The wishes of all good Men are with us – Join together and make it one CAUSE, and the Nations of the EARTH shall hail the day, when the Standard of LIBERTY shall be raised on its *Native Soil*.

SOURCE: Scottish Record Office, Home Office Papers. Placard which appeared in Glasgow and the West of Scotland on the night of 1–2 April, 1820.

DOCUMENT 56

Speech by Alexander Campbell

Campbell was a joiner in Glasgow who had been a member of the Owenite-influenced Orbiston Community between 1825 and 1828. He founded the Glasgow Co-operative Society in 1829 and was secretary of the Glasgow trades' committee in the early 1830s. The Scottish Trades' Union Gazette *was one of a number of unstamped newspapers aimed at the working class with which he was involved in these years.*

Capital is the surplus of production over consumption, and is represented by money, the object of those who possess it is always to receive more back than they lay out, never once taking thought whether the labourer received a sufficient share for his part or not. The labourer, on the other hand, is equally unconcerned as to the profits of the capitalist; he has no share in that which he produces, but his wages, and those he is always anxious to maintain at the highest rate. As capital, like everything else, is subject to be depreciated in value, by the wretched influence of COMPETITION, the capitalist often finds it his interest to suspend the employment of labour for a season, in order to keep his stock proportionate to demand; or, otherwise, to reduce the value of labour in proportion to his own decline of prices, so that the interests of labour and capital under the present system is always opposed, except where the same parties are both capitalist and labourer.

SOURCE: *Scottish Trades' Union Gazette* No 2, 21 September 1833.

The Owenite perspective: Alexander Campbell's speech to a meeting on Glasgow Green

By 1837 Campbell was a full-time 'social missionary' for the Owenite cause. Like other Owenites he was not convinced that the extension of the franchise which the Chartists were seeking would, in itself, achieve very much unless there was a commitment to a programme of social change. The severe economic depression which lasted for the next five or six years, with its accompanying working-class unemployment, encouraged many to look at the ideas being put forward by Campbell and his associates.

Mr Alex. Campbell, joiner and house-carpenter, in proposing the fourth resolution, said – Friends and fellow countrymen, the cause which has this day brought us together is one of great importance. Never were stronger motives to assemble presented to the minds of the industrious classes than hunger, want of employment, and the constant fear of starvation. These were motives which would move the greatest coward to exertion, and call into action the efforts of the brave. (Cheers.) The present state of destitution among the population of Great Britain and Ireland was not brought on by any natural calamity; there were no bad harvests, no pestilence, no earthquake, no volcanic eruption had taken place at this time, yet the industrious people were literally starving. To what then can we attribute these disastrous state of things? To nothing else than to the ignorance of our former and present rulers, and it proves distinctly that they have been totally incapable of governing the destinies of this great people – (cheers) – a nation which, within the last fifty years, has increased its power of production to be now equal to the labour of *six hundred millions* of stout active men, while we have only to support a population of twenty-five millions of men, women and children. Had the people been properly governed, instead of toiling ten, twelve, aye, and fourteen hours per day, for subsistence insufficient to maintain life, the hours of labour ought to have been reduced to eight hours a day, and the means of subsistence increased in proportion to our means of production. (Cheers.) There are also those who pretend to be the friends of the working classes, and make much noise about the corn laws, in order to produce cheap labour, that cheap goods may be sent to glut foreign markets, and say that this country ought to be the workshop of the world. Britain has already been too much a mere workshop; the beautiful and fertile plains of our beloved isle have been converted into pasture lands to feed cattle on, whose condition is much more preferable to that of the human beings, who have been driven from their rural habitations to the dens of vice and misery which exist in all large manufacturing towns. It was well observed by the former speaker, that there was something wrong in the constitution of society. Yes, society is altogether, *radically*, much more radically wrong than what Radicals generally believe; these *only* cry for universal suffrage, vote by ballot, annual parliaments, no money qualification, and no corn laws; all of which, I agree, is the right of people to have.

(Cheers.) But I also think that unless they get more than these, they will not realize that comfort and independence which it is necessary all should possess. America, for more than half a century, has been in possession of all the political institutions which the Reformers of this country demand; yet, notwithstanding they have no corn laws, no national debt, no property qualification, and have annual parliaments, vote by ballot, and nearly universal suffrage, they are labouring under similar difficulties with ourselves . . . this state of things . . . has been brought on by a set of money aristocrats, who are much worse than our landed aristocracy; they rob the working men of the value of their labour, and make bankrupts of our merchants and manufacturers. I do not say that they cheat or rob the people designedly; but it is a matter of little consequence to us whether we are robbed by knowing swindlers or ignorant knaves, if we are robbed. The working classes of this country are made to believe that they only pay their proportion of the taxes; but the fact is, they not only pay all the taxes of the government, but they support all the other classes of the society besides, till at last they have produced so much, and kept so little to themselves, that their labour is not now required, and they are consequently starving. The resolution I am about to read to you recommends that arrangements should now be entered into to produce new wealth for yourselves, and keep it to yourselves, independent of any other class whatever.

SOURCE: *New Moral World*, 1 July 1837.

DOCUMENT 58

Women and politics

Historians of class have been justly accused of ignoring the role of women in social protest. This letter published in the main Chartist newspaper, the Northern Star, *shows that at least some women did not accept the concept of women being confined to a separate sphere from men, to the private world of the home.*

'To the Women of Scotland'
Fellow Countrywoman – I address you as a plain country woman – a weaver of Glasgow. You cannot expect me to be grammatical in my expressions, as I did not get an education like many other of my fellow women, and I ought to have got, and which is the right of every human being. I am delighted to see the women of Scotland, and many other places, taking up the cause of Radicalism, and the cause of Truth; we have been too long the dupes of tyrants, but now we will be free – we will fling from us the chains that have so long kept us in bondage, and say we will

no longer be slaves. Do not listen to those who tell you that a woman has no right to interfere in politics. Has a woman not the power of reasoning as well as a man? Has she not got judgment to guide her as well as a man? Aye, and as good too, if it be cultivated. Ask them what is the meaning of the word Politics? Is it not the best way to make the people happy? Is this, then, an improper thing I would ask? No, it is their duty. It is the right of every woman to have a vote in the legislation of her country, and doubly more so now we have got a woman at the head of the government. Arouse ye women of Scotland, and demand your liberties and your rights; join heart and soul with the men in the great radical agitation – it is the cause of the suffering many. England has shown us an example – surely Scotland will not be behind, and let us not cease until we have gained what is the just right of all – Universal suffrage. The men of England have taught us many important truths – they have told us what is our rights, and how we may get them. If we do not it is our own fault. Women, I would have you look for a moment at the poor Glasgow, Paisley and Spitalfields weavers. Are they not in a state of great destitution, and nothing but starvation staring them in the face? Surely it is not the will of God that these poor then should labour hard from morning to night to obtain a scanty living for themselves and families, and that more than one half of their scanty earning should go to pay taxes to support a few individuals in luxury and idleness? No, my fellow women, it is blasphemy to God to suppose that he created man to be miserable – to hunger, thirst, and perish with cold in the midst of that abundance which is the fruit of their own labour. I conclude hoping that it will not be long before we are able to wrench the grasp from the tyrant's hand, and that will not fail doing their duty. I remain. A REAL DEMOCRAT, Glasgow, 1 June 1838.

SOURCE: *Northern Star*, 23 June 1838.

ENVIRONMENT

DOCUMENT 59

Durness described in the 1720s

Macfarlane's Geographical Collections *are a wonderful source for descriptions of Scotland before* The Statistical Account of Scotland.

The next Parish is Durness which lys westward from the former and separate from it by a peice of mossy and boggie ground of five miles length and as many in breadth stretching from the Whittenhead to the hill call'd Binnhope. Its scarce ridable but either in a very dry summer or in hard winter frost and not then without a good guide having many small loches and quagmires through it. The Parish of Durness lys much on the sea coast . . . a few places excepted. Its bounded on the East by the Whitenhead and on the West with Farohead, or Cape wrath a high promon. five miles at least betwixt both; and the shore stretches in into deep bays by the intervention of a head further in than either of the other two, called Farrars head. The more easterly of the bays is called the Loch of Eriboll, and goes inward seven miles southwards where of old was a plentifull herring fishing but has fail'd: there is yet plenty of cod and other white fish catcht there, also oisters and other shell fish.

It has an excellent road for ships of the largest burden the British fleet might ride safely at the bottom of the bay, which is covered by an island from the sea, of which more afterwards. The farms on the east side of Loch Eribol are (1) Frosgill a mile South of Whitenhead, it has a fishing port but dangerous by reason of the swelling of the sea therabouts when the wind is from the sea. (2) Inverhope two miles South of the former where there is a salmond fishing with nets & cruives. (3) Badillahamhise a mile south of the former. (4) Hunleim a mile South of the former. (5) Eribol three mile of the former and Tilinn at the Lochend.

On the west side of the Loch of Eriboll stands Portchamill a farm three miles North of the Lochend. Ruspin a mile north of the former, which has a road and harbour where boats and bark may ride safely, or lay dry. Keanbinn a mile N.W. of the former. Sangobeg a mile N.W. of the former. Sangomoar two miles N.W. of the former. Betwixt the two Sangoes at the shore, there is a cave stretching pretty far in under ground with a naturall vault above; Its called Smoa, at the mouth of it is a harbour for big boats, on the floor of the cave there is room enough for 500 men to exercise their arms, there is a burn comes out of the earth in the one side of the said cave and forms a large and deep pond there, where trouts are catched and then runs out of the pond to the sea; there is also a spring of excellent water in the other side of the said cave. A mile N.W. of Sangomoar stand the farms Baillamlulich and Durinn at some litle distance from the sea . . .

Belonging to the parish of Durness or rather to the heretor thereof the R.H. Lord Reay and betwixt the parishes of Durness and Edirachills, there are two large fforests consisting of a great many several hils stocked with red deer in abundance.

The one is called the forrest of Dirumoar, esteemed to have greater plenty of red deer than any in Scotland . . .

The Rivers of the parish of Durness are these viz. (1) The river of Hope, which takes its rise from a litle loch a mile in circuit by the hill called Glaisea; hath its course East two miles, where at a sheal or grassing place call'd Cobir-nuiskeach, it receives two other large rivulets and then it runs N. three miles in the midle of a pleasant strath called Strahuridale where it waters on the West side Ellanrighair and two miles lower on the East side a farm called Mussal, on which East side a mile above Mussall stands an old building made in the form of a sugar loaff & which a double wall and winding stairs in the midle of the wall round about, and litle places for men to ly in as is thought and all built of dry stone without any mortar. Its called by tradition Dundornigil. Below Mussall a mile the river enters the Loch of Hope and runs through it three miles N. the said Loch waters on its west bank the farms of Baddamheoir and Arnabol and on the East bank Bregisgill & Hope the river runs at last at a miles distance from the Loch into the bay called Locheriboll where stands Inverhope. (On the East side of Strahiridale which is also the side of the hill of Hope and as far down as near Bresgisgil there is a wood of birks and other timber.) Where is a salmond fishing with netts and cruives. The 2 river is called the river of Strabeg, which takes its rise at Loch Stinisaid which is half a mile long near the hill of Savoil, It runs thence N. three miles thro Strabeg, and falls into Locheriboll, at the bottome thereof, the said Strabeg hath a wood on both sides of the river, of birks, aller &^{c} particularly there grows there a parcell of large and tall hollys, whereof some have no prickles, hence their twiggs and leaves are cut down in time of snow for food to cows. The third is the river of Dinard, which takes its rise from Loch Dinard which is half a mile long near the hill called Feinnbhinn and runs thence N. eight miles and falls into the bay of Durness, at the end of that part of it called the Kyl of Grudie, on it there is a salmond fishing with nets and cruives.

The Loches of the parish of Durness besides these already named and from which ther run several burns and rivulets to the sea, are viz. the Loch of Slaness ¼ mile in circuit it stands by the farm of that name abovementioned, it hath plenty of eels. a little island in it where maws lay eggs. A litle stripe runs from it to Lochborely which bears S.E. of the former a quarter of a mile and is half a mile in circuit stands by the farms of Borley and Claiseneach it hath plenty of red belly'd trouts an Island also where fowls lay their eggs; a burn runs under ground, out of this Loch for a quarter of mile N. and falls into another litle Loch a quarter of mile in circuit calld Loch Crospuill, near to the church and the Lords Reays Mannour house, and out of which ther runs a burn into the sea. The 3^d Loch is called Loch Calladail, a large mile in circuit, and is about a miles distance from the Mannour house last mentioned bearing S.E. It has plenty of excellent trouts and a burn runs out of it to the sea at Sangomoar.

The 4th is called Lochmoadis a mile S.E. of the last mentioned Loch, about half a mile in circuit and hath good trouts, and sends a burn to the sea, at the Cave of Smoa where it comes out after having run a peice under ground.

Durness is one of the most pleasant as well as profitable spots of ground in all the highlands for corn, grass, cattle, game and fishing. All its rocks and craigs are either marble or limestone, there is also plenty of marl for gooding to the land. Its fresh water Lochs abound with a variety of trouts and eels. Its forests abound with red deer. Its grassing with black Cattle, horses and sheep and goat. Its seas abound with cod, ling, and other sea fish.

SOURCE: A Mitchell (ed) 1906 *Geographical Collections Relating to Scotland by Walter Macfarlane*, Edinburgh (Scottish History Society), 191–6.

DOCUMENT 60

Henry Home, Lord Kames, on the 'Imperfection of Scotch Husbandry'

A famous Improver castigates the traditions of Scottish farming. It was easy to be critical, but a very successful tenant once said to him, 'My Lord, to hear you talk of farming one would think you had been born yestreen' (Smout, TC 1969, A History of the Scottish People, London, 294–5).

A Man can never have thorough confidence in his road, till he be made acquainted with the by paths that mislead him; and to be made acquainted with the errors of our neighbours, is the high way to good husbandry. My present purpose, is to delineate the imperfect state of Scotch husbandry, not only as formerly practised every where, but as practised at present in most places. To contemplate the low state of their country in the most important of all arts, cannot fail to excite ambition to excel in the few who are skilful, and to rouse imitation in others.

Our crops in general are very indifferent; and how can it be otherwise, considering our instruments of husbandry, which are sadly imperfect? What can be expected from them in a poor soil, when they perform so little even in the richest? Our crops accordingly correspond to our instruments.

From many examples it is made evident, that our soil and climate are capable of producing draught horses, patient of labour, and singularly hardy. Yet the breed is so much neglected, that they are commonly miserable creatures, without strength or mettle. Did landlords attend to their interest, they would be diligent to improve the breed. Why do they not reflect, that the same farm-servants with better horses, would double the ordinary work? By improving the breed, they would draw more rent from their tenants, without laying any additional burden upon them. With respect to oxen, there is no care taken either in the breeding or feeding. How easy is it for a gentleman to procure a good bull for his tenants? and from the little care of providing food for draught oxen, one would suspect it to be a general opinion, that they require no food. In summer they are turned out into bare pasture, scarce sufficient for sheep. In winter, a small bottle of straw, not above a stone weight, is all that is allowed them in the twenty-four hours; which after the turn of the year, being dry and sapless, affords very little nourishment. What can animals so fed do in a plough? And yet such is the stupidity of many farmers, that instead of adding to the food, they add to the number; as if it would mend the matter, to add cattle that can scarce support their own weight. One unaccustomed to see ten oxen in a plough led on by two horses, cannot avoid smiling. With his goad the driver beats the horses, and pricks every ox as he advances. He then runs forward twenty yards to beat the horses a second time and prick the oxen. Some of the oxen in the mean time, instead of drawing, are found hanging on the yoke, and keeping others back. It is indeed next to impracticable, to make ten weak oxen in a plough, draw all at the same time. Nor is this the only inconvenience. A great number of oxen by such management, is requisite for stocking a farm; which is not always within the reach of the most industrious. In a year of scarcity beside, the beasts are actually starved. And what is worst of all, the tenant, in order to get straw for his cattle, is commonly necessitated to thresh out his corn, without waiting for a market, or having a granery for it.

Our farmers, led entirely by custom, not by reflection, seldom think of proportioning the number of their working cattle, to the uses they have for them. Hence, in different counties, from six to twelve oxen in a plough, without any regard to the soil. Seldom it is, that more than four good beasts can be necessary, if the proper time for ploughing be watched.

The division of a farm into infield and outfield, is execrable husbandry. Formerly, war employed the bulk of our people: the remainder were far from sufficiently numerous for cultivating even that small proportion of our land which is capable of the plough. Hence extensive farms, a small part of which next the dwelling, termed *infield*, was cultivated for corn: the remainder, termed *outfield*, was abandoned to the cattle, in appearance for pasture, but in reality for starving. The same mode continues to this day, without many exceptions, though necessity cannot be pleaded for it. But custom is the ruling principle that governs all. Sad is the condition of the labouring cattle; which are often reduced to thistles, and withered straw. A single acre of red clover would give more food than a whole outfield; yet how common is the complaint of tenants, that they are disabled from carrying on any summer-work, for want of food to their horses; a shameful complaint, considering how easy the remedy is.

Custom is no where more prevalent than in the form of ridges. No less high than broad, they are enormous masses of accumulated earth, that admit not cross-ploughing, nor any ploughing but gathering and cleaving. Custom and imitation are so powerful, as that our ridges are no less high in the steepest bank, than in the flattest field. Balks between ridges are equally frequent, though invincible obstructions to good culture. It would puzzle one at first view to explain, why such strips of land are left untilled. They must have been reserved originally, as a receptacle for stones, thrown off the tilled land; and husbandmen were led by imitation to leave such strips, even where there were few or no stones.

The proper time for ploughing or harrowing, is when the soil upon stirring moulders into small parts. This is not observed by farmers, so carefully as it ought to be. How common is it to see even a clay soil ploughed, when soaked in water, or when hard like a stone. Little attention is given to what may be termed *the frost-preparation*; which is, to open the ground before winter, in order that frost may pierce deep and mellow the soil.

Shallow ploughing is universal, without the least regard to deepness of soil. The temperance of our people may be a proper subject for ironical praise; for though nature affords commonly ten or twelve inches of soil, they are humbly satisfied with a half or third.

Ribbing is a general practice, though the slightest reflection is sufficient to make it evident, that to leave half of the land untilled, must be wretched husbandry.

Summer-fallow has of late years crept in, and is now common in three or four counties. In the rest of Scotland, for want of summer-fallow, there is a continual struggle for superiority, between corn and weeds. Do not such provoking farmers see, that it is fruitless to manure land over-run with weeds? Do they not observe, that the manure they bestow encourages weeds as much as corn; or rather, that it envigorates the weeds to destroy the corn? Make a progress through Scotland, you see stubborn weeds in every corner scattering their seed, and fouling the ground more and more. It is an easy work to cut down weeds before they go to seed. Would not one think, that work so easy would never be neglected? and yet it is never done. A Scotch farmer behaves worse than Esau: the latter got a mess of pottage for his birthright; the former surrenders his to weeds, without any recompense.

SOURCE: Henry Home, Lord Kames 1774 *The Gentleman Farmer*, Edinburgh, 359–64.

DOCUMENT 61

A Hampshire clergyman and arbiter of fashionable taste considers Scottish landscape

Mr Gilpin was very particular about what constituted an acceptable landscape to a connoisseur.

A mountain is of use sometimes to close a distance by an elegant, varied line: and sometimes to come in as a second ground, hanging over a lake, or forming a skreen to the nearer objects. To each purpose the Scotch mountains are well adapted. The distances of this country, with all their uniformity, have at least one praise, as we have often had occasion to observe, that of being bounded by a grand chain of blue mountains: and when these mountains approach, their shapes are generally such as may with little alteration be transferred to canvas.

I have however heard good judges in landscape find much fault with the Scotch mountains in general; and place them on the wrong side of a comparison with the mountains of Italy, and other countries. I can only therefore give my own opinion modestly on this head; suggesting, at the same time, that perhaps these travellers and I may have drawn our conclusions from different parts of the country. Those mountains, which I have remarked, I have generally specified in the course of my journey. – Or, it may be perhaps, that these travellers admire mountains with spiry points, instead of flowing lines; which with me are not among objects of picturesque beauty. – The affair however, after all, resolves into matter of opinion.

The lakes of Scotland are as various, as it's mountains: but they partake with them of the barrenness of the country. In the neighbourhood of water one should expect something more of vegetation. In general, however the Scotch lakes are very little adorned. You see fine sweeping lines, bays, recesses, islands, castles, and mountain-skreens; all of which, except the castles, are in the best style. But with these embellishments you must be content: wood you seldom find; at least in any degree of richness, or proportion. – At the same time if you wish to *study landscape*, perhaps you can no where study it with more advantage. For scenes like these, are the schools in which *the elements* of landscape are taught – those great outlines, without understanding which, the art of finishing is frippery.

One thing farther may be observed with regard to the lakes of Scotland; and that is their dingy colour. The lakes of Cumberland and Westmoreland have a remarkable pellucidity. They are so transparent as to admit the sight many fathoms below the surface: whereas all the Scotch lakes, which we saw, take a mossy tinge from the moors probably in their neighbourhood: at least they were all, I think, of that hue, when we saw them. And yet I know not whether this tinge is of any great disadvantage to them. It certainly affects the *general landscape* very little. In navigating the lake indeed; or in viewing it's surface from the bank, it presents an unpleasant hue: and perhaps the reflections are not so vivid, as when the mirror is brighter. Yet I have sometimes thought this dinginess is perhaps more in harmony with the moorish lands, which generally form the Scotch landscape, than if the hue of the water had been more resplendent.

SOURCE: W Gilpin 1792 *Observations relative chiefly to Picturesque Beauty made in the Year 1776 on Several Parts of Great Britain, particularly the Highlands of Scotland, II,* London, 127–30.

DOCUMENT 62

Rules and regulations of the Baron Court of Urie

The Baron Court of Urie, Kincardineshire, fears a looming environmental crisis, and tries to limit turf cutting; but notice that a partial exception is made for 'a moderate use of midden faill'.

Barony Court of the lands and Barrony of Urie, holden within the Mannour place of Urie upon the twenty fourth day of January one thousand seven hundreth and thirty years.

The said day the fiscall haveing given in a complaint that the pasturage, muirs, meadow, and sward ground within the said lands and barrony of Ury were so cast up and destroyed that in a short time it would be quite wore out and rendred useless unless timously prevented. And the same being seriously considered by the said baillie, he enacts, statutes, and ordains that for the better preserving of the said ground, pasturage, and muirs from being destroyed in time coming, and for assertaining a certain piece of hill for pasturage to each toun within the said barrony, it is hereby enacted, statute, and ordained, that no person or persons whatsomever shall, at any time hereafter, cast any turf, faill, or other fewell whatsomever for firring or other uses upon the plans following, Viz.: To the westward of the high road from the foord to the toun of Megray upon the said hill, upon the northward of the den called the Den of Woodhead, and westward of the new and present cart road of the hill of Glithno to the place called the Heathery Bridges upon north side of Bruxden, and eastward of the high road betwixt Bruxden and Montboys of the hill of the Mains, and upon the north side of the hill of Cairntoun and Balnagight from the water draught[1] of the loch of Balnagight, including the binty[2] ground along to the edge of the uppermost part of Bruxden, presently possessed by John Steinson. Also that non cast up any ground for what occasion soever within the wards[3] called the Wards of Megray and Pollbair, as the samen is bounded by the vistage of an old faill dyke round the same, nor that no ground upon what occasion soever shall be cast upon any part of the grass meadow or corne ground of the whole touns and lands of Megray and miln of Cowie, excepting upon the ground that lyes betwixt the aboun ward of Megray and George Allans croft, for a moderate use of midden faill allenarly, and upon the common brea or bogg betwixt the said toun of Megray and miln of Cowie. And likeways that no other person upon any other part of the said barrony of Ury cast up any faill or land quhatsomever upon any lands or meadow ground, nor upon any other part of their possessions, except for a moderate use of midden faill in ground not particularly excepted by this or former acts of Court, in those places they have been in use of casting for severall years bygon. And the contravenners of any of these acts to be fynd and ammerciat in the sum of twenty pound Scots money so often as they shall be found guilty of incurring the said penalty, by and attour makeing up the damnages the lands incurrs, and forfaulture of the truf, faill, divott[4] or others whatsomever so casten contrary to this act.

NOTES
1 The outlet for the water.
2 Covered with bent grass.
3 Small pieces of pasture ground, enclosed on all sides.
4 A thin flat turf, generally of an oblong form, used for covering cottages and also for fuel.

SOURCE: BG Barron (ed) 1892 *The Court Book of the Barony of Urie in Kincardineshire, 1604–1747*, Edinburgh (Scottish History Society), 130–2.

DOCUMENT 63

A consultant's report on how exploitation of natural woodland can be improved and made sustainable

Mr Monteath made his living by explaining to landed proprietors how they could make money out of their oaks.

SIR, – Having only this day had it in my power to lay my hands on the Notes of my Survey, &c. of the Woods and Wood-lands of the farms of Mackroy, and East and West Irons, the property of John M'Farlane, Esq. on Lochfine side, Argyleshire, I find there is of enclosed and unenclosed woodlands, chiefly covered with Oak and Birch, 200 acres; (I beg to say by the way, that with great propriety and advantage more could be added). The Wood-lands on these Farms are equal, both as to soil and situation, to the very best in Scotland, and will be as productive of Wood and Bark at twenty years old, as many natural Woods will be at twenty-five years. Supposing these 200 acres converted wholly into Oak Coppice, (for which purpose it only requires the blanks to be filled up with Oak, and the trash extirpated,) and divided into twenty hags or cuttings, making ten acres to cut annually. At twenty years old, the Coppice Wood and Bark, even allowing Bark to keep its present low price, will yield at least L.50 per acre, say L.500 annually; and suppose forty reserve or maiden trees to be reared up on each acre to the age of two cuttings, keeping always a regular succession of forty on each acre amongst the Coppice; these will be worth at least L.2 per tree, which at every second cutting will be worth L.80 more per acre; but to reduce the whole to an average, it will produce L.90 per acre annually, which will be L.900 Sterling of yearly income in succession, without any expense of planting, excepting one person as Forester, say at L.40 yearly; while the Bark, &c. from the thinnings will nearly pay his wages. If you take the locality of these Farms into consideration, where the whole of the yearly produce of these Barks can be disposed of to the fishermen at a fourth more price than to tanners; it will bring in a very considerable sum more than the above. If you consult the

Reports of the produce of the Duke of Montrose's Coppice Woods, and many others, you will see there I am rather, and that too considerably, under than above the annual produce; besides, the Duke of Montrose and others pay, from many places of their Woods, twenty-five shillings per ton, to take the Barks to a shipping place; whereas the Barks from the above Farms can be shipped for two shillings per ton.* As the soil of these Farms will carry timber trees to maturity, and from its beautiful situation it could be rendered particularly conspicuous and interesting as a gentleman's family residence, were a few acres of the wood-lands laid off for a cottage and garden, and standing ornamental trees reared about it; this would infinitely beautify and immensely add to its value, even 50 per cent. more than the intrinsic value of the cottage and trees, by making it so interesting in the eyes of thousands of strangers passing and repassing this estate by Steam Navigation; also, a very few small clusters of ever-green trees planted on the high knowls would greatly ornament it.

The intrinsic value of the crop in the ground at present, with the exception of the reserve trees, may be considered as not great; but when considered as Stools of trees already on the ground that will stand cutting and grow for ages, and as inseperably attached to the ground in so far as the Oak Stools go, may be, and that very reasonably, estimated at L.20 per acre.

I am,
SIR,
Your most obedient Servant,
R.M.

Stirling, 6th. January, 1827.
To A. McKinnon, Esq. Writer, Greenock, Factor.

* Locality to water carriage is of the greatest consequence in rearing woods.

SOURCE: R Monteath 1827 *Miscellaneous Reports on Woods and Plantations*, Dundee, 15–16.

DOCUMENT 64

Woods in Sutherland: their use, misuse and decay

In the light of the first part of the document, the attribution of the decline of the woods to natural causes may seem a contradiction. Elsewhere, Henderson says that tenants kept flocks of up to 60 goats apiece.

There are about 150 acres of oak copse at Criech, on the north bank of the Frith of Dornoch, the joint property of Mr. Dempster and Mr. Houston: at the age of fifteen years it is cut, principally for the bark. Mr. Sinclair from Argyleshire purchased sixty acres of it for 250*l.* and he cut the wood, which was purchased partly by the country people to repair the roofs of their cottages, and for implements of husbandry, and partly for charcoal. The oak bark sold at 15*l.* per ton, on the ground, close by the place of shipping it to market: I could not obtain any correct information of its value per acre. Birch bark is reckoned worth 7*l.* per ton.

There are some remains of a shrubbery of birch, hazel, aller, willow, and some oak bushes, in the straths of the several rivers and burns in the country, particularly on the banks of Loch-shin, and Strath-oickel, Strath-more, and Strath-naver, where there are birch and aller of considerable size, fit for agricultural and building purposes; such as ploughs, harrows, and roofs of houses for the country people, but not of so great extent as formerly, and is rapidly decaying in some places. The remains of some oak bushes among the birch and aller, in the straths of Helmsdale, Brora, &c. shew that it once flourished in these straths; but from the constant browsing of black cattle, it is not surprising that the oak is nearly gone. In some instances, where the more industrious inhabitants of these straths grub up some of this shrubbery to increase their small portion of arable land, the succeeding crops of bear or oats abundantly repay them for their labour . . .

The natural woods on the several straths in this county, to the southern, western, and northern coasts, are decaying fast, owing, as naturalists aver, to the severe frosts in the winter and spring seasons for many years past; and it is a well known fact, that in the straths where these woods have already decayed, the ground does not yield a quarter of the grass it did when the wood covered and sheltered it. Of course the inhabitants cannot rear the usual number of cattle, as they must now house them early in winter, and feed, or rather keep them just alive, on straw; whereas in former times their cattle remained in the woods all winter, in good condition, and were ready for the market early in summer. This accounts for the number of cattle which die from starvation on these straths, whenever the spring continues more severe than usual; *and this is one argument in favour of sheep-farming in this county.*

SOURCE: J Henderson 1812 *General View of the Agriculture of the County of Sutherland,* London, 83–4, 86–7.

An eighteenth-century botanist in the Cairngorms

James Robertson was sent by John Hope, Professor of Botany at the University of Edinburgh, to explore the Highlands.

Between Braemar, & Ben Awin there are several hills most of which are composed of Granite. The tops of the hills produce little but the procumbent Azalea; but their sides, likes the vallies, yield excellent pasture, and are covered with several small Copses of Birch & Hazle.

Ben Awin itself is a prodigious mass, not less, in my opinion than three miles broad, and six miles long, steep on all sides, but in some places, presenting horrid precipices altogether inaccessible. The top is flat like a large piece of gravel. On this flat top a number of natural pyramids have arisen, some of them about 30 feet high. They very much resemble the pyramids seen at the bottom of bold shores, and called in the North 'Stacks'.

In one place Ben Awin is almost cut thro' by a valley on the North, & another on the South, both extremely deep. At the head of each, the rocks are very high, similar to the steep rocks on the sea-shore.

This mountain is composed of white Granite. It's grain is coarse, and the stone is hard, tho' it easily moulders down when exposed to the air: hence the higher & more prominent parts appear as if their surface had been covered with gravel. In this hill, as well as in all those several miles East from it, & West as far as Carngorm three fourths of the Granite consist of Crystals. Of these, some are larger, adorned with a variety of beautiful colours.

In the hollows about Ben Awain I saw considerable quantities of snow, some of which has probably continued for ages, at least the people of Glen Awain assured me that neither they nor their Fathers ever remembered to have seen Ben Awin, or the hills West from it, free from snow . . .

On the sides of the mountain I saw the Dwarf Birch, Mountain Hawkweed, Mountain Saw-wort, Hairy Kidney-Wort, Trifid Sengreen, Autumnal Sengreen. Sengreen, Mountain Willow-herb and great Bilberry-bush . . .

June 11th From Gavelrig I went down the river of Awin to Camdale.

The Awin is a pretty large river issuing from Loch Awin a small lake about a mile long, situated on the West side of the foot of Ben Awin. In some places this lake reaches to the depth of several fathoms, but even there the waters are so clear, that the pebbles along the bottom, & the Trouts which glide in numbers thro' the lake, are distinctly seen. This limpidness is seldom lost even during heavy rains, & continues with the river for several miles, until it is polluted by the junction of some mossy streams. When I descended to wade the river about a mile below the lake, where the channel was smooth & the current gentle, deceived by the apparent nearness of the bottom, which shone so clearly thro' the pellucid stream, I expected the water would reach my knee only; but to my astonishment I plunged at once above my middle.

The valley thro' which the Awin runs, is very beautiful. The hills on each side are covered with Hazle, Birch, Alder, Quaking Asp, Willow, Bird's Cherry, Roses & Honeysuckle. In many places it runs out into large plains, which being well sheltered are extremely fertile, & pretty populous. Limestone abounds in most places, but is little used.

Indeed Agriculture here is neither understood nor encouraged. The small spots of arable land which are found in the valleys alone, bear a small proportion to the hilly & uncultivated parts, on which the people depend for pasture. Cattle being the chief object of attention, a man who pays £3 sterling of annual rent will perhaps have 20 black Cattle, 3 or 4 Horses, 20 Sheep & 10 Goats. During summer & autumn the pastures could maintain thrice the number, but they would perish during the winter or spring. Even the scanty stock to which the Farmer confines himself is with difficulty preserved, & not unfrequently some of them die for want of fodder. Before blaming too severely the indolence of this people, who by proper exertion might undoubtedly increase the numbers of their Cattle, & secure food for them thro' the most rigorous seasons, we must consider the difficulties under which they labour . . .

All the people here speak Erse, & many of them are Roman Catholicks. The most prevailing name is Gordon, & this country belongs to the Duke of Gordon, who has the most extensive property in Scotland, or perhaps in Britain. It reaches from the mouth of the Spey to Fort William thro' an extent of 120 english miles, & is in general 10 miles broad, so that the whole amounts to 1200 square miles.

Along the side of Awin I found some plants which I had considered as peculiar to the neighbourhood of Edinr., because I never before found them elsewhere. These were Bastard Hellebore, Wild Marjoram, French Lung-wort, Strangle Tare, Tufted Wood Vetch, Dwarf Cistus, Hairy Tower Mustard, Common Cinquefoil, Codded Mouse-Ear.

Each side of this vale is hemmed in by mountains which are covered with Moss & heath. The rocks are in general a soft Granite of a lead colour, and, in some places, a hard sandstone.

SOURCE: DM Henderson and JH Dickson (eds) 1994 *A Naturalist in the Highlands: James Robertson, His Life and Travels in Scotland 1767–1771*, Edinburgh (Scottish Academic Press), 158–62.

DOCUMENT 66

Sir William Brereton visits Edinburgh in 1636 and finds it hard going

Many Englishmen abroad found it hard to cope with native customs: those of Scotland were especially hard to take.

This city is placed in a dainty, healthful pure air, and doubtless were a most healthful place to live in, were not the inhabitants most sluttish, nasty, and slothful people. I could never pass through the hall, but I was constrained to hold my nose; their chambers, vessel, linen and meat, nothing neat, but very slovenly; only the nobler and better sort of them brave, well-bred men, and much reformed. This street, which may indeed deserve to denominate the whole city, is always full thronged with people, it being the market-place, and the only place where the gentlemen and merchants meet and walk, wherein they may walk dry under foot though there hath been abundance of rain. Some few coaches are here to be found for some of the great lords and ladies, and bishops . . .

The sluttishness and nastiness of this people is such, that I cannot omit the particularizing thereof, though I have more than sufficiently often touched upon the same: their houses, and halls, and kitchens, have such a noisome taste, a savour, and that so strong, as it doth offend you so soon as you come within their wall; yea, sometimes when I have light from my horse, I have felt the distaste of it before I have come into the house; yea, I never came to my own lodging in Edenborough, or went out, but I was constrained to hold my nose, or to use wormwood, or some such scented plant.

Their pewter, I am confident, is never scoured; they are afraid it should too much wear and consume thereby; only sometimes, and that but seldom, they do slightly rub them over with a filthy dish-clout, dipped in most sluttish greasy water. Their pewter pots, wherein they bring wine and water, are furred within, that it would loathe you to touch anything which comes out of them. Their linen is as sluttishly and slothfully washed by women's feet, who, after their linen is put into a great, broad, low tub of water, then (their clothes being tucked up above their knees) they step into the tub and tread it, and trample it with their feet (never vouchsafing a hand to nett[1] or wash it withal) until it be sufficiently cleansed in their apprehensions, and then it looks as nastily as ours doth when it is put unto and designed to the washing, as also it doth so strongly taste and smell of lant and other noisome savours, as that when I came to bed I was constrained to hold my nose and mouth together. To come into their kitchen, and to see them dress their meat, and to behold the sink (which is more offensive than any jakes) will be a sufficient supper, and will take off the edge of your stomach.

NOTE

1 To clean. Fr. *nettoyer.*

SOURCE: P Hume Brown (ed) 1890 *Early Travellers in Scotland*, Edinburgh, 140, 142–3.

CULTURE

Allan Ramsay on national realism

As one of several patriotic editors of older poetry in Scots in the early decades of the eighteenth century, Allan Ramsay, in the preface to one of his collections of poetry, The Ever Green, *speaks out in favour of a kind of realistic national integrity and against literary pollution. The contents of* The Ever Green, *however, are wide-ranging in language and literary influence, and so are not as 'pure' as Ramsay's preface might at first lead us to believe.*

. . . When these good old *Bards* wrote, we had not yet made Use of imported Trimming upon our Cloaths, nor of foreign Embroidery in our Writings. Their *Poetry* is the Product of their own Country, not pilfered and spoiled in the Transportation from abroad: Their *Images* are native, and their *Landskips* domestick; copied from those Fields and Meadows we every Day behold.

The *Morning* rises (in the Poets Description) as she does in the *Scottish* Horizon. We are not carried to *Greece* or *Italy* for a Shade, a Stream or a Breeze. The *Groves* rise in our own Valleys; the *Rivers* flow from our own Fountains, and the *Winds* blow upon our own Hills. I find not Fault with those Things, as they are in *Greece* or *Italy*: But with a *Northern Poet* for fetching his Materials from these Places, in a Poem, of which his own Country is the Scene . . .

SOURCE: Alan Ramsay 1724 *The Ever Green*, Edinburgh (Ruddiman), from the Preface.

Allan Ramsay 'Lucky Spence's Last Advice'

This poem (1718) is one of the first great social satires in Scots literature in the eighteenth century. It combines a vigorous low-style Scots, the fast-moving 'habbie' stanza and the fashionable European literary conceit of the closeness between the workings of society and of the brothel.

Three times the carline grain'd and rifted,   [old woman; groaned
Then frae the cod her pow she lifted,   [pillow; head
In bawdy policy well gifted,
    When she now faun,   [found
That Death na langer wad be shifted,
    She thus began:

My loving lasses, I maun leave ye,   [must
But dinna wi' ye'r greeting grieve me,
Nor wi' your draunts and droning deave me,   [snivels; deafen
    But bring's a gill;
For faith, my bairns, ye may believe me,
    'Tis 'gainst my will.

O black-ey'd Bess and mim-mou'd Meg,   [prim-mouthed
O'er good to work or yet to beg;
Lay sunkots up for a sair leg,   [put something by; sore
    For whan ye fail,
Ye'r face will not be worth a feg,
    Nor yet ye'r tail.

When e'er ye meet a fool that's fow,   [drunk
That ye're a maiden gar him trow,   [make him believe
Seem nice, but stick to him like glew;
    And whan set down,
Drive at the jango till he spew,   [chatter
    Syne he'll sleep soun.   [sound

    Whan he's asleep, then dive and catch
His ready cash, his rings or watch;
And gin he likes to light his match
    At your spunk-box,
Ne'er stand to let the fumbling wretch
    E'en take the pox.

Cleek a' ye can be hook or crook,   [to catch as with a hook
Ryp ilky poutch frae nook to nook;   [rake; each
Be sure to truff his pocket-book,   [pilfer
    Saxty pounds Scots
Is nae deaf nits: In little bouk   [= is no small thing
    Lie great bank-notes.

To get a mends of whinging fools,
That's frighted for repenting-stools.
Wha often, whan their metal cools,
    Turn sweer to pay,   [lazy
Gar the kirk-boxie hale the dools   [make the church-box
    Anither day.   take the winnings

But dawt Red Coats, and let them scoup,   [caress
Free for the fou of cutty stoup;   [brandy-pot
To gee them up, ye need na hope
    E'er to do well:
They'll rive ye'r brats and kick your doup,   [rob your
    And play the Deel.   clothes; arse

There's ae sair cross attends the craft,
That curst Correction-house, where aft
Vild Hangy's taz ye'r riggings saft   [= to be whipped in the
    Makes black and blae,   event of disobedience
Enough to pit a body daft;
    But what'll ye say.

Nane gathers gear withouten care,
Ilk pleasure has of pain a skare;   [share
Suppose then they should tirl ye bare,   [strip
    And gar ye fike,   [fuss
E'en learn to thole; 'tis very fair   [to put up with
    Ye're nibour like.   [neighbour

Forby, my looves, count upo' losses,
Ye'r milk-white teeth and cheeks like roses,
Whan jet-black hair and brigs of noses,
    Faw down wi' dads   [strokes
To keep your hearts up 'neath sic crosses,
    Set up for bawds.

Wi' well-crish'd loofs I hae been canty,   [greased; palms
Whan e'er the lads wad fain ha'e faun t'ye;
To try the auld game Taunty Raunty,
    Like coofers keen,   [oafs
They took advice of me your aunty,
    If ye were clean.

Then up I took my siller ca'   [silver
And whistl'd benn whiles ane, whiles twa;
Roun'd in his lug, that there was a   [whisper; ear
    Poor country Kate,
As halesom as the well of Spaw,
    But unka blate.   [shy

Sae whan e'er company came in,
And were upo' a merry pin,
I slade away wi' little din
    And muckle mense,   [much discretion
Left conscience judge, it was a' ane
    To Lucky Spence.

My bennison come on good doers,   [blessing
Who spend their cash on bawds and whores;
May they ne'er want the wale of cures   [best
    For a sair snout:
Foul fa' the quacks wha that fire smoors,   [smothers
    And puts nae out.

My malison light ilka day
On them that drink, and dinna pay,
But tak a snack and rin away;
    May't be their hap
Never to want a gonorrhoea,
    Or rotten clap.

  Lass gi'e us in anither gill,
  A mutchken, Jo, let's tak our fill;
  Let Death syne registrate his bill
      Whan I want sense,
  I'll slip away with better will,
      Quo' Lucky Spence.

SOURCE: A Kinghorn and A Law (eds) 1985 *Poems of Allan Ramsay and Robert Fergusson*, Edinburgh (Scottish Academic Press), 13–17.

Robert Fergusson 'The King's Birth-day in Edinburgh'

*Like Ramsay's 'Lucky Spence', Fergusson's poem (1772) employs a riotously
energetic language and form. This poem too, however, amid the seeming
enjoyment of the narrator, has an eye on serious issues. It pointedly shows a
royal holiday at the centre of civic and cultural disarray.*

> *Oh! qualis hurly-burly fuit, si forte vidisses.*
> Polemo-Middinia

I sing the day sae aften sung,
Wi' which our lugs hae yearly rung,
In whase loud praise the Muse has dung
    A' kind o' print;
But wow! the limmer's fairly flung;   [wench
    There's naething in't.

I'm fain to think the joys the same   [eager
In London town as here at hame,
Whare fock of ilka age and name,
    Baith blind and cripple,
Forgather aft, O fy for shame!   [often
    To drink and tipple.

O Muse, be kind, and dinna fash us,
To flee awa' beyont Parnassus,
Nor seek for Helicon to wash us,
    That heath'nish spring;
Wi' Highland whisky scour our hawses,   [throats
    And gar us sing.

Begin then, dame, ye've drunk your fill,
You wouldna hae the tither gill?
You'll trust me, mair would do you ill,
    And ding you doitet;   [beat; mad
Troth 'twould be sair agains my will
    To hae the wyte o't.   [blame

Sing then, how, on the fourth of June,
Our bells screed aff a loyal tune,
Our antient castle shoots at noon,
    Wi' flag-staff buskit,   [dressed
Frae which the soldier blades come down
    To cock their musket.

Oh willawins! Mons Meg, for you,   [alas; Mons Meg =
'Twas firing crack'd thy muckle mou;   a great gun
What black mishantar gart ye spew   [mishap
    Baith gut and ga'?   [gall
I fear they bang'd thy belly fu'
    Against the law.

Right seldom am I gi'en to bannin,   [swearing
But, by my saul, ye was a cannon,
Cou'd hit a man had he been stannin
    In shire o' Fife,
Sax lang Scots miles ayont Clackmannan,
    And tak his life.

The hills in terror wou'd cry out,
And echo to thy dinsome rout;   [blow
The herds wou'd gather in their nowt,   [cows
    That glowr'd wi' wonder,
Haflins afraid to bide thereout   [Partly
    To hear thy thunder.

Sing likewise, Muse, how blue-gown bodies,   [beggars
Like scar-craws new ta'en down frae woodies,   [gallows
Come here to cast their clouted duddies,   [patched rags
    And get their pay: [= beggars alms
Than them, what magistrate mair proud is
    On king's birth-day?

On this great day, the city-guard,
In military art well lear'd,
Wi' powder'd pow and shaven beard,   [head
    Gang thro' their functions,
By hostile rabble seldom spar'd
    Of clarty unctions.   [dirty

O soldiers! for your ain dear sakes,
For Scotland's, alias Land of Cakes,   [oatcakes
Gie not her bairns sic deadly pakes,   [strokes
    Nor be sae rude,
Wi' firelock or Lochaber aix,   [axe
    As spill their blude.

Now round and round the serpents whiz,   [fireworks
Wi' hissing wrath and angry phiz;
Sometimes they catch a gentle gizz,   [wig
     Alake the day!
And singe, wi' hair-devouring bizz,   [burning
     Its curls away.

Shou'd th' owner patiently keek round,   [look
To view the nature of his wound,
Dead pussie, dragled thro' the pond,
     Takes him a lounder,   [a blow
Which lays his honour on the ground
     As flat's a flounder.

The Muse maun also now implore
Auld wives to steek ilk hole and bore;   [shut
If baudrins slip but to the door,   [pussy
     I fear, I fear,
She'll no lang shank upon all-four
     This time o' year.

Next day each hero tells his news
O' crackit crowns and broken brows,
And deeds that here forbid the Muse
     Her theme to swell,
Or time mair precious abuse
     Their crimes to tell.

She'll rather to the fields resort,
Whare music gars the day seem short,
Whare doggies play, and lambies sport
     On gowany braes,   [daisied
Whare peerless Fancy hads her court,
     And tunes her lays.

SOURCE: A Kinghorn and A Law (eds) 1985 *Poems of Allan Ramsay and Robert Fergusson*, Edinburgh (Scottish Academic Press), 125–8.

DOCUMENT 70

David Hume on good taste

David Hume was celebrated throughout Britain and beyond for the stylistic clarity and intellectual engagement of his essays. In this extract from one of his most famous essays, Hume sounds some of the keynote beliefs of the Scottish Enlightenment about the moderate, sophisticated man of culture.

There is a *delicacy* of *taste* observable in some men, which very much resembles this *delicacy of passion*, and produces the same sensibility to beauty and deformity of every kind, as that does to prosperity and adversity, obligations and injuries. When you present a poem or a picture to a man possessed of this talent, the delicacy of his feeling makes him be sensibly touched with every part of it; nor are the masterly strokes perceived with more exquisite relish and satisfaction, than the negligences or absurdities with disgust and uneasiness. A polite and judicious conversation affords him the highest entertainment; rudeness or impertinence is as great a punishment to him. In short, delicacy of taste has the same effect as delicacy of passion: It enlarges the sphere both of our happiness and misery, and makes us sensible to pains as well as pleasures, which escape the rest of mankind.

I believe, however, every one will agree with me, that, notwithstanding this resemblance, delicacy of taste is as much to be desired and cultivated as delicacy of passion is to be lamented, and to be remedied, if possible. The good or ill accidents of life are very little at our disposal; but we are pretty much masters what books we shall read, what diversions we shall partake of, and what company we shall keep. Philosophers have endeavoured to render happiness entirely independent of every thing external. That degree of perfection is impossible to be *attained*: But every wise man will endeavour to place his happiness on such objects chiefly as depend upon himself: and *that* is not to be *attained* so much by any other means as by this delicacy of sentiment. When a man is possessed of that talent, he is more happy by what pleases his taste, than by what gratifies his appetites, and receives more enjoyment from a poem or a piece of reasoning than the most expensive luxury can afford.

SOURCE: David Hume 1777 extracted from 'Of the Delicacy of Taste and Passion', in *Essays Moral, Political and Literary*, London.

DOCUMENT 71

The perception of primitive Scotland

Tobias Smollett was a great peripatetic Scot. A former Royal Navy surgeon, widely travelled in Europe and an editor of literary periodicals in London, he was perhaps uniquely placed to observe the melting pot of eighteenth-century Britain. In this passage from his final novel, the coupling of North and South provides both laughter and serious food for thought.

There was, however, another consideration that gave Mrs. Tabitha some disturbance. At Newcastle, the servants had been informed by some wag, that there was nothing to eat in Scotland, but *oat-meal* and *sheep's-heads*; and lieutenant Lismahago being consulted, what he said had served rather to confirm than to refute the report. Our aunt being apprised of this circumstance, very gravely advised her brother to provide a sumpter horse with store of hams, tongues, bread, biscuit and other articles for our subsistence . . . The 'squire, shrugging up his shoulders, eyed her askance with a look of ineffable contempt; and, after some pause, 'Sister, (said he) I can hardly persuade myself you are serious.' She was so little acquainted with the geography of the island, that she imagined we could not go to Scotland but by sea; and, after we had passed through the town of Berwick, when he told her we were upon Scottish ground, she could hardly believe the assertion – If the truth must be told, the South Britons in general are woefully ignorant in this particular. What, between want of curiosity, and traditional sarcasms, the effect of ancient animosity, the people at the other end of the island know as little of Scotland as of Japan.

SOURCE: Tobias Smollett 1771 *The Expedition of Humphry Clinker*, Vol II, Edinburgh, from 'Jerry Melford' to 'Sir Watkin Phillips', July 18.

DOCUMENT 72

Johnson and Boswell in the Highlands

In 1773, the Scottish journalist James Boswell persuaded his friend Samuel Johnson, the grand old man of English letters, to tour Scotland with him. Both recorded their travels. In Boswell's account of this incident in the Highlands, Johnson collides with his cultural environment head first.

Before Dr Johnson came to breakfast, Lady Lochbuy said, 'he was a *dungeon* of wit'; a very common phrase in Scotland to express a profoundness of intellect, though he afterwards told me, that he never had heard it. She proposed that he should have some cold sheep's head for breakfast. Sir Allan seemed displeased at his sister's vulgarity, and wondered how such a thought should come into her head. From a mischievous love of sport, I took the lady's part; and very gravely said, 'I think it is but fair to give him an offer of it. If he does not choose it, he may let it alone.' 'I think so', said the lady, looking at her brother with an air of victory. Sir Allan, finding the matter desperate, strutted about the room, and took snuff. When Dr Johnson came in, she called to him, 'Do you choose any cold sheep's head, sir?' 'No, Madam,' said he, with a tone of surprise and anger. 'It is here, sir,' said she, supposing he had refused it to save the trouble of bringing it in. They thus went on at cross purposes, till he confirmed his refusal in a manner not to be misunderstood; while I sat quietly by, and enjoyed my success.

SOURCE: James Boswell 1786 *Journal of a Tour to the Hebrides*, London, *from* 'Friday 22d October'.

DOCUMENT 73

Robert Burns 'To a Louse: On Seeing One on a Lady's Bonnet at Church'

'To a Louse' is one of Burns' most celebrated poems. It features Burns typically at his best in making, from very local materials and a situation which is rather mundane, a poem which is finally deeply reflective on the human condition.

> Ha! whare ye gaun, ye crowlan ferlie!   [crawling marvel
> Your impudence protects you sairly:
> I canna say but ye strunt rarely,
>   Owre *gawze* and *lace*;
> Tho' faith, I fear ye dine but sparely,
>   On sic a place.
>
> Ye ugly, creepan, blastet wonner,
> Detested, shunn'd, by saunt an' sinner,
> How daur ye set your fit upon her,
>   Sae fine a *Lady*!
> Gae somewhere else and seek your dinner,
>   On some poor body.

Swith, in some beggar's haffet squattle;   [temple, squat
There ye may creep, and sprawl, and sprattle,
Wi' ither kindred, jumping cattle,
    In shoals and nations;
Whare *horn* nor *bane* ne'er daur unsettle,
    Your thick plantations.

Now haud you there, ye're out o'sight,
Below the fatt'rels, snug and tight,   [falderals
Na faith ye yet! ye'll no be right,
    Till ye've got on it,
The vera tapmost, towrin height
    O' *Miss's bonnet.*

My sooth! right bauld ye set your nose out,
As plump an' gray as onie grozet: [gooseberry
O for some rank, mercurial rozet,   [resin
    Or fell, red smeddum,   [powder
I'd gie you sic a hearty dose o't,
    Wad dress your droddum!   [thrash, backside

I wad na been surpriz'd to spy
You on an auld wife's *flainen toy;*   [flannel cap
Or aiblins some bit duddie boy,   [perhaps, ragged
    On's *wylecoat;*   [flannel vest
But Miss's fine *Lunardi,* fye!   [baloon hat
    How daur ye do't?

O *Jenny* dinna toss your head,
An' set your beauties a' abread!
Ye little ken what cursed speed
    The blastie's makin,   [bad-tempered
Thae *winks* and *finger-ends,* I dread,   creature
    Are notice takin!

O wad some Pow'r the giftie gie us
To see oursels as others see us!
It wad frae monie a blunder free us
    An' foolish notion:
What airs in dress an' gait wad lea'e us,
    And ev'n Devotion!

SOURCE: Robert Burns 1786 *Poems, chiefly in the Scottish Dialect,* Kilmarnock, 192–4.

Rapid cultural change in Scotland

In the postscript chapter to his first novel, Walter Scott is very explicitly aware that he has been depicting an element of Scottish culture (Jacobitism) which stands at the centre of great change in the national psyche. In this extract he seems evenly divided between sensible affirmation of this change and regret for it.

There is no European nation which, within the course of half a century, or little more, has undergone so complete a change as this kingdom of Scotland. The effects of the insurrection of 1745 – the destruction of the patriarchal power of the Highlands chiefs – the abolition of the heritable jurisdictions of the Lowland nobility and barons – the total eradication of the Jacobite party, which, averse to intermingle with the English, or adopt their customs, long continued to pride themselves upon maintaining ancient Scottish manners and customs – commenced this innovation. The gradual influx of wealth, and extension of commerce, have since united to render the present people of Scotland a class of beings as different from their grandfathers as the existing English are from those of Queen Elizabeth's time. The political and economical effects of these changes have been traced by Lord Selkirk with great precision and accuracy. But the change, though steadily and rapidly progressive, has, nevertheless, been gradual; and like those who drift down the stream of a deep and smooth river, we are not aware of the progress we have made, until we fix our eye on the now distant point from which we have been drifted. – Such of the present generation as can recollect the last twenty or twenty-five years of the eighteenth century, will be fully sensible of the truth of this statement; – especially if their acquaintance and connections lay among those who, in my younger time, were facetiously called 'folks of the old leaven,' who still cherished a lingering, though hopeless, attachment to the house of Stuart. This race has now almost entirely vanished from the land, and with it, doubtless, much absurd political prejudice – but also many living examples of singular and disinterested attachment to the principles of loyalty which they received from their fathers, and of old Scottish faith, hospitality, worth, and honour.

SOURCE: Walter Scott 1814 *Waverley*, Edinburgh (Constable), *from* 'A Postscript'.

DOCUMENT 75

A portentous presbyterian dream of French radicalism

Galt's Annals of the Parish, *written as the diary-account of a presbyterian minister in an Ayrshire parish from 1760–1810, is a brilliant reconstruction of the changing Scottish scene in the face of all the big movements in ideas and society in Western civilisation during this time. In this extract the events of revolutionary France impinge upon Micah Balwhidder's parish.*

On the first night of this year, I dreamt a very remarkable dream, which, when I now recal to mind, at this distance of time, I cannot but think that there was a cast of prophecy in it. I thought that I stood on the tower of an old popish kirk, looking out at the window upon the kirk-yard, where I beheld ancient tombs, with effigies and coats of arms on the wall thereof, and a great gate at the one side, and a door that led into a dark and dismal vault, at the other. I thought all the dead, that were lying in the common graves, rose out of their coffins; at the same time, from the old and grand monuments, with the effigies and coats of arms, came the great men, and the kings of the earth with crowns on their heads, and globes and sceptres in their hands.

I stood wondering what was to ensue, when presently I heard the noise of drums and trumpets, and anon I beheld an army with banners entering in at the gate; upon which the kings and the great men came also forth in their power and array, and a dreadful battle was foughten; but the multitude, that had risen from the common graves, stood afar off, and were but lookers on.

The kings and their host were utterly discomfited. They were driven within the doors of their monuments, their coats of arms were broken off, and their effigies cast down, and the victors triumphed over them with the flourishes of trumpets and the waving of banners. But while I looked, the vision was changed, and I then beheld a wide and a dreary waste, and afar off the steeples of a great city, and a tower in the midst, like the tower of Babel, and on it I could discern written in characters of fire, 'Public Opinion'. While I was pondering at the same, I heard a great shout, and presently the conquerors made their appearance, coming over the desolate moor. They were going in great pride and might towards the city, but an awful burning rose, afar as it were in the darkness, and the flames stood like a tower of fire that reached unto the Heavens. And I saw a dreadful hand and an arm stretched from out of the cloud, and in its hold was a besom made of the hail and the storm, and it swept the fugitives like dust; and in their place I saw the church-yard, as it were, cleared and spread around, the graves closed, and the ancient tombs, with their coats of arms and their effigies of stone, all as they were in the beginning. I then awoke, and behold it was a dream.

This vision perplexed me for many days, and when the news came that the King of France was beheaded by the hands of his people, I received, as it were, a token in confirmation of the vision that had been disclosed to me in my sleep, and I preached a discourse on the same, and against the French Revolution, that was thought one of the greatest and soundest sermons that I had ever delivered in my pulpit.

On the Monday following, Mr. Cayenne, who had been some time before appointed a justice of the peace, came over from Wheatrig-house to the Cross Keys, where he sent for me and divers other respectable inhabitants of the clachan, and told us that he was to have a sad business, for a warrant was out to bring before him two democratic weaver lads, on a suspicion of high treason. Scarcely were the words uttered, when they were brought in, and he began to ask them how they dared to think of dividing, with their liberty and equality principles, his and every other man's property in the country. The men answered him in a calm manner, and told him they sought no man's property, but only their own natural rights; upon which he called them traitors and reformers. They denied they were traitors, but confessed they were reformers, and said they knew not how that should be imputed to them as a fault, for that the greatest men of all times had been reformers. – 'Was not,' they said, 'our Lord Jesus Christ a reformer?' – 'And what the devil did he make of it?' cried Mr. Cayenne, bursting with passion; 'Was he not crucified?'

SOURCE: John Galt 1821 *Annals of the Parish*, Edinburgh (Blackwood), Chapter 34.

EDUCATION

Re-setting a national standard

The Scottish Parliament had already intervened in 1633 and 1646, passing acts to support the provision of parochial schools, with stipends for their schoolmasters – in 1633 on the goodwill of parishioners, but in 1646 to be supported by a tax on land, paid by owners and tenants. The 1646 act was overturned by the Restoration settlement, leaving that of 1633 as the legal standard. In 1696 the 1646 act was repeated, more or less verbatim, but with a vital distinction. In 1646 the intention was to 'found' schools (ie set them up anew where needed); in 1696 it was to 'settle' schools (ie to secure and make permanent what was already in existence).

... His Majestie with the advice and consent of the Estates of Parliament statutes and ordains that there be a school settled and established & a schoolmaster appointed in every paroch, not alreadie provided, by advice of the heritors and minister of the paroch; And for that effect the heritors in every paroch meet and provide a commodious house for a school and settle and modifie a sallary to a schoolmaster, which shall not be under one hundred merks nor above two hundred merks, to be payed yearly at two termes, Whitsunday and Martinmass, by equall portions, and that they stent and lay on the said sallary conform to every heritors valued rent within the paroch, allowing each heritor relieff from his tennents of the half of his proportion for settling and maintaining a school and payment of the schoolmasters sallary, which sallary is declared to be by and attour [over and above] the casualties which formerly belonged to the readers and clerks of the kirk session. And if the heritors or major part of them shall not conveen, or being conveened shall not agree among themselves, then and in that case the presbytrie shall apply to the Commissioners of the Supply of the shire who, or any five of them, shall have power to establish a school and settle and modifie a sallary for a schoolmaster ... which shall be alse valid and effectuall as if it had been done by the heritors themselves ...

SOURCE: Act for Settling of Schools 1696, *Acts of the Parliaments of Scotland* X, 63, c 26.

DOCUMENT 77

Meeting the people's demands for schooling

*A country parish in the South-West faces up to its educational
responsibilities. Before the 1696 act was passed, it exceeded the level of
stipend required there, and retained it afterwards: it left the master to
negotiate the fees for non-standard subjects and for non-parishioners'
children. In 1733 it faced the problem of ensuring that all children in the
parish should have access to publicly supported schooling.*

23 November 1695
The minister and elders, with consent of the heritors, taking to their consideration
the great necessity of having a schoolmaster, have, after full tryall by examination
of Mr William Chasser, constitut the said William Chasser precenter, schoolmaster
and session clerk; and for his encouragement delivers him a bond subscribed by the
heritors and elders, containing the sum of one hundred pounds yearly [L8.33
sterling], to be payed at two termes in equall proportions; and he is to have 18
shillings Scots for eache Latine scholar in the parish, and 12d for each English.
Arithmetick scholars and such as are out of the parish are at his own expense.

22 June 1733
Representation was made by the people above the Water of Minnoch that they,
lying at a vast distance from the publick school, could have no benefits from it,
though they form part of the burdine of a publick sellerie to the schoolmaster. The
session, taking into consideration the said representation, does in terms of the same
decreet, allow the people above the said Water of Minnoch twenty pund Scots
money yearly out of the said publick sellerie, with this provision, that the publick
schoolmaster be first paid his eighty pund Scots, which remains of the modifiet
sellerie . . . [and] that the man they pitch upon for teaching their children be
approven by the Session, and that the said twenty pund is to be imployed for no
other purpose but for educating children.

SOURCE: Scottish Record Office, Minutes, Minnigaff Kirk Session, Stewartry of
Kirkcudbright.

Putting Perth on the educational map

Rev John Bonar, of the West Church in Perth, had long been a protagonist of the wider teaching of science in schools and universities in Scotland. Arriving in Perth in 1756, he began to press the magistrates to set up a science-oriented school, on the pattern of an English dissenting academy. The school he proposed would have two functions: a general education to fit the new commercial age, and high-class instruction in the 'arts and the sciences' to match and improve on the restricted studies available in the universities.

Narrative of the Rise and Establishment of the Accademy in Perth for Arts and Sciences

. . . In an Age so much inlightned it is needless to say any thing in support of Learning in general, Only it may be proper to observe, that the Powers and Capacitys of the Human mind are perhaps much more upon a Level than is commonly thought, So that the Surprizing difference which we observe betwixt one Man and another is not so much owing to any Natural Superiority as to a more carefull Cultivation and more happy occasions of Exercise and Improvement.

This plainly shows that the proper Education of Youth ought to be a principal Object of attention in every Society where the Person whose mind has been carefully formed & Enlarged by Instruction will fill any Station whatever to more advantage than he could otherwise have done.

It has indeed been the misfortune of some Ages to have Education either intirely neglected or to run in a very Improper Channell. Thus in times not long past, All Learning was made to consist in the Gramatical knowledge of Dead Languages and a Skill in Metaphysical Subtiltys, while what had an immediate reference to Life and Practise was despised.

But Providence has cast our Lot in happier Times, when things begin to be valued according to their use and men of the greatest Abilitys have employed their Skill in making the Sciences contribute not only to the Improvement of the Lawyer, Physician and Divine, but to the Improvement of the Merchant, Mechanick and Farmer in their respective Arts. Must it not be then of Importance to putt it in the powers of Persons in these Stations of Life to reap that advantage which Science is Capable of affording them.

But it is obvious that only a few can, according to the present Plann of Education, reap that advantage; For tho' our different Universitys are at present filled with many men of very distinguished Abilitys, Yet both the time necessary for compleating a Course of Education there, and the vast Expense of such an attendance, must prove an unsurmountable Barr in the way of the greater part.

The People in England have been so fully convinced of this, that we find Private Accademys in almost every great Town, where not only the Languages but those parts of Science which are of most immediate use in Life, are taught in a Short Compendious & practical manner. The Example, however beneficial, has not yet been sufficiently attended to in Scotland, where scarce an Institution of that kind is to be found . . .

From this Plan it will appear how much such an Education would differ from that which is generally pursued in our Universitys, and how well it is calculated both for the service of those who being designed for an Active Life cannot afford to employ more time in the Study of Science, and as an Introduction to others who may intend to follow any of the Learned Professions, and in that view to prosecute their Studys to a greater Length . . . And the Town of Perth seems to them a place particularly proper for an Institution of this kind, for

1st   It is at a Considerable distance from any of the Universitys.

2   The Situation of the Town is remarkably pleasant, and whatever may have been said to the contrary, is certainly very healthfull.

3dly   It is the Center of a very large and populous Country, and is the place with which the Highlands of Scotland has the greatest Correspondance, So that an Institution of this kind there would co-operate with the National Plan of Improving and Civilizing the Highlands of Scotland.

4thly   Provisions of all kinds are to had at a very reasonable rate, and there is good accommodation for such Gentlemen as might either choose to send their Children to board or come with their Familys to Reside for the Benefit of the Accademy.

5thly   The People in general are of a Sober Industrious Disposition, so that perhaps the Manners of the Youth are in less Danger of being Corrupted here than in any of our great Towns.

6   To all this must be added the flourishing state of the Grammar School, where the Languages are Taught with great Success, and whose Plan would probably be enlarged, upon the Erection of an Accademy; so that young Gentlemen would have an opportunity of being perfected not only in the Latin but also in the Greek & French. And the Ushers in the Grammar School might be of great use to the Gentlemen in the Accademy in the way of private Tutors, either for the Languages or any Branch of Science . . .

SOURCE: Scottish Record Office, Perth Town Council, Minutes, 27 September 1761.

DOCUMENT 79

Taking advantage of a new medium

Newspapers of the later eighteenth century contain little coverage of local events. It is in the advertisement columns that most information about local matters, including schooling, can be found – sometimes notices of the parish and burgh schools, more usually of private schools, both day and boarding.

a) *Glasgow, 16th September 1761*
William Gordon and James Scruton continue their Academy in the Hall of Hutcheson's Hospital; and offer to the public classes in these subjects –

Writing; arithmetic; book-keeping, navigation; Euclid's Elements in Latin or English; Geography, Algebra, Trigonometry, Astronomy; classes for exchanges, the comparison of weights and measures; Landsurveying, Mensuration, etc. Lectures on Commerce, Arithmetic and Book-keeping; and the use of the Theodolite in Land Surveying.

b) *Academy at Hutcheson's Hospital, 23 February 1762*
Attentive to the importance and utility of a judicious Plan of Education, and convinced by experience of the impropriety of many different schools for the purposes thereof, William Gordon and James Scruton have been at pains to render their Academy as complete as possible, by procuring the assistance of masters properly qualified for teaching the modern languages, which our commerce hath rendered necessary for the man of business to be acquainted with, and such of the sciences as they could not (without neglecting others as essential) overtake; by which means the youth committed to their care, will be instructed in every branch of literature, proper for the merchant, the mechanic, the mariner, and farmer, under their own eye, the proper master being always at hand to resolve the difficulties that may occur, without the disagreeable necessity of strolling from school to school, at the expiration of almost every hour.

Plan of Classes: Writing and Flourishing (Mr Scruton); Arithmetic and Book-keeping (Mr Gordon), with private classes too; Practical Geometry, plain and spherical Trigonometry, with their applications in Land-Surveying; Longimetry, Altimetry, Navigation, Geography, Astronomy, Fortification, Gunnery and Dialling (Messrs Gordon and Johnston); Geography (Mr Gordon); Algebra (Mr Dow); Euclid's Elements in Latin or in English (separately) (Mr Johnston); the French Language (or Italian and Spanish if required) (Mr Johnston).

If we obtain the support of the public, it is our intention to have more masters properly qualified: by whose assistance we may be enabled to teach Rhetoric, Composition in the Latin, English, French, Spanish, and Italian Languages, History, Natural Philosophy, and the Reading of the English Language with taste and propriety; which addition it is supposed, would render their Academy as complete and extensive, as would be requisite in this City.

[In October 1763, Gordon and Scruton moved their academy to the Trongate in Glasgow, close to a rival private academy owned and taught by Messrs Stirling and Jack. By May 1764 both partnerships had been broken, and the four were advertising their own smaller schools.]

SOURCE: *Glasgow Journal* no 1050, 10–17 September 1761, Advertisement; *Glasgow Journal* no 1073, 18–25 February 1762, Advertisement.

DOCUMENT 80

An 'anxious attention to facts' needed for better government

Sir John Sinclair wanted to provide government with a better basis than mere hunch in acting to improve the living conditions of the Scottish people – hence his plan for a 'statistical account' of the country. Such was the quality of the ministers' returns to his questionnaires about the parishes that instead of summarising them, he printed them more or less in full. Here are three comments on schooling by ministers of three rather different parishes.

a) *Parish of Monzie, Perthshire: 1793*
Until of late there were 4 schools in this parish. One in the North part, another in the East, a third in the South part, and the established school near the centre. In all of these were taught English, writing, arithmetic, and book-keeping. The first of these schools, owing to the union of farms, is given up, the teacher not being able to support himself. The other 3 still continue. The salary of the one at the East end of the parish is L5 per annum, with a house and garden. It is paid by the Duke of Athol out of the bishop's rents. His fees, however, for each of the branches taught are only 1s. per quarter. The number of scholars are from 40 to 60. The school on the South side has no fixed salary, only a house and garden, given to him gratis by Mr Maxton of Culltoquhey. The fees are the same as above . . . The number of scholars are from 30 to 50. As to the established school, the number of scholars attending it are from 40 to 70. The master's salary and emoluments from the kirk session, and keeping the registers, is about L12 per annum; he has a free house and garden. The fees for English are 1s. per quarter, for writing 1s. 6d. per quarter, for arithmetic 2s. per quarter, and for a complete set of book-keeping 10s. 6d. All of these schools are very convenient for the parish. Learning is now more generally diffused than formerly. [Estimated number attending school: average, 150 (1 in 7.6); maximum, 170 (1 in 6.7)]

b) *United parish of Strachur and Stralachlan, Argyll, 1792*
There are 2 parochial schools, 1 at each of the parish churches. The salary for both schools is only L. 8:6:4 Sterling. 90 scholars, at an average, attend these schools during the winter and spring quarters. From 40 to 50 in summer and autumn . . . There are other 2 schools in the parish, in districts discontiguous to the churches. The inhabitants of 2 or more farms join and employ a young man for teaching their children. They give him board and lodging alternately in their houses, and such wages as they can agree for. At these other schools, there is about half the number of scholars that attend the parochial schools . . . [Estimated number attending school in the year is *c*135 out of a population of *c.* 1170, that is 1 in 8.6.]

c) *Parish of Hamilton, Lanarkshire, 1791*
There is a large hall for a grammar school which has had, for a long time past, a good reputation; and, besides the youth of the place, a great many boarders from a distance, have been educated at it. About 22 years ago, another school-master was established to teach English, writing, arithmetic, etc, to whose salary the emoluments of precentor and session-clerk have been added; together with the interest of L. 100, left by Mr James Naismith, for the education of poor children in the parish. Ann, Duchess of Hamilton, in the beginning of this century, mortified 2000 merks Scots [L111 sterling], under the management of the church session, for four small salaries to school-masters, in the distant villages of the parish. Two of these are still continued: the rest, from the decay of the villages, are dropt, and the money applied to other pious uses. Besides these, there are always several private schools; the teachers of which have no other income, but the emoluments of their respective scholars.

SOURCE: DJ Withrington and IR Grant (eds) 1983 *The Statistical Account of Scotland 1791–1799 edited by Sir John Sinclair*. East Ardsley (EP Publishing).
Vol XII North and West Perthshire, 738–9 (parish of Monzie).
Vol XIII Argyll (mainland), 411–12 (united parishes of Strachur and Stralachlan).
Vol VII Lanarkshire and Renfrewshire, 398 (parish of Hamilton).

Introducing the age of government-directed social enquiries

The 1803 Education Act had a clause which required government, at twenty-five-year intervals, to review parochial schoolmasters' salaries, as a means of offsetting the effects of inflation on them. Hence the enquiry mounted in 1825. The 1834 survey was mainly a response to claims by Church evangelicals about the educational deprivation of the Highlands and Islands and of fast-growing towns of the Lowlands. Here, for the same Argyll parish (or union of parishes) – Ardchattan and Muckairn – are reports on local schooling made by the Church in 1824 and by government in 1826 and 1834.

a) *Extract of return published by the General Assembly's Education Committee,* 1824
About one fifth of the population is untaught. The parish of Ardchattan is so extensive that one parochial school cannot furnish the means of education for the children of the parish: three would be required. [No mention of Muckairn at all, yet the entry is under the parish of Ardchattan and Muckairn, and the population (*c.* 2300) refers to the united parish]

b) *Parochial Education, Scotland,* 1826
[Parochial school in Ardchattan, two in Muckairn: all teach English, Gaelic, writing, arithmetic, book-keeping, English grammar; the Ardchattan master teaches Latin and Greek; one Muckairn master teaches Latin, the other mensuration. The Ardchattan school has 30 pupils, the two in Muckairn, 70 and 40.]
  There are at least five other schools in the parish of Ardchattan alone; and generally one, sometimes two, in the parish of Muckairn. [Total attendances, *c.* 260.] In the parish of Ardchattan, two of these schools are supported by two of the heritors on whose properties they are. The interest of a sum of L200, mortified for that purpose, is divided among the three other schoolmasters: this sum was left about ten years ago. The people make up whatever else the teachers get besides . . . [total of L5–L8 a year] . . . a pitifull pittance . . . The teachers are consequently very inferior and the smattering of education which they give is of little use. The teacher or teachers in Muckairn parish may make about L8 a year and that badly paid.
[Total at school *c.* 400. Population, 1948. Ratio at school, 1 in 4.9]

[Comment added by Rev Hugh Fraser, parish minister]
The above answers show that though the Act, 1803, has doubtless been a boon to Scotland, yet as to the highlands, and particularly extensive highland parishes, its enactments leave by far the greater part of the population unsupplied and untouched. This is the case even in Ardchattan and Muckairn where the heritors have interpreted the Act more liberally than it has been understood in many other

highland parishes; for here the provisions of the Act have been granted to each of the united parishes; whereas, in many other instances, both the united parishes, including often very extensive surfaces, more than some English or Scottish counties, are considered but one parish in regard to Schools; and 600 merks [c. L34 sterling] divided between two or three or even more teachers, without schoolhouse, dwelling house, garden, etc. The people are often too poor, and have besides too little interest in the station, to build a schoolhouse. The heritors do not consider themselves legally bound to provide these; hence jealousies and dissatisfactions, and the unfitness of teachers employed under such discouraging circumstances.

It is for the wisdom of the legislature to determine what remedies ought to be applied, in so far as the highlands are concerned: whether, in consequence of the greatly increased value within the last 20 or 30 years of highland properties, something additional ought to be fairly required of the properties, from the introduction of sheep-farming and the improvements enhancing the value of land, or whether government, in its bounty, ought not to provide the relief. But assuredly, unless some effective measures be taken, the highlands will unhappily continue, as they have long remained, incomparably inferior as to the advantages for education, to their more favoured countrymen in the lowlands of Scotland.

c) *Abstract of Education Returns (Scotland)*, 1834
Ardchattan
[Parochial school; two General Assembly schools. Largest total attendance: 244. Number of children aged 5–15 taught to read: 180 males, 113 females – total 293; those taught to write: 80 males, 57 females – total 137. Population = 1650: ratio of school attenders, 1 in 6.8; ratio of those taught to read, 1 in 5.6; ratio of those taught to write, 1 in 12]

Children under five years of age seldom sent to school. There may be in the parish 40 or 50 aged persons who are unable to read. Besides the above schools are one or two others, in remote parts of the parish.

Muckairn
[Parochial school; SSPCK school. Largest total attendance: 201. Number of children aged under 15 taught to read: 55 males, 47 females – total 102: those taught to write: 34 males, 32 females – total 66. Population = 770: ratio of school attenders, 1 in 3.8; ratio of those taught to read, 1 in 7.5; ratio of those taught to write, 1 in 11.7]

With the exception of very aged people, and a few strangers from remote quarters, there are not any persons in the parish above fifteen years of age who are unable to read.

SOURCE: *Extracts from Reports of the Ministers in Parishes in some synods of Scotland made in 1818 and 1819 as to Parochial Schools*, 1824, Edinburgh, 11; *Parochial Education, Scotland*, 1826, 67; *Abstracts of Education Returns (Scotland)*, 1834, 67, 89.

DOCUMENT 82

Industrialising, lowland Scotland in educational crisis?

In order to attest or to disclaim the Church's arguments that urbanising
Scotland was being demoralised by lack of schooling and of churching, the
government set up enquiries in 1834–35 to investigate both. Three of the
returns on schooling are included here – for a rural parish engulfed by
industry, a city-centre parish, and a mixed urban-rural burgh-parish.

a) *Bonhill, Dumbartonshire*
[Two parochial schools; seven others. Largest total attendance: 605. Number of
children aged 5–15 taught to read: 298 males, 203 females – total 501; those taught
to write: 175 males, 83 females – total 258. Population = 3874: ratio of school
attenders, 1 in 6.4; ratio of those taught to read, 1 in 7.7; and taught to write, 1 in
15]

About seven-eighths of the population inhabit the vale of the Leven, and are
employed at the public works, bleachfields and printfields . . . ; to these works the
children are sent, in too many cases, at and under seven years of age; and any
learning they get afterwards is at the week-day evening and Sunday evening schools
. . . There are not known to be any adults in the parish who cannot read.

b) *Dundee: St Clement's*
[No separate parish system in Dundee: hence no population figure, and much
crossing boundaries for schooling. No returns possible for numbers able or
learning to read and write.]

There never was a Parish School, properly so called, in Dundee. Public
seminaries there are, but the rates are such as to limit the access to them to the rich.
In the immediate neighbourhood of St Clement's parish there are some public and
private seminaries, at which many of the youth belonging to that parish attend –
one particularly, in which 600 children are educated in all the common branches of
an English education, one-third gratis, and two-thirds at 1s 6d per quarter,
including the use of books, slates, pencils, light and fire . . . Three other schools,
containing each 250 scholars, or rather four containing 200 scholars each, would
afford the means of instruction to all the children of the poor in Dundee, at the
small sum of 18d per quarter. The number of scholars in Dundee, in proportion to
population, will be found to be small, from various reasons, such as poverty,
carelessness on the part of parents, and idleness on that of the children; and the
temptation to which parents are exposed to employ their children from tender
years in the subordinate branches of the manufactures. Even before they are fit for
mills, a very young person can earn a shilling or two weekly, by winding yarn, no
doubt to the great hindrance of its education and the certain injury of its health.
Many thousands of Irish are here, some of whom avail themselves of the schools,
but most do not.

c) *Burgh and Parish of Renfrew*
[Parochial-burgh grammar school with two teachers; five other schools. Largest total attendance: 482. Number of children under 15 taught to read: 308 males, 260 females – total 568; and taught to write: 111 males, 78 females – total 189. Population = 2833: ratio of school attenders, 1 in 5.9; ratio of those taught to read, 1 in 5.0; and taught to write, 1 in 15.0]

In all populous and manufacturing districts the children of one parish often attend schools in another, which has the effect of raising apparently the proportion of children at school in one parish and depressing it in the other; wherefore, to obviate this difficulty, a survey of the number of children under fifteen years of age who have been taught or are now learning to read and write in the parish of Renfrew has been made, from the result of which it appears that there are 40 or 50 children of age to be at school that have not been sent; but the chief matter of regret is that they are too soon removed from school to work; on this account many who have had lessons in writing cannot write, and many in reading who cannot read with sufficient fluency to take pleasure in it. The great thing wanting in teaching is division of labour; the teachers generally have too many branches to do justice to any, and they are withal miserably paid . . .

SOURCE: *Abstract of Education Returns (Scotland)* 1834, 201, 349, 633.

DOCUMENT 83

Higher education for all? For national good or individual advantage?

As a response to widespread demands for university reform, government set up the Royal Commission on the Scottish Universities in 1826. Its report in 1830, and the later publication of four fat volumes of evidence, remained as a ready point of reference for reformers throughout the century – for arguments about the function of the nation's colleges in a modernising society, and for pointers to the best (and the worst) practices, to be removed or adapted and supported, in promoting improvements.

There are few National Institutions of long standing, which have been more powerfully modified by the circumstances of the country than the Universities in Scotland; and they have undoubtedly been gradually adapted in an eminent degree to the particular demands upon them, arising from the circumstances of the people, for whose benefit they were designed.

These Universities are not now of an ecclesiastical character, or in the ordinary acceptation of the term, ecclesiastical Bodies . . . [and are] not framed on the

principle of being mainly adapted for the education of the clergy . . . it is essential
to keep in view the peculiar and beneficent character of the Scotch Universities,
that they are intended to place the means of the highest education in Science and
Philosophy within the reach of persons in humble ranks of life, while, at the same
time, they are equally adapted to educate and enlighten the youth of the highest
class of society . . . To preserve, in the regulation of the system of the Scotch
Universities, a just balance between the claims and wants of all the different classes
of society; to continue as a sacred and almost pious duty, the blessings of
enlightened education to all who can by possibility avail themselves of such
advantages; and, on the other hand, not to lower the system of instruction, in order
to include those who are in truth necessarily removed from the advantages of a
well-conducted University, on the most moderate plan of expense, appears to be
the principle which ought to govern all deliberations on this subject.

The Universities of Scotland have always embraced Students of every variety
and description; men advanced in life, who attend some of the classes for
amusement, or in order to recal the studies of early years, or to improve themselves
in professional education, originally interrupted; or persons engaged in the actual
occupations of business, who expect to derive aid in their pursuits from the new
applications of Science to the Arts; or young men not intended for any learned
profession, or even going through any regular Course of University Education, but
sent for one or more years to College, in order to carry their education farther than
that of the schools, before they are engaged in the pursuits of trade or of commerce.
And all persons may attend any of the classes, in whatever order or manner may
suit their different views and prospects. The system of instruction, by a course of
elaborate lectures on the different branches of Science and Philosophy, continued
daily for a period of six months, is admirably calculated to answer all the objects
which such persons may have in view, as well as to afford much useful instruction
to regular Students.

To impose one particular course and plan of study upon all the Students, or
indeed to require the observance of any rules whatever on the part of persons of the
description above mentioned, would clearly be destructive of the usefulness and
prosperity of the Scotch Universities, and be injurious to the interests of society . . .
[Yet] the plan of study to be followed by regular Students may cease to be the object
of attention . . . The importance of a Course of Study for those who are intended to
follow a regular system may be neglected; and thus the Universities may remain
essentially defective in regard to some of the primary objects of such Institutions,
notwithstanding the numbers whom the eloquence or science of the Professors may
attract to their Lectures . . .

It does not appear to us that the principles applicable to trade can with
propriety be extended to the education of the country, or that it is sufficient to say,
that every one should be left to obtain where he can, the instruction and teaching
which he may require, without any provision being made by Public Institutions for
a good course of study for those who may desire it. Under any such system,
instruction, either to the extent or on the principles adapted to the state of society,

will not be adequately provided. The demand for instruction, and for the means of regular and philosophical education, is not of that description which will of itself secure a complete system which could constantly be upheld without the aid and encouragement of public establishments: and in particular, in regard to persons who are not desirous merely of information on detached or popular subjects, but are looking for a course of regular training and study, on a systematic plan, not influenced by popular prejudices, or accommodated, from time to time, to the current of prevailing tastes and fashions, we are confident that without the institutions and settled usages of an Establishment, the objects of National education could not be adequately secured . . . No one is compelled to attend the Universities unless he chooses; and all who do attend, without any particular pursuit, ought to be allowed to do so in the manner which they prefer, and to take the branches of instruction which they choose to select. But it does not follow, that for those who desire a regular and systematic course of study, the Universities should not be so regulated as to afford the best possible Course of Study and the best System of Instruction. The Universities will thereby be rendered more extensively useful, and better fitted to contribute to the improvement of the general education of the country.

SOURCE: *Report: Royal Commission on the Universities of Scotland*, 1830, Edinburgh, 9–10, 12.

DOCUMENT 84

John Stuart Blackie on universities, 1846

Reformers like John Stuart Blackie, who had also studied in German universities, found much there to admire.

The academical institutions of Scotland, while in respect of breadth and compass, and popular sympathy, they are far superior to those of England, do, in point of scientific and literary elevation, by the admission of all who know anything about these matters, stand at the lowest grade known in Europe; are, in fact, in may of their classes no UNIVERSITIES at all, in the sense in which that word is generally understood, but mere SCHOOLS, and schools of a very bad, irregular and inefficient description. All the people may not be sensible of this, but it is only too true; it stands written in legible characters to all who will read them, in the nature of the thing itself, and in the evidence given by the Professors in person, before the University Commissioners in 1826. The plain and undeniable fact is, that there are in many districts of Scotland no good Gymnasia or upper schools as there are in Germany, and in all countries where a well-regulated system of education exists . . .

It is your business, people of Scotland, to prepare the youth for academical education; and ours then – but only then – to reject them if they come not sufficiently prepared. These things are done in despot-ridden Prussia; shall a race of FREE PEOPLE not be able to touch an ounce where a tyrant lifts a ton. I say, therefore, Do the thing which circumstances require, and let us have done with this degradation for ever. Send your Inspector round the country, and let him inform you in what parts of Scotland there already exist sufficient upper schools for preparatory education (for there are good academies in many places), and in what cases these do not exist. These blanks it must be the instant duty of the Government, or of the Central Board of Education for Scotland, acting as the organ of Government, to supply; and whenever this is done, the same public authority must pass a general academical ordinance, that no student shall enter any initiatory class of a Scottish university, without having proved a fit amount of preparatory study, before scientific and literary examiners, not being professors, for that purpose specially appointed . . .

Thus much for the necessary elevation of our academical starting-point. Concerning the enlargement and extension of our curriculum, much might be said . . .

There should exist in all our universities –

I   A class of English Literature and Practical Rhetoric . . .

II   A class of Civil History, Constitutional History, and Parliamentary Law, made imperative on . . . all students whatsoever who take the highest degree, either in arts or in any of the faculties . . .

III A professorship of the Teutonic and a professorship of the Romanesque Languages . . .

IV   The Natural Sciences, especially Natural History, strictly so called, or (in the option of the student) Chemistry, should be made an essential part of the common curriculum of arts in all the universities . . . Neither need I remark that a knowledge of these sciences is of vastly more importance to the furnishing of the youthful mind than the meagre amount of Greek and Latin vocables and grammatical formulas, which we in Scotland dignify with the title of Classical Literaure . . .

SOURCE: John Stuart Blackie 1846 *Education in Scotland. An Appeal to the Scottish People on the Improvement of their Scholastic and Academical Institutions*, Aberdeen and Edinburgh (William Tait), 10–12.

Part Two
1850–1998

THE STATE

The Board of Supervision, the Representative 'Interest' and Scottish Administration, 1869

In 1868 the Government appointed a Select Committee to inquire into the rising cost of the Scottish Poor Law, which Liberal MPs had blamed on the Board of Supervision and its lack of political accountability. The extract here is from the evidence of two of its members, Patrick Fraser, the Sheriff of Renfrew, and Sir John McNeill, the Chairman, 1845–1868. Their evidence and that of other witnesses on attendance at the Board, the incorporation of vested interests and the adherence to legal procedures satisfied the Committee that much of the increased cost was due to demographic and other pressures outside the Board's control. It recommended no major alteration in Board membership or its administration. McNeill, a Tory, had been previously British ambassador to Tehran.

Patrick Fraser What is your experience of the attendance at the Board of the various members since you have been a member of it? – During these seven years I was associated with Sir John McNeill; Mr. Edward Gordon, the late Lord Advocate of Scotland, who was sheriff of Perthshire; and Mr. Shank Cook, who was sheriff of Ross-shire. We have 52 stated meetings in the year, and of these meetings Mr. Cook attended every one, except when he was absent upon official duty in Ross-shire. For the year 1862 he attended 40 meetings; 1863, 41 meetings; 1864, 42 meetings; 1865, 43 meetings; 1866, 44 meetings; 1867, 40 meetings; and in 1868, 43 meetings; and he died recently.

What was the attendance of the others? – Mr. Gordon, the sheriff of Perth, attended in 1863, 34 meetings, and in 1864, 31 meetings, and he was appointed Lord Advocate in 1866, and only attended 16 meetings in that year, and ceased to be a member of the Board. In 1863 I attended 35 meetings; in 1865, 31; in 1866, 32; in 1867, 31; and in 1868, 33 meetings. In justice to myself and Mr. Gordon I must add that we required more frequently than Mr. Cook to hold courts in our counties, and were therefore oftener absent from Edinburgh. Besides these ordinary meetings, which generally last about three hours or longer (three hours on the average), we had extra meetings, and we had consultations without formal meetings in the court; or sometimes the secretary had consultations with the sheriffs in the Parliament House . . .

The sheriffs are paid members of the Board, are they not? – Well, if you call 150*l*. a year for our labours payment, we are paid.

You have stated the attendances of yourself and your brother sheriffs; can you give the Committee the number of attendances of other members of the Board; have you any memorandum of that? – Except in the case of Mr. Smythe, and the late Solicitor General, Mr. Millar, we have really had no attendance from any other members of the Board. When we are away upon official duties in our counties, Mr. Smythe was sent for, and he attends in order to make up the quorum during the autumn and sometimes in the spring vacations . . .

Is there any particular part which the sheriffs take, as being legal members of the Board; do they moot overtures, or does the Chairman do that? . . . the legal member's work consists chiefly of this: very frequently cases of difficult points of law occur; we have not time to discuss them at the meeting, and we have not proper books to consult, and so these are, by minute of the Board, circulated among the legal members; these papers come round in little black boxes, sometimes three a week, and we are required to give our written opinions upon those questions of law, which we do; the senior sheriff, who happened till lately to be Mr. Cook, and who now is myself, has to write the first opinion; I see that since the month of June 1868, I have written 151 of these legal opinions for the Board; if we are unanimous, that legal opinion guides the Board, and we communicate it to the parties in the country who consult us; if we are not unanimous, and if we think it to be a point of difficulty and of great importance, regulating large interests, we prepare a memorial for the opinion of counsel, who are generally the ex-Lord Advocate, the present Lord Advocate, and a junior counsel; we endeavour in that way to tell the various parochial boards through the country what the law is, and how to administer it.

Is not the Solicitor General brought in if there is any difference of opinion among the sheriffs before you ask the opinion of counsel? – Yes, we ask his opinion too, but he is a member of the Board, and is not consulted as counsel.

He is consulted like the sheriffs? – Always; if we differ in opinion the papers are sent to him.

Not otherwise? – Not otherwise, since the appointment of the present Solicitor General. He put the matter to us thus: that, besides a large practice and Crown business to attend to, he had Parliamentary duties which called him away from Edinburgh, and that he could not efficiently work as a member of the Board unless he constantly attended, which he said he could not do. In these circumstances we were very glad to compromise with him, by his giving us assistance when we differed in opinion.

In fact, the sheriffs deal with all legal questions coming before the Board? –Yes.

The Solicitor General is not consulted? – He is not necessarily consulted unless we differ in opinion . . .

Sir John McNeill Would you not think that it might improve the administration of the business that comes under the jurisdiction of the Board of Supervision to reduce the Board to one responsible head, which should be responsible to Parliament? – Well, I have had 23 years' experience of the Board of Supervision, as the chairman of that Board, and I say, without hesitation, that I should deeply lament such a change as that; I have derived so great an advantage myself from the advice and assistance of my colleagues, and especially of the sheriffs, that I should pity any man left in the position in which I should have been without such assistance.

I presume that the questions upon which most frequently you would require the advice of other members would be legal questions? – The advice of the sheriffs was invaluable as regarded legal questions; but we had the good fortune to have, as sheriffs and as members of the Board, men whose opinion was of value upon every question; and I felt far more satisfied when any proposition which I had to make to the Board was fairly discussed by them (and often discussed in a hostile sense, too, by some of the members), and when the Board came to a decision, after full and free discussion amongst the members on the point at issue, than I should have felt if I had been acting solely on my own responsibility . . .

Do not you think it would be more advantageous, assuming that the constitution of the Board were continued with three official members, that those three official members should be so appointed that they should constantly attend, and have before them the regular course of business from week to week? – I do not know that; I have always thought it very important to the Board, and to the smooth working of the Board, that there should be a representation of the landed interest of the country on the Board. I do not believe that the proprietors in Scotland would have worked as smoothly with the Board of Supervision if we had not had amongst our members two recognised representatives of that class; they felt that what these men concurred in was not hostile to their interests, and we have all along, from the beginning, had landed proprietors of considerable weight on opposite sides of politics; for from the commencement I was exceedingly desirous that the Board should not only be free from any party bias, but that it should be free from the suspicion of party bias; therefore, on the first formation of the Board, Mr. Drummond, of Blair Drummond, having been appointed one of the Crown commissioners, I made a special request that the other should be Sir George Macpherson Grant, of Ballindalloch, who was on the opposite side of politics; and from that time to this the nominations have all been made with that view, that the two commissioners named by the Crown should be one on one side of politics and the other on the other.

You talk of representation on the Board; I was not aware there was anything like representation on the Board? – Well, representation in a strict sense there was not; they were not elected, and therefore were not representatives, but I think that in an essential way they represented the interests of the landed property of Scotland at that Board, and that they were there prepared to object to any proceeding which they considered undue, or unduly hostile to the landed interest.

But if you think that it is necessary or desirable that there should be representation on the Board, why are the landed interest alone to be represented? – The boroughs were represented by two of the principal Lords Provost. The Solicitor General, and the three sheriffs were men who had a great deal of local knowledge, and who did not necessarily belong to any particular section of the community. Some of them were Free Kirk men; some of them Episcopalians; some of them Presbyterians of the Established Church, and some of them of other denominations. There was, therefore, on the Board (if you will permit me to call it a representation) a representation of every class and denomination in the community . . .

[Would you] not consider that the official members would be more useful as advisers to the chairman, if they were gentlemen constantly attending to the business of the Board, instead of being summoned only on special occasions? – I should have been very glad if they could have all attended constantly; but if you are to select from men specially fitted for business, you will find very few of them so little occupied as to be able to give constant attendance; and men who are able to give constant attendance are, for the most part, men who are not engaged in much business, who have not much to do, and who have not been charged with any particular work.

In fact, they are not paid members, and they have other business to attend to? – They are not paid members.

But would it not be better that the useful working members of the Board should be paid, so that the country should get the whole of their attention to the business? – If the Government are prepared to pay a greater number of members, I have no doubt that you could thereby ensure a more regular attendance. I think that every man who is paid considers it a duty to attend.

It is not a question of regular attendance, by itself, but whether it would not be more beneficial that the country should get the whole benefit of the attendance of the working members on the Board? – It might be so. I do not know. I think that the chairman and the three sheriffs, with the occasional assistance of the other members when there is any difficulty, constitute an efficient Board, or ought to constitute an efficient Board.

SOURCE: *Select Committee on the Poor Law (Scotland)*, 1869, London.

Workers' Welfare and the Scottish Home Rule Bill, 1924

*In May 1924, during the Labour Government's first term of office, a number
of Clydeside Labour MPs introduced a bill to establish a Scottish Parliament,
with directly elected MPs. It proposed to give the Parliament control over
law and order, education, social welfare and local government. The extract
here is from the Second Reading and sets out the Labour argument that a
separate Parliament would overcome the difficulties of Westminster
'remoteness' and help rekindle a sense of national purpose. The extract also
indicates the opposition of Conservative MPs who felt the measure would
harm Scottish trade and increase political unrest. The Bill was lost ('talked
out') by the Conservatives refusing to give way during the debate and agree a
vote. Labour interest in Home Rule waned after its election defeat later that
year.*

Mr J Buchanan (Labour, Gorbals)
Let me give two striking examples that might be used as an argument for Home
Rule for Scotland. This week Scotland had two Measures that were passed by this
House. One of them dealt with school teachers' superannuation. The unanimous
wish of the Scottish Members, including, I believe, the Secretary for Scotland, was
to make the date of operation next year, but because the English Members had
agreed to accept two years, and because this Parliament is, as it must be, largely
representative of English thought, they agreed to two years. Despite the unanimous
request, despite even the agreement, in the main, of the Scottish Office, we could
not have the date that Scottish opinion wanted and should have had. Take our Poor
Persons Bill – a small, meagre Bill to deal with an urgent problem, largely arising in
Glasgow and the west of Scotland. True, we got it, but I venture to say that if we
had our Scottish Parliament, that Bill would not have been held up as it has been
for over a month. A Scottish Parliament would have had it passed, and it would
have been in law in the time it has been held up even for Second Reading. My
feeling, I think, on this question, will be accepted by most of the Scottish members.
We have our own views on education. We have our own views on religion, and on
this question may I cite one example. This House will be called upon to deal with
the Union of the Scottish Churches ere long. I must confess, for my part, I am very
open in my views. I have never committed myself on that question to either one side
or the other, but what I feel is that on a purely Scottish question, a question dealing
with the religious feeling and aspirations of the Scottish people, members largely
alien to our views should not be called upon in the main to decide a question of
which they have no knowledge or thoughts.

Take the London Traffic Bill as an example on the other side. Why should I
have been called upon to give a deliberate vote on a question that did not affect my
constituency or my country, and therefore ought to have been decided by the
Members mostly responsible for it? . . . What did we find last week? On a purely

Lanarkshire problem, a purely Scottish problem, deputations of county councils and town councils from almost every part of Lanarkshire are in London with counsel and everything else, instead of being in Scotland, where the problem is known, or ought to be known, and understood better than here. Instead of the inquiry being conducted in Scotland, we have to suffer the expense and burden of sending to London deputations from every burgh and town connected with this scheme, and have it discussed 400 miles away from the spot, where we might have had it settled within a radius of 20 or 30 miles of the place. These instances could be multiplied . . .

. . . One thing more. We are cribbed in the one thing upon which we pride ourselves most, and that is in our educational facilities. If Scotland has anything to boast of, it is in her great educational attainments. To-day we are limited in our aspirations by the outlook in this part of the country known as England. We want to be bigger and bolder in these things. We feel that a Scottish Parliament would make for better government in these things. Take the case of a great city like Glasgow, which is well known in commerce and industry. There you have the tragedy going on day after day, a death rate of four times the number of children than the death rate in a well-to-do division, and that is not because our people are poor, or Scottish, or Irish, or drunkards. It is not even because this Parliament is brutal towards our people. It is because this Parliament cannot devote the time to the work, and, furthermore, because it has no knowledge of the problems with which we are confronted . . .

Sir H Craik (Conservative, Scottish Universities)
I want the House to consider what is this national entity which you are going to cut off from the whole of Southern Britain and constitute a national item by itself. Is there that intimate sympathy of race and feeling between the remote fishermen of the Hebrides and the Orkneys and Shetland, or even Inverness-shire, and the Lanarkshire population, or that thick population in Glasgow constituted very largely by an influx during recent years of 1,500,000 from Ireland? Is that exactly a homogeneous population? Where do you think the strong sympathy exists which is to bind together the Hebrides with the coal mining districts of Lanarkshire? Do you think the Northern parts of Scotland will be so very pleased to be ruled, as they inevitably would be, by the packed population in the slums of Glasgow and the mining districts of Lanark? . . . Then have hon. Members ever considered whether there is not a very close connection between certain parts of England and Scotland? Are they aware that there are many businesses carried on in Glasgow and Manchester the partners of which live half of each week in Glasgow and half in Manchester? Manchester and Glasgow are far more closely connected in sympathy and in daily intercourse than Glasgow and Edinburgh, certainly than Glasgow and Inverness. Do hon. Members know that the pilots of Aberdeen and Newcastle know each other by name, meet each other constantly and feel like brothers to one another? Aberdeen and Newcastle are far more closely connected together than Glasgow and Aberdeen. You cannot draw these

distinctions exactly. It would not be true in race, in religion, in feeling, or in business relations.

Do you think we have not drawn enormous advantage from our brothers South of the Tweed, to their advantage too? We have sent them Prime Ministers, Lord Chancellors and Archbishops of Canterbury and of York. Do you think that will go on when you have built a high wall of division between the two countries? Do you think you will be accepted readily and easily as the rulers of your brothers South of the Tweed when you have told them 'No, you shall have nothing to say in the least to any concern of ours. We shall do you the pleasure of coming and voting upon your water Bills and anything else, but we will not allow you to intervene in anything whatever except the Post Office and Foreign Affairs.' Do you think you will get great advantage for your own country in the long run by this? Hon. Members on this side may say, 'We will have a compromise. We will go so far with you.' I am against the whole thing. It is mischievous from beginning to end. I will not temporise with it. Is it not perfectly certain that if you establish two separate Parliaments the line of political complexion of those two Parliaments will be violently opposed, that the Government of one will be absolutely different in spirit and in tone from the other? That must extend not merely to domestic affairs but to foreign affairs, and you may have two Governments ruling within this island absolutely opposed to one another, not only in private and domestic matters, but on the large issues of peace and war and of foreign policy. Will that add to the strength and respect in which we are held? . . .

Scotland has always been a very strong ally and partner under present circumstances in regard to these matters, but if those affairs are to be carried out by an Executive violently opposed to them both in domestic as well as Imperial affairs, it will be a most unfortunate conjunction. By this scheme you are risking the danger of a very serious diminishing of the weight of this Empire in foreign policy. Hon. Members say that there is a universal feeling in favour of this Bill in Scotland. I know quite well that if you go to a popular meeting and you say, 'Would you like Home Rule?' several voices will reply 'Yes.' But when those people go home they ask themselves what is really meant by Home Rule. They say 'Are we in Glasgow to be governed by a Parliament sitting in Edinburgh?' or the people in Inverness may say, 'Are we to be governed by a Parliament dominated by the half-Irish population of a great part of Lanarkshire?' Are you sure that they do not look upon this as they look upon the blessed word 'Mesopotamia,' as being something which sounds enticing and tempting, which rolls nicely from the tongue, but which has no meaning behind it? . . . I do not believe that there is any real, effective demand for this Bill in Scotland, and I feel certain that the thinking part of Scotland is not only apathetic about it, but that if they thought that it was going to take any practical form their apathy would soon be changed into bitter and active opposition.

Lieut.-General Sir Aylmer Hunter-Weston (Conservative, N Ayrshire)
. . . I am entirely opposed to this Bill, because I believe it would be, inevitably, a

precursor of friction between the two countries; and, if there be friction, it must inevitably lead to separation, which would be disadvantageous to the Kingdom as a whole, and would certainly be fatal to Scotland. No sane person, I think, would desire to go back to those conditions which obtained in this little island before the Act of Union. This island, which is the very hub and centre of our Empire, on which the whole Empire depends, is geographically too small for separation, and, I think, none but the maddest extremists really want separation. We Lowlanders of pure Scottish descent are proverbially and characteristically canny, and we know on which side our bread is buttered; and I think that all Scotsmen who have anything to do with business know only too well that separation from our larger and richer neighbour in the South would be economically disastrous. This was extremely well exemplified less than three years ago, when Sir Eric Geddes brought in what was to have been a Home Rule Bill for Scottish railways. He proposed to put all our Scottish railways in one group by themselves, so that we might have what we are always talking about, Home Rule for Scotland, in that Department. But every Scotsman made an immediate outcry. Hon. Members will remember the pressure that Scottish Members of every party brought to prevent the Government doing what we considered to be disadvantageous to everyone in Scotland, whatever his occupation, whether in or out of commerce, whether employer or employed. We were all agreed that that was fatal to us, and it was only by the great exertions made by Members of all parties and by the considerable pressure which was brought to bear upon the Government by every interest in Scotland, that that Government were induced to alter the Bill and the great English railway companies were persuaded to include Scotland in the two Northern Groups. That is an excellent example as showing that opinion North of the Tweed, though it may be in favour of devolution, is absolutely opposed to anything which would cut us off in any way from the advantages, economic and otherwise, that we at present gain by our union with England and Wales . . .

I oppose it because I consider that many of its provisions are adverse to the best interests of the working classes in Scotland, notably the division between Scotland and England in regard to national insurance, old age pensions, and Employment Exchanges. We are, I hope, on the eve of a comprehensive scheme of national insurance, and national insurance, if it is to be worthy of the name, must embrace the whole of the United Kingdom as well as embracing the major risks to which working men and working women are liable, to wit, loss of health, old age and unemployment. If Scotland is to be cut off from participation in this big national scheme it would undoubtedly be in the very worst economic interests of the working classes of my own country . . .

SOURCE: 'Government of Scotland Bill', *Hansard* 174, c 790–871, 9 May 1924.

DOCUMENT 87

Scottish Home Rule and creating a Scottish Secretary of State

*The introduction of the Scottish Home Rule Bill (see **Document 86**) caused considerable press comment in Scotland, almost uniformly hostile. The extract here is from* The Glasgow Herald. *The paper had a reputation of reflecting Glasgow business opinion and since 1919 had campaigned for elevating the Scottish Secretary into a Secretary of State, principally in the belief that it would increase Cabinet recognition of the Scottish 'interest'.*

Scottish Home Rule
The movement for Scottish Home Rule, which had been feebly sporadic among certain sections of opinion in Scotland for several generations, has within recent years taken on a certain shape and consistency. It has been galvanised into a show of political life by the operation of causes which were bound to reflect themselves in an intensification of national sentiment. One of those causes was the war, which, while it demonstrated in the most unequivocal fashion the loyal devotion of Scotsmen to the Empire, tended also to increase their national solidarity . . . The wave of unrest which swept over the world after the war had the effect of strengthening racial feeling and the desire for political change, while Scotland could not remain entirely unaffected by the European resurgence of dormant or suppressed nationalities. Another cause was the congestion of legislation in the Imperial Parliament in the period immediately following the war. This cause led to the setting up, in 1919, of the Speaker's Conference on Devolution . . . Meanwhile, however, another stimulus, of a rather equivocal nature, had been supplied by the movements in Ireland and by the grant to that country of a measure of autonomy much greater than had ever been hoped for, or even desired, by the older type of Irish Nationalist. On many people in Scotland the effect of the establishment of the Irish Free State was to cure them of any sentimental leanings they may ever have had towards Scottish Home Rule. On the other hand, not a few of the younger Scottish so-called 'intellectuals,' while mainly indifferent to the purely political side of the question, were inclined to be rather jealous of the opportunity which Ireland had obtained for an all-round development on purely national lines, which, in their view, was rendered impossible in Scotland by what they were pleased to call the political and social subservience to England . . .

The movement for national autonomy has not received any support whatever from the industrial, financial, or trading interests in Scotland. The attitude of those interests has indeed been hostile to any departure from existing arrangements. And the majority of the Scottish people have displayed a notable indifference in the matter. Such vitality as the movement possesses has been almost entirely due to the activity of a small body of extremists and idealists who have taken advantage of apparently favourable circumstances to give political shape to their aspirations . . .

The government of Scotland Bill, promoted by Mr Buchanan, which is to come up for second reading in the House of Commons on Friday, is substantially the same measure as that which was 'talked out' in the House two years ago . . .

In nearly all affairs that really count the House is not likely to be allowed to forget that the interests of England and Scotland have become practically inseparable. The question of reserved and conferred powers, for example, presents a tangle which could hardly be satisfactorily straightened out even by the brain of a Lord Haldane. The confusion is intensified by the intricate financial arrangements needed to adjust the allocation of taxation revenue as between England and Scotland. One of the advantages of a British Parliament is that it absorbs the shock of extremism which might play havoc with smaller Legislatures. The real driving power behind the present movement reveals itself in Mr Maxton's suggestion that Scotland is an ideal subject for a big Socialist experiment. We do not distrust the common sense of our own compatriots; but the Socialist advocacy of Scottish Home Rule is an additional and a very strong reason for caution on the part of the electorate. That the continued development of Scotland on Scottish lines is necessary both to the efficiency and wellbeing of Scotsmen and to the strengthening of the British Commonwealth of Nations we not merely grant but strongly maintain. And that some additional measure of devolution is necessary for that development is obvious to the most casual student of public affairs. But all the devolution that we need can be secured by a reform of Scottish administration. The elevation of the office of Secretary for Scotland into a Secretaryship of State, and the strengthening and readjustment of the Scottish Departments are among the practicable measures which, at a small expense, would make for increased efficiency of administration and for the greater consolidation and intensity of our national life.

SOURCE: *The Glasgow Herald*, Wednesday 7 May 1924.

Ministerial Responsibility and abolishing the Scottish Board, 1928

In 1927, after Parliamentary criticism, the Conservative Government withdrew a Bill to abolish the two Scottish Boards of Agriculture and Health and replace them with departments under the control of the Scottish Secretary. Sir John Gilmour, the Scottish Secretary, had inadvertently suggested that the Scottish Office in London was the 'headquarters' of Scottish administration. The Bill was re-introduced the following year and the following is an extract from the Second Reading. Despite Gilmour's vision of 'centralising' the Scottish Departments in an Edinburgh Government office, it is interesting to note the objections to 'de-nationalising' administrative control by Noel Skelton, the right-wing Conservative MP. It is also interesting to note the views on grant-aid by the Liberal 'Home Ruler', Sir Archibald Sinclair. The Bill was passed later that year and in January 1929 the Boards of Agriculture and Health were replaced by separate Departments. In 1931 Sinclair and Skelton became Scottish Office ministers under the National Government.

Sir J Gilmour (Secretary of State, Conservative)
The history of government in Scotland is very familiar to Scottish Members. They will recall a period during which the affairs of Scotland were conducted by another Department of State in England. Then came the constitution of the Scottish Office, and in order to overcome the inherent difficulties of the new system of government there was established in Scotland the system which had been used in other parts of the Kingdom; known as the Board system. The motive which led to placing the administration in Scotland in the hands of Boards, was the fact that communication at that time between Scotland and London was less easy than it is at the present; that the responsibility of whoever held the office which I have the honour to hold to Parliament and the assertion of the right of Parliament to make the Minister answerable for government in Scotland, was not then so fully developed . . .

Whether the administration of Scotland is carried on by a board or department, the House should bear in mind that the responsibility rests, and must rest, with the Minister responsible for the board or department. So far as this House is concerned in any change from a system of administration by boards to an administration by departments, which is common to this country, and is indeed working in Scotland now in regard to one of the most important administrative duties, education; the responsibility of the Minister remains the same and the opportunities for criticism by this House of the actions of the Minister remain the same. Therefore it comes down really to a practical question as to whether the system of boards is as efficient and as effective as the departmental system. I have long held the view, and it is corroborated by the fact that in England the same view is taken, that the most satisfactory method of administration in Scotland is the establishment and maintenance of a Civil Service which remains continuously and closely in touch with the work for which they are responsible and who are not liable to the fluctuations and changes of political policy.

Further, the position of the Minister in coming to decisions and taking responsibility for which he has to answer to Parliament and the country, is likely to be more efficiently safeguarded and, indeed, assisted, if he has at the head of a department a single advisor who, in his turn, takes responsibility for the advice which he tenders. In criticising the board system, I am not casting any reflection upon the good work which many of these boards have done in the past. Hon. Members can picture to themselves the position: questions coming before a board upon which there may be, legitimately, a difference of opinion and where a majority and minority report is submitted to the Minister. In such a case the Minister is unable to turn to the head advisor of the Department for advice, and he finds himself in the position of not having any responsible advice from the head of the department. He has to make up his mind on the majority and minority report of the Board. From that point of view it is wise that this should be avoided . . .

It is a difficult problem, but I think we are all agreed, no matter what party we belong to, that for these [Board] appointments patronage is undesirable. The great public service of civil servants, drawn from a class which reach and maintain their position by examination and merit, who are attached to one department or another, gain during the course of years an experience which is of enormous value to the State, to this House, and to the Minister who is responsible.

It is for that reason that I desire to see established in Scotland a system of departments. We have had experience of departmental work in Scotland. The Department of Education is not a Board of Education. I have no reason to suppose, from such evidence as I have been able to gather during my three years of administration, that there is any real criticism in Scotland that the system in the Education Department has not worked satisfactorily. The head of that Department resides in the capital of Scotland. He has, it is true, a second in command here in London. But I would emphasise at once that there appears to have been a kind of conception in the minds of some hon. Members and, indeed in the mind of some of the outside public, that this change which we propose to make is going to transfer the centre and activities of these offices from Scotland to Whitehall. On the contrary, there is no such suggestion. There never has been such a suggestion. Since I submitted the Bill last year there has been no such suggestion.

To prove that there was no intention or prospect of such a thing taking place, I have specifically inserted in the Bill a Clause which declares that the Departments shall remain in Scotland. Indeed if we achieve, as I conceive we shall, the placing at the head of these Departments of civil servants of the first class, drawn from the whole service, so that Scotland can have the best service possible without restriction of any kind except the restriction of efficiency and of examination, then we will have at the heads of the Departments men who will be capable of advising and conducting even some of the work which may, at the present moment, be carried on here at Dover House. The ambition which I have formed is not only to have first class civil servants at the heads of these offices, similar to the first class civil servants at the head of the offices here in England, but that we shall in course of time, when the clamant demands for economy shall have been overcome, centralise in Edinburgh under one roof all the Departments concerned with Scottish affairs.

Then I can visualise the linking up of Parliament and Dover House with a central office in Edinburgh, where the Minister responsible to Parliament and the Scottish Members can be in close and easy touch with the heads of every one of his Departments. The House will believe me when I say that with scattered Departments in Edinburgh now it is no light or easy task for the Minister to keep in touch with any work that is going on, and indeed to obtain from those Departments, with the rapidity that one often desires, answers to questions put to him either across the Floor of the House or by the large interests outside.

N Skelton (Conservative, East Perthshire)
. . . My right hon. Friend when dealing with this Bill seemed to treat himself as if he were the equivalent of an ordinary English Cabinet Minister, responsible for only one Department, but that is not his position. The Secretary of State for Scotland is really either a Scottish Cabinet, or, if you like to put it a little lower, he is a Scottish Prime Minister with a Cabinet consisting of his Law Officers and his Under-Secretary of State. That seems to me to be much nearer his real position . . . That being so, there appears to me to be real administrative value in having these Departments not under individual civil servants, who perhaps know little about Scotland, but under a body of representative Scotsmen who can convey to the Secretary of State, who is much occupied in London, a kind of general Scottish view upon topics.

That seems to me to be true of the Board of Health, and surely it is still more true of the Board of Agriculture. Is it conceivable that a first-class civil servant would be more agreeable to and more trusted by landlords, farmers, smallholders and others than would be a well-selected Board of Agriculture? I do not believe it. I do not believe that you can run the Navy through a first-class civil servant any more than you can run Scottish agriculture . . . The particular position of the Secretary of State for Scotland, who is more like a Cabinet than a single Cabinet Minister, seems to give an importance to these Boards which would not exist if he were an English Cabinet Minister administering one Department. Another point which ought to have been in the mind of the Secretary of State for Scotland is that the present system unquestionably gives to Scotland a certain degree of administrative Home Rule. I am not one of those who believe in a separate Scottish Parliament . . . I am certain that it is a mistake to diminish those aspects of administrative individuality which Scotland still possesses.

I feel confident that the right hon. Gentleman does not fully realise the extent to which these Boards touch various aspects of Scottish life. I do not think the right hon. Gentleman is conscious of this fact. The truth of the matter is, that the men who are drawn from independent positions in civil life do touch an infinity of aspects in Scottish life which you never can get by putting at the head of a

Department an entirely de-nationalised bureaucrat. I know the central Department will remain in Edinburgh, but there is all the difference in the world between drawing people from the rough-and-tumble of Scottish life and putting at the head of Departments people who have been civil servants from their youth upwards . . .

Sir A Sinclair (Liberal, Caithness and Sutherland)
. . . May I now say a few words from the standpoint of national sentiment. The Government in the last few years have undoubtedly derogated considerably in certain directions from the autonomy of Scottish administration. There was the Pensions Ministry, which was taken South of the Border. There was Rosyth, that fine up-to-date dockyard, which was scrapped, though a lot of out-of-date dockyards on the South Coast of England were retained. Even in a thing like summer-time, the Government yielded to the demands of the English farmers to be exempt for their seed-time and rejected the demands of the Scottish farmers to be exempted from its operation during their harvest time. All these instances have given us a feeling that we have to be vigilant when there is any question that might considerably affect the present measure of autonomy which Scotland enjoys in her public administration. It seems to me ludicrous to suggest, as some hon. Members have done, that the present system is in that regard satisfactory. It is very far from that. These Boards are held out to us as a bulwark against English domination. They are very far from that. They are the creatures of Whitehall. The Board of Agriculture cannot do anything. It cannot move hand or foot without getting the sanction of officials in Whitehall.

It is very remarkable and significant, and I commend it to all my Scottish colleagues, that the Department of Education, which is a Department and not a board, is much freer from interference and control from Whitehall than any other Department. The Department of Education gets its money voted and, provided it keeps within the limits of the Vote, it can carry on absolutely free of interference from any Treasury official or anyone else. Year after year we have tried to get the salaries of the staffs of the Scottish Colleges of Agriculture increased, but they can do nothing without consulting the Treasury at every stage. If you look into the present situation not only do you find these boards are no protection for Scottish nationality, and they can give us no security from interference from Whitehall, but that the Department is actually the freest departmental organisation. I believe a departmental organisation under the direction of a skilled civil servant, who knows the ropes, who has been trained at the Treasury and knows his way about, will give Scotland far greater administrative autonomy than she enjoys at present.

The only satisfactory solution of this great problem is, of course, some measure of Home Rule. That is a solution which the hon. Gentleman rejects, but in the meantime, if we have an opportunity of actually strengthening the autonomy of local administration in Scotland, we should be foolish to reject it.

SOURCE: *Hansard*, Vol 214, c 263–6, 28 February, 1928, 'Reorganisation of Offices (Scotland) Bill' (Gilmour extract); *Hansard* 214, c 869–70, 881–2, 5 March, 1928, 'Reorganisation of Offices (Scotland) Bill' (Skelton and Sinclair extracts).

DOCUMENT 89

The Scottish 'Interest', the Covenant Movement and Home Rule, 1949

In the period immediately after Labour's 1945 landslide election victory, the Scottish Covenant Movement, a loose coalition of Nationalists, Liberals and Communists, renewed the campaign for a directly elected Scottish Parliament. The proposed powers of the Parliament were broadly similar to those contained in the 1924 Bill (see above). The Government opposed the measure, as did the Conservatives. However, in October 1949 the Covenant announced that it would gather a petition for a Home Rule Bill and appeared to receive considerable public support. Arthur Woodburn, the Scottish Secretary, in some difficulty with the Movement's campaign, authorised his officials to prepare a detailed memorandum on Home Rule. The extract here is from a preliminary paper drafted by a senior Scottish Office official. In 1950 the Cabinet rejected the petition and, lacking the support of Scottish business, the Trade Union movement and other institutions, the Movement lost its popular appeal.

If a separate Parliament is set up for Scottish domestic affairs there appears to be some danger that the influence of Scottish Members in the Great Britain Parliament at Westminster will diminish. If the Northern Ireland precedent is followed the number of Scottish Members would be reduced to take account of the limited purposes for which the Great Britain Parliament would exercise jurisdiction in Scotland. This fact, combined with the probable reluctance of distinguished Scotsmen to serve in a Parliament in London of limited interest in Scotland, might well reduce both the quality of the Scottish contribution to the discussion of imperial and international affairs and the Scottish voting strength.

There appears to be a danger that the Scottish Ministers and their Departments would be less able, under a Scottish Parliament, to influence the course of high policy than the Secretary of State and his Departments are able to do now as members of a Great Britain Government and administration. In the realms of imperial and international affairs, foreign trade and the like, the Great Britain Government would, under the proposed scheme, presumably include no specific representative of Scotland, and the Great Britain Departments concerned would be less likely than they are now to consult with Scottish Departments in the consideration of policy. In the domestic field the Great Britain Government, whose responsibilities would be limited to England and Wales, would again proceed without having the advice of a specific Scottish Minister in the Cabinet and their Departments, with no concern in Scotland, would be unlikely to feel themselves under any obligation to consult their Scottish opposite numbers, whom they would regard as completely independent organisations answerable to a different Parliament. The co-operation which has been built up over a period of years in all domestic affairs between English and Scottish Departments with parallel interests would accordingly be greatly weakened and would probably only continue to the extent that the Scottish Department took the initiative in consulting its opposite number in the South. The consequence might well be that domestic policy would be framed in England in the light of English conditions and Scotland would be pressed to introduce North of the Border a policy in the shaping of which it had taken no effective part.

There is probably also some danger of an expansion of bureaucracy in Scotland which would be bound to lead to criticism. If it is necessary to create a whole series of new headquarters Departments in Scotland and to erect the machinery required to support a separate Scottish Parliament, there seems no escape from the conclusion that the administrative structure would have to be considerably increased. This would not only cost money, but would divert manpower from other activities.

The financial proposals in the Convention's scheme are extremely compli-cated. Further . . . their general basis is such that the British Treasury would be unlikely to agree to them as they stand. Broadly, their object appears to be to ensure an allocation of revenue to Scotland on the most favourable terms to this country that can be devised; to pay for Scottish services, on an English standard or better, out of this allocation; and to contribute to imperial services whatever happens to be left. It might well be argued that the more reasonable approach is to share the cost of imperial services on some equitable basis between England and Scotland, leaving Scotland to raise whatever funds are required to meet the allocation so made, together with the cost of maintaining domestic services.

As regards the administration of economic affairs, it must be assumed that the Convention agree to leave to Great Britain administration the Government's share in the conduct of international trade. The industry and commerce of England and Scotland are, of course, very closely integrated and there are many firms who carry on their activities in both countries. If industry and commerce are to be subject to Great Britain administration in relation to their foreign trade and to separate Scottish administration in relation to their domestic trade, the danger of their being subject to conflicting policies and possibly to conflicting directions is apparent. There may also be some danger that English rivals may benefit from the fact that, in relation both to domestic and foreign trade, they will be working under the auspices of one major Department whose concern in the sphere of domestic trade would inevitably be to further the interests of those English firms for which it had responsibility rather than those of the Scottish firms for which it had not.

SOURCE: Scottish Record Office, Scottish Office 'Memorandum on Home Rule and the Scottish Covenant's proposals', 8.12.49. SRO HH 41/454.

NATIONAL IDENTITY

Lord Rosebery, Imperialism and Scottish National Identity

Lord Rosebery (Archibald Primrose, 5th Earl of Rosebery) was a leading Liberal politician. He campaigned for the reinstatement of the office of Scottish Secretary in the mid-1880s and was an influential figure in Scottish political circles. He was also a noted 'Liberal Imperialist' and advocated that greater use be made of both the idea of a British imperial mission and the resources of the Empire. He seemed to many to combine the qualities of both Scottish and British patriotism. He served as Prime Minister briefly in 1894 after Gladstone's retirement.

a) *The Service of the State*
You will when you go forth from these learned precincts and enter upon the actual business of life – you will have in the course of your lives to help to maintain and to build that Empire. You may think that it may be in a small and insignificant manner, not more than the coral insect within the coral reef. But recollect that the insect is essential to the reef; and it is not for any man of himself to directly measure what his direct utility may be to his country. I will tell you why you must in your way exercise those functions. The British Empire is not a centralised empire. It does not, as other empires, hinge on a single autocrat or a single parliament, but it is a vast collection of communities spread all over the world, many with their own legislatures, but all with their own governments, and, therefore, resting, in a degree which is known in no other state of which history has on record, on the intelligence and character of the individuals who compose it. Some empires have rested on armies and some on constitutions. It is the boast of the British Empire that it rests on men. For that reason it is that I speak to you to-night as men who are to have your share in the work of the Empire, small or great, humble or proud. That is – unless you go absolutely downwards – your irresistible and irrevocable function . . . I would ask you to blend some memory of this Edinburgh so sacred and beautiful to us, not, perhaps the Edinburgh of Jeffrey or Brougham, but an Edinburgh yet full of noble men and wise teachers, that you will bear away some kindling memory of this old grey city, which, though it be not the capital of the Empire, is yet, in the sense of the sacrifices that it has given to the Empire, in the truest, largest, and the highest sense an Imperial City.

b) *Questions of Empire*
An Empire such as ours requires as its first condition an imperial race – a race vigorous and industrious and intrepid. Are we rearing such a race? In the rural districts I trust we are. I meet the children near Edinburgh returning from school,

and I will match them against any children in the world. But in the great cities, in the rookeries and slums which still survive, an imperial race cannot be reared. You can scarcely produce anything in those foul nests of crime and disease but a progeny doomed from its birth to misery and ignominy. That is a rift in your cornerstone of your commonwealth, but it brings some of you directly into its service. For many here [the University of Glasgow] are reared to the service of medicine. They will be physicians, surgeons, medical officers, medical inspectors. Remember then, that where you promote health and arrest disease, where you convert an unhealthy citizen into a healthy one, where you exercise your authority to promote sanitary conditions and suppress those which are the reverse, you in doing your duty are also working for the Empire . . . Commerce, then, is a bond of Empire which this University by its training may do much to strengthen. The mercantile committee at Edinburgh demand, indeed, that to our universities shall be added a commercial faculty which would stimulate the commercial side in our secondary schools, and which would be of substantial importance in attracting to the University men who are about to enter on a commercial life . . . Our University . . . has done much, but it is well aware of its weakness. It is now appealing for aid to place itself on a proper scientific footing, a footing adequate to its position in this great commercial community, which so greatly needs and which can so usefully utilise opportunities of technical and scientific training. It will not, I think, appeal to the second city of the Empire in vain . . . Are there not thousands of lads to-day plodding away, or supposed to be plodding away, at the ancient classics and who will never make anything of those classics, and who, at the first possible moment, will cast them into space? Think of the wasted time that that implies; not all wasted perhaps, for something may have been gained in power of application, but entirely wasted in so far as available knowledge is concerned. And if you consider, as you will have to consider in the stress of competition, that the time and energy of her citizens is part of the capital of the commonwealth, all those wasted years represents a deal of loss to the Empire . . . Planting a flag here and there, or demarcating regions with a red line on a map, are vain diversions if they do not imply an unswerving purpose to develop and maintain. But maintenance requires modern methods. We are apt to forget this, and to imagine that our swaddling clothes will suffice for our maturity.

I urge you, then, to realise in your persons and studies the responsibility which rests on yourselves. You are, after all, members of that company of adventurers (used in the Elizabethan and not the modern sense) which is embarked in the business of carrying this British Empire through the twentieth century. Each of you has his share in that glorious heritage, and each of you is answerable for that share. Be, then, practical partners, intelligent partners, and so you will be in the best sense practical, intelligent, industrious imperialists. Be inspired in your various callings with the thought of the service that you can do to your country in faithfully following your profession, so that in doing private you are doing public duty too. The Church, the Law and Medicine, those chaste and venerable sisters, will, I suppose, claim most of you, and in the service of each you have ample opportunities of rendering service to the commonwealth. The Law is the ladder to Parliament; and the tribunal of appeal is, and I hope will increasingly be, a constitutional bond of Empire. The missions of the Churches, and the Churches themselves, apart from their sacred functions and home labours, which directly serve the state so far as they raise their flocks, have incalculably aided in the expansion, consolidation and civilisation of the Empire. And Medicine should tend and raise the race, on which all depends. From my point of view there is not a close in the darkest quarters of Glasgow, or a Crofter's cabin in the Hebrides, which is not a matter of imperial concern.

SOURCE: Lord Rosebery, *The Service of the State*, Presidential Address to the Associated Societies of the University of Edinburgh, October 25, 1898; Lord Rosebery, *Questions of Empire*, An address delivered as Lord Rector of the University of Glasgow, 16 November 1900.

DOCUMENT 91

Scotland: An equal partner in the Union

The Scottish Home Rule Association was formed in 1886 to act as a pressure group in the campaign for a Scottish Parliament. It was motivated by Gladstone's conversion to Irish Home Rule and the belief that if Ireland should have its own Parliament, then so should Scotland. The Association was closely involved with the Liberal Party. It had little impact on political developments, however, as the period from 1886 to 1905 was dominated by Conservative governments which were hostile to both Irish and Scottish Home Rule.

Of late years a custom has grown up of applying the names England and English not only to Britain, but also the whole Empire, its people and its institutions – a custom which practically demands that Scotsmen should cease to be Scotsmen and consent to be Englishmen, that Scotland should be blotted from the map and reappear as the Northern Counties of England, and that the Articles of the Treaty of Union, which so carefully provided for the adoption of the common name 'Britain' and 'British', should be dishonourably set aside. This practice is a deliberate attempt to defraud our country and countrymen of their Treaty Rights and Privileges, and to degrade Scotsmen from their proper historical position and make their country a mere province of England . . . Scotland's claim to honourable fulfilment by England of these Treaty obligations becomes the stronger when Scotland's share in the work of the United Kingdom is considered.

Who built up the British Empire? Save a few islands in the West Indies and the plantations in North America, which were afterwards lost through criminal folly, there were few possessions. The rise of the Empire dates from the Union. Our Highland Regiments which have fought so valiantly in every part of the world, did so to maintain the honour – not of England – but of the United Kingdom. Go where you may, and you will find Scotsmen occupying foremost places, and doing more that their proportionate share in adding to the dignity and lustre of the British name. Why then insult Scotland by speaking of Britain as England, ignoring Scotland and what she has done? . . . In all maters affecting the British Empire, we acknowledge but one interest – and in regard to our loyalty, we owe none to England and never did. Our loyalty is due solely to the British crown and British government.

SOURCE: National Library of Scotland, *A Protest by the Scottish Home Rule Association against the misuse of the terms 'England' and 'English' for 'Britain', the 'British Empire', its peoples and institutions, c.* 1890.

DOCUMENT 92

Reasons for Scottish Home Rule

The Young Scots Society was formed in 1900 following the defeat of the Liberal Party in the general election of that year. It was designed to 'ginger up' the Liberal Party and set to work organising and campaigning for the party. It was more radical than the mainstream Liberal Party.

a) *Home Rule an Imperial Necessity*
Victory for the Commons now being assured, the Young Scots Society returns to its Home Rule propaganda, and intends to push that issue with all the energy it can command. Devolution is, after the Abolition of the Lords' Veto, the most urgent reform of the time. Men of all parties are recognising that this is absolutely necessary in the interests of Imperial efficiency and progress. At present the Imperial Parliament attempts to perform the work of five Parliaments. After centuries of formal Union, uniformity of legislation for the United Kingdom . . . is as impracticable as, in the higher interests of mankind, it is undesirable. Thus each of the four nations requires separate legislation and administration. In addition to dealing with the business of four distinct peoples, the Imperial Parliament has the supervision of the affairs of a great and complex Empire, with the inevitable result that its work is imperfectly done or, in large part, entirely neglected. The Imperial Parliament cannot cope with its work, and as the burden of Empire increases rather than diminishes, Devolution has become a vital Imperial necessity . . .

b) *The Neglect of Scottish Legislation*

For years and yearsScotland has been clamouring for legislation on Land, Temperance, House-letting, Education, and Poor Law Reform, but to all these demands the Imperial Parliament turns a deaf ear – [Westminster] has no time for Scottish affairs. The continual growth of Imperial business will curtail the time for Scottish affairs . . . The Government which promoted the Scottish measures might be defeated on some item of foreign policy, and although Scotland was unanimous for these local Bills, she would be helpless, and thus the reforms she demanded might be held up for another generation. If it is wrong from an Imperial point of view so to burden Parliament that there is no time to deal comprehensively and efficiently with the affairs of Empire, it is also wrong to mix up Imperial and National affairs that the one is made to suffer at the expense of the other.

SOURCE: Young Scots Society, *Manifesto and Appeal to the Scottish People on Scottish Home Rule,* July 1911, 2–30.

DOCUMENT 93

A Scottish National Policy

From the Young Scots Handbook *(see introduction to* **Document 92***).*

At the Glasgow Conference of 1907, Scottish Home Rule and the House of Lords Reform were put in the forefront of the Society's propaganda work and a parliamentary Committee was appointed to administer a fund raised for this work . . . A most extensive and successful campaign was carried out during the next three years. This campaign is undoubtedly responsible for making home rule again a live issue in Scottish politics. At the Perth conference of 1910 the development of a *National policy* was carried further by the adoption of a resolution declaring that after the effective limitation of the power of the Lords, the key to all further legislative progress in Scotland was Scottish home rule and making Scottish home rule a test question at all parliamentary elections in Scotland . . . This Conference of Young Scots, representing the whole Society, while heartily welcoming the prospect of an Irish Home Rule Bill in the next session of Parliament and promising the same its wholehearted and united support, declares that no scheme of devolution will be satisfactory which does not as an immediate result ensure self-government to Scotland; calls on Parliamentary representatives of Scotland to demand that the Government shall introduce and pass during the present Parliament a bill to establish a legislature in Scotland to control purely Scottish affairs; and declares its intention of contesting future vacancies in Scottish constituencies, if necessary, with candidates who will specifically support such a demand. The most satisfactory event falling to be noted is the remarkable progress which has been made during the past year in the cause of home rule . . . A pledge from every candidate for a Scottish constituency to insist on the granting of home rule to Scotland must be secured. Only by the formation of a strong Scottish Nationalist party can Scotland hope to secure adequate recognition of her needs.

SOURCE: Extracts from the *Young Scots Handbook*, 1911.

DOCUMENT 94

Labour and Scottish Home Rule

The Labour Party and the Trade Union movement became more powerful in Scottish society during the war. The Labour Party in Scotland had been committed to Home Rule since its inception in the 1880s.

Now that the war is ended and an era of reconstruction begun, Scottish problems require the concentration of Scottish brains and machinery on their solution. Your Committee is of opinion that a determined effort be made to secure home rule for Scotland in the first session of Parliament, and the question should be taken out of the hands of place hunting lawyers and vote catching politicians by the political and industrial efforts of the Labour Party in Scotland which should co-ordinate all its efforts to this end, using any legitimate means, political and industrial, to secure the establishment of a Scottish parliament upon a purely democratic basis, as briefly outlined below . . . Scotland, though temporarily deprived, without the consent of her people, and by corrupt means, in 1707, of the exercise of her right to self-determination, is presently, as anciently, entitled to legislate for the government of her National affairs in a Parliament of her own, the full right of that exercise is hereby restored.

Be it enacted that
1   The Secretary for Scotland, for the time being is charged with the responsibility of making necessary arrangements to summon a parliament forthwith to meet in Edinburgh.
2   Which Parliament shall be elected, on the basis of adult suffrage accruing at the age of twenty one, without distinction of sex, by the divisions within the borders of Scotland, which under the Representation of the People Act (1918), elect members to the Imperial parliament.

3   Men or Women of the age of twenty one years and upwards shall have for electoral purposes one vote each in relation to the Scottish Parliament and each of the local governing bodies appertaining to the area in which they are resident.

4   All other qualifications or disqualifications for the vote as contained in the Representation of the People Act (1918), are not to be applied so far as Scottish national and local government are concerned that (a) a person shall not be disqualified from being registered as a parliamentary or local government elector by reason that he or some person for whose maintenance he is responsible had received poor relief or alms, (b) that he or she has been, on proper medical certification, declared to be presently insane.

5   All electors resident at a greater distance than one mile from the polling station or medically certified as unfit to take the journey on foot shall have the option of exercising the right of voting in the manner presently prescribed for those on the list of 'absent voters'.

6   The elections shall be taken on the system of proportional representation, as applied at the elections to the Education Authorities of Scotland.

7   Any person entitled to the Parliamentary vote shall be entitled to be nominated for any public election to any representative governing body, whether resident in the area or not; providing that he or she shall, on nomination, sign an undertaking to attend, if elected, at not less than ninety per cent of the sittings, including sittings of any committee to which she or he may have been appointed. Failing such attendance, unless through illness or other sufficient cause certified to and accepted by the House, the seat shall at the end of the administrative year be declared vacant and a nominee of the same public connections shall be co-opted instead.

8   Public representatives shall be paid all necessary allowances to meet all reasonable expenditure upon travelling and maintenance, because of their attendance upon public duty, the rate of such remuneration to be fixed by statute.

9   A candidate for the Scottish parliament shall be required to deposit with the returning officer a sum of £20 along with the nomination papers, which money shall be returned to him at the declaration of the poll in the event of his having polled 500 or more preference votes.

10   Subject to the Constitutional veto, the Scottish house of parliament shall have powers to deal with any Scottish matters, including the levying of taxes, hitherto within the jurisdiction of the Imperial Parliament at Westminster, except such as determine the control and equipment of the Army, Navy, Civil, Diplomatic, Dominion, Colonial, and other Imperial Services.

SOURCE: Labour Party (Scottish Council) 1919, *Home Rule for Scotland: Report of the Fifth Annual Conference.*

DOCUMENT 95

John Buchan and the danger of Scottish Nationalism

John Buchan was a leading Unionist intellectual in Scotland. He was also a famous novelist. Buchan, like Rosebery, combined an acute sense of Scottish patriotism with a commitment to the ideas and values of the British imperial mission.

It [Scottish nationalism] is also found among young people who are hard headed, practical and ambitious, who are shaping out for themselves careers in medicine and law and in business. Very few of that class would agree for a moment to any of the schemes of home rule at present put forward, but they all feel this dissatisfaction. They all believe that something is wrong with Scotland and that it is the business of Scotsmen to put it right . . . This feeling has spread also to certain classes who have left their youth behind. The discontent of some of the small burghs with the Local Government Act of 1929 has caused many people, to whom home rule would have been an anathema, to question in measured terms the wisdom of the whole present system. The feeling has not gone far in the working class. They have grimmer things to think about. On the whole it has not affected the business community to any large extent. But it has infected a very important class who do a good deal of the thinking of the nation. I would have this House remember that it is not any scheme put forward that matters. Those schemes may be crude and foolish enough in all conscience. It is the instinct behind it that matters and unless we face that instinct honestly and fairly, we may drive it underground and presently it will appear in some irrational and dangerous form.

SOURCE: Speech by John Buchan in the House of Commons, 22 November 1932, *Parliamentary Papers* 272 1932, col 262.

DOCUMENT 96

Unionism and the effect of Socialism on Scottish National Identity

The Scottish Unionist Party (in 1965 the Party incorporated Conservative into its title) always made great play of the notion that the Union between Scotland and England was an equal partnership between two nations.

Union is not amalgamation. Scotland is a nation. Those who advocated and carried through the policy of Union recognised this, and made many most thoughtful and intentional provisions to secure her position . . . It is only since 1945, under the first Socialist majority, that we have seen the policy of amalgamation superseding that of Union. This must inevitably result from the fulfilment of the Socialist creed, which is basically one of amalgamation and centralisation. To this policy we are fundamentally opposed . . . The effect of the Socialist policy has been to transfer the management and control of the State-owned industries of Scotland to Whitehall. The act of Union never contemplated this unnatural state of affairs. Those who drafted it did not foresee this new despotism. The concentration of all power at the centre, the denial of effective action to any authority except the central one, these are symptoms of the disease of Socialism.

SOURCE: National Library of Scotland, *Scottish control of Scottish affairs: Unionist policy* 1949, 1–2.

THE HIGHLANDS

DOCUMENT 97

Sir John M'Neill on the problems of the Western Highlands and Islands, 1851

Sir John M'Neill (1795-1883) was a career civil servant who had served in India and Persia. He was born on Colonsay and was a Gaelic speaker. During the famine he had been in close contact with Charles Trevelyan, who had been in overall charge of famine relief in Ireland and in the Scottish Highlands. M'Neill was the first Chairman of the Board of Supervision, the body established to oversee the administration of the new Scottish Poor Law in 1845. The government had been extremely reluctant to become involved directly in Highland social administration and M'Neill was sent north to investigate the problems of the area and come up with recommendations which would obviate future intervention. M'Neill's investigation created a panic among landowners that an 'able bodied poor law' was about to be introduced, but M'Neill's conclusions favoured assisted emigration as a 'solution' and the report led to the legislation of 1851 and the establishment of the Highlands and Islands Emigration Society, in which both M'Neill and Trevelyan were heavily involved.

Of the various measures that have at different times been proposed, on speculative grounds, by intelligent and benevolent men, to enable the inhabitants of those districts to produce the means of subsistence, all that are not impracticable appear to have been tried, and have hitherto failed. Where position or facility of communication long established, has led to increased intercourse with other parts of the country, and to the habit of seeking employment at a distance, or where the population have long relied more on other occupations than cultivating their own lands for the means of living, though less has been expended for their employment at home, the condition of the population generally is not so depressed as where proprietors have expended the largest amount, and the inhabitants have been more dependant on the produce of their crofts. In every parish, with one or two exceptions, men of all classes and denominations concur unanimously in declaring it to be impossible, by any application of the existing resources, or by any remunerative application of extraneous resources, to provide for the permanent subsistence of the whole of the present inhabitants; and state their conviction that the population cannot be made self-sustaining unless a portion removes from the parish . . . The working classes in many parishes are convinced that the emigration of a part of their number, affords the only prospect of escape from a position otherwise hopeless; and in many cases individuals have earnestly prayed for aid to emigrate . . . It has rarely happened that so many persons, between whom there was or could have been no previous concert or intercourse, and whose opinions on many important subjects are so much at variance, have concurred in considering any one measure indispensable to the welfare of the community; and there does not appear to be any good reason for supposing that this almost unanimous opinion is not well founded.

There is good reason to hope that this season will pass away, not certainly without painful suffering, but without loss of any life in consequence of the cessation of eleemosynary aid. But if henceforward the population is to depend on the local resources, some fearful calamity will probably occur before many years, unless a portion of the inhabitants of those parishes remove to where they can find the means of subsistence in greater abundance, and with greater certainty, than they can find them where they now are.

SOURCE: Report to the Board of Supervision by Sir John M'Neill, G.C.B., on the Western Highlands and Islands *Parliamentary Papers* XXVI 1851, xxxv; xlvii.

DOCUMENT 98

The Napier Commission report into the conditions of the crofters of the Highlands and Islands of Scotland, 1884

The Napier Commission report has usually been interpreted as a grand theoretical statement on the organisation of Highland society. The fact that its recommendations were overtaken by events and ignored by the government, which looked to Ireland for precedents in land legislation, has contributed to this perception. The section of the report which dealt with land was drawn up by the Chairman in the absence of consensus among his commissioners. Indeed, several of them repudiated this section of the report, some in formal notes of dissent, others more privately, and more vociferously. Security of tenure for the whole crofting community was rejected and assisted emigration of cottars was recommended. These are only two of the most important differences between the report and the subsequent legislation of 1886.

. . . it is in our opinion desirable to seek a basis of operation in the customs of the country; and we believe that such a basis may be found in the recognition of the Highland township as a distinct agricultural area or unit, endowing it at the same time with certain immunities and powers by which it may attain stability, improvement, and expansion.

We have no hesitation in affirming that to grant at this moment to the whole mass of poor tenants in the Highlands and Islands fixity of tenure in their holdings, uncontrolled management of those holdings, and free sale of their tenant-right, good-will, and improvements, would be to perpetuate social evils of a dangerous character. It would in some districts simply accelerate the subdivision and exhaustion of the soil, promote the reckless increase of the people, aggravate the indigence, squalor, and lethargy which too much abound already, and multiply the contingencies of destitution and famine which even now recur from time to time, and are ever impending. The proper basis for agricultural improvement in the crofting districts we deem to lie in the right of a respectable and competent occupier to claim from the owner an improving lease.

It may be objected to the scheme which has been proposed, that the protection and encouragements afforded to the higher class of crofters above the level of the £6 line are withheld from those of an inferior condition, forming in most localities, we regret to say, the vast majority, and who may need such safeguards equally or more. This must be admitted. The poorer sort are here endowed with no formal security against eviction or excessive rents. The inequality of treatment is manifest and may appear unjust. If we allow it we do so not from a want of sympathy for the class excluded – we accept an evil to avoid a greater evil still. To invest the most humble and helpless class of agricultural tenants with immunities and rights which ought to go hand in hand with the expansive improvement of the dwelling and the soil, would tend to fix them in a condition from which they ought to be resolutely though gently withdrawn. These people ought either to pass as crofters to new holdings of a higher value, or take their position among the cottars as labourers, mechanics, or fishermen, with a cottage and an allotment, or migrate to other seats of labour here, or emigrate to other countries.

SOURCE: Report of the Commissioners of Inquiry into the Condition of the Crofters and Cottars in the Highlands and Islands of Scotland, *Parliamentary Papers* 1884, xxxii, 17; 33; 39.

DOCUMENT 99

Social unrest in the Isle of Skye, 1882

The Celtic Magazine *was edited by Alexander Mackenzie who was a well-known journalist, historian and genealogist. During the 1870s it concentrated on articles of a historical and cultural nature and when venturing into more controversial political areas confined itself to linguistic and educational issues. Mackenzie, however, regarded himself as a representative of crofter opinion and as a radical on the land issue. This extract was one of the first public comments on the outbreak of the Crofters' War at Braes in April 1882 by a Highland journal sympathetic to the crofters and it shows awareness of the grievances which produced the protests at Braes but also a desire to keep the protest within respectable limits.*

That we were and still are on the verge of a social revolution in the Isle of Skye is beyond question, and those who have any influence with the people, as well as those lairds and factors who have the interest of the population virtually in their keeping, will incur a grave responsibility at a critical time like this unless the utmost care is taken to keep the action of the aggrieved tenants within the law, and on the other hand grant to the people in friendly and judicious spirit, material concessions in response to grievance respecting any real hardships which can be proved to exist . . .

The most material grievance, however, as well as the most exasperating, is the gradual but certain encroachment made on the present holdings. The pasture is taken from the crofters piecemeal; their crofts are in many cases sub-divided to make room for those gradually evicted from other places, in a manner to avoid public attention, to make room for sheep or deer or both. The people see that they are being gradually but surely driven to the sea, and that if they do not resist in time they will ultimately and at no distant date be driven into it, or altogether expelled from their native land. A little more pressure in this direction and no amount of argument or advice will keep the people from taking the law into their own hands and resisting it by force. The time for argument has already gone. The powers that be hitherto refused to listen to the voice of reason, and the consequence is that scarcely any one can now be found on either side who will wait to argue whether or not a change is necessary. It is admitted on all hands that a change must take place at no distant date, and the only question at present being considered is, What is to be the nature of that change?

SOURCE: *Celtic Magazine*, May 1882, 335–6.

The Crofters' Holdings (Scotland) Act, 1886

*The Crofters' Act was modelled closely on the Irish Land Act of 1881 and
not on the recommendations of the Napier Commission published in 1884.
An attempt had been made in 1885 to pass a Crofters' Bill but this attempt
failed as the Liberal government fell in the summer of that year. The second
bill was largely the work of Sir George Otto Trevelyan, the Secretary for
Scotland. The act provided for security of tenure for all 'Crofters' in the
seven crofting counties provided they met certain conditions regarding the
payment of their rents, the prohibition of subdivision and sub-letting, and
the upkeep of their land and buildings. A Crofters' Commission was
established to administer the Act and to adjudicate on fair rents for crofters.
The crofters' movement held that the Act was deficient as it contained only
very limited provisions to increase the amount of land available to crofters.
Much debate had surrounded the geographical scope of the Act and the
definition of a 'crofting parish'.*

A crofter shall not be removed from the holding of which he is tenant except in
consequence of the breach of one or more of the conditions following (in this Act
referred to as statutory conditions), but he shall have no power to assign his
tenancy.

The landlord or the crofter may apply to the Crofters' Commission to fix the
fair rent to be paid by such crofter to the landlord for the holding, and thereupon
the Crofters' Commission, after hearing the parties and considering all the
circumstances of the case, holding and district, and particularly after taking all into
consideration any permanent or unexhausted improvements on the holding and
suitable thereto which have been executed to paid for by the crofter or his
predecessors in the same family may determine what is such fair rent, and
pronounce an order accordingly.

It shall be lawful for any five or more crofters resident on neighbouring
holdings in a crofting parish, where any landlord or landlords after application
made to him or them have refused to let to such crofters available land on
reasonable terms for enlarging the holdings of such crofters, to apply to the
Crofters' Commission setting forth that in the said parish or in an adjacent crofting
parish there is land available for the enlargement of such holdings which they are
willing to take on lease, but which the landlord or landlords refuse to let on
reasonable terms.

In this Act 'crofter' means any person who at the passing of this Act is tenant
of a holding from year to year, who resides on his holding, the annual rent of which
does not exceed thirty pounds in money, and which is situated in a crofting parish
and the successors of such person in the holding, being his heirs or legatees.

'Crofting parish' means a parish in which there are at the commencement of
this Act, or have been within eighty years prior thereto, holdings consisting of

arable land held with a right of pasturage in common with others, and in which there still are tenants of holdings from year to year, who reside on their holdings, the annual rent of which respectively does not exceed thirty pounds in money, at the commencement of this Act.

SOURCE: *Crofters' Holdings (Scotland) Act*, 1886, Sections 1; 6(1); 11; 34.

DOCUMENT 101

The differences between the Highlands and the Special Areas

The context of the comments in this extract is the debate within government as to the best response to the report of the Hilleary Commission of 1938. One of the recommendations of the Commission was the appointment of a Highland Development Commissioner, similar to the Special Areas Commissioner, who had responsibility for areas of high unemployment under earlier legislation. The government was not keen to appoint such a person and the memo details the perceived differences between the Highlands and the Special Areas of industrial Scotland. The details of the report were not acted on immediately because of the outbreak of war but a body very like the one recommended towards the end of the memo was created in 1949 as the Advisory Panel on the Highlands.

The two problems are, of course, different. The Special Areas have a long industrial history related to a few large industries, and when these industries became subject to severe and sudden depression the Areas suffered acutely. They required special and speedy treatment in the spheres of public works, social service and diversification of industry if their condition was again to compare favourably with more fortunate districts. This is not the Highland problem. This, unlike the problem of the Special Areas, is as old as the physical conditions which gave rise to it, and unless the whole economy of the Highlands is revolutionised by the introduction of big industry – a course the Committee deprecates – its fundamental characteristics will persist. The question is how to enable a scattered but huddled population to live tolerably under natural conditions probably more difficult than those existing in any other part of Great Britain. For years the special features of Highland life have been recognised and its needs reflected in many statutes. As a result of state action and expenditure in many directions, there is little doubt that life in the Highlands today is more tolerable than it has been previously. The people are better housed, better educated, better doctored, and thanks to the benefit of social legislation they have more cash. This does not mean that the Crofter's life may not still be difficult and that further efforts to improve his economic position and in this way to make his lot more attractive to the younger generation may not be desirable, but the peculiar and temporary urgency of the Special Areas problem is non-existent. Thus it is largely true that the Highland problem is different in kind from that of the Special Areas and does not contain the same elements of urgency. If the proposal for a Commissioner is rejected, the question remains whether any step can be taken in order to facilitate the consideration of Highland problems by the government. It may be noted that today there is no distinctive organ of government dealing with Highland affairs exclusively or as a whole. It may, therefore, be argued firstly, that government departments with their manifold activities may tend to overlook at times the special needs of the north and secondly that the government has within its sphere no permanent body which considers Highland policy as a whole, and to which government can turn for advice. In these circumstances consideration might be given to the appointment by the Secretary of State of a Highlands and Islands Advisory Council, representing the various aspects of Highland life which come within the cognizance of government.

SOURCE: Scottish Record Office, Memo Concerning Highland Development Commissioner, 1939, Development Department Files, DD 15/12.

Finlay J MacDonald on Highland life in the inter-war years

The distinguished journalist Finlay J MacDonald published his memoirs in the 1980s. The volumes are a valuable source of information on Highland life in the inter-war period. They are not merely collections of anecdotes concerning amusing characters in a crofting and weaving township in Harris, but they also shed light on the difficulties Gaelic-speaking children had when faced by an education system which only understood English. Further, they demonstrate clearly the perception held universally in the Highlands at the time that to 'get on' one had to leave the area. The difficult economic circumstances of the inter-war period emerge clearly from the books.

The only reason why we, in our new village, were aware of the recovery of the thirties probably more sharply than most of the rest of the kingdom was because a whole avalanche of progress and novelty overwhelmed us in a very short space of time. We were on the periphery of modernization in the early thirties, still without regular public transport, without electricity or gas, without running water in the vast majority of our homes, with 82 percent of the population around us suffering from tuberculosis, with no radio and with only the most rudimentary telephone service. Having advanced so little we couldn't slip back so very far, and what we were missing most were luxuries and conveniences to which we had barely had time to become accustomed. We had had, after all, a major local slump of our own in the mid-twenties when Lord Leverhume's great plans for the industrialization of Harris had collapsed overnight, and all that remained of them now was the decaying town of Leverburgh – named after the great magnate.

When the world and the nearest bit of it to us, the mainland, began to pull out of the Depression, the effects of the mainland recovery had no immediate impact on us; but when it began to have, it began to have it very noticeably. When the cities could again afford fish, the fishing of the Northlands boomed; when the cities began to afford luxuries again and when the nation began to export, the Harris Tweed industry boomed: it is an industry that collapsed and boomed very rapidly in those days, and because it was so cottage-based its fluctuations were felt immediately. And then, within the space of a couple of years, radio, the aeroplane, daily bus service, mobile vans, and people to teach us how to make the most of life all began to descend on us at the same time. The markets of the south were obviously bursting at the seams and Calum the Post's van began to sag on its springs under the weight of advertising that poured in on our newly discovered land. Even the margarine companies convinced themselves that there was a market in a part of the world where every house had at least one cow, and most frequently two, and an unending supply of free fresh butter. The remarkable thing was that the margarine companies had spectacular success, not because people particularly liked their products but because people liked the varieties of gifts and bonuses that they were prepared to dish out in a bid to cut each others' throats and profits.

SOURCE: Finlay J Macdonald 1983 *Crotal and White*, London (Macdonald), 136–7.

INDUSTRIAL SCOTLAND

DOCUMENT 103

The manufacture of iron

During 1868, The Scotsman carried a series of articles by David Bremner on 'The Industries of Scotland'. Edited and revised, these articles were subsequently published in book form to create what has become a valuable source for the industrial historian. While acknowledging the appalling pollution and the exhausting and dangerous toil of the workforce, the extract conveys something of the awe with which the great works were regarded and the excitement engendered by the rise of industry in Scotland.

The most valuable deposits of ironstone are in Lanarkshire and Ayrshire, and in the former county two-thirds of the pig-iron made in Scotland is produced. The blast furnaces are chiefly concentrated in the vicinity of Coatbridge, Airdrie, and Wishaw, all of which towns were rapidly raised to importance by the development of the mineral treasures which lay beneath and around them. Coatbridge stands within a crescent of blast furnaces, and in the town are a large number of rolling mills, forges, and tube works, the hundred chimneys of which form quite a forest of brickwork capped with fire.

Though Coatbridge is a most interesting seat of industry, it is anything but beautiful. Dense clouds of smoke roll over it incessantly, and impart to all the buildings a peculiarly dingy aspect. A coat of black dust overlies everything, and in a few hours the visitor finds his complexion considerably deteriorated by the flakes of soot which fill the air, and settle on his face. To appreciate Coatbridge, it must be visited at night, when it presents a most extraordinary and – when seen for the first time – startling spectacle. From the steeple of the parish church, which stands on a considerable eminence, the flames of no fewer than fifty blast furnaces may be seen. In the daytime these flames are pale and unimpressive; but when night comes on, they appear to burn more fiercely, and gradually there is developed in the sky a lurid glow similar to that which hangs over a city when a great conflagration is in progress. For half-a-mile round each group of furnaces, the country is as well illumined as during full moon, and the good folks of Coatbridge have their streets lighted without tax or trouble. There is something grand in even a distant view of the furnaces; but the effect is much enhanced when they are approached to within a hundred yards or so. The flames then have a positively fascinating effect. No production of the pryotechnist can match their wild gyrations. Their form is ever changing, and the variety of their movements is endless. Now they shoot far upward, and breaking short off, expire among the smoke; again spreading outward, they curl over the lips of the furnace, and dart through the doorways, as if determined to annihilate the bounds within which they are confined; then they sink low into the crater, and come forth with renewed strength in the shape of great tongues of fire, which sway backward and forward, as if seeking with a fierce eagerness something to devour.

The most extensive ironmasters in Scotland are Messrs Baird and Co., who own forty-two blast furnaces, employ nine thousand men and boys, and produce about three hundred thousand tons of pig-iron per annum, or one-fourth of the entire quantity made north of the Tweed. Twenty-six of their furnaces are situated in various parts of Ayrshire, and the remaining sixteen are concentrated at Gartsherrie, in the neighbourhood of Coatbridge. Gartsherrie Ironworks are the largest in Scotland, and it is stated, there is only one establishment in Britain which has a greater number of furnaces. The quantity of pig-iron made is one hundred thousand tons per annum, and the number of men and boys connected with the works is three thousand two hundred. More than a thousand tons of coals are consumed every twenty-four hours; and, as showing how well chosen is the site of the works, it may be mentioned that nineteen-twentieths of the coal required is obtained within a distance of half-a-mile from the furnaces. One coal-pit is situated close to the furnaces, and has been in operation since the works were established, forty years ago. The coal from this pit is conveyed to the furnaces by means of a self-acting incline. Most of the ironstone was at one time obtained from pits in the neighbourhood, but now it has to be brought from a distance of from two to twenty miles; and a complete system of railways connects the pits with the works. The total length of the railways is about fifty miles, and the traffic is carried on by means of six locomotives and an immense number of trucks. The establishment is also connected with the great railway systems of the country, and possesses additional facilities for transport in a branch of the Monklands Canal, which has been carried through the centre of the works. For the canal traffic, there is a fleet of eighteen barges, of about sixty tons each; and eight of these are screw steamers. A great proportion of the manufactured iron is sent out by the canal.

As the Gartsherrie Ironworks have a wide-spread reputation for producing iron of a superior quality, and are among the best organised manufactories in the country, a description of them may be interesting.

The furnaces, sixteen in number, stand in two rows, one on each side of the canal, and about forty yards distant from it. A constant supply of coal and ironstone can be reckoned upon, and therefore only a small stock is kept at the works. The mineral trains are worked with unfailing regularity, and their cargoes are deposited conveniently for immediate use. There is thus no superfluous shovelling about of the materials, nor is any expense incurred by piling them into heaps. The proportions of ironstone, coal, and limestone, laid down are exactly what are required in the process of smelting. Manual labour has, by a variety of ingenious appliances, been reduced to a minimum, and the amount of waste is infinitesimal. Everything is done according to a well-defined system, and nothing connected with the works is considered to be too insignificant to merit attention. No heaps of rubbish are allowed to accumulate, no scraps of iron or cinder lie about, and every nook and cranny about the vast place is as tidily kept as it can possibly be. The workmen are liberally treated, but they must do their work carefully and well. Negligence and irregularity are unfailingly punished, while merit is as certainly rewarded. All the men employed about the furnaces, even the firemen and engineers of the blast engines, are paid according to the quantity and quality of iron produced. This arrangement is found to work admirably, as each man knows that, by attending to his work, he is not only putting money into the pockets of his fellow-labourers, but also improving his own earnings.

Before the ironstone is ready for smelting it has to be calcined, which operation is performed at the pits. The object of calcining is to separate carbonic acid, water, sulphur, and other deleterious substances, which are volatile at a red heat; and it is performed in this way: – A layer of rough coal is first laid down, and on that the ore, mixed with a certain quantity of small coal, is piled. The blackband ironstone, as it contains a large proportion of carbon, requires less coal to calcine it than the clayband. When the heap is completed, fire is applied to the windward side, and combustion goes on gradually until the desired effect is produced. When the ore cools, it is ready for the furnace; but when the heat has been too intense, the ore is found to have run into large masses, the breaking up of which takes a considerable amount of labour.

Having been built at different periods, the Gartsherrie furnaces are of various patterns. The general shape is cylindrical, the diameter twenty-two feet, and the height sixty feet. The Nelson Monument, on Calton Hill, Edinburgh, would, were it less lofty, bear a close resemblance to one of the most recently erected furnaces. The furnace is fed from the top, and, in order to protect the 'fillers,' the mouth of it is surrounded by a light wall of brick, pierced with convenient openings. This brick wall is so much thinner than the main wall of the furnace on which it stands, that a gallery or footway several feet in width is left clear all round. Externally, there are four arched recesses in the base of the furnace, three of which are occupied by the 'tuyeres,' or pipes conveying the 'blast;' while the fourth contains a doorway by which the 'slag' is drawn off, and also the opening through which the molten iron is discharged. The interior of the furnace consists of a circular cavity, seven and a half feet in diameter at the lower part or hearth. At a height of five or six feet from the bottom of the hearth, the cavity begins to increase in diameter, until, at half the height of the furnace, it measures eighteen feet across. It is then gradually contracted, and at the top the diameter is eleven feet. The materials with which the furnace is fed are roasted ore, coal, and limestone. The proportions of these vary according to their quality. In some cases, a small quantity of red-iron ore or hematite is used along with the blackband ironstone, and then the portions of what are called a 'charge' are these: – Coal, about 10 cwt.; roasted ore, 6½ cwt.; red ore, ½ cwt.; and lime, 2⅝ cwt. About sixty 'charges' are thrown into the furnace in the course of twelve hours, and at six o'clock in the morning and at six at night the furnace is 'tapped' and the iron run off. The chemical changes undergone by the materials introduced into the furnace are thus described: – The iron ore consists of iron, oxygen, and sand, and the object of the iron smelter is to separate the two latter substances from the former. The coal introduced has two functions to fulfil – in part it is burned so as to raise the contents of the furnace to such a high temperature that they will be enabled to act on each other; and, at the same time, it carries away the oxygen which was originally in combination with the iron in the roasted ore. The lime plays the part of a flux, and combines with the sandy matter to form a slag. During the whole operation, hot air is being constantly forced in the lower part of the furnace, so as to aid in the necessary combustion. The roasted iron ore being thus deprived of its oxygen by the coal, and of its sand by the lime, allows the other constituent – the iron – to trickle down through the mass of red-hot cinders to the lower part or hearth of the furnace.

In front of each furnace is a level piece of ground covered with coarse sand, in which before the 'tapping' takes place a number of small furrows are formed. These communicate with larger channels leading from the opening in the furnace; and when the iron is let out, it runs along the main channels in a glowing, bubbling stream, and distributes itself into all the hollows. The large channels are called 'sows,' and the small ones 'pigs;' hence the term 'pig-iron.' Two men are employed to feed each furnace. One fills half a charge of coal into a large iron barrow, and the other half a charge of the other materials into a second barrow. The men and the barrows reach the staging communicating with the mouth of the furnace by means of a hydraulic lift. The coal is thrown in first, and the other materials immediately afterwards. The occupation of the 'fillers' appears to be a somewhat dangerous one, as the flames at times shoot out upon, and almost surround them. Two men are employed at the hearth scooping out the slag and cinders with a huge spoon suspended from a crane, and from time to time stirring up the contents of the furnace. This is very severe labour, and the faces of the men engaged in it have a half-roasted appearance. The slag is poured into iron trucks, and, when it consolidates, is wheeled away to be emptied on the waste heap – which, it may be mentioned, contains as much material as would build a copy of the Great Pyramid. The pig moulds are formed in the sand by boys, the operation being a very simple one.

Up till about forty years ago the air forced into blast-furnaces was cold, and the process of smelting was slow, and also costly, in consequence of the great quantity of coal that was required. In 1827, Mr J. B. Neilson, engineer of the Glasgow Gas-Works, conceived the idea of heating the air before injecting it into the furnace; and two years afterwards a most successful trial was given to the invention at the Clyde Ironworks. With the cold blast coke had to be used, and 8 tons $1\frac{1}{4}$cwt. of coal converted into coke was required to reduce one ton of iron. It was found that when heated air was employed the coal might be used raw, and that 2 tons $13\frac{1}{4}$ cwt. was sufficient to smelt a ton of iron, including 8 cwt. required for heating the air. This discovery gave an extraordinary impetus to the iron trade, and the patentee and his partners are said to have realised L.300,000 by the invention. At Gartsherrie there are three immense engines for generating the blast – two for one range of furnaces, and one for the other. The engines are on the beam principle, and their united 'duty' is equal to about 500 horse power. The steam cylinder of the largest is five and a half feet in diameter, and ten feet deep, and the air cylinder is ten feet in diameter and depth. The air cylinders are simply gigantic pumps, which force the air into receivers, whence it flows at an equal pressure through the tubes of the heating oven, and into the furnace. By passing through the oven the temperature of the air is raised to 800°. It has been calculated that the quantity of air thrown into a blast-furnace in full work exceeds in weight all the solid material used in smelting.

In the vicinity of Gartsherrie there are about five hundred houses belonging to Messrs Baird & Co., and occupied by their workmen. Nearly all the houses have two apartments, and a few have a third room. A bit of garden ground is attached to each house, and all are supplied with water and gas at a cheap rate. The miners get as much coal as they require without payment – only they must dig it out for themselves; and the other workmen are charged only 3s. 6d. for a cartload. Liberal provision is made for the education of the children of the workpeople. There are three schools in direct connection with the works, each being divided into separate apartments for infants, boys, and girls. The workmen seem to appreciate highly all that has been done for their welfare, and few of them leave the place. They own one of the most successful co-operative stores in the country. It is managed by a committee of the workmen, but its prosperity is in a great measure owing to the fostering care of the employers, who, however, have no interest in the concern beyond seeing that it is properly conducted. There are seven hundred members in the society, nearly all of whom are heads of families, and the business done amounts to about L.1200 a-month. In addition to general grocery goods, wines, spirits, butcher meat, and potatoes, are sold in the store.

SOURCE: David Bremner, *The Industries of Scotland, Their Rise, Progress and Present Condition* (originally *The Scotsman* 1868, first presented in book form by A & C Black, 1869, and reprinted, with new introduction by John Butt and Ian Donnachie, 1969). Extract relating to the 'The Manufacture of Iron', Butt/Donnachie edition, New York (Augustus M Kelley), 35–40.

The Brassert Report of 1929

Confronted by terrible market conditions throughout much of the 1920s, the major Scottish iron and steel manufacturers feverishly sought salvation for their firms by price-fixing agreements, methods of limiting output, amalgamation and the pursuit of government protection; but the most radical solution to the industry's problems was envisaged by the American firm of consulting engineers, H A Brassert & Co of Chicago. Commissioned by a leading Scottish industrialist, Lord Weir of Eastwood, on behalf of a number of companies, Brassert's produced a report which argued that only a fully integrated iron and steel-making plant built on the Clyde would permit the rehabilitation and long-term survival of the Scottish iron and steel industry. The report, sent to Lord Weir in May 1929, was prefaced by the letter reproduced below. Only now, with the disappearance of this once great Scottish industry, can its prescience be fully appreciated.

Dear Lord Weir

Having completed our investigation of the Scottish iron and steel industry, we beg to give you herewith a résumé of our conclusions and recommendations, pertaining particularly to the immediate problems, the solution of which you entrusted to us.

As I told you the other day, we are strongly impressed with the fact that the Scottish iron and steel industry is intrinsically based on a sound foundation. Nature has endowed it with a plentiful and high grade supply of fuel, with a geographic location which makes possible the assembly with it of the best ores from the world's markets to replace the local ores which have become exhausted. These natural advantages are combined with a large and industrious population in its immediate vicinity in which the fitness to do mechanical work has become pre-eminent through generations of training, with very large home markets for the very products which form the bulk of the Scottish steel production and with shipping facilities overseas which cannot be surpassed.

Unfortunately, these advantages while utilized in the past century in the best manner then apparent, have not been followed up through progressive development in more recent times. The basis of the industry, the production of low cost pig iron, was allowed to fade away with the exhaustion of the local fuel and ore supply upon which the original blast furnace plants were founded. The proximity of tide water harbours to the centre of population and the reserves of coking coal, and the opportunity these harbours afford for cheap assembly of ore and fuel for the manufacture of pig iron on tide water were not utilized. Instead large expenditures were made for increased steel and plate production at existing plants, though unfavourably located. True, that a great deal of this was due to the pressure of war. We are greatly impressed with the excellence of some of the departmental improvements which have been made, and we see in the works no evidence of lack of ingenuity and of capacity to deal with large units and progressive methods. We remember that the great American iron and steel industry was very largely conceived, constructed and developed by men from Scotland, and we believe that a plant built on the Clyde according to modern principles from the assembly of fuel and ore down to the finished product, will be operated as efficiently and economically as any modern plant could be anywhere in the world.

If the rehabilitation of the Scottish iron and steel industry is not undertaken in the broad spirit which we have assumed and by concentration of its basic production in the most favoured location, the Clyde, we believe that it is doomed, sooner or later, to failure. Developments are taking place elsewhere which will hasten the economic collapse of steel industries which are not soundly entrenched. Some of these, because they no longer have the proper basis, cannot escape the inevitable result, but the Scottish iron and steel industry, we repeat, can be remade into one of the soundest, as clearly shown by the costs of production which we estimate will be realized with a modern plant situated on the Clyde.

Yours very truly,

HA Brassert

SOURCE: Letter from HA Brassert & Co, Consulting Engineers, to Lord Weir of Eastwood, concerning the manufacture of iron and steel (in Scotland), 16 May 1929.

DOCUMENT 105

'A real harum scarum crowd': Shipyard riveters

The great liners, naval and merchant vessels for which the Clyde became famous, were to the end largely built by labour-intensive techniques. Therein lay both the strength of the industry and its weakness. This extract provides an evocative glimpse of a world we have lost and represents the value of oral history in the recreation of the lives of those who, until recently, constituted the workforce of Scotland's heavy industries.

The metallic din which characterised shipyards before 1940 was the sound of manual rather than mechanised work, of hand rather than power-driven tools. This was particularly true of the riveters. The riveters fastened plates and beams onto the ship's skeleton by hammering red hot metal rivets to make a watertight connection. A manual riveting squad consisted of four members: a left-handed riveter, a right-handed riveter, a holder-on and a boy rivet heater. Before the widespread introduction of welding during World War Two, the way in which riveting work was performed changed little from the nineteenth century:

> You had a furnace and the boy put five or six rivets in the fire; he had a bag of rivets at the side of his fire. He throws the hot rivet to the holder-on and he picks up the hot rivet, sparking hot, and puts it through the hole, rams it through wi' a back-hammer. The riveter drives it in wi' alternate blows on the outside of the shell and that way you fill up every hole wi' rivets.

Riveting was a physically rather than technically demanding trade. Hull riveting involved long runs of identical work; simple hammering repeated time after time. But because the ship's internal structures were also riveted, riveters had to be capable of coping with considerable variations in their job, often in awkward corners in which it was impossible to stand upright or maintain the natural rhythm of their trade:

> In the bulkheads you could be bent nearly double and riveting heavy beams and plates. That was twice as hard as ordinary shell riveting. You had to work just as fast because the rivet had to be hammered while it was red hot.

The hallmark of the best riveting gangs was the combination of strength, stamina, speed, accuracy and coordination. 'A good riveting squad, a really good squad, you would think you couldnae slide a piece of paper between the two men as they worked.' Even when pneumatic hammers replaced hand squads on the heaviest work this did not lessen the physical demands of riveting. Pneumatic hammers weighed around 20lbs and demanded 'tremendous strength to handle properly' especially since one man was expected to use it 'all day, every day'.

While the riveters served a five year apprenticeship and were members of the Boilermakers' Society the harsh nature of their work meant that other tradesmen tended to look down upon them. As one electrician put it: 'You only went to the riveting if you were half daft; at least that was our opinion of them. You battered your brains out knocking down rivets; you destroyed your ear drums with the constant noise; continual noise; continual harassment, fighting for your wages all the time. They were mostly a harum scarum crowd, wild men'.

The squalid, dangerous working conditions endured by the riveters reinforced their reputation as 'hard men'. During the Depression working conditions deteriorated as management rushed shell riveting by crowding gangs onto the ship. There were good reasons for management to hurry – the yard received payment from the ship's future owners as each major stage of construction was completed. By rushing through this vital work, management was not only paid more quickly but reduced their vulnerability to lightning strikes. As a result, riveting gangs would be working directly above one another until the hull resembled an 'ant's nest'. During such periods even basic safety precautions were ignored:

Men would be riveting 80 to 100 feet up, sometimes higher. Men would be working – swinging hammers – on two wooden planks, sometimes only one, without any guard rail. The plank would be bouncing as they worked – we'd have been safer trying to work on a tightrope!

Not only did riveters work outside exposed to the elements all the year round, they also dealt with dangerously sharp, ragged edged iron and steel plates that were filthy with oil and rust. It was conditions like these which earned the riveters (as well as the other boilermakers) their nickname – the black squad:

> You couldnae get a dirtier job . . . You were black from head to foot; grime and sweat. Every riveter's shirt was torn – we walked about the shipyard like ragbags. There were no overalls, the only thing they gave you was a pair of gloves and you had to pay for them. Moleskin trousers were the favourite with riveters because they were hardwearing: they got so thick wi' oil they were like leather . . . You bought a pair of moleskins for your work and they had to last you six months. When you took them off at night they could stand up themselves. Nobody ever washed moleskins, when a riveter came home he just dropped them off and put them into the press until the next morning. Moleskin trousers and a grey flannel shirt to soak up the sweat was the attire for the summertime. In the winter time it was all sorts of gear – all sorts of old jackets and cardigans, all patches. We were like walking ragbags.

In the enclosed, masculine world of the shipyard, the riveters won the grudging respect of other shipyard tradesmen for their ability to win a wage at such demanding work in such a dangerous environment:

> A ship is such an awkward thing; a great big lump of steel – it's so unrelenting, unyielding. You've put it through the furnace, you've did everything to try and shape it, to impose your will on that steel. And then you take it to the boat and it not only has to be joined onto the next plate but also fixed to the frame which has been shaped and is already in place. I used to wonder they could ever get the prow of a ship together. Now, the riveters were always left with the thankless job of overcoming any deficiencies: even the smallest error by the platers was magnified a hundred times once the plate was on the berth. And these men [the riveters] had to manhandle these huge plates, to get them fitting together, with all the holes in line then they had to rivet it and make it watertight. Not an easy task!

Riveters were paid strictly by piecework; they were only paid for the work they completed, not for the time they spent in the yard. Of course, the very nature of riveting 'lent itself to a count'. It was a simple task to measure the riveters' output by counting the rivets knocked down and marking them with different coloured paint at the end of each day:

The piecework system was where you put in hundreds of rivets and the
counter came along and counted your rivets. They paid you maybe 12/6 per
hundred or 25/- a hundred or whatever it was. You had to put in thousands
of rivets to make up your wages at the end of the week.

Riveters were not paid for any wasted time caused either by bad weather or
delays in delivering materials. Quite literally, as one Brown's worker put it, the
employer 'bought our sweat'. To the riveters the calculation was straightforward:
'lost time, lost wages'. During the winter riveters had a cruel, simple choice to
make: either work in the bad weather or go home with no pay. Quite apart from the
obvious saving to the employer in wages it also meant that the riveters required
little supervision on the job since they had a financial incentive to work constantly
even in wintertime:

> It was cruel in the winter. You had to lift pneumatic machines that stuck to
> your hand. I've got frostbite in my finger wi' using the trigger. You wore a
> leather glove to protect your hand but you wore it mostly on your left hand
> because you couldnae grip the machines too well wi' a leather glove on. You
> had a big pad on your left hand to save it getting burned by the machine.
>   Riveting in winter was really cruel. You had the furnace and the first
> thing you did was get a heat – heat your hands in the morning next to the
> furnace. Then you had to lift this cold machine to drive in the rivets. Ye
> drove in about ten rivets and your hands were freezing again. The riveter
> had no chance of getting a heat if he was up on the deck or outside the shell,
> so he kept a wee pail of coal to heat his hands. Conditions were pathetic in
> the shipyard.

For the riveters, the piecework system meant that they always had to struggle
to maintain their earnings and customary workloads. During the Depression, the
employers cut the prices paid for riveting, forcing the riveters to work increasingly
harder as they desperately tried to maintain their earnings. The riveters' only
protection was their ability to halt production at short notice if they disputed their
earnings:

> 'Putting the tools in the store' was if you had a fault in your wages. We were
> on strict piecework – and if your wages didnae tally up tae what we thought
> they should be, we just said OK we're chucking it – put the tools in the
> store. So we'd all pull the tools off the boat and drop them in the store and
> just walk out the gate.

Until the widespread introduction of welding in World War Two riveting
remained almost entirely manual work performed outside in all weathers. In many
ways, this suited the employers, who avoided the investment needed to mechanise
this work and build the sheds which would enable hull construction to continue

uninterrupted throughout the year. The piecework system meant that the employer only paid for completed work and that during bad weather or slack periods John Brown's was not liable for wages. In turn, the uncertainties of casual employment meant that the riveters were in constant conflict with the yard to maintain their earnings. It was this daily economic battle as much as the arduous nature of their work which earned the riveters' reputation as 'hard men'.

SOURCE: Alan McKinlay (no date) *Making ships making men . . . Working for John Brown's – Between the Wars*, Clydebank District Libraries, 26–30.

DEMOGRAPHY

DOCUMENT 106

Concerns over the numbers emigrating from Scotland in the early twentieth century

This extract is from evidence presented to the Dominions Royal Commission which, among other things, was concerned with migration from the United Kingdom to the self-governing Dominions up to 1912. Here the Right Honourable J Burns MP raises some concerns about labour shortages – skilled and unskilled – in certain parts of the country because of the high levels of emigration. He also raises some interesting points about how the combination of declining birth-rates, lower death-rates and high levels of out-emigration saw the youngest and most productive go abroad, while an older, less fertile population was left behind.

In the six months ending September 1912 under the new scheme – these are reliable figures – the English emigrants were 171,000 in round figures; the Welsh were 3,167; the Scottish were 45,824; and the Irish were 29,588, or a total outwards of 249,470 from the four parts of the United Kingdom. The English inwards were 31,000; the Welsh were 876; the Scottish were 7,107; and the Irish 3,938, or a total inwards of 43,184 under the various nationalities as against 249,470 outwards. The net total outwards, therefore, in the six months ended September 1912 was 206,000 . . .

. . . Now I come to Scotland. Scotland had a natural increase of population by births over deaths of 51,791 in 1910, but the passengers leaving Scottish ports numbered 55,344 in the same year, that is, 3,500 more than the natural increase of the population by births over deaths. In 1911 in Scotland the difference was greater than in 1910; the departures exceeded the natural increase by more than 7,000. As regards 1912 the more accurate figures we are now obtaining already show for six months an excess of 14,000 in net emigration over the natural increase by births over deaths. So we have Ireland with a population reduced by emigration sending more than its natural increase, and Scotland, for the first time I think for 100 years, is showing an emigration in 1912 considerably beyond its natural increase. The total for the whole year may, or may not, be twice the figures for the six months, but from all we hear the emigrants are leaving in large numbers. It has been stated that some of the Territorial regiments are losing many of their best men. A large number of young farmers, the sons of farmers, and mechanics, are going, and in some parts of Scotland, as I think some members of your own Commission may know, there is a dearth of certain sections of skilled and unskilled labour, mainly through emigration from Scotland, at the present time. It is interesting to give the nationality of emigrants. The English provided 63 per cent.; the Scottish 20 per cent.; the Irish 13 per cent.; the Welsh 1 per cent.; and the colonial 3 per cent. of the total of the 397,000 emigrants gross, outwards in 1910 . . . With regard to the Scottish emigration, the males increased in the 10 years 228 per cent.; the females 434 per cent., and the children 431 per cent. With regard to Ireland, the males increased only 20 per cent.; the females dropped 6 per cent., but the children show an increase of 20 per cent., the same as the males. Taking the United Kingdom, we find this: in the 10 years male emigration had increased 131 per cent., females 156 per cent., and children 275 per cent. I have put those figures in that way to answer, as accurately as one can, several points in your memorandum. Now I want to add to what I have said in the matter of statistics. I want to say something on the relation of public health and the saving of life to emigration. In the 10 years 1901 to 1910, the death-rate of the United Kingdom dropped to 15.7, compared with 18.2, which was the death-rate for the 10 years 1891–1900. This drop in the death-rate represents 1,079,985 lives saved in the United Kingdom in 1901–1910 by the reduction of the death-rate alone. In 1911 the saving was 152,000 for that year, or a saving in life of 18,000 more than emigrants to Canada from this country in the same year. And in ten years the saving of life through the lower death-rate is 1,079,985, or nearly twice as much as the emigration to Canada in the same period. With Ireland emigrating more than its natural increase, and with Scotland exporting much more, I mention the last fact to indicate that it is mainly from the lower death-rates that we have been able to secure the larger increase in emigration during the last 10 or 20 years. I will put it, if I may, in a shorter way. The natural increase of population in the United Kingdom in 1911 was 432,000; the saving in life was 152,000 for that year. That is, the natural increase would have been only 280,000, but for the saving of life. The emigration during 1911 was 262,000. If we had emigrated 262,000 in 1911 without the saving of life due to the lower death-rate, there would have been a surplus only of 18,000 people. Now the percentage of emigration to natural increase is very important, and I have done my best to secure it for you. In 1901 from the United Kingdom the emigration was 16 per cent. of the natural increase; the average for the last 11 years was 33 per cent. of the natural increase. The 1910 emigration was 47 per cent. of the natural increase, and in 1911 it was 60 per cent. That shows that with Ireland minus and Scotland minus, England and Wales alone supply a margin for emigration by natural increase of births over deaths. And, if I may put it finally in connection with this branch of what I have to say, where you have a declining birth-rate coinciding with a very high rate of emigration, notwithstanding that you have a much lower death-rate than you previously had, it means an older population whom emigration leaves behind. I may be pardoned if I have given you these figures, because they convey, only as figures can, the real essentials of the questions that on this subject you put to me.

SOURCE: Royal Commission on the Natural Resources, Trade and Legislation of Certain Portions of His Majesty's Dominions: Minutes of Evidence, Part 1: Migration. *Parliamentary Papers* 1912, Cd 6516, 186–89.

DOCUMENT 107

The issue of voluntary and assisted emigration from Scotland in the early twentieth century

These letters are from the Dominions Royal Commission, submitted as written evidence appearing in the Appendices. The first letter was sent to the Secretary of the Association of County Councils in Scotland by the Secretary of the Dominions Royal Commission. The Chairman of the Royal Commission was concerned that no information had been collected and presented by the Scottish county councils and that they had not availed themselves of their statutory right to borrow money to finance emigration. The letter also refers to 'a memorandum of question on the subject of migration' (also reproduced here) which gives a good indication of the remit of the Commission and the information required from local authorities. The reply suggests that money raised by individuals and through the work of active voluntary emigration agencies meant that the powers available through the Local Government (Scotland) Act, 1889, had not been invoked.

The following letter was sent to the Secretary of the Association of County Councils in Scotland: –

> Dominions Royal Commission,
> Scotland House
> Embankment
> London, S.W.,
> 19th August, 1912

Sir,

I am desired by the Chairman of the Dominions Royal Commission to forward, for your perusal, a copy of the terms of reference of the Commission, together with a memorandum* of questions on the subject of migration from the United Kingdom to the self-governing Dominions, which has been widely circulated by the Commission to private organisations interested in the subject.

It has been brought to the notice of the Commission that by the Local Government Act (Scotland), 1889, section 67, County Councils are empowered to borrow moneys for emigration purposes subject to certain conditions. It is understood that these powers have not in practice been exercised, and the Commission is desirous of obtaining a full staement and, if necessary, hearing evidence as to the precise reasons for this.

It has been suggested that reference might usefully be made to your Association on the subject, and the Commission will be much obliged by any information and observations which you may have to offer.

I am, &c.,

W. A. Robinson

The Secretary,
The Association of County Councils in Scotland.

The Executive Committee of the Association of County Councils in Scotland did not meet until December the 19th, 1912, after which meeting the following letter was received from the Secretary:–

County Rooms,
Edinburgh,
21st December 1912

Sir,

It was only on Thursday that I had an opportunity of submitting to the Ececutive Committee of the Association of County Councils in Scotland the correspondence which has passed between us regarding the request that the Association should furnish the Commission with information as to the reasons why County Councils in Scotland have not availed themselves of the powers conferred on them by sec. 67 of the Local Government (Scotland) Act, 1889, to borrow moneys for emigration purposes.

The Association are of the opinion that the number of persons who have emigrated from Scotland on their own account and through the assistance of voluntary agencies is so great that there has been no occasion for County Councils to put in force their powers in the matter.

As far as the Executive Committee are aware no application, either by persons or by bodies of persons, corporate or unincorporate, has ever been made to any County Council in Scotland for assistance in the matter of emigration.

I am, &c.,

A. G. G. Asher,
Secretary.

The Secretary
Dominions Royal Commission

Memorandum

The Dominions Royal Commission appointed in pursuance of the 20th Resolution of the Imperial Conference, 1911, and representing the United Kingdom and the self-governing Dominions, viz., the Dominion of Canada, the Commonwealth of Australia, the Dominion of New Zealand, the Union of South Africa, and Newfoundland, proposes, inter alia, to enquire into the existing arrangements for the migration of population between the United Kingdom and the self-governing Dominions, with a view to considering whether it can make any practical suggestions in connection therewith for the consideration of the respective Governments.

To assist in this enquiry, the Commission will be glad to receive answers to the following questions: –

1   What are the objects of your organisation with reference to migration from this country?
2   What methods do you adopt for the promotion of migration to and settlement in the Dominions?

3   Can you give figures of migration to the Dominions under the auspices of your organisation back to the year 1901, a statement of the cost of such migration per head, and figures to show what proportion of those who migrated have, in your opinion, proved successful? Can you state what classes of population were most concerned in such migration?

4   From what sources is the income of your organisation derived, and what is the amount from each source?

5   To what extent do the persons who migrate themselves contribute to the cost of their migration and settlement?

6   Do you consider that the methods now existing, whether public or private, of organising, encouraging, directing, assisting, and controlling migration and settlement should be expanded, and, if so, can you suggest any definite directions in which this could be done?

7   Generally, will you give any views which you may have on the subject of migration from the United Kingdom to the Dominions, and settlement therein, not covered by the foregoing questions?

It is requested that answers to the above questions may be sent, in writing, if possible before the 31st of August, to the Secretary, Dominions Royal Commission, Scotland House, Victoria Embankment, S.W. Due notice will be given when the Commission will be ready to hear oral evidence and witnesses will be invited to attend.

SOURCE: Royal Commission on the Natural Resources, Trade and Legislation, of Certain Portions of His Majesty's Dominions. Minutes of Evidence, Part I: Migration, Appendices and Written Submission, 220–1; 250. *Parliamentary Papers* 1912, Cd 6516, 250.

DOCUMENT 108

Lower birth rates and fertility of marriage in Scotland from *c* 1860

The Report on the Fifteenth Census of Scotland *sought to identify those factors particular to the cause of the decline in family size in Scotland by the early 1950s. The report notes that the problem is closely linked to population shift and 'heavy Scottish losses by emigration'. But it also stresses factors more closely associated with the shift in social attitudes, noting that the community as a whole had come to accept the notion of the smaller family as normal. The impact of two world wars was significant, but so too were changing economic conditions, particularly at times of high unemployment. When compared with the conclusions arrived at through* **Document 109***, however, it is clear that factors such as the changing attitude of women to childbirth and child-rearing are not considered, or materialist explanations for the decline in family size. The impact of the Second World War is considered in terms of the loss of life, but not from the standpoint that the living experience of that war helped influence and promote significant shifts in social values.*

Decline in family size – The natural increase in the population of Scotland, resulting from the excess of births over deaths, has in proportion to the population been falling since the 1870's. In 1871–81 it amounted to 14.0 per cent. of the population of 1871. In 1941–51 it was no more than 5.8 per cent of the population of 1941. The heavy Scottish losses by emigration, mainly from the younger age groups, have assisted in the decline by taking away prospective parents, but the main cause is a long continued and heavy decrease in the fertility of marriage. This is plain from the fact that the average number of children per family in the 1870's was about 6 whereas today it is about 2.5.

Fertility trends 1861–1951 – In 1860–62 there were 316.0 births for every 1,000 married women in Scotland under the age of 45, which is taken as the upper limit of the normal child-bearing period. By 1900–02 the number had fallen to 271.8 or 86 per cent. of the figure in 1860–62. By 1950–52 it had fallen to 132.3 children per 1,000 married women or 42 per cent. of the rate in 1860–62. (The figures are taken for three-year periods around census dates to allow in some degree for temporary fluctuations.) Thus the rate fell by 58 per cent. between 1860–62 and 1950–52. Between 1860–62 and 1900–02 the fall was 14 per cent. and between 1900–02 and 1950–52 51 per cent. The heavy weight of the fall has been in the present century.

Variations since 1901 – The following table looks a little more closely at the experience in the present century.

Legitimate Births per 1,000 Married Women aged under 45

Three year period	Rate	Percentage of rate for preceding period	Percentage of rate for 1860–62	Percentage decrease from rate of preceding period	Percentage decrease from rate for 1860–62
1890–92	296.4				
1900–02	271.8	91.7	86.0	8.3	14.0
1910–12	233.2	85.8	73.8	14.2	26.2
1920–22	226.7	97.2	71.7	2.8	28.3
1930–32	169.0	74.5	53.5	25.5	46.5
1940–42	136.9	81.0	43.3	19.0	56.7
1950–52	132.3	96.6	41.9	3.4	58.1

The rate of decrease from one decade to another varies widely but there is always a fall. It was low in 1920–22 but that is unrepresentative because the birth-rate rose sharply following upon the first world war, largely as a consequence of the depression of the rate while so many men were absent for long periods during the war. For that reason the increased population from the temporarily high birth-rates after the first world war was really more in the nature of a compensation for the losses sustained by the birth-rate while the war was running its course. Had normal trends continued without the interruption of the war, it is estimated, somewhat conjecturally, that the fall in the fertility rate in 1920–22 from that of the preceding decade would probably have been nearer 12 per cent. than the 2.8 per cent. shown in the table.

The high fall of 1930–32 came in the early years of the world-wide economic depression of the 1930's, which followed upon years of heavy unemployment in Scotland. Apart from the discouraging effect of such conditions on the growth of a population, they caused in the decade 1921–31 the heaviest recorded loss by emigration from Scotland in any decade since figures became available after the 1861 census. Nearly 400,000 men, women and children left Scotland in those ten years, and they would include in their ranks as usual a high proportion of younger people and children. Losses on such a scale from the younger ranks of the population would increase the average age of the remaining population and help to reduce the fertility rate.

The rate of decrease recorded in 1940–42 was less but nevertheless heavy and still probably bore the mark of the economic depression as well as the disturbing conditions of the war.

Post-war increase in birth and marriage rates – After the second world war, as after the first, there was a sharp increase in the numbers of births. In part they were again a compensation for losses to the birth-rate due to absence from home of men serving with the forces, but in general the periods of absence were considerably less than in the first world war and consequently the weight of this compensating factor would be less than after the first world war. There was a heavy increase in marriages after the second world war and a general consideration of the position suggests that many of these additional marriages would not in the ordinary course of events have been contracted until later. The increase in the numbers of new marriages would make a material contribution to the temporary improvement in the fertility rate. It rose as high as 163.9 per 1,000 married women in 1947 but by 1952 it was back to 131.3, noticeably lower than the rate before the war began.

Influence of lower mortality – Taken as a whole the experience shows that very widely throughout the community a smaller family has come to be accepted as normal. The improvement in the death-rate has something to do with this. Mortality among children was very heavy no more than 50 years ago. Out of every 1,000 children born in the five years 1896 to 1900 no less than 129 on the average did not reach their first birthday, and if account is taken of all who died before reaching the age of ten, the figure rises to 230 in every 1,000. Today the comparable figures are 30 in every 1,000 for children under one and 40 for children under ten.

Of the typical family of about 6 children in the 1890's hardly more than 4½ children on the average (it is unfortunately not possible to avoid fractions when dealing with the single family) survived to the age of 10. Today the typical family of two or three children have a very much more certain prospect of survival to and well beyond the age of 10. But even so the number of children surviving in a typical family of the 1890's was still about twice the number in a family of the present day. It is plain therefore that the fall in the birth and fertility rates is not attributable in the main either to the results of emigration or the improvement in the death-rate but to a change springing from other causes that influence the population in their attitude to the size of the family.

SOURCE: *Report on the Fifteenth Census of Scotland*, Vol V: Fertility of Marriage, 1956, Edinburgh (HMSO), 111–12.

DOCUMENT 109

Reasons for lower fertility rates and rates of family formation in Britain after the Second World War

The following is from the Royal Commission on Population 1949. Here the principal reasons for the decline in fertility rates and rates of family formation since the late nineteenth century are considered. Such issues were particularly important in light of the impact and effect of the Second World War. The passage is illuminating in one other regard. The main features identified by the Royal Commission on Population 1949, which help explain lower birth rates, are also the main features of change brought about by the commercial and industrial transformation of Scottish economy and society in the nineteenth century. The shift from high to low rates of family formation is, therefore, a result of the impact of industrial change.

The main features of these changes are well-known. They include the decay of small scale family handicrafts and the rise of large scale industry and factory organisation; the loss of security and growth of competitive individualism; the relative decline in agriculture and rise in importance of industry and commerce, and the associated shift of population from rural to urban areas; the growing prestige of science, which disturbed traditional religious beliefs; the development of popular education; higher standards of living; the growth of humanitarianism, and the emancipation of women. All these and other changes are closely inter-related; they present a complex web, rather than a chain, of cause and effect; and it would be exceedingly difficult to trace how they acted and reacted on each other or to assess their relative importance.

SOURCE: *Report of the Royal Commission on Population. Parliamentary Papers* 1948–49 XIX, 684.

URBANISATION

DOCUMENT 110

Four manufacturing towns

Francis Groome's Ordnance Gazetteer of Scotland *continued a long tradition of Scottish topographical description dating back to* The Statistical Account of Scotland. *This edition used the population figures of the 1891 Census and reflected the local government changes of the 1880s. The four extracts represent contrast. The two border textile towns, though very different, had a long experience of urbanism and a rich institutional structure. The two metal towns were of recent and rapid growth with very different social and cultural resources.*

a) *Selkirk*

Selkirk, a post and market town, a royal and parliamentary burgh, and a parish in Selkirkshire. Selkirk is the county town, and is situated on a rising-ground flanking a fine haugh on the right bank of Ettrick Water, 6¼ miles S by W of Galashiels, 7 SW of Melrose, 11 N by W of Hawick, 22 ESE of Peebles, and 38 SSE by road and 40 by rail from Edinburgh. It stands at the terminus of a branch line, 6¼ miles long, from Galashiels, formed under an act of 1854, and amalgamated with the North British in 1859. Its site on an eminence, rising from 400 to 619 feet above sea-level, is eminently favourable for sanitary arrangements; and its environs comprise the beautiful pleasure-grounds of Haining and picturesque reaches of Ettrick and Yarrow Waters to Oakwood Tower and Newark Castle. At the beginning of the 19th century the town presented the appearance of an ill-built, irregular and decaying place, fast hastening to extinction; but since then it has suddenly revived, has undergone both renovation and extension, and is now a pleasant, prosperous, and comparatively ornate place, including various lines of new thoroughfares, elegant private residences, several good public buildings, and a number of busy factories. The plan of Selkirk is far from being regular. A spacious triangular market-place occupies the centre of the town; and thence the chief streets branch off in different directions. On the shortest side of the market-place is the town-hall, a neat modern edifice surmounted by a spire 110 feet high. The county buildings, occupying a site on the side of the road leading to Galashiels, were erected in 1870, and contain a handsome courtroom with an open timber roof, and well-planned apartments for various official purposes . . . A tunnel under the intervening street communicates with the sunk floor of the county prison, which stands opposite, and which was altered and enlarged in 1865–66 at a cost of £2000. In the open area of the market-place stands Handyside Ritchie's monument to Sir Walter Scott, erected by the gentlemen of the county in 1839 . . . Another monument, by Andrew Currie, was erected in High Street in 1859 to Mungo Park, the African traveller, who was born at Fowlshiels, in the parish of Selkirk . . . The railway station stands in the haugh at the foot of the rising ground occupied by the town . . . A public hall was erected in 1894–95 in Viewfield Gardens at an estimated expense of £5000.

The present parochial church was built in 1862, and contains 1100 sittings . . . A chapel of ease was opened at Heatherlie in 1877, and cost £3856. Early Decorated in style, it is a cruciform and apsidal structure, containing 600 sittings . . . The Free church was built soon after the Disruption, and contains 700 sittings. There are two U.P. churches in the town. The first U.P. congregation occupy a church, opened in 1880, with 850 sittings, and a hall behind. It is in the Early Gothic style, with a spire 130 feet high, and cost about £5000. The new West U.P. church (1890) has 700 sittings. The E.U. chapel contains 130 sittings. There are also Congregational and Baptist chapels. St John's Episcopal church, with 156 sittings, is an Early English edifice of 1869; and the Roman Catholic church of our Lady and St Joseph contains 250 sittings, and was erected in 1866. Three schools – Knowe Park, Burgh, and Roman Catholic – with respective accommodation for 420, 541, and 121 children, had (1893) an average attendance of 382, 407, and 56, and government grants of £402, 14s. 10d., £356, 2s. 6d., and £47, 13s. 6d. The Selkirk Science Class (Physiography) meets in the Burgh School. There is also the Scott and Oliver Trust, with an income of over £160.

Selkirk has a post office, with money order, savings bank and telegraph departments, branches of the British Linen, the National, and Commercial Banks, and of the National Security Savings Bank, and six hotels. The disused prison of Selkirk was purchased by Provost Craig Brown, who converted it into a library and reading room, and presented it to the town . . . Among the miscellaneous institutions and associations of the burgh are the South of Scotland Chamber of Commerce, the Border Counties Association, a subscription library founded in 1772, a choral union (1872), a cottagers' horticultural society (1852), a farmers' club (1806), an association for the improvement of domestic poultry (1863), an ornithological association, a Conservative club, the Ettrick Forest Bowling Club (1788), two Co-operative societies, two friendly societies, a provident building society (1859), Freemasons', Free Gardeners', Foresters', and Good Templar lodges, an angling association, curling, cricket, football, bowling, and golfing clubs, a total abstinence society, and various religious and philanthropic associations. There are also a gaswork, a volunteer drill hall, with accommodation for 800 persons; the Union Hall, for 400; the Chapel Street Hall, for 150; and the Baptist Chapel Hall, for 400. The *Southern Reporter* (1855) is published in the town every Thursday. The *Selkirk Advertiser*, containing chiefly advertisements, is published every Saturday, and distributed gratis in the town and neighbourhood . . .

Industries – The present staple manufacture of Selkirk is woollen goods – tweeds, tartans, shawls, and such articles – similar to those produced at Galashiels. This manufacture was introduced in 1835, has since steadily increased in importance, and is carried on in large factories employing very many hands. There are now half-a-dozen mills engaged in spinning woollen yarns, and a dozen in the manufacture of tweeds and tartans, etc. One of these, the Scotch Tweed

Manufacturing Society's mill, is carried on on Co-operative principles. Besides these there are a number of hosiery manufactories. The other industrial establishments are of less importance; they include an engineering and millwright work, saw-mills, corn-mills, and the usual commercial institutions of a country town . . .

Selkirk was made a royal burgh in the reign of David I. It is governed by a provost, 2 bailies, a dean of guild, a treasurer, and 10 councillors. The corporation revenue in 1892–93 was £1524; and in 1893 the municipal constituency was 1161, of whom 249 were females. The police force is incorporated with that of the county, and since 1884 has been under the chief constable of Selkirkshire. Justice of peace courts for the whole county are held as occasion requires. Sheriff courts for the county and sheriff small debt courts are held weekly during session; small debt cases, ordinary cases, and cases under the Debts Recovery Act, on Fridays . . . Valuation of real property in the burgh (1885) £22,898, (1893) £23,632. Pop. (1831) 1880, (1861) 3695, (1871) 4640, (1881) 6090, (1891) 6397, of whom 3436 were females . . .

The landward schools are Selkirk public and Bowhill schools, with respective accommodation for 317 and 53 children, and (1893) an average attendance of 239 and 35, and grants of £229, 5s. 6d. and £47, 17s.

b) *Hawick*

Hawick, a parliamentary and municipal burgh and parish in Roxburghshire. The town is the largest seat of population in the eastern Border counties . . . It is situated on both sides of the Teviot, which enters the town from the SW after passing through the haughs and woods of Branxholme and Wilton Lodge . . . The town is in a basin, the principal streets being built on the level land on both sides of the rivers, from which other streets ascend the slopes, and above these are the mansions and villas of the principal inhabitants . . . The town is regular in form, and the streets are well built and spacious . . . The Municipal Buildings, the foundation stone of which was laid in 1885, were completed in 1887 at a cost of £13,000. They . . . contain the Free Library and a public hall capable of seating 1000 people . . . On the ground floor are the police office, officials' rooms, and cells; the second floor contains the council room, the burgh court-room, etc . . . The Science and Art Institute was erected as a memorial to his Grace the late Duke of Buccleuch, who had long been the munificent benefactor of the burgh. The Cottage Hospital and Dispensary, opened in 1885, stands on an elevated site in Buccleuch Street granted by the late Duke . . . The post office, with money order, savings bank, and telegraph departments, was removed to handsome new premises at the corner of Bridge Street and Croft Road in 1892 . . .

The first bank established in the town was a branch of the British Linen Co. in 1797 . . . The other branch banks are the Commercial Bank (1820), the National Bank (1852), the Royal Bank (1856), the National Security Savings Bank (1815), and the Hawick Heritable Investment Bank. There are also the Temperance Hall, 2 Masonic halls, several hotels, the Museum, and a large Combination Poorhouse. Hawick has three weekly newspapers – the *Hawick Advertiser*, the *Hawick Express*, and the *Hawick News*. Among its numerous associations there are the Teviotdale Farmers' Club, the West Teviotdale Farmers' Club, the West Teviotdale Agricultural Society, Archaeological, Horticultural, and Ornithological societies, the Working Men's Building Society, and several political and educational associations. There is a public library, the Public Libraries Act having been adopted by the burgh in 1877, and several clubs for recreation and amusement. The cricket club has a spacious park near the town, and the bowling clubs have two attractive greens. Wilton Lodge estate was purchased as a public park in 1890 for £14,000; and in the same year the Miller's Knowes were leased for ten years for a similar purpose . . .

The original parish church is St Mary's, which dates from 1214 . . . St John's church, built in 1879–80 by subscription at a cost of £6000, is a fine Early English structure with 800 sittings . . . Wilton parish church, built in 1860, is a beautiful edifice, and contains 950 sittings. Wellington church, a chapel of ease to Wilton church, was opened in 1886. St Cuthbert's Episcopal church, a fine building in the Early Decorated style, was erected and endowed by the Duke of Buccleuch. There are also three Free churches, four U.P. churches, and an Evangelical Union, Baptist, and Roman Catholic church, etc . . .

. . . The following are the statistics of . . . average attendance . . . for the school year ending 30 Sept. 1891: – Buccleuch school (. . . 868 . . .), Trinity (. . . 536 . . .), Drumlanrig (. . . 443 . . .), Wilton (. . . 531 . . .), St Mary's (. . . 149 . . .). Besides the board schools there are academies and private schools, and schools receiving government grants in connection with the Episcopal and Roman Catholic churches. There are also Art and Science classes . . .

. . . now there are in Hawick several of the largest and most prosperous tweed factories in Scotland . . . There are now about a dozen and a half woollen factories, supplied with the most improved machinery. Great extensions in the hosiery manufacture have been made by the introduction of power knitting machines, of very complex and costly mechanism, into the larger factories . . . There are at present about 20 hosiery manufactories at work. Besides these, the great staple industries, there are dye-works, tanneries, an oil manufactory, quarries, saw-mills, etc.

. . . The situation and prosperity of the town have made it a great market of grain, and especially of live stock . . . One of the first originators of these sales in Scotland was the father of the present Mr Oliver of Thornwood, who has long been known as one of the most extensive salesmen by auction of live stock in the kingdom, and at whose principal sales, attended by breeders from all parts, as many as 25,000 sheep and lambs have been disposed of in a single day. Besides his principal sales at the mart . . . there is a weekly auction every Monday. The weekly corn market is held on Thursday, and hiring, cattle, wool, and sheep and lamb fairs are held at periods between springtime and the beginning of winter . . .

The municipal constitution of the burgh was established by a special act of parliament in 1861. It is governed by a provost, 4 bailies, and 10 councillors, who also act as Police Commissioners. The Burgh Police (Scotland) Act of 1892 made no difference in the governing body of Hawick. In 1867 it acquired the rank of a parliamentary burgh, and, united with Galashiels and Selkirk, returns one member to parliament . . . Pop. of burgh (1861) 10,401, (1871) 11,356, (1881) 16,184, (1891) 19,204.

c) *Coatbridge*

Coatbridge, a municipal burgh of Old Monkland parish, Lanarkshire. It stands, at 300 feet above sea level, on the Monkland Canal, and in the midst of a perfect network of railways, being 2 miles W by S of Airdrie, 8E of Glasgow, and 34 W by S of Edinburgh. Fifty years since it was only a village; and its rapid extension is due to its position in the centre of Scotland's chief mineral field. The Airdrie and Coatbridge district comprises some twenty active collieries; and in or about the town are several establishments for the pig-iron manufacture, malleable iron and steel works, and numerous rolling mills. Nor are these the only industries; boilers, tubes, tinplate, firebrick and fireclay, bricks and tiles, oakum, railway waggons, etc., being also manufactured. It is governed by a provost, 4 bailies, and 15 councillors, with a treasurer and dean of guild. Splendid municipal buildings are in course of erection. Coatbridge, in its growth, has absorbed, or is still absorbing, a number of outlying suburbs – Langloan, Gartsherrie, High Sunnyside, Coats, Clifton, Drumpellier, Dundyvan, Summerlee, Whifflet, Coatdyke, etc. Fire, smoke, and soot, with the roar and rattle of machinery, are its leading characteristics; the flames of its furnaces cast on the midnight sky a glow as if of some vast conflagration. It has stations on the Caledonian and North British railways, a post office with money order, savings bank, insurance, and telegraph departments, branches of the Clydesdale, Commercial, National, Royal and Union banks, several hotels, the Alexander Hall, a reading room, gas-works, a water-supply conjointly with Airdrie, and a Wednesday paper, the *Coatbridge Express*. A theatre and music hall, seating 2000 spectators, was opened in 1875; at Langloan is the West End Park, where in 1880 a red granite fountain, 20 feet high, was erected in memory of Janet Hamilton (1795–1873), the lowly Coatbridge poetess; and a fine public park towards the north-east was in 1887 gifted by Mr Weir of Kildonan. There are also a literary association, temperance organizations, masonic lodges, and cricket and football clubs. Gartsherrie *quoad sacra* church (1839; 1050 sittings) cost over £3300, and is a prominent object, with a spire 136 feet high; and Coats *quoad sacra* church (1875; 1000 sittings) is a handsome Gothic edifice, built from endowment by the late George Baird of Stitchell. Of 4 Free churches – Middle, East, West and Whifflet – the finest was built in 1875; and other places of worship are 3 U.P. churches, a Congregational church, an Evangelical Union church, a Baptist church, a Wesleyan church (1874), St John's Episcopal church, and two Roman Catholic churches. Besides other schools noticed under Old Monkland, Coatbridge and Coats public school, Langloan public school, and St Patrick's and St Augustine's Roman Catholic schools, with respective accommodation for 1682, 552, 588, and 489 children, had (1891) an average attendance of 1102 day and 102 evening, 385 day and 81 evening, 403, and 416, and grants of £1242, 11s. 6d. and £52, 12s., £407, 11s. 8d. and £48, 12s., £395, 14s. 6d., and £364. There is, besides, the

Coatbridge Technical School and West of Scotland Mining College. Valuation of burgh (1892) £132,024, 4s. 3d. Pop. (1831) 741, (1841) 1599, (1851) 8564, (1861) 12,006, (1871) 15,802, (1881) 24,812, (1891) 30,034. – *Ord. Sur.*, sh. 31, 1867.

d) *Motherwell*

Motherwell, a town in Bothwell, Dalziel, and Hamilton parishes, Lanarkshire, on the Caledonian railway . . . occupies flat ground, 300 feet above sea level, amid richly cultivated and well-wooded environs. Founded in the early years of the 19th century, Motherwell having previously had no existence, it is said, even as a village, it consists largely of the dwellings of miners and operatives employed in the neighbouring collieries and ironworks, and serves, in connection with the railway junctions, as a great and bustling centre of traffic . . . In 1887 a handsome town-hall was erected, the cost of the building being about £7000. Motherwell has a post office, with money order, savings bank, insurance and telegraph departments, for which new and extensive premises were provided in 1894, branches of the Bank of Scotland, the British Linen Co., the National, and the Clydesdale Banks, several hotels, a new hospital (1893–94), a Co-operative Society for which new buildings were erected in 1894, the Conservative Club (a handsome building erected in 1892 and costing £3000), two building societies, the combination poorhouse for Dalziel, Bothwell, Cambusnethan, and Shotts parishes, with accommodation for 120 inmates, and a Saturday paper, the *Motherwell Times*. In 1877 a splendid water supply was brought in from two burns on the estate of Lee at a cost of over £14,000, and in 1894 a large extension cost the burgh over £30,000. In the latter year also an extension of the gasworks took place, by the erection of an additional gasometer by the gas company, and in 1887 the Dalzell Jubilee Park was gifted by Lord Hamilton of Dalzell. In Merry Street is the new parish church of Dalziel, erected in 1874 at a cost of £5700 . . . A new Free church in Windmill Street, built in 1892 at a cost of about £1900, has 410 sittings . . . One of the two U.P. churches was built in 1881, at a cost of £3750 . . . There are also a Primitive Methodist chapel, an Evangelical Union chapel, a Baptist chapel (1894), an Episcopal church (1894), and the Roman Catholic church of Our Lady of Good Aid (1873; enlarged 1883) . . . No Scottish town has grown so rapidly as Motherwell, such growth being due to the vast extension of its mineral industries. These, at the census of 1891, employed 3412 of the 6100 persons here of the 'industrial class' – 1000 being engaged in coal-mining, 1318 in the iron manufacture, 617 in the steel manufacture, etc. Besides the works of the Glasgow Malleable Iron and Steel Company – the largest in Scotland – there are several other extensive iron and steel works. In or about the town are also boiler works, bolt and rivet works, brick, tile and fire-clay works, quarries, steam crane works, and spade and shovel works . . . Valuation of the Burgh (1893) £75,540. Pop. (1841) 726, (1861) 2925, (1871) 6943, (1881) 12,904, (1891) 18,726, of whom 10,270 were males, and 3585 were in Hamilton parish.

SOURCE: Francis H Groome (ed) 1893 *Ordnance Gazetteer of Scotland*, London, vol vi 328–30; vol iii 249–53; vol i 273; vol v 74–5.

Housing and work in Glasgow

Henry Broadhurst, English trades union leader, is questioning one of Glasgow's reform-minded Lord Provosts. The answers give some indication of the complex decisions working people took when they decided where to live and the factors which influenced this decision. The later answers show that he and his medical officer were ready to advocate the regulation of houses by the municipal council but were very cautious about direct intervention.

Mr Broadhurst to Sir William Collins

What is your opinion as to the reason why men came from the outlying districts into the city to live when they work at factories outside; would it be partly for the sake of the education of their children? – I think it is very largely due to the fact that if they live in town a larger number of the members of their family can find employment than can find employment in those outlying districts where the works are of a special kind, such as the shipbuilding yards. For instance, taking the case of Thompson's Yard, there is no employment for females in that neighbourhood. There is a railway from that district into Partick by which a number of workmen go backwards and forwards; I think the charge is only 6*d.* per week, so that the cost is really not much. Another train runs up to the Cowlairs district on the North British Line. I think the reason why they live in the town is chiefly because it is more convenient for their families.

And it has nothing to do with the question of school accommodation you think? – In Govan, for instance, there is ample school accommodation at their very doors for all the families that live there, but that is only a proportion, and still a large number come up by steam tramcar from Govan, and a large number come up from Dalmuir and Clyde Bank, either to Partick or to Cowlairs.

Do you think that the fluctuating nature of the trade by the river side has something to do with it also? – That was the case at first when first the shipbuilding yards were established, but the population is becoming a great deal more consolidated year by year, and they are choosing Partick and Clyde Bank as their permanent residences. The only proprietors who have made provision for their men are the Thompsons at Clyde Bank who have made considerable provision for their own workers.

Does the firm of John Elder and Company do anything in that direction? – No, nothing.

Although the wages in the shipbuilding trade were very good some three years back, I suppose things are much worse now and the wages have gone down? – The wages are reduced by a certain percentage; I could not say how much. It was only a certain class of the workers in those yards whose wages were abnormally high, such as the rivetters and holders on. In the wages of the regular engineers there was no very great rise.

The very high wages that were paid were confined to rivetters and platers? – Yes.

And the ship joiners and the engine fitters, that is to say, the engineers of the vessels, shared to scarcely any extent whatever in that abnormal prosperity? – The wages of fitters down there would not be much, if any, more than those of engineers in town engaged in the ordinary branches of engineering.

And of course that would apply to blacksmiths as well? – Yes.

And it would apply especially to ship joiners? – Yes, it applies especially to them. In very busy times a great number of house joiners were drafted into the ship-building yards.

Chairman to Sir William Collins

There have been a good many discussions, have there not, in the town council as to the propriety of the town council themselves rehousing the people who are displaced? – It has been discussed several times; but the decision has always been adverse to it. In the first place it was believed that they would never be able to erect or manage them so economically as private builders would.

The general tendency in Scotland is to believe in private enterprise for re-housing is it not? – I think we have had experience in Glasgow that is quite sufficient, and more than sufficient, to provide for the requirements. In fact if the town council had shown any tendency to build on their own account it would have paralysed the efforts of outside parties; and therefore I believe we should have had a great deal of unprofitable work done, and not so much good work.

Have you your Act with you? – I am sorry to say that I have not.

Do you remember the 28th and 29th sections of that Act with regard to the protection from hardship of the poorer inhabitants who were dispossessed? – The provision was that the sheriff should hold an inquiry, and proof was required to be led before him that there was sufficient accommodation for those who were going to be displaced.

That was the point as to which I asked you before? – Yes.

Are you in the habit of doing anything in the way of giving monetary compensation to the people you turn out? – That would only apply in the cases of shops where there were leases.

You do not give compensation to working people? – No, they have no leases; they only take the place at most for a year; so that they would just be allowed to let their term of let to run out.

You give them long notice? – Yes.

I suppose you think that money compensation might in some cases be spent in drink? – If some people have too much money in their pockets they sometimes dispose of it in that way.

Mr Goschen to Dr Russell

Do the people shift much from house to house in Glasgow? – They do; it is quite the habit of the population.

Mr Lyulph Stanley
You stated that the rule of the corporation with regard to cubic space was 300 cubic feet to each person and 900 cubic feet for a single room; have you found as a matter of fact that rule is often broken through? – I do not know whether you are aware that a constant inspection is kept of these houses of one, two, and three apartments in size and not exceeding 2,000 cubic feet, to the extent of 38,000 to 40,000 visits every year to that class of house; and the proportion of cases in which overcrowding is now found varies between four and five per cent. of the houses visited. In the year 1866 when the Act was passed and the inspection began it was over eight per cent.

Then at this moment in the single-roomed tenements, which are about 35,000 or more in number, and in the other tenements of two rooms, and so on, you find that at present there is from 4 to 5 per cent. of overcrowding? – That is the result of our visits to those of the worst class which are ticketed.

SOURCE: Royal Commission on the Housing of the Working Classes, *Parliamentary Papers* 1884–85, 31, c19, 473–93.

Glasgow and the 'ring of burghs'

By the 1880s Glasgow was surrounded by a series of independent police burghs. The debate on the extension of the boundaries of Glasgow to include these burghs revealed the nature of the resources which urban places needed to regulate and sustain themselves.

a) *Partick*

The 'village of Partick' (of which the Boundary Commissioners of 1832 wrote), had been for centuries an inhabited place on the west bank of the Kelvin near its junction with the Clyde. It had in 1831 'some six or seven mills' (flour-mills), 'a weaving factory employing about 150 hands, a bleaching-work and dye-works, and some other smaller industries.' At that time the population is said to have been about 1800. From 1831 Partick does not appear to have made any perceptible progress, until the extension of the Glasgow quays, consequent on the deepening of the Clyde, compelled the removal of the shipbuilding yards to a lower part of the river. Several of them were accommodated in Partick about 1845. The development of shipbuilding soon made Partick a populous place, and in 1852 steps were taken to form it into a police burgh under the Act of 1850. At that time it contained a population of over 5000, which has since increased to 30,500. The rateable value, which was £18,880 in 1852, is now £156,405. The area of the burgh is 1006 acres, its frontage to the Clyde extending to 1½ miles. There are twelve commissioners (including three magistrates) of police, all of whom are resident within Partick, but the present chief magistrate is in business in Glasgow as well as in Partick. The burgh maintains a separate police force of 38 men of all ranks. It has a fire brigade of 11, but only one of these is on permanent duty. They are provided with a steam fire-engine, a manual engine, and other appliances. With Maryhill and Hillhead, it shares a fever hospital and a small-pox pavilion at Knightswood, with accommodation for 100 patients. Very complete municipal buildings have been provided; and an excellent public park containing about 45 acres.

The rates, exclusive of water-rate, amount to 2s. 2½d. per £, viz., 1s. 9⅛d. on occupiers, and 5⅜d. on owners. If the differential water-rate were added, the rates in Partick would practically be the same as those in Glasgow on rents above £10, and considerably higher than on those below £10.

As respects water supply and tramway accommodation, Partick is dependent on Glasgow. While it is within the compulsory gas-supply area of Glasgow, it can also use the gas of the Partick, Hillhead and Maryhill Gas Company.

If Partick was isolated, no serious objection could be taken to the provision made for the security and health of its inhabitants. But it must be kept in view that it adjoins the buildings of Glasgow, Hillhead, and Kelvinside, along its eastern and north-eastern boundaries (between two and three miles in extent), thereby forming a continuation of the great urban community of which Glasgow is the real centre.

The feeling in Partick in favour of annexation to Glasgow appears to be growing; but the commissioners are unanimously opposed to it.

b) *Maryhill*

The Forth and Clyde Canal, constructed nearly 100 years ago, attracted to its banks some manufactories of which the Boundary Commissioners of 1831–2 take notice, and which they plainly indicate they were only prevented from including, even then, within the Parliamentary boundaries of Glasgow because, had these manufactories and the 'Village of Partick' been included, the Kelvin and the Canal must have been lost as boundaries, and none so good could have been found. For many years after 1832 Maryhill did not increase in size or population, and, although the point is contested, we see no reason to doubt that its ultimate enlargement was due to the overflow of Glasgow population and the establishment within it of works belonging to Glasgow citizens. Be that as it may, Maryhill had become so populous that in 1856 it was formed into a police burgh under the Act of 1850. At that time it contained a population of between 5000 and 6000, which has since increased to over 16,000. It does not appear what the rateable value was in 1856, but it is now £67,499. The area of the burgh is 1183 acres. There are twelve commissioners (including three magistrates) of police, one of whom carries on business in Glasgow. Maryhill maintains a separate police force of nineteen men of all ranks. It has a fire brigade of 12 men; but only one, who is also borne on the police strength as its sole detective officer, is wholly in public employment. The brigade is provided with one manual engine. Provost Craig, when asked (Q. 13144) whether the fire apparatus was adequate, candidly replied, 'Well, for a small fire, I daresay it would be, but for a great blaze we would require more assistance.' Maryhill has a share in the joint hospital at Knightswood. It has also erected municipal buildings and a handsome burgh hall. The condition of the side streets is not satisfactory, nor are the sanitary arrangements all that could be desired.

The rates, exclusive of water-rate, amount to 2s. 4d. per £, viz., 1s. 11⅛d. on occupiers, and 4⅞d. on owners. If the differential water-rate were added, the rates in Maryhill would be higher than those in Glasgow on all rents, whether under or above £10.

As respects water supply and tramway accommodation, Maryhill is dependent on Glasgow. While it is within the compulsory gas-supply area of Glasgow, it can also use the gas of the Partick Hillhead and Maryhill Gas Company.

The Barracks for the troops stationed at Glasgow are situated at Maryhill.

We are unable to say that the urban equipment of Maryhill is satisfactory.

The evidence indicated that a considerable number of the ratepayers desire annexation to Glasgow. The majority of the commissioners are opposed to it.

c) *Pollockshiels*

The district of Pollockshiels is, like Crosshill, entirely of a residential character; but while the western portion of it consists of villas, the eastern consists of terraces and streets of flatted tenements. In both divisions the inhabitants are, in the great majority of instances, either actual or retired citizens of Glasgow. The original application under the Act of 1862 was to form the whole district into a single police burgh; but on an appeal to the Home Secretary the application was refused in regard to the eastern portion, while it was granted in regard to the western. Pollockshields (West) then was formed into a police burgh in December 1876. The area at its formation was 166 acres, but it has since been extended under the statutory procedure to 216 acres. So entirely residential is the burgh that the Case for it states that there is no 'shop, factory, or other place of business, within its boundaries.' In 1876 the population was 1864 and the rateable value £18,756. They are now respectively 2856 and £35,339. There are nine commissioners (including three magistrates) of police. The burgh is policed by the county of Renfrew. It has no fire brigade, but has made arrangements for obtaining assistance, in case of fire, from Glasgow and Kinningpark. Being composed of self-contained villas, it has not felt it to be necessary to make any arrangement for the treatment of infectious diseases. The rates amount to 1s. 2½d. per £, viz., 8¾d. on occupiers, and 5¾d. on owners.

Although the Commissioners of Pollockshiels at first appeared in opposition to annexation, they withdrew at an early stage of our inquiry, the majority of the Commissioners and of the inhabitants being in favour of the extension of the boundaries of Glasgow so as to include the burgh.

d) *Statement by the Ratepayers Committee for the Burgh of Hillhead and the District of Kelvinside*
. . . The district [Hillhead and Kelvinside] has no police of its own. The police in Hillhead and Kelvinside number only 25 men, and they are part of the County force. In the event of any sudden riot or disturbance arising in the surrounding labouring or mining districts of Maryhill, Anniesland, Knightswood, or Partick, or in the City, and coming into Kelvinside or Hillhead police reinforcements would require to be drawn from the total force of 235 men of Lanarkshire Police, widely scattered over a large county. However well organised the County Police may be, there must be considerable delay in concentrating an extended force upon any particular point of the country, and especially on this district, which is detached from the rest.

C. The capabilities, or rather incapacity, of the County Police to cope with a sudden riot were well illustrated in the month of February of this year, 1887, during the riots among the miners at Blantyre. The Chief Constable of the county sent for reinforcements of men to Glasgow, and on 8th February 172 men were sent to his assistance, and 40 more were held in reserve in Glasgow. Twenty eight men were sent to Coatbridge, and 40 were in other parts of the county for some days. The remainder were not required beyond one day. The Committee do not reflect on the Chief Constable or the men under his charge; they know the Chief Constable to be a zealous and energetic officer, and the men under him to be well disciplined. They merely point to the incident as showing the absurdity of continuing part of a large town under the control of a small force of county police. In Glasgow, on the other hand, the police force numbers over 1000 men; and being confined to a comparatively small area, a force of several hundred men can with facility be collected on short notice, as when 172 men were sent to the county and 40 held in reserve in February last; and when on the occasion of a recent Socialistic meeting between 500 and 600 men were collected in the Green.

The detective department of Glasgow would be made more effective by the area adjoining the City being included, and the advantages of its extensive system for the recovery of stolen property would be available to the inhabitants. During the summer of 1887 several cases of house breaking and robbery occurred in Kelvinside and Hillhead, in none of which were the parties discovered.

SOURCE: Glasgow Boundaries Commission 1888, *Parliamentary Papers* 46, xvi–xxii; 131–3.

RELIGION

DOCUMENT 113

The Home Missionary

John G Paton (1824–1907), born in Dumfriesshire the son of a stocking-maker, spent ten years in city mission work in Glasgow whilst undertaking study at Glasgow University. In 1858 he was ordained a minister of the Reformed Presbyterian Church, and spent almost twenty years conducting a mission in the New Hebrides. In his autobiography, quoted below, he recalled his mission work in the east end of Glasgow during the years 1847–57, first employed by the Glasgow City Mission and subsequently by a congregation of the Reformed Presbyterian Church.

[Working for the Glasgow City Mission,] we were expected to spend four hours daily in visiting from house to house, holding small prayer meetings amongst those visited, calling them together also in evening meetings, and trying by all means to do whatever good was possible amongst them. The only place in the whole district [of Calton in Glasgow's east end] available for a Sabbath evening Evangelistic Service was a hay-loft, under which a cow-feeder kept a large number of cows, and which was reached by an outside rickety wooden stair. After nearly a year's hard work, I had only six or seven non-church-goers, who had been led to attend regularly there, besides about the same number who met on a week evening in the ground-floor of a house kindly granted for the purpose by a poor and industrious but ill-used Irishwoman . . . [Her husband] became a Total Abstainer, gave up his evil ways, and attended church regularly with his wife . . .

We instituted a Bible Class, a Singing Class, a Communicants' Class, and a Total Abstinence Society . . . [Meetings amongst the Calton Division of Glasgow Police bore fruit when] the men got up a Mutual Improvement Society and Singing Class also amongst themselves, weekly, on another evening. My work now occupied every evening in the week; and I had two meetings every Sabbath.

[After a year, Paton changed to working for Great Hamilton Street Reformed Presbyterian Church as its home missionary, and was given the use of a block containing church, halls and manse.] Its situation at the foot of Green Street gave it a control of the whole district where my work lay; and so the Church was given to me in which to conduct all my meetings, while the other halls were adapted as Schools for poor girls and boys, where they were educated by a proper master, and were largely supplied with books, clothing, and even food, by the ladies of the congregation . . .

Availing myself of the increased facilities, my work was all re-organised. On Sabbath morning, at seven o'clock, I had one of the most deeply interesting and fruitful of all my Classes for the study of the Bible. It was attended by from seventy to a hundred of the very poorest young women and grown-up lads of the whole district. They had nothing to put on except their ordinary work-day clothes, – all without bonnets, some without shoes. Beautiful was it to mark how the poorest began to improve in personal appearance immediately after they came to our class; how they gradually got shoes and one bit of clothing after another, to enable them to attend our other meetings, and then to go to church; and, above all, how eagerly they sought to bring others with them, taking a deep personal interest in all the work of the Mission. Long after they themselves could appear in excellent dress, many of them still continued to attend in their working clothes, and to bring other and poorer girls with them to that morning class, and thereby helped to improve and elevate their companions . . .

What would my younger brethren in the Ministry, or in the Mission [in the 1880s], think of starting out at six o'clock every Sunday morning, running from street to street for an hour, knocking at the doors and rousing the careless, and thus getting together, and keeping together, their Bible Class? This was what I did at first; but, in course of time, a band of voluntary visitors belonging to the class took charge of all the irregulars, the indifferents, and the new-comers, and thereby not only relieved and assisted me, but vastly increased their own personal interest, and became warmly attached to each other . . .

[At the Wednesday evening Prayer Meeting,] the attendance often more than half-filled the Church . . . On Thursday I held a Communicants' Class, intended for the more careful instruction of all who wished to become full members of the Church . . . Each being thus trained for a season, received from me, if found worthy, a letter to the minister of any Protestant Church which he or she inclined to join. In this way great numbers became active and useful communicants in the surrounding congregations, and eight young lads of humble circumstances edu-cated themselves for the ministry of the Church, – most of them getting their first lessons in Latin and Greek from my very poor stock of the same! Friday evening was occupied with a Singing Class, teaching Church music, and practising for our Sabbath meetings. On Saturday evening we held our Total Abstinence meeting, at which the members themselves took a principal part, in readings, addresses, recitations, singing hymns, etc . . .

From five to six hundred people were in usual weekly attendance, consisting exclusively of poor working persons, and largely of the humbler class of mill-workers. So soon as the circumstances improved, they were constantly removing to more respectable and healthy localities, and got to be scattered over all the city.

About eight or ten of my most devoted young men, and double that number of young women, whom I had trained to become visitors and tract distributors, greatly strengthened my hands. Each of the young men by himself, and the young women two by two, had charge of a portion of a street, which was visited by them regularly twice every month. At a monthly meeting of all our Workers, reports were given in, changes were noted, and all matters brought under notice were attended to . . . Several Christian gentlemen, mill-owners and other employers in the Calton, Mile-end, and Bridgeton of Glasgow, were so interested in my work that they kindly offered to give employment to every deserving person recommended by me, and that relieved much distress and greatly increased my influence for good . . .

Almost the only enemies I had were the keepers of Public-houses, whose trade had been injured by my Total Abstinence Society. Besides the Saturday night meetings all the year round, we held, in summer evening, and on Saturday afternoons, Evangelistic and Total Abstinence services in the open air. We met in Thomson's Lane, a short, broad street, not open for the traffic conveyances, and admirably situated for our purposes. Our pulpit was formed by the top of an outside stair, leading to the second flat of a house in the middle of the lane . . .

All through my City Mission period, I was painfully carrying on my studies, first at the University of Glasgow, and thereafter at the Reformed Presbyterian Divinity Hall; and also medical classes, at the Andersonian College . . . I struggled patiently on through ten years.

SOURCE: John G Paton 1889 *Missionary to the Hebrides. An Autobiography* (London, 4th edition), 55, 57–65, 81.

DOCUMENT 114

The Fisherwoman

Christian Watt (1833–1923) was a fisherwoman from Broadsea, a village near Fraserburgh on the Moray Firth coast. She was a woman of poor means, and many of the fishermen in her family were claimed by the sea. She followed her mother into the Congregationalist Church, but the Church of Scotland kirk session in her parish still tried in the 1850s to claim a right of superintendence on her. Her memoirs were written as a personal account of her life whilst a resident in later life in a mental institution in Aberdeen.

. . . I entered into a marriage contract at the end of January [1859]. It was a bond of handfast, drawn up by the lawyer. Within a year and a day we could produce evidence of a forthcoming child; or failing, by mutual consent, we could end the contract with no liability. If we married and I died the following week, my legacy, and (under my granny's will) both 35½ and 72 Broadsea became the absolute property of my mother and father jointly. If my husband died, 13 Pitullie, which was his also his grandparents' house 50 Pitullie, became the property of his mother; without such a contract, in the event of a death, the property passed to the remaining spouse. My father insisted on it, he had a business streak of his deceased mother, old Siccary. I felt perfectly happy and my mother was glad for me.

In April my mother was quite ill with chest trouble. She had been sheeling and baiting to my father who was at the small lines. She was admitted to Aberdeen Royal Infirmary. My father went through to stay with the Nobles at 4 South Square, Footdee; they were distant relations. I was alone in the house and thought many thoughts as I poked the fire to kindle the peats into a blaze, as generations before me had done the same. The white reek went up the lum where the steam of a million broth pots had gone before it. I thought how short is man's life. Should I bother to marry? I had been to Aberdeen, my mother was getting on fine and would soon be home. I had the house shining for her return. My mother was aye fond of nice things and had a lot of bonnie linen and bedding and bonnie china which she told me, if I married, to take the lot with me apart from my own bottom drawer providing.

It was a Saturday night, the boats did not go out the next day, I had no fish to split and smoke. James Sim came over to see me. It turned out a terrible night of wind and rain, I suggested he stay and sleep in the closet, but eventually he ended up in my bed in the butt end. Rain was lashing on the window. He was six foot three in his stocking soles. My brothers had been as tall and when they grew up the butt box bed had been extended, which made the wardrobe at the end shorter. Life had given me its last and final hidden secret, a moment poets have all written about. I was under contract, but still felt a sense of guilt having taken advantage of my parents absence. The rain ceased to pelt down. At four in the morning I told him to draw the back window and leave that way. I had left the ben lamp still burning and I intended leaving it till daylight came in; the reason was for prying eyes across the road. Our neighbour, Annie Gatt, in 71 (she was Onty's second wife and a born clake, gossip to her was like sun and water to a flower) – from the darkness of her butt window I noticed a shaft of light from the other end and her face on the glass. She had seen my lad arrive but did not see him go. My parents were away, the light was still on, so she would have the teem errand of sitting up all night seeing nothing! I laughed to myself.

Two weeks later James Sim left for the whaling at Greenland. He had pleaded to be married right away, but I wanted more time to think. When I went to hack mussells from our scaup west of Mawcraig, the lovely ozone on my face awakened desires in me as the fresh sea breeze quickened my nostrils. I was once again heaving and tossing on the Atlantic, and I could feel the wind filling the topsails and I knew part of my heart would always be in America. My sweetheart had been there at the sailing but had no love for it. The cold grey German Ocean did not hold the same romance. Lying in my bed when the rummel root was singing in the auld butt lum, I could hear the roar of the Atlantic in my ears, but now my consideration was for the child that was with me. I had let the father away and should there be delay with ice at the arctic, my child would be born illegitimate in January, which meant I would have to go before that bunch of hypocrites the Kirk Session – if so I would very quickly clean all their dirty neuks. During the conflict between Episcopalians and Presbyterians several times my ancestors had wrecked the church, now I would wreck the session. I would ask to appear in the body of the kirk not the vestry, and I would start on one elder, a Fraserburgh business man who had in the past been known to frequent bawdy houses in Aberdeen. In fact I toyed with the idea of turning down the father and keeping the child – today I wish I had made that decision . . .

During the weeks of waiting, I read nothing but my Bible, and to my own joy and astonishment I found the Lord Jesus as my own personal saviour. Only in my own personal experience did I discover how man was alienated from God, and how we were reconciled by his death on Calvary's cross. In my own room that night I knew I had passed from death unto life.

'Oh joyous hour when God to me a vision gave of Calvary, my bonds were loosed my soul unbound, I sang upon redemption ground.'

My duty lay in carrying out my betrothal contract, for whatever happened nothing could separate me from the love of Christ, whose very purity can see through the false, swicks, liars and cheats. His very majesty can make the greedy, envious and covetous hang their heads in shame.

SOURCE: D Fraser (ed) 1988 *The Christian Watt Papers*, Collieston (Caledonian Books), 67–8, 71–2.

DOCUMENT 115

The Church and Youth, 1960

John Highet was the pre-eminent sociologist of religion in Scotland between the late 1940s and the late 1960s. In this extract, he opens the first serious discussion of the emerging youth crisis in the Scottish churches.

No one knows the proportion of Scotland's young people who are connected with its Churches. Most, but not all, of the Churches who supply adult membership figures also publish figures of Sunday School enrolment and the number attending Bible Class or its equivalent. But even if all these were gathered up the aggregate would be but a minimum index. Not only that, it would be virtually impossible to relate it meaningfully to the total young people in the country. There are several reasons for this. The most important is that the age-ranges to which the figures refer differ (not only as between one denomination and another but, sometimes, as between individual churches), and there is no means of knowing what to add or deduct to get comparability. Another is to decide which categories to include and which to exclude. Should one take only Sunday Schools and Bible Classes, or include the membership of other youth organizations attached to the church? If the latter, how can one control, from the available statistics, the probable element of duplication? Church youth statistics are notoriously intractable.

Then there is the question of how many young people – in their late teens – may be full members of a Church. No information about this is available. An attempt was made through the sample survey to obtain data about the number of such young people in membership and about their attendance performance, but the figures provided proved unusable because while some ministers restricted their returns in the way desired, others clearly included Sunday School and Bible Class scholars and did not separate their number from that of young people in full membership.

For the younger age-groups, such figures as there are show that some denominations – for example, the Church of Scotland and the Baptist and Congregational Unions – show increases in their Sunday School and/or Bible Class enrolment since 1947, while others – for example, the United Free Church and the Episcopal Church – report decreases; and that, in the case of the Church of Scotland, the number of Sunday School scholars in 1957, at 307,218, represented 33.0 per cent of children of school age. This compares with nearly 470,000 in 1901, or more than half of the school population at that time, while between the two world wars the proportion was always between two-fifths and one-half. While the 1957 percentage compares very favourably with most of the figures for the post-Second World War period, which recorded a fairly steady upward movement compared with 1946, the 1957 enrolment was down by nearly 18,000, and the school population percentage by 2 points, on those for 1956. Bible Class enrolment, at 54,155 in 1957, or 24 per cent of the young people aged fifteen to seventeen, also compares very unfavourably with the position fifty years ago and in the 1920's and 1930's, and is down by several thousand compared with the mid-1950's.

This, however, tells us only about the church connection of some of the nation's children and younger teen-agers. As stated, one can only guess at the proportion of young people (in the sense of older teen-agers) who are members of a Scottish Church. Some sample returns indicated that a fair number of young people were about the congregation, and some ministers, in answering a later question, spoke of the thriving 'younger life' of their congregations and the promising quality of these young people. But this does not take us very far. As another partial guide, I asked the panel of supplementary respondents if their experience bore out a suggestion that is sometimes made, that the 1950's have witnessed a 'revival' of interest in the Church on the part of young people. Of the thirty-two who replied, more than half (seventeen) said there was no evidence of a revival, five said that while there were no signs of a 'revival' there were signs of growing interest (one of this group mentioned the university population in particular), four that there was 'steady' interest (in one case, 'young people are as responsive as ever'), three that there was 'some' or 'general' interest on the part of some young people, two that 'keen and realistic' interest was being taken and 'honest searching' being done (again by some), and one that 'young people are not as heathen as we sometimes suppose'. In their replies one or two mentioned that the average age of their Kirk Session was lower than they could remember, this showing that the 'keenly interested' young people of a few years ago had maintained their interest and even deepened it . . .

While one cannot put a measure on it, it is evident enough that there is a considerable body of the country's young people standing apart from its Churches, and what 'keeps them away' is often said (and not only by non-church adults and young people) to be the fact that the Church 'doesn't get across to young people' or 'doesn't do enough for them' in a way that would help them with their difficulties or even indicate to them that it understands, or is trying to understand, what these difficulties are; so that to young people it appears that the Church has little to say to them that is relevant to young adulthood in the conditions of today. Perhaps it is partly that young people superficially think that they do not need help or make help difficult for those offering it. 'However hard one tries', said David Reid of Castlemilk, 'it is not easy to make young people feel part of the "family" of the Church. They like to think of themselves as a breed apart.' At all events, I asked our panel for their views on this alleged obstacle. Six did not answer the question directly, and, of the remaining twenty-nine, seventeen were definitely of the opinion that the Church was not 'doing enough' (two said 'because it hasn't the resources' and one added that it realized it should do more); six said it was doing what it could, and four that it was doing a lot but could do more; one said it was doing 'too much' and another that 'youth should do more for the Church'. Among the replies were . . .

> Increasingly teen-agers are being, unconsciously perhaps, thrust outside the range and influence of the Church. One hears much about their hostile attitude to older people, but is this not due to the fact that they cannot trust older people?; we have not tried to understand them. I have discovered that among teen-agers, many of them of the teddy-boy and -girl type, there is a deep basic honesty. They are willing to examine and discuss the Christian faith provided they do not think you are going to 'sell' them something. They are perhaps looking for truth in their own way. (Ian MacTaggart)

> The Church is talking to young people in terms of a bygone age. Ministers do not talk to them as intellectual equals, though they sometimes are (and sometimes their superiors). (Dr Donald M. Macfarlan) . . .

Sex is, of course, only one of the problems people think the Church should be helping young people with, but our society is characterized by an incessant emphasis on and playing up of sex through the media of mass communication, and there is evidence that not all young church people put the teachings of the Church on sexual morality into practice.[1] The majority on the panel said that the Church was not facing up squarely enough to unorthodox behaviour, either by its own people or in society at large, or to helping young people, again both inside and outside the Church. Some replied that the Church should, and could only, make its own teaching quite plain, but others saw it as a wider problem, one asking, for example, 'Is it not time that we called a halt to this incessant stimulation?' (through the mass media), and another stating: 'In competition with the "new morality" fed to young people by the cinema, wireless and TV plays, modern periodicals and literature, the Church stands as helpless as do parents'. I was surprised that none mentioned the support by some Scottish Churches of, for example, the Marriage Guidance movement and the fact that some ministers in recent years have been inviting lecturers on that movement's panel to address the engaged or newly married couples in their congregations. On the whole, the answers seemed of the kind that would strike our 'objector' as bearing out his contention that in matters such as this the Church is not really 'getting across' to young people very helpfully.

NOTES

1 See, for example, *Youth at Leisure*, a report by a Special Commission set up by the Youth Committee on instructions from the General Assembly, and published by the Committee in 1956.

SOURCE: John Highet 1960 *The Scottish Churches: A Review of Their State 400 Years after the Reformation*, London (Skeffington), 180–6.

DOCUMENT 116

The Church and Youth, 1973

This extract comes from an extensive sociological study of Falkirk conducted in the late 1960s for the Church of Scotland and the Hope Trust. Written by Peter Sissons, the inquiry sought practical advice for the General Assembly's Church and Ministry Department on how – particularly – to respond to the growing problem of nonchurchgoing. It took Falkirk – lying roughly midway between Edinburgh and Glasgow – as a suitable community for intensive study. Whilst other reports followed in 1980 and 1987 on economic and 'lifestyle' aspects of the Church of Scotland in society, the Sissons Report was by far the most ambitious in sociological terms.

Some social correlates of religious affiliation amongst two hundred and fifty-eight school children in the burgh of Falkirk: A preliminary report of the first stage of a pilot study conducted in the Graeme High School, Falkirk

... Church was attended with varying degrees of regularity by 45% of the children in the sample [of 258]. The Registrar General's classifications were used for distinguishing socio-economic class which was measured by the occupation of the father, or, when this was unknown, by the occupation of working mothers. By these criteria 64% of the church attenders were in the Registrar General's first three classifications, whilst 5% were placed in the fifth classification reserved for those engaged in unskilled occupations. The highest percentage of church attenders was to be found in the third of the five classifications, indicating that more than half of the children attending church had one or both parents engaged in a skilled occupation of either manual or white collar in nature. The percentage of church attenders in this category was higher than the comparable percentage of either of the other sub-samples. The children who attend church are predominantly from lower middle-class homes. This was reflected in their career expectations. Almost 36% of those who attended church hoped to go on from school to further education or to enter one of the professions, whilst 11.8% expected to be employed in manual work and 22.6% expected to be engaged in skilled work in offices or laboratories. The fact that 34.4% of the church attenders expected to engage in occupations which currently engage 86.8% of church attenders' parents, whilst 36% aspire to occupations which currently engage less than 10% of church attenders' parents is indicative of an expectation of high mobility typical of lower middle-class families of a certain type and, in our sample, it is typical of those who attend church ...

More girls attended church than boys, and they attended more often. 77% of the church attenders attended their churches regularly, but 84% of the girls attended regularly including 50.7% who attended every Sunday. The girls were more likely to attend the same church as other members of their families than were the boys, although fewer girls than boys said that they attended church because of their parents. 64% of the children who attended church were girls, whilst girls generally had a marginally higher degree of participation in all organisations. A consideration of the attitudinal questions, unsophisticated as these were, suggests that the girls possess a higher level of religiosity than the boys and that the boys related to the church through their families or through their friends rather than because of internal convictions. Only 37% of the male church attenders believe in God, whilst 76% of the girls do so. A higher percentage of girls believes that God created and rules the world and that God guides the choice of career, although the percentage decreased with each of those questions. Similarly 38.7% of the girls said that they attended church because they wished to worship God as opposed to 12.2% of the boys; 75% of girls who attend church said that they prayed alone on some occasion, and 60% of the girls added comments to the questionnaire about their need for the church and the importance of Christianity in their lives. In their behaviour and in their expressed beliefs the girls are more religious than the boys, although they appear to relate to the church through their parents, particularly through their mothers, more than the boys . . .

The former attenders differed most markedly from the church attenders in that they were more often to be found in the younger age groups. Almost 60% of the fourteen year olds had ceased to attend church, whilst only 20% of the seventeen year olds no longer attended. Factors which might adversely affect the weighting of these figures have already been outlined. More interesting than the age distribution is the fact that 83% of the children who had ceased to attend church had done so before their fourteenth birthdays. This is undoubtedly related to disenchantment with the Sunday school, but as the analysis above has suggested there are other variables to be taken into account, particularly the role of the family . . .

Belief in the existence of God was expressed by 52% of those children who had ceased to attend church, whilst 13% and 12% respectively believed that God rules the world and that God influences the choice of careers, and 34.6% of the sub-sample believed that the world had been created by God. The boys who had ceased to attend church showed a higher incidence of belief than those who continued to attend, 46% against 37% of the male former attenders believed that God rules the world as against 12.1% of the male attenders. One boy who had ceased to attend church expressed his awareness of this apparent contradiction when he wrote on the questionnaire, 'I do not believe that it is necessary to attend church in order to believe in God'; he went on to express positive belief in God as the creator, the ruler of the world and as an influence in occupational choice. This supports the hypothesis suggested earlier that boys who go to church consciously relate to the church in social terms rather than in terms of commitment or belief . . . A smaller percentage of female former attenders subscribed to all four beliefs than in the sub-sample of church attenders. The bible was read occasionally by 34% of male former attenders and 35.3% female former attenders, compared with 31% and 60% respectively of the boy and girl church attenders, and a similar ratio existed for the offering of private prayer. Indication of what has been described as 'residual belief' is high for former attenders, and the boys who formerly attended church compare remarkably in these limited criteria of religiosity with the boys who attend church . . .

Secularisation is evident in this sample in institutional rather than ideological terms. The cessation of church attendance was not necessarily a cessation of religious belief for these children, it was rebellion against a form of institutionalisation, the imposition of an unwelcome ecclesiastical routine and it was an inability to identify with the church in communal or associational terms. The attitudinal data were unfortunately not sufficiently refined to permit an exploration of the relationship between church attendance and degree of overt and covert identification with the church through participation and subscription to orthodox or unorthodox religious beliefs. Some theories of secularisation begin with the proposition that in an increasingly fragmented and specialised society religion is assuming a fragmented and associational character in which it is identified with a part of life rather than with the whole of life. This appears to be borne out by the apparent influence of the family upon the sub-samples of church attenders and former attenders inasmuch as the loss of identity with the religious institution coincides with the family's disinterest in religion, and the loss of the family's communal identity. At the same time the children have difficulty in achieving an associational relationship with the churches . . .

Summary . . .
I   The children who attend church are those who belong to lower middle-class families, whilst those who do not attend include the children who belong to lower-middle class families, and almost all of the children who belong to working-class and better educated middle-class families.
II   The girls in the sample were more religious than the boys in terms of both behaviour and belief.
III   Most of the children who attended church did so with their families or had parents or siblings who attended other churches.
IV   The boys were more conscious than the girls of the fact that they related to the church through their families, whilst the girls cited belief and the desire to worship as their primary motivations for church attendance.
V   The member of any of the families most likely to attend church was the mother.
VI   Those who attended church were the children most likely to attend voluntary associations, and the associations which they attended were of a communal rather than an associational nature.
VII   The children who attended church predominated in the older rather than the younger age groups.
VIII   Those who attended church were more certain of their career expectations and were more ambitious (in that they expected to engage in occupations with a higher social status than their parents) than were the children who did not attend church.
IX   Those children who had ceased to attend church had for the most part done so before their fourteenth birthdays.
X   The children who had ceased to attend church and those who had never been

church-goers belonged mainly to families in which church going was not a custom. XI These children were not such avid joiners of voluntary associations as those who attend church, and the bodies to which they belonged were associational rather than communal in character.

XII The reasons which were given for the cessation of church attendance were attitudinal rather than behavioural, reflecting disinterest in the central activities of the churches, but in some cases expressing complete disenchantment with religious teaching and antagonism to the beliefs, practices and adherents of the churches . . .

SOURCE: PL Sissons 1973 *The Social Significance of Church Membership in the Burgh of Falkirk*, Edinburgh (Church of Scotland), 292–3, 301–14.

GENDER

DOCUMENT 117

Oral testimony: Stirling women

*Social historians of nineteenth- and twentieth-century Scotland can draw
upon a vast range of primary sources relating to their areas of interest.
However, much of the experience of women and gender relations before the
Second World War remains poorly documented, not least because women
were largely denied access to positions of power and had a relatively low
profile in public affairs. This was the product of an intensely patriarchal
society, where the prevailing attitude was that a woman's 'proper' place was
in the home. Hence sport, politics and trade unions were largely male
domains and the records of related institutions offer few insights into the
lives of women and gender relationships. This is especially true of the inner,
private world of the home and family. Recently, some historians have
exploited and developed the methodology of oral history – interviewing and
recording respondents' memories on tape – to open up a window on such
experiences. Their findings have helped to recreate the sexual division of
labour within the home and vastly extend our understanding of gender
relations within the family. The following are a few extracts selected from
one of the oral history projects in Scotland funded by the Manpower Services
Commission in the mid-1980s and directed by the late Jane Stephenson. The
Stirling Women's Oral History Project produced 80 transcribed interviews
covering all aspects of women's lives – work, home, family, religion, leisure,
public affairs – relating predominantly to the period c.1900–1950.*

Interview conducted:	29/6/87
Name:	Mrs C2
DOB:	1912
Occupation:	Hairdresser & clerical worker

Q)   So did your mother have any jobs before she married?
A)   Yes, she was in charge of a finishing place where they curled ostrich feathers
and cleaned feather boas and things like that. They had a lot of branches this firm
and she was sort of in charge of the office side of that. These were the days when
furs and feather boas and all these sort of things were very fashionable.
Q)   Did she work after she was married?
A)   No, oh no, you didn't work after you were married in those days. She worked
but worked a lot harder than anybody ever works nowadays because to start with
everything had to be starched. And I remember, my pram had broderie anglaise lining
and broderie anglaise round the hood and it had a frill and that all had to be starched
and ironed with a goffering iron. All the clothes that babies wore were starched and

white broderie anglaise with frills had to be done with this goffering iron and of course the washing was done in a wash house – the fire had to be built there first thing in the morning and then mothers had to take their prams and their babies down, if they were in a flat. And they had to . . . they washed most of the day . . .

Q)   You mentioned that your father played golf. Did your mother play golf?

A)   No, she didn't play golf. Women didn't play golf so much in these days. I don't know – a woman's role was much more that of a homemaker, they didn't seem to have so many outside interests you know as . . . I remember my mother went back to Edinburgh every week-end, perhaps the Saturday or the Sunday. The return fare in the bus was one and thruppence in the old money y'know and she was so homesick for Edinburgh to start with, that she went back. Well of course she had a modern house with a bathroom, electricity and a living room with a little scullery off, and when we came here we had to take a furnished house in the Abbey and it had oil lamps and the great big range which had to be lit before you could do any cooking.

Q)   So did your mother do all the housework?

A)   Everything. She had – because she wasn't very strong – she had a woman once a week to do the rough work, always. She always had that because she really wasn't able to do scrubbing and polishing and cleaning you know. So she had this woman for, I think it would be from about eight 'til one. Mind you that only cost half a crown in these days. And you could get – a farthing was legal tender. When you got your penny on a Saturday you got four farthings, not a penny, so that you could spend a farthing at a time you know. It made it last out better.

Q)   Was the washing sent out?

A)   No, at that time she did the washing. Much later on some things went to the laundry – linen and so on, but that was a long time after, not initially. And of course in the house in Riverside we had a gas boiler there and a big garden, and the washing was very easy compared to what it had been in this furnished house.

Q)   So did your mother make or mend family clothes?

A)   She made all my clothes until I would be perhaps about seven. She made trousers for the boys and knitted all our socks and my father's socks and all these sort of things, and I think she also knitted cardigans for us and things like that. In fact I can remember you didn't seem to buy many new clothes because if I was getting anything special a dressmaker came. We bought the material, and mother . . . there was a lot of dressmakers about, good ones you know. My party frocks and things like that, were made by a dressmaker. There wasn't so many ready made things at that time when I was seven – that's a long time ago, sixty-eight years ago.

Q)   Did your father help your mother with any jobs in the house?

A)   (Laughs) No, they weren't expected to, they were never asked to in these days – at least most men who had the kind of jobs my father had weren't expected to do anything. I can remember when my mother; she had migraine headaches, and about almost every month she would be in bed for about three days with the curtains drawn and vinegar cloths on her head, and everybody had to creep around. And of course being the only girl I had the dishes to do and things like that – I generally left the pots. Poor mother, she got the pots to come down to. But my father would offer to dry the dishes. Now he wore stiff white collars and stiff white cuffs and he was immaculate, always immaculate as if he came out of a bon box. Now, he would take off his jacket, hang it on the back of the chair, roll up his sleeves, fix them up here, tie a clean tea towel round his waist and then he would start. It was like performing an operation drying these dishes and he took so long to do it you know – he was very particular.

Q)   So did you have to do any jobs around the house, like housework? Did you do any yourself?

A)   Oh yes, we all got jobs to do. We weren't allowed out on a Saturday until we all did our jobs, the boys too. My job was to clean the bathroom, I remember that, and my brother who was near me, he scrubbed the boards in the kitchenette and they were well scrubbed – he was very thorough and my younger brother cleaned the cutlery – you know it had to be cleaned every week in these days. When you think of it you know, the work that people had then, I don't think they would believe it if they came back and saw nowadays.

Q)   And how much did your husband have to do with the children when they were young?

A)   Not so much as nowadays, not nearly so much. All he . . . if the baby cried at night, through the night, I'd probably get up and see that there was no wind or anything – change the nappy and put her down. If she continued to cry he would say to me, he would nudge me, and say, 'You're not much of a mother letting the child cry!' I said, 'There's nothing wrong with her, I'm a very good mother and if you're worried you get up!' But he didn't. Men didn't do so much. In fact the first child he took out in the pram was John. And I said to him once, 'You know you never took the girls out,' and he said, 'Oh no, but this is a boy.' I said, 'But how are people going to know when he's in a pram and all covered up that it's a boy?' I couldn't understand that reasoning, you know. But he did a bit more with the children as they got a wee bit older. You know he was really good, and he looked after them at night if I was going out. And he got to the stage that, I think, probably my having this asthma he had to do more. And he got gradually used to it. But he never changed nappies or things like that. Men didn't do that in these days, you know, unfortunately.

Q)   And how did you and your husband manage the housekeeping in the early years of your marriage?

A)   Well I managed it, he wasn't . . . I was the one who always seemed to see to everything, I seemed to be – though he had a business – I seemed to be more the business head, though I was younger. And I always managed the money. And he used to . . . , if we were going anyplace I'd say, "You tell me where you want to go," and he said, "Just please yourself!" That was usually his attitude. Or if we were going on holiday and if anything was wrong with it, it was my fault you see. It's a very sensible thing for a man to do. To put the onus on his wife for . . . you know he'd never make up his mind where he wanted to go. Just left it to me. Left everything to me.

Interview conducted: 29/6/87
Name: Mrs B.2.1
DOB: 1907
Occupation: Clerkess in butcher's shop

Q)   And did your mother do all the housework herself? Did she ever get anybody to come in?

A)   Oh no, when we were young, but as we grew older you had to do your bit. My sister, oh my sister was a far better worker than me. I would go and sort the flowers and I would go and do the garden but oh I hated doing pots. Of course they were big black pots you know and they got all . . . but we had the grate and of course there was an awful lot of steel about them and on a Friday morning, Saturday morning rather, we would get up and we had to clean this, polish this and oh, my sister was a great worker and it'd all to be blackleaded and polished 'til your face shone in it and then there was a steel fender and everything and we had to clean that. Oh no, you didn't get away with it, you had to take your share, but you thought nothing of it.

Q)   What about your father, did he help in the house at all?

A)   No, oh dad would . . . I mean if my mother wasnae very well certainly, but in these days you see the wife did everything, and it was exceptional for the father.

Q)   So what about birth control in those days, did you know anything about birth control?

A)   Well we knew about it but of course Jimmy was away three and a half years and if we'd got another baby good and well, but it didn't happen you see, but well you knew there was the rubber goods and there was the rhythm method and that but . . . you just learned as you went along.

Q)   Could you get advice anywhere? Or how did you learn of it?

A)   Just picked it up here and there you know, there was no place you would go for advice – your doctor I suppose but we never asked the doctor, we didn't bother.

Q)   So did you feed your baby yourself?

A)   Oh yes, uh-huh, I believe in breast feeding, it gives the child a great start.

Q)   Now when you first got married then who did the housekeeping? Was that all left up to you?

A)   Yes. My husband handed over his pay packet every month and he got so much back for pocket money, and I got his cigarettes along with my groceries and the money was mine, if I couldn't keep within it that was my fault – that was the whole thing as I say, you had to keep within your housekeeping. Of course I had had a good training, my mother trained us well and we were brought up, and she said, 'Now you're going away from the house,' and she says, 'Remember you've your own home and you'll always be welcome back here. But unless anything terrible happens you stay with your husband.' See, the attitude was different then and like every other couple we never really fell out, but you had your arguments – you wouldn't be human to say you never argued – 'well they must be something wonderful!' (laughs). But you never thought of leaving your husband, I never had any reason to of course 'cause Jimmy didn't drink, he smoked and he was a manager in the church.

Interview conducted:	25.3.87
Name:	Mrs B.1.1
DOB:	1907
Occupation:	Domestic service

Q) Did your husband help you with the kids at all?

A) Well he was good with the bairns, but no' about the house. He was very good with the kids, oh aye.

Q) So how did you and your husband manage the housekeeping in the early years?

A) Oh, you had your lean times being married to a miner, there were ups and downs all through your married life, 'til the family grew up and started work, but I managed.

Q) Did you know what your husband earned?

A) Not his full wage, no, never. They weren't any good at telling you that long ago (laughing).

Q) So he would just give you some of his wage?

A) Uhuhm.

Q) And how did you work out when you should get an increase in that housekeeping?

A) Oh, I couldnae tell you about that. I just never thought I suppose, took it when it come likely.

Q) Did you pay the bills or did your husband?

A) No, no, I paid everything.

Q) What about decisions about things like new furniture?

A) I did that. I got the money and I had to get on with it.

Q) If you were ill or perhaps confined to bed having children or something, did you get help from neighbours or friends?

A) Oh, aye, they were good neighbours. I was always fortunate I helped and they helped sort of thing.

Q) You all sort of mucked in?

A) Oh yes, aye, oh yes.

Q) Would somebody come in when you were having one of your children, say a neighbour, and perhaps do the cooking.

A) Aye, up until my own daughters grew up.

Interview conducted: 23.3.87
Name: Mrs A.1
DOB: 1911
Occupation: Fabric block printer (Cambusbarron Mill)

Q)   Can you remember what hours you worked?
A)   From eight to one . . . from eight to twelve and from twelve to one and some days it was to depending on whatever they were doing you got to half past one. Then you finished at five thirty and you couldnae leave the mill down here, you didnae get out the gate till a quarter to six and there was a man standing at the gate. One of the men liked to see that the lassies didnae take anything. See it was material like that, all designs and some used to wrap a bit round them and they had to watch.
Q)   What did you wear for work? Did you have a uniform?
A)   No. Over and above that I worked on Saturday. On Saturday we didnae work down there and well we did half day, twelve o'clock and then I got a job in Woolworths. I started at about one o'clock and I worked to six at night in Woolworths. Five bob for the week, it wasnae much when you think on it.
Q)   Which job did you prefer?
A)   Well, I think I liked the mill because Woolworth was quite em . . . the pattern, there was a handle on it y'see and you stamped it there and you stamped it there the whole eighteen yards down you stamped it with a different bit of the design.
Q)   So did you think it was more skilled in the mill than working in Woolworths?
A)   Eh, working in Woolworths was nothing 'cause they could put you anywhere and eh, I only took the job in Woolworths for the sake of the extra five bob. The old man he only gave us a tanner off of that money.
Q)   In the mill can you remember if it was men and women working together?
A)   No. We made the material, printed it right, maybe sixty-two yards of material and they had about seven or eight men on the other side of the yard down here in the mill and they had long, it would be about the length of the room, long sinks they could put the material into for all that colour to come out. But before they put it into there, I should have mentioned it they put it on pulleys and put it into this room and steamed it and that steam done when we buy our material likes of.
Q)   Like you showed me before?
A)   Aye, you steamed it in for about three quarters of an hour and then washed it and when they washed it the design didnae come out y'see because the colour was steamed in. You had to be pretty careful about the colours.
Q)   Did you get on with the girls that you worked with?
A)   Oh aye, we aye had to because there werenae that many of you, there maybe just be about eleven and twenty, I think there'd only be about sixteen of us. There was eight tables, I'm right enough eight twos is sixteen, then they'd maybe have four extra lassies in case somebody didnae turn up and when you printed it that material had to go across the yard down here in the mill to a place. We just printed it with the colour that went on the linen.

Q)   Were you all doing the same job in your room?

A)   Aye.

Q)   There was nobody doing a different job?

A)   No, no just that. They took it off to this shed and these two men steamed it, they put it on rollers like a pully and they would shut the door and it was steamed for about an hour and then they opened and they took the material out and they brought it back over to us and we had to wash all that dye out of it.

Interview conducted: 1.4.87
Name: Mrs H.1
DOB: 1907
Occupation: Textile worker

Q)   Did each family do their own?

A)   No, mother done the washing but periodically I'd be going at night and do a big wash and boil it in the boiler, then it was a wringer that I've got ben there and she would hang it out next day, just to save her, give her more time y'know with the children.

Q)   Did you do that quite a lot?

A)   Oh yes, I liked house work. I do yet in fact.

Q)   Did your brothers and sisters help?

Everybody had their share, my father laid that rule down. Some would make beds, some would do windows. There were no carpets remember, it was just linoleum, some would scrub that and I had the spoon drawer to do, all the cutlery. Polished them, washed them, put them in their line. I also had the big grate to do, big black leaded grate, that was my job, I liked that and the brasses that was my job as well.

Q)   What sort of things did your brothers do?

A)   Well, there was so many years between the girls and the boy. He was just brought up with us as a baby and he always clung to me, he does yet and he's sixty-eight. He lost his wife three years ago.

Q)   Was there anyone else living with your parents and brothers and sisters, any other relative or anything?

A)   No, not really.

Q)   Did your mother ever get anybody to come and help her in the house?

A)   No, we always helped, that was our rules and regulations. We never got out unless we done our work. We had to do that job and when we were coming from the factory, my father was going down to the Ordnance, back to his work after lunch. He used to turn round and he used to shout, 'If you girls are going out tonight remember you must do your work.'

Q)   Did your dad keep quite a close eye on what household duties you were doing?

A)   Oh yes, very, very much. He was a very particular man.

Q)   Did he do any himself?

A)   Well, he done the garden, no he didnae need to do it, he did, when my mother had the girls, when they were young he took over bath time and done our hair. The ones that had curls which I had, he used to put them round his finger and pull his finger down and dry it. It was lovely and the ones that had long hair in plaits, he used to plait it all, birl it round at the bottom and that was how you went to bed. Your hair done and yourself washed, no bathroom just a great big bath on the floor. You each took a turn and had a bath. When your body was washed, your face, and your hair was washed, we all done our feet and I don't mind telling you we were cleaner than what they are now, some of them and they've all got bathrooms.

Q)   Were there any other tasks that your father did in the house?

A)   Well, after we started growing up and going to school, father mended the shoes. We never put any shoes to the cobblers. He got a last and all the tools and he used to sole and heel all our shoes. That saved a bit of money.

Q)   Were there any other housework tasks that you did?

A)   The windows, the washing, and do the curtains and the ironing, clean the pots. I had to take the pots out to the back yard with a knife and scrape the pot because they were just fires to cook on.

Q)   Did men and women work together in your bit of the factory?

A)   No, it was mostly women. But what we called the gaffer, the head one, then an under chap he took over when he was away doing something. Then that chap I told you went round with the barrow collecting all the waste. Three of them on the floor head.

Q)   And those managers were the ones that would sometimes walk around and maybe stop and watch?

A)   To see that everybody was doing their work, that second one walked around.

Q)   How did you get on with the other people that you worked with?

A)   Oh great, everybody. There were people from Cowie, Bannockburn, St. Ninians, Plean and Stirling all worked in that factory. You got on with every one of them and mind the ones that had come from Plean and Cowie had to get a bus maybe at half past seven and if that bus wasnae going at half past seven there was no use in coming because they didnae arrive to eight o'clock and that's when the big gate got shut. Well, they knew when the bus was going and when it was coming back.

Q)   But they didn't get shut out often?

A)   Once I told you I got shut out. I didn't go home that day I went away for a walk then I got no pocket money (laugh).

Q)   How did you feel about your work at Templetons?

A)   Oh, I loved it. It was sort of dirty but we loved it. We always took a change of clothes. We worked with different clothes. I did anyway. I used to change my stockings and my shoes and my skirt and put this big overall on because when the machine was going round it was splashing out oil and you got it all on your clothes and my father objected to us dressing going to our work. He thought when we went to our work and when he had a wee job at night in the bar as well as the Ordnance he thought we were going out that night if we went dressed to work.

Q)   So when did you give up your job at Templetons?

A)   When I got married, twenty-one.

Q)   Was it usual to stay on or to leave after you got married?

A)   Well, I don't remember very many girls going back when they got married but I remember a few going back but not very much. They just left that time and stayed at home. Of course a lot of them had to stay at home if you know what I mean.

Q)   What do you mean?

A)   They were pregnant some of them (laugh) innocently.

Q)   Was that quite common?

A)   Not very often. I wasnae one of them, don't think it.

Q)   So what did you do then?

A)   Well, when my husband went to work I used to go up and help mother to do her work, and her washing, and her ironing and take my own washing up and get it done at the same time. No washing machine though. Hands rubbing on the boards.

SOURCE: Transcripts of the Stirling Women's Oral History Project. Courtesy of the late Jane Stephenson and Elspeth King. The tapes and transcripts can be consulted at the Smith Museum, Stirling and at the Scottish Oral History Centre, History Department, University of Strathclyde.

LOWLAND AGRICULTURE
AND SOCIETY

DOCUMENT 118

Harvesting in Ayrshire, 1856

*At the time of writing his diary, Peter Wright, Bruntwood Mains, Galston,
Ayrshire, was seventeen years old. This extract, 4 to 17 September 1856,
describes the end of the hay harvest and the start of the grain harvest.*

Thursday, 4   In the morning we cut the Timothy hay which was for seed their
was 160 sheaves of it, we brought up a cart of grass from the meadow to the horse;
this was Bruntwood Hill hay stack. Alex, Janet, Isabella and I, with Sharp [a horse]
was at it. There was 6 horse leeding [carting] in and plenty of hands, 4 from
Lowholehouse and a horse, 4 from Killock and a horse, 4 from our house and a
horse, 3 from Meckleyard and a horse, 3 from Beut and a horse, 2 from Righead,
1 Bruntwood. We had past before six and danced in the Barn till between 11
o'clock and 12, this was a good day.

Friday, 5   Alex, Isabella and I and a horse was at Mouk. gathering a cart of
thrashes [rushes]. The were very thin and we had a small cart of them. We came
home by Burnam and Burnhead, we came home about 7 o'clock. My Father was
at Kilmarnock and my Mother was at Galston. This was a good day but rather
cold at Mouk. The thrashes are to thick [thatch] the hay ricks [stacks]. Beut and
Littleson are commenced there harvest. Ours is late but heavy. Wm Wright took
down 19 bolls of ryegrass seed to Kilmarnock to-day. The cows are not giving so
much milk now.

Saturday, 6   In the morning Alex and my Father went down to Galston station
with 10 bolls of old corn he sold it yesterday at Kilmarnock to Andw Aitken, Dalry.
In the forenoon we brought down some thrashes . . . from the Knows and Quarry
and drew [sorted them for length] them and those which came from Mouk. In the
afternoon we thatched 2 of the largest ricks. Janet and Isabella made the rops
[ropes]. At night we brought down a cart of grass for the horse. I milk night and
morning. This was a dull day and a little rain at evening.

Monday, 8   In the morning and forenoon Alex and I mowed out all the thrashes
which was in the Little Getterland, and brought down a cart of grass to the horse,
with Bell [a horse]. Sharp went to Kilmarnock with Bruntwood ryegrass seed to-
day. In the afternoon, Alex, my Father and I with Bell went down to Galston Bar
and took out near 6 loads of meal to Alex White and brought home 1 load to Mouk
and I load ½ boll and ten lb. It is all out the Garnel now. Their was 74 bolls of it,
at 46/6 per load. This was a dull day but warm. We bought 2 hooks [sickles] and 1
syth to-day.

Tuesday, 9   In the morning and forenoon Alex and I mowed all the thrashes and
some grass in the Plantain. Their was a cart of thrashes and one of grass. We

brought them up with Sharp. My Father thatched one off the little ricks. In the afternoon Alex brought up two carts of coals from Dykehead Collery. This was a warm day thunder and rain on the afternoon. We put out 7 calves into the Plantain to graize. My Father mending the gates and hedges. I drew some of the thrashes for thatch. Bell was at the Smithy to-day. My Uncle weeding thistles in the Bruthole.

Wednesday, 10   In the forenoon Alex brought two carts of coals from Dykehead coal pit. I mowed all the dyke backs round the Smithy park [field]. In the forenoon and part of the afternoon my Uncle and Isabella drew thrashes in the stackyard for thatch, and I put them into sheaves. Alex brought up two carts of coals from Gauchline coalpit in the afternoon and brought down a large cart of grass for the horse which I mowed in the afternoon. My father was working about the house. This was a warm day, and sunny. The most of people have commenced their harvest now.

Thursday, 11   In the morning Alex and I drew the remainder of the thrashes which is in the stackyard. Alex brought two carts of coals from Dykehead coalpit in the forenoon. We had the seedmen to-day in the forenoon. My uncle drove [hand cranked] the fanners [winnowing machine]. 2 seedmen and my father reeing [sieving] and I filling the fanders [ie *fanners* or winnowing machine]. In the afternoon my Father went to a burial at Townhead. We had the seed all through twice before night. Their is 33 bolls of it the weight of the bushel lucky 23 lb it is ready to take . . . This was a fine day. Sharp was working at Mikleyard.

Friday, 12   In the morning Alex and my Father went to Mr Dickie seedmerchant with 2 carts of ryegrass-seed, 31 bolls. Wm Wright getting 2 bolls for seed. My father and I took 2 bushels of seed out from among the caff [chaff] weight 20lb per bushel. Alex brought 2 carts of coals home with him from Dykehead. In the forenoon I mowed some of the dyke backs round the Farmuir. Isabella digged pottatoes all day in the Farmuir. The are very bad. My uncle wed thistles in the Wee Getterland. Andrew Paton Flesher Galston killed a swine at our house to-day. Brought down a cart of grass from the Farmuir.

Saturday, 13   In the forenoon my Father went down to Galston. 45 stones of cheese to Alex White at 11/ per stone, and a swine to Andrew Paton, weight of it 7½ stones at 12/ per stone. Alex, Isabella and I cut and quiled [ie *kyled*, or put into rows] the grass round the Meadow and the goat. In the afternoon Alex and I brought down a cart of grass from the Smithy park. My Father, Uncle, and Isabella brought up two carts of grass from the Meadow and the Timothy hay which was for seed. We thrashed and cleaned it. We have commenced to give the cows sheaves of beans [ie whole plant] at night. This was a good day.

Monday, 15   In the morning Alex and I cleaned the roads about the house we commenced to mow our corn to-day about 11 o'clock. My Father and Alex mowing. We cut near 7 rigs [cultivation ridges] all but a little piece at the head and foot. Janet, Isabella and John lift bind and make straps [sheaf bands] to Alex. Robert Alexander from Newmilns and I do it to my Father. This was a very good day for mowing, a strong west wind, but showery. The corn we cut to-day is not very heavy. Yesterday was my 17 birth day. We have visitors to-day from Irvine lately arrived from Port Ellen Islay. All people are shearing now.

Tuesday, 16   We went out to mow corn this morning at half past 5 o'clock. I syeth till near 10 o'clock. Breakfast at twenty minutes past 8, dinner twenty minutes past 1 o'clock supper after 7. My father and Alex mowing the same as yesterday the corn is not very ripe. On the crowns of the rigs, we were working on the head half of the field, a fine wind for mowing. Some at the head of the field is lying. Robert Alexander [seasonal labourer] wages are 12/ per week food and bed. The horses graze in the we park throughout the day. We have a small crop of apples this year. No rain but cloudy to day.

Wednesday, 17   Their was some rain this morning so that we could not go out to the corn till after break fast time. Then the two syeths commenced and their was a good piece of it cut before dinner time. There was a good wind for mowing to-day. All the top of the Longcroft is cut now. A good deal of the apples in our garden was blown down last night. I have stopped milking now. It is dark now at half past 7 o'clock. The cows get beans at night. This was a good day but cloudy, and makeing for rain. My Aunt and cousin are still at our house.

SOURCE: *Diary of Peter Wright*, Bruntwood Mains, Galston, Ayrshire, 4–17 September, 1856. Courtesy of Mrs Margaret Skilling, Peter Wright's descendant. Private collection.

DOCUMENT 119

A late nineteenth century small factory for field machinery and carts

This report on JD Allen and Son's works at Culthill, Perthshire, is from the Dundee Courier, *17 July 1896. Such small manufacturing plants were a common feature of small towns throughout lowland Scotland, nearly all on the railway network.*

The Workshops are extensive and comprise a regular blacksmiths' workshop, for the shoeing of horses, repairing of farm implements, machines, &c., a joiners' workshop, where all kind of country joiner work is executed, and a very commodious and well-lighted workshop, containing the most modern and ingenious machinery, tools, and other appliances for the making of new farm implements and machines. The machinery is driven by water power supplied by a stream which passes the works, the large overshot water wheel which drives the outside circular saw also supplying the power for the machinery within the works. The water power is for the most part ample, but in case of scarcity the 6-horse power steam engine has been fitted up within the works, which, however, is not required more than three or four days in a year. Mr Allan says that all makers of implements are alive to the fact that it is only by the aid of labour saving, power-driven machines, which will accomplish the maximum amount of work with the minimum expenditure of handlabour, that such works as his can nowadays be made lucrative. In the large workshops are machines for tenoning the spokes of wheels, and for boring the felloes to suit; shearing and punching machines capable of cutting iron bars 1 inch thick, or punching holes through same; emery grinding machines, which are driven at a very high speed, and are very effective, and also common stone grinding machines; a heavy geared turning-lathe capable of turning shafts 4_ inches in diameter; circular and band saws; vertical and horizontal drills, the boring tools being an American patent, which ensure the holes made through even the thickest iron or steel plates to be perfectly circular. In the blacksmiths' department are six forges, the wind for which is supplied by a fan blast making 3000 revolutions a minute. Each forge has its accompanying anvil and hand tools, and in connection with the blacksmith department is an oven for heating wheel tyres, its capacity being four of the heaviest sized tyres at a time. A cool tyre is put in as a hot one is taken out, and this keeps the hands going, and facilitates the work. Connected with the fitting department are all kinds of modern appliances, such as vices and hand tools, machines for punching out key seats, mandrels, and templates, to ensure the procuring of duplicate parts for any machine when wanted. In front of the works is the large, well-lighted and well-ventilated paint shop full of farm implements, such as farm carts, reaping-machines, potato-diggers, turnip-slicers, &c., in preparation for the Highland Show at Perth. Mr Allan has been remarkably successful with his output of potato-diggers for which he has gained very high repute both at home and abroad. They are specially well known and very highly appreciated in the three sister countries – England, Scotland, and Ireland – a great many going over the Border and across the Channel every year, so much so that difficulty is experienced in keeping up with the orders.

SOURCE: *Dundee Courier*, 17 July 1896.

DOCUMENT 120

Farm servant life in Aberdeenshire, 1890–1940

In this extract, the late W Smith, a native of the Buchan countryside and a retired teacher, describes aspects of the working life and conditions of a farm servant in Aberdeenshire between 1890 and 1940.

During this 50 year period the life and work of the farm servant saw little change until the start of the First World War. From what I could gather from veterans of the 1890s, wages, work, food and hours remained on a fairly static scale until 1914. Up till then the normal rate of pay would have been – Grieves, Cattlemen, Foremen (1st Horseman) £16 to £18. Exceptional cases a little extra. Others on a sliding scale according to age and ability and down to loons around £6, all per 6 months. Cottars were on a different footing, as all were engaged for 12 months at pay around £30–£32 with meal, milk and potatoes as prerequisites, the same as men who lived in bothies.

The staff on a farm of say 500–600 acres would have been – A Grieve, 4 or 5 Horsemen, 2 Cattlemen, an Orra man, a loon or strapper to attend to the farmer's pony and trap, etc. In all instances the Foreman (1st Horseman) took precedence, also at mealtimes in the farm kitchen, if he was married and lived in a cottar house the next in seniority took the lead to the kitchen.

Meal times were Breakfast 5 or 5.30. Dinner 11.30. Supper 6.30 pm, allowance for meals ¼ hour each.

Meals
Breakfast – Brose, milk and oatcakes. In later years – one slice of loaf-bread with syrup and a cup of tea.

Dinner – Stoved Tatties, Kale and Kale Brose. Tattie Soup (mashed and hired with a lump of butter). Neeps and neep Brose. Barley broth made with milk. Cabbage and Cabbage Brose. Tatties and Skirlie. Milk and oatcakes were always on the table but never beef. Those farmers who killed and cured a 'mairt' helped greatly to augment the variety and some probably was sent through to the kitchen en'. A little variety possibly on Sunday, some cases tea.

Supper – Porridge and milk. Sowens, a milk diet, whole rice, or cut loaf-bread (saps or velvet soup – so called in different areas). 'Brochan' – a thick gruel mixed with onions and cheese and served very hot. All this before tea was much in use.

There were no breaks for mid-meal refreshments except in harvest time when an afternoon bite was carried out to the field, probably milk or home brewed ale with oatcakes and cheese, or a pailful of curds to be shared out along with oatcakes and perhaps cheese, all a satisfying meal. Some farms provided large home-baked scones spread with jam or jelly. No tea at these times either.

As was always the case, some farms were noted for being 'better fed' while others got the name of being the opposite. Here it was where oatcakes were baked different from what was sent 'ben the hoose'.

Hours of work

On many farms a 60 hour week was adhered to, throughout the year. On others a 9 hours day was the rule, during the winter months until 1st March when the 10 hour day was resumed. Horsemen rose at 5.40 or 5.45, attended to horses, breakfasted and ready to yoke at 6 a.m. Generally plenty work awaited in the barn until daybreak during the winter months, but it seemed ridiculous to have men out in the fields ploughing, or driving turnips, etc, until 6 p.m. during winter. (I can vouch for one instance when the 2nd Horseman was sent to the plough while the Foreman went to meal mill for the meal. The ploughman was overcome by darkness and rather than stand at the end of the rig, which they often did, he decided to 'lowse' a twenty minutes or so earlier. As he was drawing up to the stable door the farmer appeared with the order: – 'Ging doon and gie Fraser a trace up the brae'. Well there is surely a moral to that).

Probably the Kitchie 'deem' or maid, had the longest day of all, and the least pay. She had little spare time to herself, and when she got a few hours off on a Sunday afternoon, her presence was required at milking time – 8 p.m.

Holidays and amusements

Recognised holidays were (1) Feeing market, (2) Fast Day – the Thursday be' Sacrament, and of course New Years Day. Any other time off had to be made up by working overtime. Following the end of the First World War, a gradual relaxation took place, and ultimately reached the half day on Saturday, and followed up later by an 8½ or 9 hour day.

Amusements – in many cases farm servants had to find their own amusement. Those living in outlying areas found it very lonely at times, and would often spend the dark evenings sitting at the kitchen fire until 9 p.m., when it was time for stable, and then off to bed. In the more populated districts the winter evenings were often spent in visiting their neighbours the general conversation would be about their horses, harness, ploughs and ploughing, etc. A game of cards, draughts, a sing-song accompanied by a melodeon, or fiddle, and in fact anything of a light-hearted nature that helped pass the evening. In the summer evenings more attractive items were to be found. Quoits and other competitions were popular, and perhaps a travelling circus of side-shows were always a draw, and amusements at feeing markets were seldom awanting.

SOURCE: National Museums of Scotland, Scottish Country Life Archive, 'Notes on Farm Servant Life in Aberdeenshire 1890–1940, compiled by W Smith', MS 1970/49, 1965.

DOCUMENT 121

Rural Housing – a call for action

The following extract from The Scottish Farm Servant, *the official publication of the Scottish Farm Servants' Union, draws attention to some of the problems with rural housing in the 1930s, and calls on the farm workers to take action.*

When the Tories Ruled
In the early months of 1929 we tried to persuade Sir John Gilmour, who was then Secretary for Scotland, to meet a deputation from the Executive Committee of our Union to discuss the administration of the Housing Acts in rural Scotland. He declined to meet us, and referred us to the Secretary to the Department of Health, whom we met in March, 1929. As a result of that meeting, a special circular was issued to landward local authorities requesting them to carry out their statutory duties.

When Labour Rules
Nothing happened, and on 5th April, 1930, we sent a deputation to meet the present Secretary for Scotland, Mr Wm. Adamson, to draw his attention to the continued neglect of their statutory duties by the local authorities in rural districts. We placed before him evidence which could be confirmed by the Department of Health, not only that local authorities were not carrying out their duties, but that when complaints were lodged with them about particular farm cottages, most of the authorities did everything they could to evade their duties. Mr. Adamson promised to give due consideration to the matters we had brought before him, and assured us that every assistance would be given to remedy the neglect of rural housing.

Our Charge
Nothing has happened since then. Local authorities do not carry out systematic inspection of the houses in their area. Local authorities do not require proprietors to make or keep houses in all respects reasonably fit for human habitation. Local authorities do not require proprietors to provide every house with water in the house and a water closet, where practicable, and where not practicable with water immediately outside the house and a separate earth closet. Even when complaints are lodged that these statutory requirements are not being met it is practically impossible to get most of the authorities to act.

Some Instances
Complaints which were lodged as long ago as 1927 in Midlothian have not been remedied. In Ross-shire we have one glaring example which is now three years old, and the local authority is still giving the proprietor an opportunity to remedy the complaint. In West Lothian a complaint lodged in June, 1929, about the cottages on two farms belonging to a wealthy peer, is where it was when it was lodged. We could go on in county after county with similar instances. The one thing the

County Councils seem to be anxious about is to spare the feelings of the lairds; they are utterly indifferent to the conditions the workers have to live under.

Promises and Sympathy

We are promised that further circulars will be sent to County Councils, pointing out their duties under the Housing Acts. The County Councils know these duties perfectly well. They do not sin in ignorance; they do not mean to carry out their duties. The proprietors are offered public money to carry out the repairs which they ought to have been compelled to carry out ten years ago. The workers are assured of the usual sympathy, but sympathy does not make a damp, unhealthy house any more tolerable.

You Can Help

If we could get every worker who is living in a house which is not in all respects reasonably fit for human habitation to send us particulars of the defects, we could wear down the County Councils and create such a scandal in every county that action will have to be taken. Until the workers are prepared to take such action themselves, little progress will be made. We regret to have to say it, but it is unfortunately the fact, that two years of a Labour Government has made no improvement in the administration of rural housing.

SOURCE: *The Scottish Farm Servant*, 1931

DOCUMENT 122

Government plans to increase food production

This signalled a continuation of the wartime agricultural effort and its institutionalisation into a peacetime framework of government support. Prosperity followed for those who remained on the land, but the euphoric prediction of the labour requirements would prove to be hopelessly inflated.

The Government's plans to step up home food production by £100,000,000 by 1951–52 were announced simultaneously in London and Edinburgh yesterday. They include price incentives for approved crops and livestock products, acreage payments for wheat and potatoes, and entirely new subsidies and grants.

'This is no temporary measure,' said Mr Joseph Westwood, Secretary of State for Scotland, speaking in Edinburgh – first to the National Farmers' Union Council and later to the Chairman of A.E.C.s. 'This programme signifies the Government's recognition of the need for permanency by substantially raising the minimum prices for livestock products up to 1951–52.'

What was wanted was nothing less than the maximum production of which the agricultural industry was capable. That was essential to meet the needs of the situation. The Government had set a production programme, but it was hoped that it would even be exceeded.

'Everyone,' Mr Westwood declared, 'must play his or her part. Farmers', he said, 'raise your holdings to the highest stage of technical performance of which they are capable. Farm workers – maintain and intensify your labours, be willing to work overtime when the needs of the farm require it and readily accept all foreign and other additions to the agricultural labour force.'

'Landowners – be ready to play your part in providing, within the limits of your available resources, new farm buildings, water supplies and drainage and, particularly, new accommodation of the larger numbers of livestock.'

Finally, Mr Westwood called on the organisations of farmers, farm workers and landowners 'to support to the utmost the initiative of the Government and explain and interpret to their best endeavours the needs of the nation.'

The estimates of expansion . . . represent, it is stated, an expansion of 50 per cent, compared with pre-war, of 15 per cent, compared with the wartime peak of 1943–44 and 20 per cent, compared with 1946–47.

The targets set out in a recent White Paper are considerably exceeded – 'An immense effort greatly surpassing the highest known output of the agricultural industry hitherto.'

The Government estimate that £50,000,000 of the total extra output demanded will be represented by increased efficiency of the industry – an improvement in efficiency of 2 per cent, per annum, stated to be well within the capacity of the industry.

'The total expansion of one hundred million pounds should therefore fall into two reasonably equal parts – fifty million pounds from higher efficiency and fifty million pounds from additions to the resources of the industry.'

A uniform expansion, product by product, is not envisaged, but the emphasis has been deliberately placed on dollar-saving products – a departure from the war years, when the emphasis was on saving ships. There is a particular emphasis on pig meat, eggs, beef, mutton, cereals and linseed. The Government's programme, therefore, is essentially one of emphasising and expanding the production of meat and eggs, restoring part of the wartime expansion of wheat and barley, and adding to the cropping area no less than 400,000 acres of linseed.

Labour
Additional labour required – One hundred thousand, representing 9 per cent of the total existing labour force in the United Kingdom – will be drawn partly from British and partly from foreign sources. Mr Westwood, however, did not state a figure. He contented himself by saying that many thousands more workers would be needed.

SOURCE: *Farming News (& North British Agriculturalist)*, 22 August 1947

The Common Agricultural Policy explained

The following is an extract from the speech of the Secretary of the Scottish National Farmers' Union (DS Johnson) to the Executive Committee of the Scottish Council Development and Industry, 1 June 1988. Johnson was not the first, nor will he be the last, to explain the CAP to a largely urban-based audience.

I am uncomfortably conscious that it takes a bout of something approaching temporary insanity to volunteer for an enterprise which involves any attempt to explain, far less defend, the CAP.

But despite the rich crop of absurdities which the CAP has spawned, I want to start by asserting that it is a largely successful attempt to ensure security of food supplies for a population in the EEC now in the region of 350 million people. This is a deeply serious purpose. The CAP exists to influence an industry whose business depends on the inter-action of the climate with the top few inches – no more than that – of the earth's land areas.

That sounds a chancey business, and so it still remains. Enormous strides have been made in applying technology to agriculture – to make the process more certain and more controlled. But no technology could save great areas of Scotland from the appalling physical and financial damage caused by the rains of 1985, or the harr which destroyed much of Grampian region's harvest in 1987 and had the combines out in some places on New Year's Day 1988. No technology is available to save the great areas of the USA this summer from crop and financial disaster – and the prospect of higher food prices too – unless the temperature falls and the clouds bring rain.

These considerations are the beginning of a rationale for specific policy provisions in the farming sector.

Add to that the fact that although supply is variable, demand for food is inelastic. If prices drop, people may be tempted to buy, say, two cars – but if food prices drop they will not – in advanced economies – double their calorie intake.

And finally, in this introduction, I invite you to consider that all the available evidence suggests that the most efficient resource allocation in farming seems to be in those countries where the production unit is of a size which can be managed by a farmer, his family and perhaps some hired help, rather than in units which match the size necessary for economies of scale in many parts of manufacturing industry. And since the biggest farmer is insignificant in relation to the commodity markets which he is supplying, it follows that farmers in the absence of countervailing measures are doomed to the role of price takers, not price makers.

Mr Chairman, I have taken some little time with these introductory remarks because I shall be talking about changes in farming policy, and it seemed to me to be worthwhile to offer a brief explanation as to why there is a CAP – why most advanced countries run agricultural policies too – and in passing let me observe that by international comparisons, the CAP is not particularly costly to operate.

Now let me give you some notion of the scale of Scottish agriculture.

It is an industry which gives work directly to nearly 60,000 people, as farmers or as farm workers. We estimate that something like 150,000 people in Scotland are employed in industries directly supplying the farming industry and processing and transporting its products. There are always problems of definition, but the Scottish Agricultural Colleges calculate that in 1984 the food and agriculture sector accounted for over 14% of Scottish output (excluding oil and oil related industries), and provided nearly 6% of total employment. The figures are naturally much higher in rural areas – 31% of output in Grampian Region, for example, and 15% of employment.

The gross value of Scottish farm output is £1,400 million.

The industry's net income is very volatile – a catastrophic low of £27 million in 1985; £95 million in 1986; and £125 million in 1987 – better than the two previous years, but still in real terms a third of its value 10 years ago.

In addition to farmers' incomes, the industry pays £220 million to farm workers, £40 million in rents to landlords, and £95 million to banks, the interest bill on an outstanding debt of £900 million. From 1976 to 1986 farmgate prices rose by 153%, retail prices for food by 217%, and the general retail price index by 245%.

SOURCE: National Museums of Scotland, Scottish Life Archive, 'Extract from the speech of DS Johnston, Secretary of the Scottish National Farmers Union, to the Executive Committee of the Scottish Council Development and Industry, 1 June 1988', MS 1989/28/18.

CLASS

DOCUMENT 124

Extracts from the Minutes of the Clyde Shipbuilders and Engineers Association

The Clyde Shipbuilders and Engineers Association was formed in the 1860s. The Association included most major shipbuilders and some engineering firms and its main concern was to control the conditions of employment. Generally the Association sought to do so by securing a collective agreement among members on rates of pay and other conditions and relying on member firms to enforce them. Its deliberations are directly relevant to the debate on how far West of Scotland employers were more 'autocratic' than their counterparts in England.

At Glasgow and within the Chambers of the Secretary, No 30 Gordon Street on the 11th Day of September 1882. Met the Members of the Association, the Employers Associated therewith and Kindred Employers.

Present
Mr. Walker (of Lobnitz & Co.)
Mr. Kinghorn (of The London & Glasgow Co)
Mr. Kemp (of Alex Stephen & Sons)
Mr. Maclean (of Barclay Curle & Co.)
Mr. Inglis Jr.
Mr. Connell
Mr. Mansel
Mr. Pearce

Mr. Pearce in the Chair

The Minutes of last Meeting were read and approved of.
Read letter from Mr. W.B. Crawford, Secretary of Master Painters Association enclosing offer of Joiners from England from English Agent.
Authorised Secretary to place £5 in Mr. Crawford's hands to defray expenses of English Agent coming here on Thursday at 3 o'clock and appointed the Chairman and Messrs. Inglis Jr., Kinghorn, Maclean and Kemp a Committee to meet said Agent. Meantime instructed Secretary to write to Employers that offers have been made of Joiners from England and requesting them to state before one o'clock on Thursday how many they can take.

At Glasgow and within the Chambers of the Society, No. 30 Gordon Street on the 14th day of September 1882. Met the Members of the Association the Employers associated therewith and Kindred Employers.

Present
Mr. Kinghorn
Mr. A. Maclean (of Barclay Curle & Co.)
Mr. John Inglis Jr.
Mr. Kemp (of Alex Stephen & Sons)
Mr. Pearce
Present also Mr. Connell

Mr. Pearce in the Chair

[Hereafter only the date of the meeting will be given and other introductory materials omitted to save space]

Read letter from Messrs. James & George Thomson stating that they had not conceded advance to Joiners as reported in the newspapers.

Read replies received from Employers in answer to enquiry as to how many English Joiners they would take.

Conferred with English Agent. Agreed to employ him for a month (say four weeks) at £3 per month and his travelling expenses. Instructed him to ascertain how many Joiners he can procure on the following terms 7d per hour, their railway fare here to be paid, to remain not less than two months and if they leave before that time to refund their fare here to allow the Employers to retain their tools till said fare be refunded, their fare back to be paid by the Employers if they discharge them without fault before the end of said two months, and to report progress daily to the Secretary of this Association. Authorised Secretary to advance him money as required.

Adjourned Meeting until Monday 25th current at 3 o'clock if no earlier Meeting be required.

21st day of September 1882
The Minutes of last Meeting were read and approved of.

Read Telegram and Letters from English Agent. Considered as to bring English Joiners by steamer or by railway. Instructed Secretary to inform English Agent that it had been fixed that he was to bring down 120 Joiners certain by railway on Monday night to be allotted to the various forms as per list furnished to Secretary. Further instructed Secretary to arrange with North British Railway Company for the men's fares.

25th day of September 1882
The Minutes of last General Meeting were read and approved of.

The Secretary, in the absence of the Chairman of the Sub-Committee on employing English Joiners, reported the action taken by the Committee of which the Meeting approved.

Read letters and telegrams from English Agent. Instructed Secretary to arrange with North British Railway Company for conveyance of men from Hull.

Allotted men expected to arrive tomorrow morning as per instructions given to Secretary.

26th day of September 1882. Met the Sub-Committee on employing English Joiners and Employers requested to consult with them.

Present
Mr. Connell
Mr. Walker (of Lobnitz & Co.)
Mr. McKnight (Aitken & Mansel)
Mr. John Stephen
Mr. John Inglis Jr.
Mr. Shepherd (Elder & Co.)
Mr. Kinghorn

Mr. Stephen in the Chair.

The Minutes of last Meeting were read and approved of.

Conferred with English Agent. Resolved to bring down more Joiners from England. Also to bring in Joiners from other parts of Scotland. Instructed Agent accordingly. Instructed Secretary how men are to be allotted.

11th day of October 1882
The Minutes of the last General Meeting were read and approved of.

The Minutes of the last meeting of the Committee on Employing English Joiners were reported and approved.

Considered letter from Sir Donald Currie. Instructed secretary to acknowledge same and to state that after mature consideration the meeting did not see their way to accept the services which he so kindly offers towards settling the dispute now existing with the joiners.

The Secretary reported that English Agents engagement terminates tomorrow. Resolved to re-engage him for a fortnight on same terms as formerly with power to Secretary to engage him for a fortnight further if he thought fit. Further authorised Secretary to continue to advance him money as required.

23rd day of October 1882
The Minutes of the last meeting were read and approved of.

Considered letter from Secretary of Joiners addressed to Mr Rowan dated 10th inst. Instructed Secretary to write to Secretary of Joiners direct stating that the letter had not been handed by Mr Rowan to this Association until the 21st inst. and that in reply to the Resolution of the joiners the Employers are prepared to appoint four representatives to confer with an equal number of workmen and adding that if at any time the men had requested a conference it would not have been refused.

Further instructed the Secretary to inform Mr Rowan that the Secretary of the Joiners had been written to direct acquainting him that the Employers were prepared to meet the men in conference and hand a copy of the letter to that effect to Mr Rowan.

Nominated Mr Pearce, Mr John Stephen, Mr John Henderson Jr and Mr Connell whom failing Mr Kinghorn and Mr Maclean as Representatives to confer with the men.

Read telegram from Sir Donald Currie to the effect that he had been asked by the men to endeavour to bring about a settlement with the Employers. Instructed Secretary to acknowledge receipt and to state that he had been instructed to write to the secretary of the Joiners direct acquainting him that the Employers were prepared to meet the men in Conference handing to Sir Donald copies of the letter from the Secretary of the Joiners to Mr Rowan dated 10th inst. containing the resolution of the Joiners proposing a conference and of the reply by this Association thereto agreeing to confer and thanking him for his kind offices.

Read letter from Messrs Dobie and Co. Deferred further consideration thereof under the circumstances in the meantime.

Considered as to bringing down more joiners from England. Requested Secretary to instruct English agent that if not less than 100 joiners (or at least not less than 90) could be procured in Manchester willing to work here during the strike to bring them down on Thursday night one third to be sent to each of the three following yards viz. Messrs Elder and Co, Messrs A Stephen and Sons and The London and Glasgow Coy.

30th day of October 1882

The Minutes of the last meeting were read and approved of.

Read letter from Secretary of Joiners. They were willing to accept one farthing now and the other farthing on the 1st March 1883. Resolved unanimously to decline the proposal. Agreed on terms of letter to be sent to the Secretary of Joiners in reply and instructed Secretary of this Association to write to him accordingly.

Instructed Secretary to write to the English Agent to Manchester not to bring them men tonight but to hold them over until Thursday night.

Again deferred consideration of Messrs Dobbie and Cos letter in the meantime.

6th day of November 1882

The minutes of the last meeting were read and approved of.

Instructed Secretary how next squad of joiners from England were to be allotted and empowered him in his discretion to re-engage English agent from time to time until further instructions on the same terms as at present and to continue to advance money to him as required.

Resolved in consequence of the continued strike of ship joiners to anticipate the Levy of February next and hereby call up from each Member of the Association the sum of six pence sterling for each person stated to be employed by such Member in the return made by them in January last.

Considered letter from Sir Donald Currie. Agreed on terms of Telegram to be sent to him in reply and instructed Secretary to telegraph to him immediately accordingly.

11th day of November 1882

The Minutes of the last Meeting were read and approved of.

Read letter from Secretary of Joiners stating that they are willing to resume work on terms stated in Sir Donald Currie's letter. Instructed Secretary to state in reply that no advance will be conceded.

Considered as to allotment of joiners from Liverpool and instructed Secretary thereon.

27th day of November 1882

The Minutes of the last Meeting were read and approved of.

Read letter from Messrs D and W Henderson offering to contribute their proportion of the expences incurred by the Association in bringing joiners' strike to a termination. The Secretary stated that Mr Walker of Messrs Lobnitz and Co had made a similar offer on behalf of his firm at one of the meetings of Employers. Instructed the Secretary to write to these firms and enclosing Returns to enable their proportion of said expences to be calculated.

Considered and approved circular to be sent to the other Employers not Members of this Association in the Upper and Lower reaches enclosing Returns to be made by them if they the like manner wished to bear their proportion of the expences of the strike and instructed Secretary to issue said circular forthwith.

Read application of English Agent to be permanent employed by this Association. Resolved not to employ in the meantime a permanent Agent . . .

Extracts from November 1883 to January 1884

At Glasgow and within the Chambers of the Secretary No. 30 Gordon Street on the 21st day of November 1883 met the Members of the Clyde Shipbuilders and Engineers Association and the Employers associated therewith.

Present

Mr. McIntyre (of Messrs. McIntyre of Paisley)
Mr. D.S. Porteous
Mr. Robertson (of the London & Glasgow Coy)
Mr. Ferguson (of Messrs. Barclay Curle & Co.)
Mr. Pearce
Mr. Connell
Mr. John Stephen
Mr. John Inglis (of Messrs. A. & J. Inglis)
Mr. D.J. Dunlop
Mr. James Thomson (of Messrs. J. & J. Thomson)

Mr. Rodger (of Messrs. Russell of Port Glasgow)
Mr. Howden
Mr. Maclean (of Messrs. Barclay Curle & Co.)

Mr. Pearce in the Chair

[Hereafter only the date of the meeting will be given]

The Minutes of last meeting were read and approved of.

Considered rates of wages. It was unanimously agreed that a reduction of ten per cent be made from the 1st of December on the wages of the Iron Workers in the Shipyards; and as the tonnage in hands is so much less than it was at the close of 1881 and the prospects of the trade so very much worse than they were at that time, it was also unanimously agreed that on resuming work after the New Year the rates of wages of all classes in the Ship Engine departments be reduced to those that existed at the end of 1881.

Considered Basis for proposed General Association. Instructed secretary to issue a circular stating that a Meeting of Employers will be held on an early day for the special purpose of considering the Basis and requesting the employers to let the proposed Basis receive their consideration in the interim.

Read letter from Chamber of Commerce wishing opinion of the Association on Mr. Chamberlain's proposals for the establishment of Local Marine Courts and Merchant Shipping Commissioners. Remitted to Messrs. Pearce, Englis, Connell and Ferguson as a Committee to consider and report. Mr. Pearce Convener.

Passed the following Accounts
1   Strathaw & Co. – Printing £27.5/-
2   John Miller – Envelopes 6/-
3   Do.   – Notepaper £1.0.3d.
4   – Envelopes 6/6

Instructed Secretary to order 50 copies of the Books of Iron Workers Rates to be printed off but to be retained by him as private types thereafter to be taken down.

1st Day December 1883

The minutes of the last meeting were read and approved of.

Mr Pearce explained the object of the present meeting and moved that those present constitute themselves as a Committee to meet Mr Knight, Mr O'Neill and the members of the Executive Council.

The Meeting then resolved itself into a Committee of the Association accordingly.

The following Deputation from the Executive Council of the Iron Shipbuilders was then introduced
1   Mr. Knight, Newcastle on Tyne
2   Mr. McGill, Tyne and Wear

3   Mr. Craig, Govan

4   Mr. McLerie, Paisley

5   Mr. John Kelly, Glasgow

6   Mr. Henry Carberry, Port Glasgow

    The Deputation enquired

1   Will Employers accept Rates to be mutually agreed upon.

2   Will Employers recognise the Workmen's Society's Delegate to regulate disputes as to Rates.

The Committee agreed to report these two questions to the Association for consideration and the Deputation withdrew.

Read letter from Amalgamated Engineers, Glasgow. Instructed Secretary to acknowledge receipt and to state that Committee has not power to deal with the question of the reduction of wages in any other way than that determined on by the General Meeting of Employers held on the 21st Nov. but that it was clearly laid down at that Meeting that the Rates for Engineers are to be the same as in the end of 1881.

The meeting then by Resolution was re-constituted as a General Meeting. Considered further rates of wages, and unanimously agreed to adhere to the Resolutions of 21st November last.

4th day of January 1884

The Minutes of last Meeting were read and approved of.

Considered communications from Boilermakers and Shipbuilders and Associated Blacksmiths. Adhered to Resolution to reduce the wages of these workmen to the rates paid in the end of 1881.

Considered also letters from the Amalgamated Engineers the Associated Shipwrights and the Clyde Ship Joiners. Resolved from special circumstances laid before the Meeting to alter the Resolution by modifying the reduction as regards Engineers to an average of one halfpenny per hour, the Shipwrights to one halfpenny and the Joiners to one farthing. Remitted to the Chairman Messrs. Ferguson and Macgregor to frame the replies to be sent to the various communications from the Workmen's Societies.

28th day of January 1884

The Minutes of last Meeting were read and approved of.

An Audited Statement of Accounts up to the 21st December 1883 was laid before the Meeting in terms of the Rules.

The Meeting then proceeded to elect a Chairman.

SOURCE: Strathclyde Regional Archives, Mitchell Library, Glasgow: TD 241\1\2.

DOCUMENT 125

Joint Meetings of the Executive Committees of the Engineers' and Shipbuilders' Associations, held within the Offices, 105 West George Street, Glasgow

These meetings of the two most powerful employers' organisations on Clydeside were held at the height of the 1919 Forty Hours strike. The first, a joint meeting of the executives, took place on 30 January. The second, on 31 January, was virtually a mass meeting with 123 employers present representing almost every major firm on Clydeside. It was held a couple of hours after the confrontation between police and strikers just four hundred yards away in George Square and before the situation elsewhere in the city had been brought under control.

30th day of January, 1919

Reduction in working hours: Irregular strike
Reported that the number of men which the Unofficial Strike Committee were able to take out on strike on Monday, 27th January, did not exceed 25% of the workpeople; that the Leaders recognising that a collapse of the whole movement was only a matter of time unless they could make headway by some other means had resorted to 'mass picketing' – the assemblage of large numbers of Strikers in a complete body round the works gates in such a manner as to prevent workmen either entering or leaving the works; that the methods adopted were being extended to districts outwith the Glasgow area, and that the office and management staffs were, in some cases, being threatened.

Mr Biggart reported that after consultation with the President of the Engineers' Association, he had called upon the Chief Constable of Glasgow who stated that he was quite alive to the position and had already issued instructions throughout the area under his charge: that the police could not prevent peaceful picketing, but he regarded the massing of large numbers calculated to overawe the workpeople, or any action which prevented freedom of coming and going, as illegal, and the constables were to do all they could to keep free passage ways. The Chief Constable's great difficulty was that he still required 600 men to bring the Force up to its usual strength; the requests for constables at the works were coming from so many directions that it was quite impossible to send sufficient numbers to the different places, and it looked as if effective assistance could only be secured by obtaining the assistance of the Military. It had been mentioned that the Employers did not view with favour – at least up till now – the bringing in of the Military, as the strike was against the Trade Union Officials and the strikers' fellow-workmen, rather than against the Employers, and therefore the latter did not wish to appear in the matter.

It was also explained that the Engineering & Shipbuilding Employers' Federations were in close touch with Lord Pirrie of Messrs Harland and Wolff Ltd., during the time he was in London, and that they were hopeful his firm would act in conjunction with the Federations in regard to the hours question.

Action of A.S.E. and Boilermakers' Local Officials in connection with strike – After discussion agreed to report to the Federations that Mr Harry Hopkins, Secretary, of the Glasgow District Committee, Mr William Kerr, Local Organiser of the A.S.E. and Mr William Mackie, District Delegate of the Boilermakers' Society, are taking a very active and prominent part in the irregular strike in this district, and to suggest that unless the Executive Councils of these two Societies secured the withdrawal of the active opposition of these local officials to the Agreement come to between the Federations and the Unions for a 47 hour week, the Employers would be compelled to consider seriously whether they could continue to recognise these local officials in any negotiations and conferences with the Unions; that the Employers had no desire to interfere with the internal arrangements of the Unions, but if the state of affairs referred to were permitted to continue the Societies must be prepared to find that Employers may be forced to the decision that the officials in question are no longer acceptable to them as representatives with whom they can deal. Agreed further to request the Federations to send to the Unions a strong and emphatic protest against the present state of affairs and intimate to them how seriously the employers in this district would regard its continuance.

31st day of January, 1919

Shorter working week
The Chairman reported that the Meeting had been agreed upon at a Joint Meeting of the Executive Committees of the Engineers and Shipbuilders Associations held the previous day in order that Members might be kept fully informed of developments in connection with the Unofficial Strike . . .

The Joint Executive Committees at their Meeting on 30th January, had considered the action of the Glasgow Corporation in shutting off the supply of electric current. In view of the Provost's seeming disposition to regard, and treat with, the Deputation as responsible Trade Union Leaders, it was considered desirable to place the position and policy of the Engineering and Shipbuilding Employers Federations and the Associations before the Lord Provost. For this purpose a Deputation consisting of Messrs J.R. Richmond, Archibald Gilchrist, Noel E. Peck and Allan M. Connell had been appointed. The Employers Deputation had interviewed the Provost during the forenoon of Friday 31st January when he had been asked where the Corporation stood in the matter and in what way they proposed to treat with the unruly mob which was then meeting outside the City Chambers. The Chairman on behalf of the Associations had outlined the various steps taken in connection with the 47 hour week and from which it appeared the Lord Provost had not been made familiar with the actual position of affairs.

The Deputation had explained to the Lord Provost that Joint Committees composed of representatives of the Engineering and Shipbuilding Employers Federations and the Trade Unions had been appointed; that they had met and discussed the question and came to a joint recommendation for a 47 hour week;

that the recommendation had been before the Members of all the Unions represented at a Joint Conference and the ballot vote had favoured acceptance, and that the shorter week was put into operation on 1st January, 1919.

It had been further explained that the Employers and Unions recognised that many questions of detail required to be discussed, and the Employers had suggested that the 47 hours week should be postponed until the more important details had been fixed. This however, had not been agreed to by the Unions who pressed for the shorter week coming into operation on 1st January 1919. It had also been pointed out to the Provost that arrangements were made for discussing questions of detail, and further, that on Thursday of last week, the representatives of the Employers and Unions had met in London when it was pointed out to the Union representatives that they would require to secure the return of the men on strike before further discussion could take place. The Trade Unions had agreed and promised to endeavour to get the men to resume work on Monday, 27th and the Employers had promised to meet the Unions on Wednesday 29th January, provided the men on the Clyde and North East Coast were back at work.

The Lord Provost in reply had explained –
1   The position in which he was placed when the Deputation of the Strikers met him and stated that he had simply conveyed a request, from a section of the Community to the Government.
2   That he had worded a telegram to the Prime Minister in such a way as to impress upon the Authorities that the situation was most serious and required immediate action on their part.
3   That he had endeavoured to get the Authorities to realise that they had a certain responsibility and would now require to take definite action; and
4   That he was out to preserve law and order for the City and would endeavour to do so according to the law.

Reported also that after the Employers' Deputation had left a riot had occurred during the course of which Sheriff Principal MacKenzie, Chief Constable Stevenson, and others had been injured and Messrs Gallacher, Kirkwood and others arrested.

Further reported that the Federation had recently met the leaders of the Unions and pointed out that they must take steps to have the recalcitrant Strikers brought to book; that the first Agreement entered into since the war broke out was in danger of being scrapped and that unless the Unions were able to carry out the terms of the Agreement, it was useless to carry on collective bargaining. There had been considerable difficulty in bringing one or two sections of the Trade Unions to book but finally the Federations had got them to pass a recommendation undertaking to do all within their power to get their Members back to work.

Management and Clerical Staffs
Reported that the Management and Clerical Staffs of a number of firms had been

informed by the Strikers that they would not be allowed to enter the Works after Saturday 1st February 1919.

Exaggerated Statements in Press

This question had been under consideration by the Joint Executive Committees when it was arranged that Mr Biggart should interview the Press Representatives with the object of a judicious cutting down of statements in the Press concerning the unofficial strike and the eliminating from Reports the names of the Strike Leaders.

Civic Guard

It was arranged that the Deputation when again interviewing the Lord Provost of Glasgow should suggest the formation of a Civic Guard, it being felt that quite a number of the loyal workmen and Employers would join the Guard with a view to opposing the Strikers and protecting workmen against 'massed picketing' or intimidation.

Demobilised Soldiers

Discussion took place on whether the Employers should issue a manifesto to the effect that two months from this date should there be a number of demobilised soldiers still out of employment, the Employers would either by reduced hours or other means give them employment. It was remitted to the Deputation to consider what action, if any, should be taken in the matter.

SOURCE: Strathclyde Regional Archives, Mitchell Library, Glasgow: TD 241\1\18.

DOCUMENT 126

Reports by government agencies on unrest on the Clyde

The Cabinet received intelligence briefings on internal discontent from a variety of sources. The information was of considerable volume, uneven quality and often from conflicting vantage points. All members of the Cabinet would be supplied by the Special Branch with the weekly digest of materials on revolutionary organisations. Those with defence portfolios received additional materials from military intelligence, focusing in particular on unrest in the army and among demobilised soldiers. The Ministry for Munitions had its own intelligence wing covering the wide span of industries supplying defence materials.

a) *Fortnightly Report on Revolutionary Organisations 28 January 1919*
[These reports were compiled for use of the Cabinet and mainly derive from Metropolitan Police Special Branch sources]

'The outlook during the past fortnight has been rather dark . . .
   My Glasgow correspondent reports that the revolutionary movement is certainly gaining ground, and he thinks that the strike threatened for next week must be very carefully watched . . .

[John Maclean]
Since his release from prison, this man has been making a series of revolutionary speeches in Lancashire. He appears to be convinced that the Social Revolution will come this year. His programme is for the miners to come out first on some economic question, the other members of the Triple Alliance will follow suit, and then the unofficial workers movement will come in. He thinks that with the miners, the transport workers, the railway workers and the engineers on strike, and the Army, Navy and the Police either sympathetic or powerless, the Government of the country can be transferred to the workers either peaceably or forcibly. He hopes therefore that the government will refuse the six hours to the miners.

Though Maclean is mentally unstable, there is sufficient method in his speeches to attract large audiences. He begins by telling them how he has been extraordinarily successful among soldiers and sailors. He then relates his sufferings in prison . . . Then he goes on to introduce the subject of the Revolution.'

b) *Ministry of Munitions Day Book for January 1918*
[The Ministry of Munitions had its own intelligence wing which supplied regular reports]

Labour Report dated 30 January 1919

'The strike on the Clyde is spreading chiefly owing to mass picketing. The works of Messrs. Beardmore and John Brown at Dalmuir and Clydebank are closed. Upwards of 40,000 men are idle and the strikers are being so threatening that it is unsafe for anyone to remain at work. The public services are being maintained much as usual with the exception of the tramways which are being carried on under difficulties owing to a considerable portion of the tradesmen having joined the strikers.

Rosyth [Fife]

The engineers at the Dockyard, 1200 left work yesterday, but so far unrest is confined to the engineering trades.

Labour Report dated 1 February 1919 [but apparently compiled the previous day]

'While at the present time practically all the large shipbuilding and engineering shops on the Clyde are completely idle, it is not considered that the strike will last much longer.'

Reports coalminers in Fife as returning to work but those in Lanarkshire as still out.

'NB since the above report the following news has come to hand. About 60,000 strikers assembled this morning outside the Municipal Chambers. The strikers have come into collision with the police.'

c) *Intelligence Report Scottish Command 13–19 April 1919*

[Military Intelligence compiled its own weekly reports for circulation to all branches of the armed forces. At the time Military Intelligence were particularly concerned with unrest among servicemen and ex-servicemen. The Clyde Defence Propaganda Committee was set up to campaign on behalf of those arrested in the aftermath of the police charge on 31 January]

'The advanced socialists represented in the organisation of the Clyde District Defence Propaganda Committee are now entirely given over to the principles of Bolshevism, and such men as Arthur McManus of that committee and Mr McPhee, lately General Secretary of the Glasgow Federation of Discharged Soldiers and Sailors . . . are nothing more than active Bolshevik agents. The doctrines of socialism are being spread in a quiet and insidious way, and the worst type of discharged soldier and sailor becomes an easy convert. McFarlane, the witness in the 40 hours strike trial who created a scene in court the other day, is a discharged soldier and Secretary of the Tradeston Branch of the Glasgow Federation [of Discharged Soldiers and Sailors]. Proper counter propaganda against Bolshevism is still urgently necessary, and if the government could do something to relieve unemployment, a settlement would likely be gained.'

SOURCE: Public Record Office a) PRO CAB 24/74 GT 6713; b) PRO MUN 5/18; c) PRO AIR 1 553 16/15/41.

DOCUMENT 127

Now's the day and now's the hour

This article took up the front page of The Call, *the weekly paper of the British Socialist Party, on 23 January 1919, three days before the beginning of the Forty Hours strike. Its author was John Maclean, then in Lancashire conducting meetings among the miners following the all-British conference of the Miners Federation of Great Britain in Southport on 14–15 January. Just a few weeks previously Maclean had been released from almost a year's imprisonment for conducting anti-war propaganda. The article situates the struggle for shorter hours within wider international events occurring during the first few weeks of January 1919: British military intervention in Russia and the execution of the German socialist leaders Rosa Luxemburg and Karl Liebknecht in Berlin (announced in the same issue).*

We witness today what all marxists naturally expected, the capitalist class of the world and their governments joined together in a most vigorously active attempt to crush Bolshevism in Russia and Spartacism in Germany. Bolshevism, by the way, is socialism triumphant, and Spartacism is socialism in process of achieving triumph. This is the class war on an international scale, a class war that must and will be fought out to the logical conclusion – the extinction of capitalism everywhere.

The question for us in Britain is how we must act in playing our part in this world conflict. Some are suggesting a general strike to enforce a withdrawal of British troops from Russia and, I suppose, from Germany as well. That, to some of us on the Clyde, is too idealistic. Were the mass of the workers in Britain revolutionary socialists they would at once see that their well-being depended on the peaceful development of Bolshevism in Russia and would, in consequence, strike for the withdrawal of British forces, at the moment attempting the downfall of Russia's social democracy. But the workers are not generally of our way of thinking, and so are unable to see that their material interests are bound up with Bolshevist stability in Russia. It necessarily follows that we will have no success in urging a strike on this issue, especially as the government has the majority of trade-union leaders in the hollow of its hand, and can easily manipulate them against us – with comparative safety to the leaders at that.

Some of us on the Clyde, therefore, think that we must adopt another line, and that is to save Russia by developing a revolution in Britain no later than this year. We socialists know that the capitalists can only realise their profits by selling a great part of their goods abroad. We know that America is in exactly the same predicament as Britain, and we further know that America intends to assume the economic position in the world that Germany has just failed to attain. If it is true, as well-informed commercial papers assert, that in 1918 America built more ship-tons than Britain, we may take it that America is in a position to lick Britain in the 'navy race'.

In five years' time such will be the glut of goods on the market that fear of revolution through unemployment and hunger may force these two powers into war. If capitalism lasts, then war is inevitable in five years; yes, and a war bloodier than the present war. Humanity is in a very tight corner, and so those who will be called on to kill in the next war will have to make up their minds or fight capitalism to death this year . . .

The next question for us is the start of the fight. How can we get the mass on the move and pulled onward by the young, who wish to save their lives? We have the opportunity at hand. The demobilisation has already created a menacing unemployment problem. We can get the support of the unemployed if we can suggest a means whereby they can get a living. The only possible solution is a drastic reduction of hours per week. This reduction will appeal to the employed if they are assured of at least a pre-war standard of living. Here we have the economic issue that can unify the workers in the war against capitalism.

The Miners' Reform Movement in South Wales and Scotland, in view of this, adopted as their minimum programme the six-hour day, five-day week and one pound a day. I place my services primarily at the disposal of the Miners' Reform Movement and am recognised as one of their spokesmen. I am as proud of that honour as the one conferred by our Russian comrades. My first campaign was among the Lothian miners, and as the result of a week's mission, we have there now a powerful unofficial committee and movement. Shortly a Lancashire County Conference will be held at Bolton, when the movement will spread like wildfire.

On the Clyde and amongst the miners the cry was 'All eyes on Southport'. It should be borne in mind that the Clyde Workers' Committee has issued a leaflet urging the thirty hours' week, and pledging its support to the miners. The Miners' Reform Movement decided that, if the Miners' Federation at the conference at Southport on Tuesday and Wednesday, 14 and 15 January, did not make up its mind to have the programme enforced, they would call a strike about the middle of February. Thanks to the advance guard, the MFGB has at Southport agreed to the six-hour day. The government is asked to enforce it by amending the Eight Hours Act. My good old friend, Bob Smillie, at the Conference pointed out that 'we can produce enough in less than a six-hour day if we were not producing to make millionaires'.

The Executive Committee has now to interview the Prime Minister and the government and, failing satisfaction, must convene another conference. From our point of view that is all to the good. The onus for the strike is thus thrust on the government, and will add to the fierceness of the fight when it comes off, as we know the government will never concede the miners' demands. This will also give the Reform Movement time to expand their propaganda in the various coalfields and knit up more closely than ever. Let all miners who read this article buckle to and build up a powerful group in their own area . . .

To convince the simple-minded worker who believes his master ought to have a profit, I am providing my audiences with the following illustration. Shortly since, the chairman of the Darracq Motor Company at the annual general meeting stated that since August 1914 their employees had increased fourfold, but that their output had increased sevenfold. That means that one worker now in four hours is producing as much as formerly in seven hours. Seven sevens are forty-nine. Add two and that makes fifty-one, a very common pre-war number of hours per week. Seven fours are twenty-eight. Add two and that makes thirty. So that in thirty hours the Darracq workers are doing as much now as formerly in fifty-one hours. Once we get the mass on the move on this issue, we shall be able to take control of the country and the means of production at once, and hold them tight, through disciplined production under the workshop committees and the district and national councils. Through the co-operative movement we shall be able to control the full distribution of the necessaries of life, and so win the masses over to socialism.

All revolutions have started on seemingly trifling economic and political issues. Ours is to direct the workers to the goal by pushing forward the miners' programme and backing up our 'black brigade'.

The condition of the army, the navy, and even the police strengthens us in the fight. Capitalism is in the last ditch. Let us this year cover over this dripping monster and prepare the way for human solidarity on a sound world-wide workers' owned and controlled economic solidarity.

SOURCE: *The Call*, 23 January 1919.

EDUCATION

DOCUMENT 128

Physical education in Scottish schools

Once education became universal, governments were tempted to use the school to train citizens and promote social welfare. Physical education, initially in the form of drill, had become a standard feature of elementary schools, and this circular, issued to school boards during the Boer War, stresses the value of military drill. It reflects the ideas of the Conservative Secretary for Scotland, Lord Balfour of Burleigh, and also of the Secretary of the Scotch Education Department, Henry Craik. The last paragraph suggests the formation of local cadet corps for recent school leavers; these uniformed corps were already popular in secondary schools. This line of policy eventually led to the appointment of a Royal Commission on Physical Training in Scottish Schools, whose report in 1903 revealed the poor physical state of working-class children.

SIR

I am directed by Lord Balfour of Burleigh to bring under the attention of School Boards and Managers of Schools a subject which is one of great public importance, and which in his Lordship's opinion concerns not less the interests of the pupils of State-aided schools than the welfare and security of the Empire. It is that of physical exercise, and particularly of those forms of military drill which most effectively develop the physical capacities of the pupils, and train them in the habit of the combined and dexterous employment of these capacities.

Lord Balfour is convinced that such exercises, apart from any other consideration, would be a most important aid in attaining some substantial objects at which all education must aim. Not only do they tend to improve manual dexterity and to render more alert the faculties of observation, but they are also pre-eminently useful in developing those habits of comradeship, of responsibility, and of individual resource, which are of supreme importance, not only to the nation as a whole, but to the individual pupil. Indirectly they bring the individual into contact with the principles which lie at the foundation of national defence, and they bring home to him his duties and responsibilities as a citizen of the Empire, while at the same time giving him an opportunity of strengthening and developing his physical powers, and rendering him more fit for his ordinary employment. Whatever form the military service of our country may hereafter assume, it is evident that the strength and security of the Empire as a whole, as well as that of every individual citizen, must depend upon the extent to which the moral elements of responsibility, duty, and readiness of judgment, along with the physical capacities, may be developed. Success in this can only be achieved by careful consideration of the best methods, and by employing these strenuously and zealously during school life.

Attention to physical training becomes all the more urgent owing to the tendency of population to gather to the larger towns, where the opportunities for physical exercises are necessarily restricted.

. . . the main object will best be attained by the action of School Managers in combination with Local Associations, which he trusts may be formed in different centres by leading and public-spirited inhabitants. Such Associations might greatly contribute to the work; and in particular, apart from the immediate work of the school, they might aid in providing the most simple and essential elements of military drill, and in the formation of Cadet Corps for those who have just left school. The formation of such corps would not only encourage the pursuit of a healthy and useful physical training, but would be an effective means of promoting intercourse and sympathy between different classes, and of influencing young men for good at an important crisis in their lives.

SOURCE: Report of the Committee of Council on Education in Scotland, 1904–5, *Parliamentary Papers* 1905, 29, 278.

DOCUMENT 129

Supplementary courses in Scottish schools

The Education (Scotland) Act of 1901 made fourteen the effective leaving age, and required more thought to be given to the education of older children in primary schools. This circular of 1903 drew a clear distinction between secondary education, suitable for the few, and the more vocational education needed by the great majority. It argued that the two sorts of education should be given in different types of school, and that potential secondary pupils should be transferred by the age of twelve to appropriate schools. The circular was controversial – see Document 132 *– because it had been traditional in Scotland, especially in rural areas, to teach secondary subjects in the ordinary school. 'My Lords' means the Scotch Education Department, which was constitutionally a committee of the Privy Council.*

3   . . . while there is no doubt a certain disciplinary value in the study of even the rudiments of certain distinctively secondary subjects, as e.g., a language (ancient or modern), or geometry deductively treated, such subjects imply a new departure for which there has been little, if any, preparation in the previous studies of the pupil, and they demand, to be effectively studied for any practical purpose, much more time than can possibly be given to them by children who are to leave school at the

age of 14. These subjects, therefore, cannot be made a necessary element of the curriculum. Nor should the curriculum which such pupils are to follow during the concluding portion of their time at school be dictated by the special requirements of a few exceptional pupils. The educational interests of the different sets of pupils should be provided for, but this should be done, wherever possible, in separate schools. My Lords are of opinion, from a careful consideration of the facts, that the tendency – not confined to any one class of school – to make one and the same school with one and the same staff serve many different functions is the weak point of educational organisation in Scotland as compared with that of other countries, with which, in other respects, Scotland might justly challenge comparison, and They are satisfied that increasing division of function as between different types of schools is an essential condition of further educational progress. This division of function, as will be apparent from what follows, does not necessarily imply a distinction of higher and lower, but simply a difference of aim and purpose with a corresponding difference in the subjects of instruction. They would accordingly urge, in the case under consideration, that the exceptional pupils for whom instruction in secondary subjects (in languages particularly) is desired, should, wherever possible, be transferred at a sufficiently early age (say before 12 years of age) to schools, whether schools under the Code or Secondary Schools, in which these subjects form the staple of the curriculum. Such transference should nearly always be possible in towns and populous districts, and it is clearly to the advantage of both sets of pupils – those for whom instruction in secondary subjects is desired and those for whom it is not – that the transference should be made. But They recognise that there are many cases, particularly in rural districts, where such transference is difficult or impossible, and They have no desire to limit the freedom of instruction in such cases, provided always that the real interests of the majority of the pupils are not sacrificed to the special requirements of one or two.

4   The case, then to be specially considered is that of those pupils who having reached a certain well defined stage of general education, will not enter upon the study of the specifically secondary subjects. Obviously the curriculum of study for such pupils in the remaining portion of their school life must be in the main a continuation and development of their previous studies. My Lords have already expressed the opinion that no mere repetition of previous work will in itself be sufficient; but They are equally of opinion that it is possible to give a fresh interest to the previous studies of the pupils, and at the same time to enhance their value, by putting in the forefront, at this stage, their bearing upon the probable practical requirements of the pupils' after-school life. What these requirements may be cannot, of course, be specifically determined in each particular case, but it will probably be found that sufficient definition will be given to the pupils' studies if the requirements of certain well defined groups of occupations are kept in view.

5   Guided by these considerations the following differentiated lines of work are suggested: –

Preparation for commercial pursuits. (Commercial Course.)
Preparation for manual occupations and trades. (Industrial Course.)
Preparation for rural life. (Course for Rural Schools.)
For girls – Preparation for domestic duties. (Household Management
    Course.)

Suggestions as to the kinds of work suitable for each of these courses will be found
in the Appendix . . .

6   But School work has for its end and aim objects more important than
preparation in the narrow sense for any particular occupation. It should aim at
producing the useful citizen, imbued with a sense of responsibility and of obligation
towards the society in which he lives. It should render him – so far as the school can
do so – fit in body and alert in mind, and should prepare him for the rational
enjoyment of his leisure time, as well as fit him for earning his living. These are
ideals, no doubt; but they are ideals towards which the school should constantly
strive. It follows that instruction in certain matters of general import should in all
cases be combined with, and should even take precedence of, the instruction special
to each of the course, of the preceding paragraph . . .

[The Appendix makes suggestions for the different types of course, including:]

Course for Rural Schools
1   The special instruction relative to this course should obviously be in matters
pertaining to Agriculture and Horticulture. The Nature Study lessons given in the
earlier stages of school life should now be so amplified and extended as to be useful
afterwards in the work of field or garden. School gardens, such as are now
common in America and on the Continent would prove a most valuable adjunct to
the lessons, and the time spent in giving practical instruction therein would, under
reasonable restrictions be reckoned as part of the school course. Much, however,
may be done with window boxes and flower pots in the way of experiment and
observation on plant reproduction and growth, the influence of various manures in
increasing the fertility of a soil, etc. The rocks and soils in the neighbourhood
should be carefully studied and their relations established. The suitability of
different soils for particular crops might afterwards be considered from the farm
practice of the district. The life histories of weeds and insect pests could be worked
out and simple remedies against them tested. Wind and insect pollination of plants
would also prove a most interesting study, and would naturally lead to observation
on bees and bee-keeping at the nearest bee-hives. A few well-illustrated lessons in
the rudiments of chemistry would serve to bring home to the pupils the more
important facts connected with the nutrition and work of plants, and the relations
of air, water and soil, to both vegetable and animal life. This gives a brief outline of
the nature of the instruction which may be undertaken, but the intelligent teacher,
knowing his ground, will be able to suggest many other lines along which the

school time may be advantageously spent. From the observations made, inference as to the farming practice may from time to time be drawn; but it is important that the course should be a training of the observing and reasoning faculties, such as will be of value to the pupil whatever his future occupation may be, and not simply a committing to memory of facts relating to any branch of Natural History or Agriculture.

In any inferences as to farming practice that may be drawn, the teacher should be careful to be guided by the best expert opinion available, and full use should be made, both for purposes of illustration and for drawing inferences as to correct farming practice, of any Experiment Stations conducted in the neighbourhood by the Agricultural College of the District.

2   As subsidiary subjects, the following should find a place in the course.

(a) Instruction in Geometry on the lines already indicated for the Technical Course, but leading up to land measuring and simple exercises in surveying. (b) The study of newspaper market reports and exercises in calculations based upon them. (c) The keeping of accounts.

Household Management (Girls' Course)

1   The special aim of this course should be to give the pupils an intelligent and well-grounded preparatory knowledge of the essential branches of housewifery. The course should comprise a series of carefully co-ordinated lessons in housekeeping (the care of rooms, furnishing, and clothing; marketing and the keeping of household accounts; cookery, laundry work, and needlework, especially mending, darning, and cutting-out). It is important that these various branches should be treated, not as isolated subjects to be taken in separate courses and then dropped, but as parts of a whole conducing to one end.

While this course must, from the nature of it, be mainly practical, yet it may be made a valuable instrument of mental discipline, if care be taken to secure that practice is always intelligently based upon reasoned and well-illustrated theory. By clear explanation, illustrated whenever possible by simple experiments, the pupils should be made to understand and appreciate the 'reason why' of the detailed practical methods taught; and they should be trained and encouraged to observe, test, note, compare, and infer for themselves.

In Girls' Courses thus treated, some extension would fitly be given to certain of the topics of general education enumerated under head (B) (*a*). In particular the subject of proper feeding and care of infants should receive attention.

SOURCE: Report of the Committee of Council on Education in Scotland, 1904–5, *Parliamentary Papers* 1905, 29, 281–2; 289–90.

DOCUMENT 130

Continuation classes for school leavers

This circular was issued following the Education (Scotland) Act of 1908, which gave new responsibilities to school boards, including the provision of school meals and medical inspection. Evening classes for adolescents had a long history, and by the 1900s were organised as 'continuation' classes, which sought to carry on general education alongside technical or vocational training. There was a movement – inspired like many innovations at this time by the German model – to make part-time continuation classes compulsory for recent school-leavers, and the Act allowed school boards to do this within their own areas; they were also encouraged to organise juvenile employment services. The policy was introduced in Scotland before England as an experiment.

2   The importance of this new departure in legislation has been recognised on all hands, but certain aspects of it deserve more than a passing notice. For the first time a direct responsibility is placed upon School Boards for at all events certain aspects of the education of adolescents. Hitherto the statutory duties of School Boards have not extended beyond the provision of the means of education for children of school age, i.e. from five to fourteen. The latter age, indeed, denotes a comparatively recent extension of the period during which the great majority of school children have been in point of fact subjected to systematic discipline and instruction. During these years a certain amount of moral training has been given and a certain modicum of instruction in Reading, Writing and Arithmetic (and incidentally in other subjects) imparted, in the hope, apparently, that the education so given will be of material assistance to the child in its future occupation, whatever that may be, and that he or his parents may be trusted to turn it to good account. It has been no part of the duty of a School Board under the Statutes (or, indeed, of any other public body) to take cognisance of the period of adolescence; to reinforce parental control at the time when it is most needed but is, in point of fact, weakening from natural causes; to guide and advise young persons as to choice of occupations or even to put before them much needed information on the subject; to ascertain what further systematic instruction is needed to enhance the efficiency of young persons in their several occupations and to make them more useful citizens; or to see that suitable means of further education with these practical ends in view are actually provided. True, very many School Boards, to their credit be it said, have exerted themselves to provide instruction for young persons beyond the statutory school age either in schools giving instruction of a 'secondary' character or in Continuation Classes for those engaged in all manner of wage-earning occupations. But these efforts have been sporadic and in large part unsystematic, and it remains broadly true that School Boards as such have hitherto stood in no sort of relation to young persons over 14 years of age or had any responsibility for providing for the educational needs of adolescents.

3   It is becoming increasingly clear that a national system of education founded on such principles can be at best but a qualified success. That is the experience of other countries as well as of our own, and everywhere the progressive nations of the world are bestirring themselves to make the proper instruction, control and discipline of adolescents a matter of State concern. In these circumstances it will probably be regarded as a source of legitimate satisfaction by the School Boards and people of Scotland, and as a tribute to the soundness and efficiency of Scottish educational traditions, that the Legislature has seen fit to permit this momentous experiment to be made first of all in that portion of the United Kingdom. It has further shown its confidence in the School Boards of Scotland by entrusting them with the discretionary use of the very comprehensive powers conferred by the third subsection of section 10 of the Act – a confidence which will doubtless be justified by experience of the use which School Boards make of these powers and by their discharge of all the responsibilities placed upon them by the recent Act in this connection.

SOURCE: *Scotch Education Department. Reports, & c., Issued in 1908–09. Minutes and Circulars*, 55.

DOCUMENT 131

Post-qualifying courses for twelve to fifteen year olds

The Education (Scotland) Act of 1918 merged school boards into county-wide Education Authorities, which had to draw up schemes for the systematic organisation of secondary education. It also provided for raising the school leaving age to fifteen, and although this was indefinitely postponed, the 1921 circular still assumes that it will take place. There were widespread hopes that the different types of 'post-qualifying' course (ie those for the twelve to fifteen age group) would be brought together, but this circular reasserted the bifurcated system of 1903, and was widely criticised at the time.

Post qualifying organization
4   In face of the contemplated extension of the school age the question of the best form of 'post-qualifying' organization assumes an urgency that has never attached to it before. In considering it, Authorities would do well to concentrate their attention upon two main groups of pupils – those who are likely to complete a full course of Secondary education and those who, for one reason or another, will leave the Day School at 15 or thereby, and subsequently give a year's attendance at

Continuation Classes. So far as the former group is concerned, but little difficulty is likely to be encountered. Despite defects and imperfections which experience is gradually remedying, the present organization of Secondary education in Scotland may be regarded as fairly satisfactory. Moreover, the force of public opinion is strong enough to ensure the maintenance of the immemorial Scottish tradition that, subject to the overriding condition of intellectual fitness, no child, whatever his home circumstances, shall be debarred access to the Secondary School and the University by lack of opportunity. There is abundant evidence that, so far as this particular obligation is concerned, the liberality of Education Authorities has brought Scotland nearer to the ideal than she has been at any previous period in her educational history. Indeed, the only point as to which doubt arises is whether due attention is always paid to the overriding condition.

5   The second, and much larger, group of pupils is in far less happy case. After all, however hard the saying may seem, there is no denying the fact that in every country only a relatively small percentage of the population will be endowed by nature with the mental equipment which they must possess if they are to profit by Secondary School or University study. A frank recognition of this truth is essential, if a proper organization is to be established. As bearing upon it, the figures of enrolment and wastage in our Intermediate and Secondary Schools during recent years are most significant. Of the boys and girls who pass the Qualifying Examination, it is only a small majority, in some important districts it is actually a minority, who are to be found at any given time in Supplementary Courses. The natural and inevitable result is that, of those who choose the Intermediate curriculum, a very large proportion drop off at the end of the first or the second year. Such a record means much fruitless effort on the part of the teachers, much disappointment and loss of time on the part of the pupils. The extension of the school age will only aggravate these evils, unless the situation has been adequately prepared for.

6   Nineteen years ago, in their Circular Letter of 16th February, 1903, the Department laid down certain principles which ought, in their opinion, to govern all endeavours to frame courses suitable for other than distinctively Secondary pupils. These principles still hold good. Up till now, however, it can hardly be said that they have been translated very effectively into practice. The reasons for this are not far to seek. A new departure on a scale so extensive involved the definite abandonment of certain conventional ideas as to what was or was not implied in the use of the word 'education'. In a limited number of cases the situation has been courageously faced, with altogether admirable results, but as a general rule the Supplementary Courses have tended to be starved and neglected. Managers and teachers alike have been inclined to regard them as of second-rate or even of third-rate importance. As a result, their prestige has never been high. Pupils have avoided them and have preferred to enrol in Intermediate Courses, even when they had no serious intention of carrying the Intermediate curriculum to a conclusion. The

apathy which was responsible for this state of affairs was no doubt partly due to the feeling that it was hardly worth while troubling much about courses where the average boy or girl would spend only one or at most two years. Now that this limitation is likely to be removed before very long, it is imperative that Authorities and teachers should bend their minds to constructing a system which will enable them to meet the demand with which they will be confronted when sections 14 and 15 come into operation. They will be legislating for the majority. Of all the problems with which Education Authorities have to grapple, this is at once the most severe and the most immediately pressing.

SOURCE: *Education (Scotland). Reports & c., Issued in 1921–22.* Section G, Circular 44, 2–4.

DOCUMENT 132

'Centralising' advanced subjects in secondary schools

Simon Somerville Laurie (1829–1909) was the leading Scottish educational expert of the late nineteenth century, and his many books and lectures on educational philosophy were standard fare in teacher training. He was the first professor of education at Edinburgh University, retiring in 1903. He also acted for many years as inspector for the Dick Bequest, an endowment which supported rural schools in the North-East, especially encouraging them to keep up the classics and other university-oriented subjects. This extract is from Laurie's report to the governors of the Bequest. The bill to which he refers was an unsuccessful precursor of the 1908 Act, but his general target was the Scotch Education Department's policy of 'centralising' advanced subjects in secondary schools.

Concluding remarks
It is no part of my duty to criticise generally the Bill which has been withdrawn, and which, it is understood, will be re-introduced next year. I would merely submit to the Governors that there can be no assurance that the Bequest will be able to fulfil its purposes unless, in any Act that may be passed, the Department be *instructed* in its Codes to recognise the (so-called) 'secondary subjects' of Languages and Mathematics in rural schools. So long as these subjects are essential for a university graduation course, instruction in them sufficient to prepare for the Preliminary Examinations of the universities, or, at least, for entering with advantage some accessible secondary school, is indispensable. If this be not available, then assuredly the rural schools will fall into the same grade as the 'common' schools in

England and elsewhere, the class of teacher will degenerate by their being restricted to elementary subjects, and country children will be permanently cut off from their present privileges.

It is true that neither the Department nor the Secretary for Scotland, in framing the Bill, showed indifference to the interests of clever boys and girls in rural districts. Their policy was, and I presume still is, to transfer the more ambitious pupils at an early age to Higher Grade or Central Schools, and to provide a certain number of local bursaries to facilitate this. On this policy I would remark, first, that while parents above the industrial classes would doubtless take advantage of these bursaries, and supplement them, others could not do so. And secondly, that the majority of parents will have strong objections to lodge their children away from home before they have attained the age of fourteen at least. And thirdly, that there is no evidence that the brighter boys and girls gathered in centres will make more rapid and solid progress than they do under a system which secures for them the close personal attention and interest of the teacher, while giving him an opportunity of showing his own efficiency and securing professional distinction. Schoolmasters, as well as schools, will be divided into two classes with a gulf between them. The wisdom of such a division of schools and of the teaching class is more than doubtful, although it looks well on paper. It certainly is not in the educational interests of Scotland, if we take a large view of these and recognise that the living education of a country depends mainly on two things, the interest which adults take in the work of the schools, and the class of teacher who can be drawn into the profession of schoolmaster as offering a field for the exercise of the highest intellectual and moral attributes.

It will not be supposed that I advocate the maintenance of the principle of the Dick Bequest solely in the interest of a few boys and girls who may be thereby enabled to rise in the world. This is only an advantage incidental to the system. It is the effect which disciplinary subjects have on the mind of the whole school that is of importance. The object of the State in educating the people is not so much the equipping of future citizens for their work in this or that special industry as the disciplining of the young to the vigorous exercise of their intelligence; and above all, training them up to the moral and religious ideal of the nation to which they belong. If the school-time is pre-occupied with fragments of utilitarian instruction, that which is higher and better must necessarily be driven out. Whatever may be the amount of practical information the pupils may gain, it is a truism to say that it will all be useless to the State if the great motive force be wanting; and that must always be a moral and religious force. Given this, all else will come. If intellectual discipline and the moral and religious elements of education be pushed into a corner during the impressionable years of childhood, it must be remembered that those years come only once. The primary school, above all, should, in my opinion, be sacred to a liberal education, and technical instruction should be postponed to a later stage.

SOURCE: *Dick Bequest Trust. General Report to the Governors, 1890–1904, by Professor SS Laurie* 1904, Edinburgh, 42–5.

LEISURE AND RECREATION

DOCUMENT 133

'Mountain Men'

Before the 1930s mountaineering in Scotland was the sport of a minority of middle-class intellectuals – usually university academics who had long vacations and no financial worries. From around 1840–1900, it became the custom for these professional men to pioneer routes in the Alps and in Britain and write about their experiences. Mountaineering was a gentleman's sport and after a hard day's climbing their nights were spent in comfortable hotels or inns with a good dinner to end the day. In the 1930s in Britain a very different kind of mountaineer emerged, men from the industrial cities such as Glasgow. They were men from working-class backgrounds who worked in the shipyards, in shops or as apprentices, but all had in common the uncertainty of unemployment and the bleak prospect of being young in a large industrial city at a time of dole queues and recession. For many of them getting out of the city was the great escape.

Alistair Borthwick:
'You have to understand what Scotland was like in those days. It was a grim place. There were a million people in Britain out of work and more, was it two million? People were on the dole, there was absolutely no hope at all. It really was grim and you were a youngster in this and you accepted this, you had been brought up to this, this was normal, this grimness, then suddenly to find this escape route, this climbing thing and it absolutely bowled you over. Here was an entirely different world where it was alive and things were happening. And the people in it were all young and full of enthusiasm and so on. And the escape from the city at the weekend, it's something that I don't think any youngster today could possibly believe. I mean, today they go off and they hitch-hike to Istanbul and nobody thinks anything of it, but in those days, the idea of simply getting out of the city, even as far away as Glencoe, people just didn't understand it, they didn't realise that this could be done. It was an explosion, it was a wonderful thing.'

Jock Nimlin:
'Some of us in those bad old days when jobs were hard to find were working in shops and when you were working in a shop you had to work a six-day week until 9.00 p.m. on a Saturday. The lucky people only worked a five-and-a-half-day week, they got off at noon, and they could catch trains and buses going away out into the Highlands.

'But those of us who worked in shops and quite a lot of my friends did, would have to take late trains and late buses to some point in the countryside as close as you could get to the mountains. If you were going to Arrochar, for example, you got as far as Balmaha and Loch Lomond and we had an arrangement with the boat hirer there to leave out a boat and two sets of oars and we would board the boat perhaps eight of us, sometimes ten of us, we sometimes had the boat overloaded and off we would go about midnight from Balmaha and we would row fourteen miles up to Tarbet.

'Then we would pull the boat ashore, snatch a few hours' sleep under trees until daylight and then we'd have a very early breakfast and walk across to Arrochar and from Arrochar we would climb the Cobbler, Ben Ime, Ben Narnain, any of the mountains in that vicinity, and in the early evening, we would make a point of getting back to the boat, back into the loch again and we had that fourteen miles to row, back to Balmaha. Of course we always tried our best to get the last bus at Balmaha but on one or two occasions we were held up by headwinds and we missed the last bus at Balmaha which meant that we had to walk from Balmaha right back into Glasgow again to start work on the following morning. And some of these weekends were super-strenuous, we were absolutely exhausted when we got into work on a Monday morning and I can always remember the manager of the music shop I worked in at this time, he met an acquaintance of mine, he didn't know this man was a friend of mine, and he met him because he had a rucksack on. He spoke to him and he said that he had a youth working in his music shop who went away climbing at weekends and came back so tired that he didn't wake up until Wednesday of the following week, which I think was gross libel because I used to be fully awake by Tuesday!'

Alistair Borthwick:
'The first time I realised the wonderful kind of society that I had landed in was one weekend early on, we went up to investigate Bruce's Cave in Glen Loin, that's just above Arrochar. And the advice I'd been given was to go beyond the hostel and there were various other instructions about where to turn off.

'And after that I was told to wait until I smelt kippers, and then to follow my nose and we did this, and we came to a place where a cliff had collapsed and there was a great jumble of boulders and sure enough half way through this, I smelt kippers and I followed my nose and there was a hole in the ground and I dropped through this hole, about six feet down onto the floor. This took me under the boulder which was the size of a church and there was a great room inside, speaking from memory perhaps twenty yards one way by a roof maybe fifteen feet high. There were a dozen chaps in, sitting around in among the rocks and there was a fire going with kippers. And in all stages of dress and undress, we sat that night and discussed anything from football to philosophy.

'And every ten minutes or so somebody else would drop in through the door because you see they were all hitch-hiking and some had got a lift early in the day and some hadn't managed to get one and they were still coming through the door at midnight.'

Jock Nimlin:

'We stayed in some of the most enchanting places you can imagine. We stayed in what we called 'howffs'. It could be an old Scottish word, but I'll tell you how we came to use this word: a group of us in the late '20s were sleeping under an overhang on Loch Achray. It was a sort of cave which had been formed perhaps thousands of years earlier when the loch had a higher level and during the 1926 strike, miners fed up with no work had gone out into the countryside to fish and possibly to do a bit of scrounging of potatoes and turnips from the fields. But anyhow, you used to meet quite a lot of miners at that time in the countryside and they had improved this overhung section of the bank and they had put in one or two wooden shores they had collected from the driftwood of the loch and we were all sitting here one night with a fire going and a bit of smoke coming out when an old tramp wandered in.

'And the tramp told us he wasn't staying the night, he was going to a meeting of tramps in a barn a few miles further along the road but he asked if he could boil his can on our fire and of course he did and just before he left, his last words were, "Ye've a real guid howff here."

'So we got onto this word "howff" and we looked up the Oxford Dictionary and we found that it had quite a number of meanings. One being a resort or a haunt; it could be a tavern; it could be a graveyard; in other words, a resting place. So all our resting places were known as howffs and we applied them freely to old bothies in the mountains and sometimes under bridges – some bridges were favourite howffs – you got shelter from the weather to some extent and when I go through the Highlands nowadays with friends, I'm always pointing out the howffs I've slept in and sometimes I'm still able to point out the trees I've slept under.

'I know some of our members joined youth hostels eventually, some of them became more civilised, but some of us kept to this old business of hunting for howffs and we still do.'

Hamish Hamilton:

'Ironmongery in these days was frowned upon, you know. If you carried a piton with you, you were regarded as a softie. But now the whole approach has changed and unless you go about bristling with pitons, you're really not supposed to be a man at all. Which I think is a pity, because I think free climbing had much more to offer than the present sort of mechanised approach but then I'm one of the older school and this is understandable.'

SOURCE: Ishbel MacLean 1980, *in* Billy Kay (ed) *Odyssey – Voices from Scotland's recent past*, Edinburgh (Polygon Books/BBC Scotland), 79–87.

DOCUMENT 134

Poem found on the door of Ryvoan Bothy

Catharine Loader dedicated her book about the Scottish Centre of Outdoor Training at Glenmore Lodge in the Cairngorms (published in 1952), to 'all the young people of all countries'. She added, 'May you learn to enjoy the thrills and adventure of life in the open air, and . . . realise that in your hands you hold a sacred trust: the heritage of the hills and the country to which you belong'. This was an era of progressive education, of taking children out of the classroom to seek a spiritual union with the natural world, to make them better adults for the future. This poem was found written on the door of Ryvoan Bothy and was fortunately copied before the door was destroyed. From 1948, the children staying at Glenmore Lodge wrote such songs and verse which they then read out at the Friday ceilidh evenings.

I leave tonight from Euston

I shall leave tonight from Euston
By the seven-thirty train,
And from Perth in the early morning
I shall see the hills again.
From the top of Ben Macdhui
I shall watch the gathering storm,
And see the crisp snow lying
At the back of Cairngorm.
I shall feel the mist from Bhrotain
And pass by Lairig Ghru
To look on dark Loch Einich
From the heights of Sgoran Dubh
From the broken Barns of Bynack
I shall see the sunrise gleam
On the forehead of Ben Rinnes
And Strathspey awake from dream.
And again in the dusk of evening
I shall find once more alone
The dark water of the Green Loch,
And the pass beyond Ryvoan.
For tonight I leave from Euston
And leave the world behind;
Who has the hills as a lover,
Will find them wondrous kind.

ANON.

SOURCE: Catharine Loader 1952 *Cairngorm Adventure at Glenmore Lodge*, Edinburgh (William Brown), 49–52.

DOCUMENT 135

The New God, Tourism

In the 1990s tourism is seen to have a dominant role in the Scottish economy. Every year, especially during the summer months, thousands of Scots holiday abroad or within the UK, and thousands of overseas visitors come to Scotland. In the 1930s the majority of tourists in the Highlands would have been Lowland Scots or the English, brought there by the transport revolution of cheaper motor cars and bus travel. This prose by the writer Neil Gunn is an attack on those who believed that tourism would solve all the economic ills of the Highlands. Gunn predicted that the new god, tourism, would enslave the Highland spirit, as hotels and B & Bs opened up across the North, run by proprietors keen to make quick money.

Tourist traffic is becoming a matter of importance in the affairs of most nations, and generally there is a department or semi-official body ready to hand out pamphlets to allure the traveller. Even the intricate matter of money exchange may to a slight extent be manipulated in favour of the visitor as anyone contemplating a tour in Germany should know. The underlying idea is the apparently simple one that money brought into a country and spent there adds to the wealth of that country.

Apparently simple – because the business of the wealth of a country is in reality extremely complex. I got my first lesson here when as a lad I read 'Progress and Poverty', and learned that in proportion as the wealth of a nation increased so did poverty amidst the workers of that nation . . . The increase in recent years in unemployment in this country has been accompanied by an increase in the national wealth and by an incalculable increase in the potential national wealth. And the reason for this is simple enough: the perfecting of machinery by invention and scientific discovery at once increases production and displaces labour. That fact is now generally admitted, and the political fight is concentrated on the nature of the remedy required. We are not concerned here with the nature of the remedy, but we are concerned with the underlying facts.

For in the Highlands at the moment a fight is going on over the question of whether or not a limited liability company should be given statutory powers to use the waters of a certain area of a county for the production, by hydro-electricity, of a commercial commodity within that county. The inevitable questions of local rights or jealousies do not concern us here. What is pertinent to our purpose is that prominent opponents of this water-power scheme base their general opposition on two points: (1) they do not desire to see the water power of the Highlands used in creating private industry, and (2) they consider that the tourist traffic should solve all the economic ills of the Highlands.

Now this is a matter of grave, perhaps of crucial, importance to the Highlands at this particular moment in time. For the decline in every phase of Highland life is becoming alarming. It is easy to quote census figures showing a progressive depopulation of the Highland counties, but it is not so easy to grasp precisely what that implies by way of emigration of the youthful best, and the leaving behind of an ever-preponderating number of the aged and unfit. The old croft is no longer a self-supporting unit. The sea-fisheries are in desperate straits. There have been more economic tragedies on the Moray Firth coast in recent years than should last a whole sea-faring nation for a century. The distribution of national or public relief has been constantly increasing, until at last a problem has arisen, particularly in the Outer Isles, that the Department of Health is finding it difficult to solve: the problem of the 'manufacture' of work by men and women, so that, within the meaning of the Act, they may get thirty stamps affixed to a card and so qualify for the dole. The suggestion that one should 'blame' them for this is merely a piece of insufferable moralism. But there is the picture. All vital statistics of the Highlands point the same way. And not least those of insanity.

A correspondent in these pages last month referred to the increase in the inmates of the Inverness District Asylum, which serves the counties of Inverness, Ross, Sutherland, Moray and Nairn. Not only is the pauper lunacy rate for this area far higher than for any other part of Scotland, but it is more than twice as high as that for the congested industrial towns of Lanark, where conditions amongst the vast mass of the poor have been and are surely dreadful enough. The General Board of Control in its report on pauper lunacy in Scotland states: 'At the top of the list stands without a break the whole Highland and insular region of Scotland'.

And the Scottish Committee of the British Medical Association, in its Memorandum of Evidence, comments thus: 'One causative factor is depopulation, which has drained the Highlands and Islands of much good stock, leaving behind weaker and older people who are unable to stand up to the strain of daily life on the sea coast or among the hills. Nothing has been done by way of a really serious attempt to preserve the fine type of people, mentally and physically, which the Highlands and Islands have hitherto possessed and produced'.

But the decline of what we call our Highland heritage is even more marked on – if I may be allowed the phrase – the cultural side. We may have the finest folk music in the world, and, in the Gaelic, one of the finest folk literatures. Is any music being created to-day, or any literature of the slightest significance? And what about Gaelic itself? Dying steadily.

Now, painting this negative side is not pleasant. None of us likes evidence of 'gloom'. The Highlander, despite all writing to the contrary, is a cheerful fellow. But then so is the consumptive. In short, whether we are made uncomfortable or not, whether our pride is hurt or not, we must face up to facts so long as we are truly concerned about the future of our land. If we are no longer so concerned, then nothing matters but the self-induced warmth of make-believe until the feast or the famine is over and the bones left for the inevitable antiquary.

Taking then the Highlands as we know them to-day, can the tourist industry in fact restore the economic life of the people, can it revive what have so long been its whole way of living, namely crofting and sea-fishing?

First let us revert to our opening remarks. Tourists who come to this country do spend money. That money, let us say, increases national wealth. But how far does this tourist money as spent in the Highlands increase the wealth of the working Highlander? Could we, as in 'Progress and Poverty', have an increase of apparent wealth floating about the Highlands coincident with an actual impoverishment of the crofter and fisherman? In short: (1) how does the tourist traffic directly affect the general industries of crofting and sea-fishing, and (2) in how far are the hotels which tourists patronise dependent on the products of Highland labour?

Let me take a certain wide area of the Caithness coast which I visited a few weeks ago. Many townships are there: many scores of crofts. There is a harbour that in its heyday had over a hundred fishing boats sailing from it and now has five motor boats. There is the usual hotel, though not a sporting one. Most of the folk I know personally. The highway to John o' Groats passes through this region. I went into the matter closely. In this whole area there are two families that benefit, to a certain degree, from the tourist traffic: the family that runs the hotel and the family that runs the garage. No other families benefit . . .

And as with that Caithness region so with nearly all the rest of the truly crofting and sea-fishing areas of the Highlands. Individual houses here and there may be encountered along the great main roads where a night's accommodation can be obtained, and in a few special areas, as in Badenoch, there is a regular house-letting business, run for the most part by women who otherwise have only slender means of support. But I am concerned here with the true crofting and fishing areas, with the crofter and fisherman who have their own homes and their own families, and my experience satisfies me that the three months' tourist season does not affect one per cent. of them to the value of one pound sterling.

Now for the hotels, particularly as we know them in the West, complete with sporting privileges. I suggest that the food for these hotels is purchased not from local shops or other local source, but direct from the great city stores, wholesale or retail. In fact, in view of the table that has to be provided for high-paying guests, this must be done. The hotel proprietor has no option. Such fresh foods as milk or vegetables he generally takes care to provide from his own byre or garden. And as for sea fish, he keeps in touch with the nearest town or provides it himself. Last year a friend of mine, staying in a West Coast hotel, went for a day's sea-fishing in the hotel boat and helped to swell a very considerable catch. For this privilege he was charged thirty shillings.

These hotels, in the season, give employment to some maid servants and gillies, and wages got in this way over a month or two may affect the economy of a few fishing or crofting families. But I suggest the effect over all is negligible. Most of the money drawn at the hotels goes to pay Southern stores, and the profit retained by the hotel-keeper finds profitable investment neither in crofting nor in sea-fishing . . .

. . . If I were an unemployed man in the Highlands, a broken fisherman, a three-months gillie, I should prefer to work in a factory in the Highlands rather than in one in Lanarkshire, South Wales or the Midlands of England. The folk who object to the scheme because it is to be run for private profit would not impress me, because each one of them runs his own business for private profit. Even their objection on the basis that it would destroy the tourist traffic I should see to be specious, inasmuch as countries like Switzerland, Norway, and Sweden, with hydro-electric works all over them, have an immense tourist traffic; and even in the Irish Free State, since the erection of the Shannon scheme (in the most lovely part of the country), with its pylons marching across the breadth of Ireland, tourism has increased enormously.

But tourism one way or the other wouldn't matter. I should demand a man's work, and I should demand it in my own land. I might hate the forces, national or local, that had so misgoverned and impoverished the Highlands as to compel me away from my fishing or crofting and into a factory. But better a factory than starvation; better a self-respecting worker in my own trade union than a half-sycophant depending on the whims of a passing tourist. For I should know that so long as Highlandmen are employed in the Highlands, so long as they constitute the mass of the workers there, then there is hope for the Highlands. In virile life, however employed, there is a future, because free men will not bear indefinitely the evils of our present industrial system. But when this free virile life is absent, then not all the deserving old women attending to all the tourists of the world and prattling of the scenic beauty of empty glens can save the ancient heritage from decay and death.

SOURCE: Neil M Gunn 1937 ' "Gentlemen – The Tourist!" The New Highland Toast', *Scots Magazine* New Series, Volume XXVI, No 6, March 1937, 410–15.

CULTURE

DOCUMENT 136

Hugh Miller on religion

Hugh Miller (1802–56), journalist and folklorist, in defence of the religion of the Scots.

The merry unthinking serfs, who, early in the reign of Charles the First, danced on Sabbaths round the maypole, were afterwards the ready tools of despotism . . . The Ironsides, who, in the cause of civil and religious freedom bore them down, were staunch Sabbatarians . . . the preponderance of enjoyment lies on the more credulous side. I never yet encountered a better-pleased people . . . unthinking, unsuspicious, blue-eyed, fair-complexioned, honest Saxons.

'You Scotch are a strange people', said one of the commercial gentlemen. 'When I was in Scotland two years ago, I could hear of scarce anything among you but your Church question. What good does all your theology do you?' 'Independently altogether of religious considerations', I replied, 'it has done for our people what all your Societies for the Diffusion of Useful Knowledge, and all your Penny and Saturday Magazines, will never do for yours: it has awakened their intellects, and taught them how to think.'

SOURCE: Hugh Miller 1847 *First Impressions of England*, London (John Johnstone), 45–6, 369, 10–11.

DOCUMENT 137

Edwin Muir 'Scotland 1941'

Edwin Muir (1890–1959), poet and critic, on Calvinist Scotland.

> We were a tribe, a family, a people.
> Wallace and Bruce guard now a painted field,
> And all may read the folio of our fable,
> Peruse the sword, the sceptre and the shield.
> A simple sky roofed in that rustic day,
> The busy corn-fields and the haunted holms,
> The green road winding up the ferny brae.
> But Knox and Melville clapped their preaching palms
> And bundled all the harvesters away,
> Hoodicrow Peden in the blighted corn
> Hacked with his rusty beak the starving haulms.
> Out of that desolation we were born.
>
> Courage beyond the point and obdurate pride
> Made us a nation, robbed us of a nation.
> Defiance absolute and myriad-eyed
> That could not pluck the palm plucked our damnation.
> We with such courage and the bitter wit
> To fell the ancient oak of loyalty,
> And strip the peopled hill and the altar bare,
> And crush the poet with an iron text,
> How could we read our souls and learn to be?

SOURCE: from Edwin Muir 1960 'Scotland 1941', in *Collected Poems*, London (Faber and Faber), 97.

DOCUMENT 138

'Let every herring hing by its ain head'

Rob Roy *is the most popular of Sir Walter Scott's works in Scotland. In this extract, Bailie Nicoll Jarvie, a Glasgow magistrate and a successful businessman, gives his views on the Union.*

'Let ilka ane roose the ford as they find it. I say, "Let Glasgow flourish!" whilk is judiciously and elegantly putten round the town's arms by way of bye-word. Now, since St. Mungo catched herrings in the Clyde, what was ever to gar us flourish like the sugar and tobacco trade? Will ony body tell me that, and grumble at the treaty that opened us a road west-awa yonder? . . .

But I maun hear naething about honour – we ken naething here but aboot credit. Honour is a homicide and a bloodspiller, that gangs about making frays in the street; But Credit is a decent honest man, that sits at hame and makes the pat play . . . '

Mr Jarvie answered some objection which Owen made on the difficulty of sorting a cargo for America, without buying from England, with vehemence and volubility. 'Na, na, sir, we stand on our ain bottom; we pickle in our ain pock-neuk . . . let every herring hing by its ain head, and every sheep by its ain shank and ye'll find, sir, us Glasgow folk no sae far ahint but what we may follow'.

SOURCE: Sir Walter Scott 1817 *RobRoy* Edinburgh (Constable), from Chapters 27 and 26.

DOCUMENT 139

'A sick state and an ailing people'

John Buchan, Lord Tweedsmuir (1875–1940), novelist, historian and Tory politician, on Scotland's political problems.

There is but one master in the land and its name is Law – which is in itself a creation of a free people under the inspiration of the Almighty. That law may be changed by the people's will, but till it be so changed it is to be revered and obeyed. It has ordained the King's prerogative, the rights of the subject, and the rights and duties of the Kirk. The state is like the body, whose health is only to be maintained by a just proportion among its members. If a man's belly be his god, his limbs will suffer; if he use only his legs, his arms will dwindle. If, therefore, the King should intrude upon the subject's rights, or the subject whittle at the King's prerogative, or the Kirk set herself above the Crown, there will be a sick state and an ailing people.

SOURCE: John Buchan 1927 *Witch Wood*, London (Hodder and Stoughton), from Chapter 3.

DOCUMENT 140

Thomas Carlyle on the values of Scottish society

The following extracts from the writings of Thomas Carlyle (1795–1881), historian and social critic, give a flavour of his views on a range of subjects, from Calvinism to the railways.

a)   Instruction, that mysterious communing of Wisdom with Ignorance, is no longer an indefinable tentative progress, requiring a study of individual aptitudes, and a perpetual variation of means and methods, to attain the same end; but a secure, universal, straightforward business, to be conducted in the gross, by proper mechanism, . . . with such intellect as comes to hand.

b)   A country where the entire people is, or even once has been, laid hold of, filled to the heart with an infinite religious idea, has 'made a step from which it cannot retrograde.' Thought, conscience, the sense that man is denizen of a Universe, creature of an Eternity, has penetrated to the remotest cottage, to the simplest heart. Beautiful and awful, the feeling of Heavenly Behest, of Duty God-commanded, over-canopies all life.

c)   It is in Society that man first feels what he is; first becomes what he can be. In Society an altogether new set of spiritual activities are evolved in him, and the old immeasurably quickened and strengthened.

d)   . . . railways have set all the Towns of Britain a-dancing . . . confusedly waltzing, in a state of progressive dissolution, towards the four winds; and know not where the end of the death-dance will be for them, in what point of space they will be allowed to rebuild themselves.

e)   Call ye that a Society . . . where there is no longer any Social Idea extant; not so much as the Idea of a Common Home, but only of a common, overcrowded Lodging-house? Where each, isolated, regardless of his neighbour, turned against his neighbour, clutches what he can get, and cries 'Mine!' and calls it Peace, because, in the cut-purse and cut-throat Scramble, no steel knives, but only a far cunninger sort, can be employed? . . .

f)   . . . many men in the van do always, like Russian soldiers, march in to the ditch at Schweidnitz, and fill it up with their dead bodies, that the rear may pass over them dryshod, and gain the honour . . . How many earnest rugged Cromwells, Knoxes, poor Peasant Covenanters, wrestling, battling for life, in rough miry places, have to struggle, and suffer, and fall, greatly censured, *bemired*, before a beautiful Revolution of Eight-eight can step over them in official pumps and silk-stockings, with universal three-times-three!

SOURCE: Thomas Carlyle:
'Signs of the Times', *The Edinburgh Review* 1829, reprinted in *Scottish and Other Miscellanies*, London (Everyman/Dent *c.* 1900), 227.
'Sir Walter Scott', *London and Westminster Review*, i–iv, reprinted in *Scottish and other Miscellanies*, London (Everyman/Dent *c.* 1900), 71.

'Characteristics', 1831, reprinted in *Scottish and other Miscellanies*, London (Everyman/Dent *c*. 1900), 194.

Latter-Day Pamphlets, 1850, London (Chapman and Hall), 228–30.

Sartor Resartus, 1836 (reprinted by Everyman/Dent, London 1956), 174.

'Baillie the Covenanter', 1841, reprinted in *Scottish and other miscellanies*, London (Everyman/Dent, *c*. 1900), 146.

DOCUMENT 141

'Greedy as corbies and chattering like pyets'

John Galt (1779–1839), novelist on local and national government.

a   [I] got the cart up the brae, and the whole council reduced into a proper state of subjection to the will and pleasure of his majesty, whose deputies and agents I have ever considered all inferior magistrates to be, administering and exercising, as they do, their power and authority in his royal name.

b   'Till Governments, and Houses of Commons, and those institutions which the sinful condition of man renders necessary, are made responsible to a tribunal of appeal, whose decisions shall control them, there can be no effectual reform. The first step is to take away all will of its own from Government – for statesmen are but mere men, rarely in talent above the average of their species, from what I have seen – and oblige it to consider itself no better than an individual, even with respect to its own individual subjects. Let the law in all things be paramount, and it will little matter whether the lords or the vagabonds send members to Parliament . . . '

I had, indeed, a sore heart when I saw the Whigs and Whiglings coming louping, like the puddocks of Egypt, over among the right-hand benches of the House of Commons, greedy as corbies and chattering like pyets.

SOURCES: John Galt
1822 *The Provost*, Edinburgh (William Blackwood), 21.
1832 *The Member*, London (James Fraser), 138, 268.

DOCUMENT 142

The End of an Old Song

The following extract is from The End of an Old Song: A Romance, *a novel by JD Scott (1917–1980). In these extracts, Scott's hero, Alastair Kerr, decides to ditch both Scotland and Britain.*

'As a successful English barrister I would have been a stinkeroo . . . I don't know which is worse – the real God-given English upper-class arrogance or imitations of it. I never did like that country very much, Patrick, and now I'm through with it.' He paused for a long moment. 'I've finally decided to become an American citizen.' "Sir Alastair Kerr, KC, and Lady Kerr with Jeremy, aged eight, and Curia, aged ten, on the lawn at Owlets Pastern." Sounds well, doesn't it? But there was a picture something like that in the minds of the most diverse people, Levantine Jews and Irish navvies and clever wee Scotties, for maybe a couple of hundred years. And now we have to give it up for an apartment on Fifth Avenue. It isn't the same thing.

(Edinburgh) seemed different now; it had the mild Welfare State look . . . Now, after London, I was once again struck by the hardness, the *stoniness* of the streets . . . everything looked slightly proletarianized. This was the Scotland of the nineteenth century, the grim, competitive little country that exported successful men. Then, a few hundred yards on, I turned into George Square, and at once moved back into that earlier Scotland with its special manifestations of grace and homeliness, elegance and dignity. I thought of Kingisbyres; and then, a little later, I thought of Catherine.

SOURCE: John D Scott 1954 *The End of an Old Song: a Romance*, London (Eyre and Spottiswoode), Parts 6.1, 3.1.

Hugh MacDiarmid on Scottish culture and nationalism

Hugh MacDiarmid (Dr Christopher Murray Grieve, 1892–1978), poet, on Scottish culture and nationalism.

a)   'A Drunk Man Looks at the Thistle'

Thou, Dostoevski, understood,
Wha had your ain land in your bluid,
And into it as in a mould
The passion o' your bein' rolled,
Inherited in turn frae Heaven
Or sources fer abune it even . . .

Is Scotland big enough to be
A symbol o' that force in me,
In wha's divine inebriety
A sicht abune contempt I'll see?

For a' that's Scottish is in me,
As a' things Russian were in thee,
And I in turn 'ud be an action
To pit in a concrete abstraction
My country's contrair qualities,
And mak' a unity o' these
Till my love owre its history dwells,
As owretone to a peal o' bells.

And in this heicher stratosphere
As bairn at giant at thee I peer . . .

b)   'Unconscious Goal of History'

If there is ocht in Scotland that's worth ha'en
There is nae distance to which it's unattached
– Nae height, nae depth, nae breadth, and I am fain
To see it frae the hamely and the earthly snatched
And precipitated to what it will be in the end
A' that's ephemeral shorn awa' and rhyme nae mair
Mere politics, personalities, and mundane things,
Nor mistak' ony philosophy's elaborate and subtle form
That canna fit the changed conditions, for your trend
Drawin' a life's threids thegither there
Nor losin' on the roonabouts, nor gainin' on the swings

But like the hairst that needs baith sun and storm,
Simmer and winter, Life and Daith . . . A' roads are closed;
North, South, East, West nae mair opposed.

Withoot a leg to stand on, like a snake
Wi' impossible lustres I shake.
Earth contracts to a single point of licht
As men, deceived by their een, see stars at nicht,
And the religious attitude has found
In Scotland yet a balancin' ground . . .

c)   'The outlook for the Scottish race is exceedingly grave . . . our race and our culture are faced with a peril which, though silent and unostentatious, is the gravest with which the Scottish people has ever been confronted.'

SOURCE: Hugh MacDiarmid
1930 'A Drunk Man Looks at the Thistle', *in* M Grieve and A Scott (eds), *The Hugh MacDiarmid Anthology: Poems in Scots and English*, London (Routledge and Kegan Paul), 82.
1930 'Unconscious Goal of History', *in* M Grieve and A Scott, (eds), *The Hugh MacDiarmid Anthology: Poems in Scots and English*, London (Routledge and Kegan Paul), 117.
1926 *Albyn or the Future of Scotland*, London (Kegan Paul), 72.

DOCUMENT 144

Greenvoe

For George Mackay Brown (1923–1996), poet and novelist, nationalism implied a revived medievalism, and also the regional variety of Scotland, exemplified by the history and landscape of his own Orkney.

The Lord of the Harvest took the black cloth from the niche where the horse-shoe had been secreted. The horse-shoe had vanished. In its place was a loaf and a bottle.

The Master Horsemen raised the Harvester to his feet. They put a white cloak over his shoulders. They brought him over to the niche where the whisky and the bread stood.

Slowly the sun heaved itself clear of the sea. The cliff below was alive with the stir and cry of birds. The sea moved and flung glories of light over Quoylay and Hrossey and Hellya, and all the skerries and rocks around. The smell of the earth came to them in the first wind of morning, from the imprisoned fields of the island; and the fence could not keep it back.

The Lord of the Harvest raised his hands. 'We have brought light and blessing to the kingdom of winter,' he said, 'however long it endures, that kingdom, a night or a season or a thousand ages. The word has been found. Now we will eat and drink together and be glad.'

The sun rose. The stones were warm. They broke the bread.

SOURCE: George Mackay Brown 1972 *Greenvoe*, London (Harmondsworth: Penguin), 249.

DOCUMENT 145

Alasdair Gray on Scotland in the 1980s

Alasdair Gray (b 1934), novelist and painter, on Scotland in the 1980s.

a)   A blast of cold wind freshened the air. The rushing grew to surges and gurglings and up the low road between Necropolis and cathedral sped a white foam followed by ripples and plunging waves with gulls swooping and crying over them. He laughed aloud, following the flood with his mind's eye back to the river it flowed from, a full river widening to the ocean. His cheek was touched by something moving in the wind, a black twig with pointed little pink and grey-green buds. The colours of things seemed to be brightening although the fiery light over the roofs had paled to silver streaked with delicate rose. A long silver line marked the horizon. Dim rooftops against it grew solid in the increasing light. The broken buildings were fewer than he had thought. Beyond them a long faint bank of cloud became clear hills, not walling the city in but receding, edge behind pearl-grey edge of farmland and woodland gently rising to a faraway ridge of moor. The darkness overhead shifted and broke in the wind becoming clouds with blue air between. He looked sideways and saw the sun coming up golden behind a laurel bush, light blinking, space dancing among the shifting leaves. Drunk with spaciousness he turned every way, gazing with wide-open mouth and eyes as light created colours, clouds, distances and solid, graspable things close at hand. Among all this light the flaming buildings seemed small blazes which would soon burn out. With only mild disappointment he saw the flood ebbing back down the slope of the road.

b)   By the last chapter our man has been employed for several months, his only close friend has died of drink and exposure, and he has been arrested as accessory to an unusually futile crime. Heavy drinking has so washed out his chances of a sex-life that he has never considered one, and this is lucky. In his community sex leads to children and marriage, and who would gladly bring children into such a community? It is collapsing. The only choice is, collapse with it or clear out. If he had children his decent instincts would lead him to collapse with it. So his worst habit allows him a happy ending.

c)   'Bluster has no effect on the British public when uttered with a regional accent. You've got to be damned hard, and dry and incisive. Use an Anglo-Scots accent. The Scotch do change their accents when they get into positions of power.'
    'Thomas Carlyle didn't!' said the writer loudly.
    'As far as I know Thomas Carlyle was never in a position of power,' said the actor, 'fortunately for Britain.'
    'You English are cunning bastards,' said the writer, and walked out.

SOURCE: Alasdair Gray
1981 *Lanark*, Edinburgh (Canongate), from Chapter 44.
1984 'Postscript', *in* Agnes Owens *Gentlemen of the West*, Harmondsworth (Penguin), 141.
1984 *1982 Janine* London (Jonathan Cape Ltd), 248